Grant's River Campaign

ALSO BY JACK H. LEPA AND FROM MCFARLAND

The Civil War in Tennessee, 1862–1863
(2007; paperback 2011)

*Breaking the Confederacy: The Georgia
and Tennessee Campaigns of 1864*
(2005; paperback 2011)

The Shenandoah Valley Campaign of 1864
(2003; paperback 2010)

Grant's River Campaign

Fort Henry to Shiloh

JACK H. LEPA

McFarland & Company, Inc., Publishers
Jefferson, North Carolina, and London

LIBRARY OF CONGRESS CATALOGUING-IN-PUBLICATION DATA

Lepa, Jack H., 1949–
Grant's river campaign : Fort Henry to Shiloh / Jack H. Lepa.
      p.   cm.
Includes bibliographical references and index.

ISBN 978-0-7864-7477-6
softcover : acid free paper ∞

1. Tennessee—History—Civil War, 1861–1865—Campaigns.
2. United States—History—Civil War, 1861–1865—Campaigns.
3. Grant, Ulysses S. (Ulysses Simpson), 1822–1885.   I. Title.
E472.9.L47 2014   973.7′359—dc23   2013035697

BRITISH LIBRARY CATALOGUING DATA ARE AVAILABLE

© 2014 Jack H. Lepa. All rights reserved

*No part of this book may be reproduced or transmitted in any form
or by any means, electronic or mechanical, including photocopying
or recording, or by any information storage and retrieval system,
without permission in writing from the publisher.*

On the cover: Battle of Fort Donelson, Capture of General
S.B. Buckner and his army, February 16, © 1862, by Kurz & Allison,
Art Publishers, Chicago (Library of Congress)

Manufactured in the United States of America

*McFarland & Company, Inc., Publishers
Box 611, Jefferson, North Carolina 28640
www.mcfarlandpub.com*

For Jack and LaVerne —
thank you for everything

Table of Contents

Preface 1

1. Getting Ready for War 3
2. War Comes to the West 13
3. The Opening Moves 20
4. Taking Fort Henry 26
5. On to Fort Donelson 34
6. Two Attacks and Two Defeats 40
7. The Confederates Strike First 47
8. The Battle for Fort Donelson 53
9. A Most Important Victory 60
10. Johnston Saves What He Can 68
11. On to Nashville 76
12. Problems for Grant 84
13. Pittsburg Landing 92
14. The Forces Gather 100
15. Johnston Risks All 108
16. The Approaching Battle 116
17. A Lovely Day for a Battle 124
18. Fighting and Falling Back 133
19. Disaster Approaches 142
20. Slaughter in the Afternoon 149
21. Grant Hangs On 156
22. A Terrible Night for All 163
23. The Second Morning 169
24. Reversal of Fortune 177
25. After Shiloh 184

Chapter Notes 193
Bibliography 204
Index 209

Preface

For both sides the first year of the American Civil War was one of confusion and working hard to build up their military forces for the coming bloodbath. For the final Union victory no area was more important than the Western Theater and the state of Tennessee, especially the rivers that ran through the state. Control of the Tennessee and Cumberland rivers would eventually provide Union forces with a virtual highway into the Deep South. The first Union victories of the war occurred in this region and many of the officers who would end up commanding the victorious Union armies at the end of the war received much of their command experience here. This book describes events during the first few months of 1862, when, quite possibly, the outcome of the Civil War was decided.

I would like to thank the staff of the University of Nevada, Las Vegas, for their help with research and locating material used in this book. The staff of the Interlibrary Loan Department of the Las Vegas–Clark County Library District provided significant assistance in finding older and rare books that I would not have had access to otherwise. In addition, the Honnold/Mudd Library at The Claremont Colleges in Claremont, California, has an excellent selection of nineteenth-century books that I was allowed to use.

1

Getting Ready for War

Long before the United States tore itself apart in a long and terrible Civil War it was a simple fact of life for most of the nation that poor roads and a scarcity of railroads made the major waterways like the Mississippi, the Ohio, the Tennessee, and the Cumberland rivers the most important avenues for the growing population to be able to communicate and trade with one another. With the secession of the Southern states in 1861 and the formation of the Confederacy it was especially critical to the economic well-being of what was then considered the Northwest that the Mississippi and its major tributaries remain open for navigation. There were, of course, railroads that ran east and west, but they were relatively few in number and could not begin to transport the volume of goods needed to replace water transportation. The only economically viable way for the bulky farm products of the Northwest to be transported to markets in the East and Europe was by ships that traveled along the great rivers of the region.[1]

Even before the conflict grew into open warfare the newly formed Confederate government thought, or at least hoped, that the threat of closing the Mississippi and other rivers might force the states of the Northwest to peacefully accept the existence of the new nation. The Southerners miscalculated, however, because this threat to their economy caused the states that were most dependent on the region's waterways to support the war effort even more enthusiastically than they otherwise might have. When President Abraham Lincoln issued his first call for volunteers to fight for the Union governors Richard Yates of Illinois and William Dennison of Ohio both promised that their states would provide an abundance of enthusiastic volunteers to fight to preserve the nation.[2]

In addition to the dire economic consequences of losing control of the Western rivers there were political and military considerations as well. With the country literally falling apart it was imperative for the Lincoln Administration to keep the support of the states in the Northwest for the coming war. From a military point of view the value of controlling the major rivers as supply routes and avenues of invasion into Tennessee and the Deep South was pretty obvious to anyone who could read a map. Later in the war General William T. Sherman wrote to Admiral David Porter about how important the rivers of Tennessee had been to the war effort, "We are much obliged to the Tennessee, which has favored us most opportunely, for I am never easy with a railroad which takes a whole army to guard, each foot of rail being essential to the whole; whereas they can't stop the Tennessee, and each boat can make its own game. I think also we can clear out anything except occasional shots at passing boats."[3]

The area that became known as the Western Theater contained all the territory between the Appalachian Mountains on the east and the Mississippi River on the west. Included in this vast region were the Confederate states of Alabama, Georgia, Mississippi, and Tennessee and one state that remained in the Union, Kentucky. The Eastern region along the Appalachians was made up of mostly rugged terrain with little food or population. The lack of railroads and the poor surface roads meant that conducting a military campaign in this area would be next to impossible. In the West the Mississippi River created a natural barrier. It was mostly in the center of the Western Theater that military operations could be conducted with relative ease. There the terrain held few serious physical obstacles to moving large numbers of men, with most of the region consisting of flatland or relatively low rolling hills until you began approaching the south-central part of Tennessee moving toward Chattanooga. From one point of view the rivers in the region could be considered barriers to armies trying to cross them, but on the other hand they also provided highways to most of the important economic and military locations. The ability to transport large numbers of troops and massive amounts of supplies on the rivers and railroads in the region would allow campaigning in all but the worst weather.[4]

Tennessee was especially important to both sides, as the rivers that traversed the state in all directions provided open avenues of transportation to the Deep South. If these rivers were to fall under the control of Union forces the rest of the Confederacy would be exposed to invasion and ultimate defeat. Other than the Mississippi, which formed Tennessee's western border, the state's two main waterways were the Tennessee River and the Cumberland River. The Tennessee River wanders through the state from the mountains near Knoxville in the east flowing southwest down to Chattanooga near the border with Georgia. Heading west from Chattanooga the river crosses the northern end of Alabama before making a sharp turn north to head back through Tennessee again until it empties into the Ohio River at Paducah, Kentucky, about forty-five miles from Cairo, Illinois, a small border town at the southern tip of state.[5]

The other major waterway in Tennessee, the Cumberland River, began in Eastern Kentucky and flowed south into Tennessee past the state capital of Nashville. The river then headed northwest back into Kentucky until it met the Ohio River several miles east of Paducah. Control of the Cumberland would give Union forces easy access to

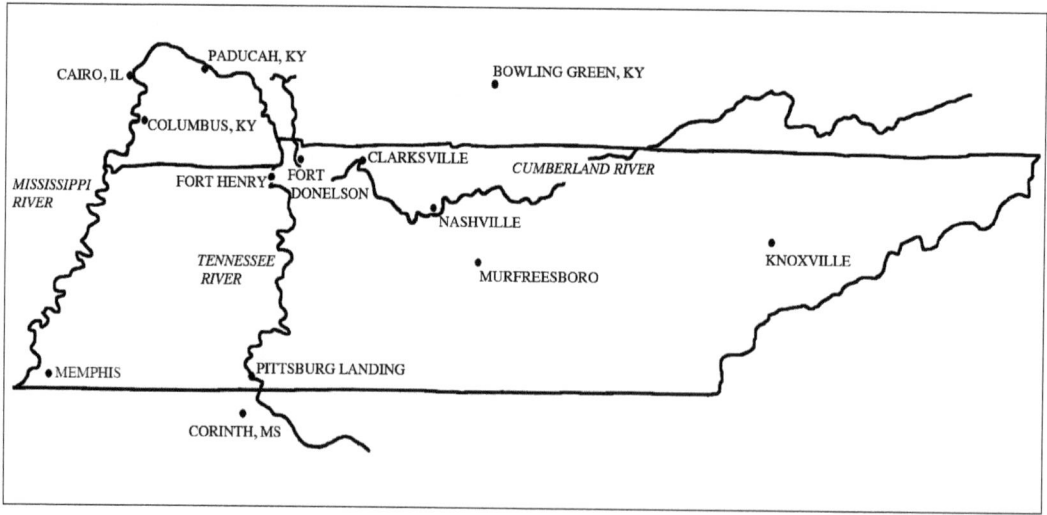

Operations in Tennessee

Nashville. In addition to being the state capital, Nashville was a major rail center and the city itself and nearby areas along the river contained one of the South's largest concentrations of munitions manufacturing and numerous other machine shops, foundries and other industries.[6]

In Kentucky, while there was more support for the Union than in her neighbor to the south, the situation was fluid enough for both sides to be optimistic about their chances to control what was perhaps the most important of the border states. If Kentucky were to stay with the Union it was unlikely that Missouri would ever be able to become an active member of the Confederacy due to simple geography. In addition, with Kentucky under Union control the western portion of Tennessee would be constantly threatened by invasion. If Federal forces could take Memphis and control Tennessee's western border along the Mississippi that indispensable waterway would be open as far south as Vicksburg, Mississippi.[7]

Conversely, a Confederate-controlled Kentucky would provide a shield for Nashville and the food-producing region of Central Tennessee. The North would also face the constant threat of offensive actions by the Confederates against Southern Indiana, Ohio and Western Pennsylvania. What might be the most important result of a Confederate Kentucky, however, would be that the border of the Confederacy would be advanced to the Ohio River. Not only would the Ohio form a natural barrier to invasion from the North, but also Confederate forces would almost certainly attempt to close the river to Union traffic. The military and economic consequences of this would have been disastrous to the Union cause. William T. Sherman wrote to his brother U.S. Senator John Sherman in October of 1861 that "whatever nation gets the control of the Ohio, Mississippi, and Missouri Rivers will control the continent. This they know, and for this they will labor."[8]

As war approached, the initial Confederate strategy for defense in the West was to combine fortifications that would block Federal access to the major waterways with several interior defensive positions and mobile forces that could block any Federal overland advances. The Confederates planned to include the states of Missouri and Kentucky under this defensive umbrella, even though they had not yet left the Union. This anticipated main line of resistance had its anchor at Columbus, Kentucky, which was the most northern point on the Mississippi where the bluffs on each side of the town were high enough to dominate the river below. From Columbus the proposed line ran to a point in Central Tennessee where the Tennessee and Cumberland rivers were closest and fortifications could close both those rivers to any Federal ships. There were also plans to build a fortified camp at Bowling Green, Kentucky, as a forward point that could not be ignored and left in the rear of an advancing Federal force. The defensive line would then run east following the Cumberland River, defending Nashville, and to the Cumberland Gap. Such a defensive line would have protected the most important avenues of invasion, the rivers, and provided strong points that would enable the defenders to cut off from their supply lines any army that tried to advance between them. Overall this was not an unreasonable plan except for two problems the Confederate government seemed to overlook. There were not nearly enough Confederate troops in the region to properly defend such a huge amount of territory and Kentucky was still part of the Union.[9]

During much of 1861 Kentucky's official position toward secession was indecisive and inconsistent. Despite the fact that many inhabitants believed in states' rights and were sympathetic to their neighbors to the south, there was a decided lack of public support for seceding from the Union. The government of Kentucky was just as divided on the issue of secession as were the people with Governor Beriah Magoffin supporting it while most of the state legislature was committed to remaining in the Union. This impasse led the Kentucky legislature to pass a bill proclaiming that the state would take no part in the conflict but would remain friendly with both sides and would observe strict neutrality. When Fort Sumter was attacked and President Lincoln issued his call for troops to put down the rebellion Governor Magoffin stated, "Kentucky will furnish no troops for the wicked purpose of subduing her sister Southern states."[10]

Anyone with any common sense could see that should the conflict degenerate into serious warfare Kentucky's strategic position simply would not allow the state to remain above the fight. When Tennessee seceded in June of 1861 Kentucky's position became even more important. In the North it was widely believed that Kentucky's neutrality was nothing more than a sham to protect Tennessee. Whatever Kentucky's true motives, it was certain that for the Confederacy having that state act as a buffer that was closed to Federal forces between the Appalachians and the Mississippi River provided a shield for the South was almost as helpful as if Kentucky actually joined the Confederacy. Even though both sides were skeptical of Kentucky's motive for claiming neutrality, they respected the state's stance, at least on the surface. It was feared by many on both sides that some blunder, like being the first to send troops into Kentucky, would push the undecided majority of citizens into the opposite camp.[11]

North of the Ohio River there was naturally serious anxiety about the intentions of their neighbor to the south. Indiana governor Oliver P. Morton sent a telegram to Assistant Secretary of War Thomas A. Scott at the end of August saying, "I earnestly hope the Government will not lose a moment in preparing for the crisis in Kentucky." Morton wanted arms and artillery to defend towns along the river. In a second message urging preparations should be made for possible action Morton wrote, "Civil War in Kentucky is inevitable," adding, "A force should be provided, ready to march to the support of Union men at a moment's warning."[12]

Kentucky's neighbor to the South was also important to both sides but for different reasons. While a neutral Kentucky provided a sort of protection against Federal incursions, the rivers of Tennessee were like open highways right into the heart of the Confederacy and had to be held at all costs. And there was no question about which side Tennessee was on. Tennessee governor Isham G. Harris, the state's dominant politician and a determined secessionist, responded to President Lincoln's request for volunteers by saying, "Tennessee will not furnish a single man for coercion, but fifty thousand if necessary for the defense of our rights or those of our Southern brothers." After the act of secession was passed in June volunteers flooded into militia organizations across the state. Tennesseans were ready to fight.[13]

The Provisional Army of Tennessee was created in the spring of 1861, but Tennessee, like most states at that time, was totally unprepared for war. One of the governor's first orders was for the commanders of the various militia units to hold their men ready and begin training. Harris also appointed Gideon J. Pillow a major general and commander of the Provisional Army of Tennessee with headquarters in Memphis.[14]

A graduate of the U.S. Military Academy and veteran of the Mexican War, General Pillow was Tennessee's most recognizable soldier at this time. Pillow came from a wealthy family and grew up in the rich plantation district around Columbia, Tennessee. He was a lawyer who owed his appointment as brigadier general during the Mexican War to his former law partner President James K. Polk. Pillow was distinguished looking and energetic, with a magnetic personality and confidence that allowed him to believe that he was actually qualified for the position he held.[15]

General Pillow immediately began fortifying positions along the Mississippi River at Memphis, another location above Memphis, and yet another position a few miles farther north at a horseshoe bend of the river, which ended up being called Fort Pillow. Just off the northwestern corner of the state Island No. 10 was fortified, as was the Tennessee side of the river. When Tennessee joined the Confederacy Governor Harris transferred control of the state military to the Confederate government, which became the nucleus of the deservedly famous Army of Tennessee. Although he knew that Pillow was unqualified to command this new army, Jefferson Davis could not afford to insult Tennessee by refusing to use that state's senior officer in the Confederate service. Davis decided to leave Pillow in charge of defending Tennessee but to put a superior officer over him in command of the Western region. On July 4 newly commissioned Major General Leonidas Polk was appointed to the command of Department No. 2 with headquarters in Memphis. Polk's new command contained Western Tennessee, Northern Alabama, Mississippi, and Louisiana and Eastern Arkansas.[16]

Leonidas Polk was an unusual choice for such an important command. A graduate of West Point, he resigned his commission soon after beginning active service and joined the Episcopal Church to study for the ministry. Over the years he had risen in the church to become Bishop of Louisiana. Polk's lack of military experience didn't seem to matter to Davis, probably because they were old friends from the Military Academy and Davis felt that the situation on the Mississippi needed immediate attention. Clearly Davis trusted Polk to take care of the basics of defending the region and not do anything that might force Kentucky into the arms of the Federal Government.[17]

When Polk took over his new command Pillow was reduced in rank to brigadier general in the Confederate Army. Pillow was naturally upset, but he and Polk were able to work together to improve the defenses along the Mississippi and organize and train troops as they were mustered into the Confederate army. Polk began fortifying the town of New Madrid, Missouri, which lay near the center of one of the river's many horseshoe bends near Island No. 10. With both of these positions properly armed and manned they would present a formidable obstacle to any Federal gunboats descending the Mississippi. There was another position about sixty miles farther up the river that was an even better location to fortify, Columbus, Kentucky. Both Polk and Pillow recognized that the high bluffs overlooking the river at Columbus could be turned into an impregnable fortress that would effectively close the Mississippi less than twenty miles below Cairo, Illinois. Unfortunately, as both generals were well aware, President Davis had declared Kentucky off-limits for any incursions by Confederate forces.[18]

While the Confederacy was building up its forces in the West the Federal Government was working hard to do the same. The first Union commander for the Western region was Major General John C. Frémont, former explorer and presidential candidate, who made his headquarters in St. Louis. His assignment was to hold Missouri for the Union and prepare an expedition to take control of the Mississippi River down to New Orleans. Frémont won his appointment more from his political connections than because of his military abilities. Within a few months the command was awash in corruption and so disorganized that little progress could be made in actually fighting the war.[19]

In November 1861 George B. McClellan became general-in-chief of the Union army and quickly decided that a change needed to be made in the West. Later that same month McClellan chose Major General Henry W. Halleck to replace Frémont. Halleck had been born in New York in 1815 and graduated third in his class at the Military Academy as an engineer in 1839. During the Mexican War he served in California and saw no action. In 1854 Halleck resigned from the army and built a successful law practice in San Francisco. During the next several years he prospered financially, helped draft California's constitution, and was offered a seat on the California Supreme Court, which he decided not to accept. When it became apparent that war was on the horizon many retired officers were recalled back into the service. The general-in-chief at the time, Winfield Scott, recommended Halleck to President Lincoln and he was quickly offered a commission as major general in the regular army and was seriously considered for the position of general-in-chief that ultimately went to McClellan.[20]

Henry Halleck had a bad temper and could be overbearing and rude to subordinates and others he did not consider his intellectual equals; his nickname "Old Brains" was not used as a sign of affection. However, his obvious success in previous endeavors and his effectiveness as an administrator inspired confidence in his ability to bring order out of the chaos that reigned in the West. When Halleck replaced General Frémont as commander of the Department of the Missouri the territory under his command encompassed the states of Missouri, Iowa, Minnesota, Wisconsin, Illinois, Arkansas, and Kentucky west of the Cumberland River. Halleck inherited a number of problems from his predecessor. Frémont's incompetence resulted in irregularities with contracts for supplies, a serious shortage of arms of all kinds, and a general lack of organization in the department and the loss of large quantities of stores and arms to profiteers.[21]

While Leonidas Polk worked to build up the Confederate defenses east of the Mississippi there was little he could do to organize the forces west of the river to provide a coordinated front against Federal incursions. Polk recommended that one commander be assigned for all the Mississippi Valley on both sides of the river and he and President Davis agreed that the best man for this important command was Albert Sidney Johnston, one of the most distinguished soldiers on either side. Born in Kentucky in 1803, Johnston graduated from West Point in 1826. He served on the frontier and later with Jefferson Davis in the Black Hawk War in 1832. In 1834 Johnston resigned his commission to care for his dying wife, and after her death he moved to Texas. Joining his adopted home's war for independence from Mexico, Johnston becoming a brigadier general in the new nation's army and later served as secretary of war for two years.[22]

Union general Henry W. Halleck. Major general, former attorney in California and commander of the Department of the Missouri (Library of Congress).

When the United States went to war with Mexico, Johnston commanded a regiment of Texas volunteers seeing action at Monterrey. Returning to service in the U.S. Army as a major and paymaster for the troops stationed in Texas, the restless Johnston was ill suited for this type of administrative job but in 1855 he was promoted to colonel and given command of the elite new 2nd Cavalry Regiment. Serving in this regiment were several future Civil War generals, including Robert E. Lee. In 1857 Johnston was put in command of the expedition to put down the unrest in Mormon-controlled Utah, a difficult assignment that brought him a brevet promotion to brigadier general. Johnston's last assignment for the U.S. Army was as commander of the Department of the Pacific stationed in San Francisco.[23]

At first supporting the Union, Johnston eventually decided to follow his heart when his adopted home of Texas seceded. Johnston again resigned his U.S. Army commission and after a long and difficult journey across the Southwest he arrived in Richmond in August. Warmly welcomed by his old friend Jefferson Davis, Johnston was quickly appointed a full general ranking second in the entire Confederate army. Davis would later say that while he hoped he had other men who would prove to be generals he knew he had at least one, Johnston.[24]

Confederate general Albert Sidney Johnston. Highest-ranking officer on either side killed in action during the war (Library of Congress).

Albert Sidney Johnston was fifty-eight years old when he committed himself to the cause of the Confederacy. A little over six feet tall, he was strongly built, with a dignified and commanding personality. He was said to be a strong-willed man who could quickly lose his temper but then regain his self-control just as quickly. To most people who knew him he looked and acted like a general. Even his enemies could say little negative about Johnston. His opponent at Shiloh, Ulysses S. Grant, later wrote that many of the Union officers who knew Johnston before the war expected him to be the most formidable opponent they might meet on a battlefield.[25]

On September 10 President Davis assigned Johnston to command the newly expanded Confederate Department Number Two with the imposing title of General Commanding the Western Department of the Army of the Confederate States of America. Johnston's new command stretched from the Appalachian Mountains in the east through the Indian Territory in the west. Included in this vast area were the states of Tennessee, Arkansas, Western Mississippi, Kentucky, Missouri, Kansas, and present-day Oklahoma. Johnston inherited approximately seventy thousand Confederate troops currently under arms in the region, a force totally inadequate for any kind of proper defense. Leaving Richmond as soon as possible, the new commander of the Confederate forces in the West arrived at Nashville on September 14.[26]

As the opposing forces were being formed, Federal commanders were making plans to take control of the all-important waterways of the West by building a powerful naval force. James B. Eads, an engineer and mechanical genius from St. Louis, was consulted and hired to begin building ships. Naval Captain John Rogers came out west to work with Eads, and by June three passenger steamers and been purchased and redesigned in Cincinnati to serve as gunboats. These ships were the *Conestoga, Taylor,* and *Lexington,* each carrying several large-caliber guns and protected by heavy oak bulwarks.[27]

Although these first three gunboats were powerful ships, they would not be able to stand up to the pounding of heavy guns from enemy forts along the rivers, so in July the government advertised for bids to construct a new class of ironclad gunboats that could survive heavy fire and also be able to navigate on the shallow rivers in the region. James Eads won the contract to build seven new vessels that would be about six hundred tons, draw only six feet of water, carry at least thirteen heavy guns and have iron plating for protection. Built simultaneously in several river towns, these ships were as unusual looking as they were powerful. The new ships were flat-bottomed paddle wheelers protected by two and a half inches of iron plating across the front with thinner plating along the sides reinforced with a thick layer of wood on the inside. The ships were about 175 feet long and just over 50 feet wide, with sides sloped down to the waterline so that when struck by enemy shot there would be no flat surface to receive the shock. This sloping casemate caused the ships to be nicknamed "turtles." These ships were underpowered and ungainly in appearance, but their heavy guns and iron plating made them more powerful than any vessels the Confederates could send against them. At the same time it was believed that the heavy guns on board the ironclads would allow them to bombard enemy fortifications from a safe distance or move in close and stand up to the fire of all but the heaviest guns.[28]

During the summer months Eads and Rodgers pushed hard to complete the ships as soon as possible. In addition to the seven new ironclads, thirty-eight mortar boats and numerous other supply ships were also being built. New dockyards, machine shops, foundries, and sawmills had to be created to supply the shipbuilders with the tools and parts needed to build the new fleet. Delays in making payments caused Eads to use up his own credit and go deep into debt to keep the work going; in fact, some payments were so late that during a few of the gunboat's early engagements they still technically belonged to Eads.[29]

As the building of the fleet continued through the summer there was an important change in command. On September 6 Rogers was replaced by Flag Officer Andrew Hull Foote. Born in New Haven, Connecticut, in 1806, to a future U.S. Senator, Foote briefly attended the U.S. Military Academy but resigned in 1822 to become a midshipman in the Navy. He served in various ships as he worked his way through the ranks, serving as first lieutenant on the *Cumberland* in 1843.[30]

As commander of the brig *Perry* from 1849 to 1852 Foote was involved in the suppression of the slave trade off the coast of Africa. After spending several years ashore working on naval reform he returned to sea as commander of the sloop *Portsmouth*, and in 1856 Foote personally led a landing party that destroyed four forts guarding the approaches to Canton, China, in retaliation for attacks on U.S. ships. Foote was in charge of the Brooklyn Navy Yard when he was chosen to command the flotilla being built for use on the Western rivers. Foote was deliberate in making decisions but tough and stubborn when it came to taking action. A very religious man, he liked to preach to his crew on Sundays. About average in size and appearance, Foote was well built and physically tough. He was soft-spoken and blunt in his speech, but, also honest and fair-minded, he was considered by many to be a good man to have for a friend.[31]

When Foote took over the command of the fleet it consisted of the three wooden gunboats already in service, with the ironclads and mortar boats still under construction. Frémont authorized Eads to purchase and convert two other ships to ironclads in addition to the original seven. Frémont also gave Foote pretty much of a free hand when it came to getting the ships ready, telling him, "Use your own judgment in carrying out the ends of government," and to "spare no effort to accomplish the object in view with the least possible delay."[32]

Foote spared neither himself nor the contractors, and on October 12 the first of the ironclads, the *St. Louis*, was launched at Carondelet, Missouri. It took only three more weeks for the remaining ships of the original contract to splash into the waters of the Mississippi and Ohio. These seven ships, the *Cairo, Carondelet, Cincinnati, Louisville, Mound City, Pittsburg* and *De Kalb* (the *St. Louis* was later renamed), along with the two other larger ships being converted to warships, the *Benton* and the *Essex*, were the nucleus of the Western fleet that would eventually clear the Mississippi, Tennessee, and Cumberland rivers of enemy fortifications.[33]

By the time the ships were nearing completion the biggest problem Foote had to contend with was that there were only about one hundred trained seamen available for the fleet when the ships began sliding into the water. Recruiting offices as far away as the Great Lakes brought in few experienced sailors. In November the Navy Department sent out five hundred men from the east, but the blockading squadrons operating along the coastline always had first choice of available trained seamen. Over time several hundred volunteers from the army joined the fleet, mostly to man the guns, but trained sailors were always in short supply.[34]

Unlike the recruiting difficulties faced by the Navy, the land armies had all the volunteers they could use, at least in 1861. Still, mobs of civilians anxious to fight do not an army make and before the generals could carry out any of their grand strategies regiments had to be recruited, trained and armed. Most of the states had some form of militia, but these were usually poorly armed and trained amateurs more interested in dressing up and playing soldier to impress their friends and families. When Fort Sumter was attacked in April and a real war was suddenly on the horizon these militia units became critical building blocks for the armies of both North and South. During the summer and fall of 1861 a frenzied mobilization for a war that no one was prepared to fight took place with the usual chaos that one might expect.[35]

Both North and South farmers, clerks, teachers, and others from all walks of life volunteered to fight for their separate causes. The men who formed the armies that eventually fought the battles came from similar backgrounds, religious beliefs, and social and economic situations. They were quite alike in most ways except what they were willing to fight and die for. Most Southern soldiers would probably say they were not fighting in support of slavery but for the freedom to form a new nation, while most Northern soldiers would probably say they were not fighting to end slavery but to preserve the Union.

After Fort Sumter was fired on and President Lincoln issued his call for seventy-five thousand troops, like everywhere else recruiting offices in the West were inundated with volunteers. Indiana was asked to provide six regiments for Federal service; in a week Governor Morton was informed that there were enough volunteers to form thirteen regiments. In Illinois the legislature authorized the raising of ten additional regiments, above the six requested, offering to pay these ten thousand extra men until the Federal Government took them into service. Despite their enthusiasm, the new recruits could do nothing without weapons, and one of the biggest problems facing both sides that summer was obtaining arms for the thousands of budding soldiers. Neither the Union nor the Confederacy had nearly enough military-grade weapons to arm the flood of new recruits, and in short order agents of both governments were purchasing arms all over Europe. For months many of the new soldiers did their training unarmed or with whatever rusty and outdated weapons their state armories might provide.[36]

Fortunately for these poorly trained and equipped volunteers, the first assignments during the summer of 1861 were mostly garrison duty at important towns and positions along the Ohio and Mississippi rivers. Even the inexperienced military commanders and political leaders of the Western states could see how important it was to safeguard the cities along the rivers. Especially important was Cairo, Illinois, a small, dirty little river town where the Ohio ran into the Mississippi at the southern tip of the state. It was not just the junction of the rivers that made Cairo important but also the southern terminus of the Illinois Central Railroad. By water and by rail Cairo was one of the most strategic locations in the region for commerce and war, and it was one of the first locations to host a Federal garrison. It would not be much of an exaggeration to suggest that the coming struggle for the rivers of Tennessee and the eventual Union victory in the West began at Cairo, Illinois.[37]

2

War Comes to the West

September of 1861 saw the end of Kentucky's unrealistic attempt at neutrality as the reality of the military situation overcame all other considerations. The most important Federal post in the West at that time was Cairo, Illinois. The small town near the meeting of the Ohio and Mississippi rivers gave the Federal forces based there a great strategic advantage over the Confederates who were still in the process of completing defensive works at New Madrid and Island No. 10, both well south of Cairo. Along the Tennessee shoreline there were few locations on the Mississippi that were suitable to build fortifications that would be strong enough to survive the battering they were sure to receive from the Federal ironclads. As it turned out, however, there was one place that both Generals Polk and Pillow had already decided would be perfect for closing the great river to Federal ships, Columbus, Kentucky.[1]

The Confederates had been prohibited from entering Kentucky by President Davis, just as the Federals had been banned from taking action in that state by President Lincoln, both leaders wanting to preserve the imagined neutrality as long as possible, unless the other side acted first. On September 3, possibly in reaction to rumors of a Federal movement down the Mississippi, General Polk sent Pillow with six thousand men into Kentucky to take and hold Columbus and, more important, the high bluffs above and below the town. His mission was easily accomplished and suddenly the Confederates had a strategic position that commanded nearly five miles of the river and was only eighteen miles below Cairo, effectively closing the Mississippi at that point.[2]

The Confederate incursion into Kentucky was roundly condemned. Governor Harris of Tennessee quickly wrote to Governor Magoffin of Kentucky that he had no advance notice of the invasion and asked Confederate president Davis to pull his troops out of any positions they occupied. Seeing that the damage could not be undone and realizing how important Columbus was to the defense of the Confederacy, Davis wired General Polk, "The necessity justifies the action." In Kentucky the legislature, which happened to be meeting at that time, passed resolutions calling for the removal of the Confederate troops and the calling out of the state's militia under the command of General Thomas L. Crittenden to oppose the invaders if they did not withdraw.[3]

By taking Columbus when he did Pillow had only just beaten the Federals to the same prize. General Frémont had already ordered General Ulysses S. Grant, one of the most nondescript officers in the army at the time, to mount an expedition into southeastern Missouri to drive out enemy detachments in the area and attack any enemy force in Belmont, across the river from Columbus. In his instructions Frémont stated, "It is intended, in connection with all these movements, to occupy Columbus, Kentucky, as soon as possible."[4]

After Grant learned that Columbus was no longer a viable target he was quick to realize that there was another strategically important position that the Union could not afford to lose: Paducah, Kentucky, a few miles above Cairo, where the Tennessee met the Ohio River. Without specific orders and with no time to waste, as there was news that Polk was already heading for Paducah, Grant quickly pulled together a small force of less than two thousand men and prepared to move out. Grant twice sent messages to Frémont asking for permission to move on Paducah, saying, "I am nearly ready to go to Paducah, and shall start should not a telegram arrive preventing the movement." Deciding he could wait no longer, Grant sailed up the river on the night of September 5, arriving at Paducah the next morning. The sight of hundreds of Union soldiers disembarking from their ships convinced the few Confederates in the town to leave, and Grant took over Paducah without firing a shot.[5]

Grant could hardly have timed his arrival in Paducah better, as less than half a day's march away a Confederate force, much larger than Grant's, was approaching from the south. Upon learning the Federals had taken over the town and were already busy building defensive fortifications the Confederates turned back. Leaving troops to garrison the town, Grant returned to Cairo, where a dispatch from Frémont was waiting authorizing him to "take Paducah if you are strong enough." Grant's quick action taking the responsibility on his shoulders prevented the Confederates from seizing a valuable position at the mouth of the Tennessee River and possibly compromising the Ohio River as well. The importance of Paducah was noted by Confederate general Simon Bolivar Buckner in a message to Richmond on September 13: "Our possession of Columbus is already neutralized by that of Paducah."[6]

With the mirage of Kentucky neutrality smashed to bits there was no reason for either side to put off taking as much territory as they could as quickly as possible. General Johnston wrote to Richmond on September 16, "So far from yielding to the demand for the withdrawal of our troops, I have determined to occupy Bowling Green at once." General Buckner promptly led an expedition north and took over Bowling Green on the eighteenth. At the same time another Confederate force led by Brigadier General Felix Zollicoffer entered Eastern Tennessee through the Cumberland Gap to subdue the inhabitants of that mostly Union-supporting area. Now that their state had been invaded by the Confederacy the Kentucky legislature authorized the enlistment of forty thousand volunteers to fight the invaders and also approved that these troops would enter the service of the United States.[7]

General Johnston quickly had men working to establish their defensive lines along the route that had been previously proposed. From the Cumberland Gap the Confederate defenses ran west to the large fortified camp at Bowling Green, then continued south and west to positions established just inside Tennessee blocking access to the Tennessee and Cumberland rivers, then west to the fortress at Columbus. Writing from Bowling Green to Confederate adjutant and inspector general Samuel Cooper on October 17, General Johnston explained that he expected Federal attacks to be forthcoming "from Cairo by the river, and Paducah by land." Also noting that the Federal command "of the Ohio and all the navigable waters of Kentucky, and better means of land transportation, give them great facilities of concentration." Johnston also informed Cooper that he was going to have to wait to see what the Federal forces were going to do before reacting because "[a]s my forces at neither this nor either of the other points threatened are more than sufficient to meet the force in front, I cannot weaken either until the object of the enemy is fully pronounced." Closing with a rather ominous but realistic note, Johnston stated that he "will use all means to increase my force and spare no exertions to render it effective at every point; but I cannot assure you that this will be sufficient."[8]

Johnston's concerns were very valid considering that the major rivers in the West could all be used by Union forces to make deep inroads into Confederate territory. The Mississippi River was the most important waterway in the nation and as such received the most attention. The fortifications at Columbus were the first line of defense for the Confederacy on the Mississippi, and General Polk quickly turned that position into an unassailable fortress, at least from the river side. With as many as 140 guns on the bluffs stretching as much as two hundred feet above the river, the fortress at Columbus was favorably compared to the British fortress at Gibraltar. Farther down the river were several other forts or fortified positions, including New Madrid and Island No. 10. Taken altogether, the Confederate defenses on the Mississippi effectively closed that waterway to Union shipping.[9]

While the defense of the Mississippi understandably commanded much of the Confederacy's time and resources, the other two important waterways that Johnston had to defend, the Tennessee and Cumberland rivers, were provided with relatively modest defenses in comparison. Only two positions, Fort Henry on the eastern bank of the Tennessee and Fort Donelson on the western bank of the Cumberland, defended these crucial waterways that guarded the doorways to the heart of the Confederacy. Fort Henry held only seventeen guns with a garrison of two to three thousand men. Built during the summer months when the river was low, the fort was poorly planned and located and was subject to frequent flooding during the rainy months. Fort Donelson, on the other hand, was much more imposing with about forty guns on several levels overlooking the Cumberland. Including the outer works the fort could support a garrison of over fifteen thousand. In November Brigadier General Lloyd Tilghman was assigned to command the defenses of both the Tennessee and Cumberland rivers. Seeing the poor location of Fort Henry, he began construction of Fort Heiman on the opposite bank of the river but on much higher ground so that the fort's guns would look down on any approaching vessels.[10]

While it was obvious that Johnston had to vigorously defend the major rivers against Federal naval incursions, it was also important to defend Southern Kentucky and Tennessee from attack by land-based forces. One of the places that were considered imperative to hold was Bowling Green, Kentucky, a small town located on the Big Barren River and the important Louisville and Nashville Railroad. After the Confederates took control of the town in mid–September it was quickly fortified and soon became home to about twenty thousand Confederate troops commanded by Major General William Hardee. With the military requirements in Virginia always taking precedence over those of the West, Johnston could never get adequate resources to match the number of Federal troops he had to contend with. In prophetic comments to General Cooper in January, Johnston wrote, "No matter what the sacrifice may be, it must be made, and without loss of time. Our people do not comprehend the magnitude of the danger that threatens. Let it be impressed upon them." Adding to his argument for more troops, Johnston noted that the winter weather might postpone enemy operations in the East, but he was convinced that considering the ease of movement "the well-filled rivers of the Ohio, Cumberland, and Tennessee give for active operations, that they will suspend them in Tennessee and Kentucky during the winter months is a delusion." As he would soon learn, Johnston's assessment could not have been more correct.[11]

General Johnston did not know it at the time, but the man who would give him the most to worry about was Ulysses S. Grant, one of the last men anyone would have considered a formidable enemy at this point in the conflict. Born in Ohio in 1822 and a graduate of the Military Academy in 1843, Grant was twice noted for bravery during the Mexican War.

Married in 1848 and assigned to the Pacific Northwest, Captain Grant became bored and lonely, developed a fondness for drink, and resigned from the army under a cloud. As a civilian he failed at most of his endeavors before the war, including working in his father's leather shop. Experienced officers were in high demand at the beginning of the war and Grant quickly found himself the colonel of the 21st Illinois Volunteers and almost as quickly a brigadier general serving in General Frémont's command. In early November Grant was once again in southeastern Missouri trying to root out enemy guerrillas when he learned that enemy forces at Columbus were preparing to send out a force of their own into Missouri. Hurrying back to Cairo, Grant put together a force of about three thousand men and set sail downriver on November 6 with an escort of two gunboats.[12]

On the morning of the seventh Grant's troops landed about three miles above Belmont, Missouri, which is opposite Columbus on the western side of the river. As the Federal troops approached the town they came under fire from the Confederates stationed outside town. Originally the Confederates were only in regimental strength, but they had been reinforced by troops from Columbus. In a letter to his father Grant wrote that after he deployed the troops in line they moved forward and "fought our way from tree to tree through the woods to Belmont, about two and a half miles, the enemy contesting every foot of ground." Forcing the Confederates back, Grant's men eventually drove them away and captured their camp, where the Union soldiers burned pretty much everything they could not carry off.[13]

While the fighting was taking place at Belmont, across the river at Columbus General Polk wasted little time putting together a relief force of several regiments that crossed the river with the intent of cutting the Federals off from their transports. Grant's men had to make a rather hasty withdrawal back to their ships with the Confederates following close behind. Overall the battle was basically a draw, with the Federals defeating the original Confederate force and then being driven off by a large group of enemy troops. The casualties for Grant's first real battle were relatively light, about 350 for the Federals and 500 for the Confederates. Putting the most optimistic interpretation on the event, Grant wrote, "Taking into account the object of the expedition the victory was most complete. It has given me a confidence in the officers and men of this command, that will enable me to lead them in any future engagement without fear of the result."[14]

There had been little offensive movement by any of the Union forces in the West other than Grant's little excursion to Belmont, and by the end of 1861 President Lincoln was tired of waiting for someone to take action. In fact, as early as November 22 Brigadier General Don Carlos Buell wrote to McClellan regarding his plans for a offensive against Bowling Green that "it will be important that Halleck shall strike at the same time that I do, and I think you will agree that his blow should await my preparation." Buell later suggested that the movement of expeditions up the Tennessee and Cumberland rivers would be essential to the success of any campaign against Nashville. General Buell again wrote to McClellan, who had recently been too sick to do much of anything, on December 29, still advancing his ideas of where the main blow should fall: "It is my conviction that all the force that can possibly be collected should be brought to bear on that front of which Columbus and Bowling Green may be said to be the flanks. The center, that is, the Cumberland and Tennessee where the railroad crosses them, is now the most vulnerable point. I regard it as the most important strategical point in the whole field of operations." Buell also noted that while the Confederates controlled the area between the rivers "it secures their force and gives access through the two rivers to the very center of their power. While they hold it, at least two-thirds of the whole force on that front may safely be considered available for any one point that is threatened." General Buell's proposals for piercing the Confederate defensive line were quite sound and realistic, but as usual no one in command wanted to take the responsibility of actually acting on one of them.[15]

Don Carlos Buell would play a major role in the early part of the war in the West, but not always a positive one. General Buell was appointed by his close friend George McClellan to command the new Department of the Ohio consisting of Ohio, Michigan, Indiana, Tennessee and Kentucky east of the Cumberland River. Many of Buell's colleagues considered him to be an excellent officer who was a tough disciplinarian with an established record of turning new recruits into well-trained soldiers. He was also methodical to a fault and usually considered the enemy as an inconvenience that might disturb his perfect plans. Buell wrote that he had learned from his studies of military history that the only reason to fight a battle was for some important object and that "success must be rendered reasonably certain if possible — the more certain the better; that if the result is reasonably uncertain, battle is only to be sought when very serious disadvantage must result from a failure to fight or when the advantages of a possible victory far outweigh the consequences of probable defeat. These rules suppose that war has a higher object than that of mere bloodshed."[16]

There was little doubt that General Buell was committed to the cause of preserving the Union; he was also a conservative Democrat with no interest in destroying the institution of slavery, having been a slave owner himself. Believing that political methods could still work to end the rebellion, he did not really approve of escalating the war to the point of subjugating the South by military means. Regrettably for Buell, his belief in taking it easy on the enemy put him one step behind the current thinking in Washington and affected the war effort in the West in 1862.[17]

It would be safe to assume that Halleck probably agreed with Buell's opinion that in order to be successful any major Federal campaign in Tennessee had to include taking control of the Tennessee and Cumberland rivers. Unfortunately, part of the reason for the delay in implementing any plan was that both Halleck and Buell wanted to be the one to claim that victory. Halleck was hesitant to mount what would almost certainly be a costly assault on Columbus or send thousands of his troops up the two rivers in order to make it easier for Buell to capture Bowling Green and Nashville. Buell, reasonably enough, believed that Nashville was the most important prize in Tennessee, and since the city was in Buell's department he wanted to receive the credit when the city was taken. Taking Nashville was the kind of victory that could propel a man to overall command of the West and Buell was not particularly interested in sharing that credit with anyone, but especially not with Henry Halleck, his main rival.[18]

Even on the last day of the year President Lincoln was still trying to get Halleck and Buell to cooperate. Lincoln sent a message to Halleck asking, "Are General Buell and yourself in concert? When he moves on Bowling Green, what hinders it being re-enforced from Columbus? A simultaneous movement by you on Columbus might prevent it." The next day the president wired Buell mentioning that he had already written to Halleck and commenting that "I think you better get in concert with General Halleck at once." The problem in coordinating any meaningful operations in the West was that the two top commanders were more concerned with their rivalry for the top command than they were with accomplishing anything that might actually earn them that position.[19]

President Lincoln was having a tough time of it just then. There were constant complaints from Congress asking why the war effort was moving so slowly. General McClellan had shown that he was in no hurry to initiate any major offensive movement in the East until he was fully prepared, which apparently looked to be a long time coming. Lincoln only wanted someone to start fighting and didn't really much care where. Now the president's frustration with the generals reached new highs when he received messages from both Buell and Halleck on January 1. General Buell replied, "There is no arrangement between General Halleck and myself. I have been informed by General McClellan that he would make suitable disposition for concerted action." In other words, Buell would take no action in concert with Halleck and no action on his own without orders to do so from McClellan. An eerily similar reply was received from General Halleck: "I have never received a word from General Buell. I am not ready to co-operate with him. Hope to do so in few weeks. Have written fully on this subject to Major-General McClellan. Too much haste will ruin everything." Halleck was also in no hurry to make war and would apparently wait for the perfect opportunity to take action, which seldom occurs in wartime.[20]

While the generals commanding the armies in the West were not anxious to work together to attack the enemy, they were certainly willing to write to each other either asking for assistance or turning down requests for assistance. On January 2 Halleck wrote to Buell basically warning him that there would be no help coming from Halleck's forces in the immediate future since "I have had no instruction respecting co-operation." Making any serious movement against Columbus to support a move by Buell against Bowling Green was simply out of the question as "all my available troops are in the field except those at Cairo and Paducah, which are barely sufficient to threaten Columbus." Maybe in a few weeks Halleck could put together a plan to assist Buell but certainly not now.[21]

Even from as far away as Washington the general-in-chief could see the proper strategy for the initial campaign in the West depended on Halleck and Buell cooperating with each other. On January 3 McClellan wrote to Halleck, "It is of the greatest importance that the rebel troops in Western Kentucky be prevented from moving to support the force in front of General Buell." The most obvious way to prevent this was for Halleck to send an expedition "up the Cumberland River, to act in concert with General Buell's command." McClellan even suggested that the expedition be made up of two divisions escorted by gunboats. He also mentioned that even if it was not possible to carry out a serious movement against Columbus some sort of demonstration would be very helpful in drawing Confederate strength away from the area where the actual campaign would be directed. McClellan requested that Halleck report back with his views on the subject.[22]

General Buell also wrote to Halleck on the third putting forth his own idea of how they might cooperate in a major campaign. Buell began by stating what was pretty obvious to both generals, that the greatest strength of the Confederates was between Columbus and Bowling Green. The most important point strategically was the relatively small area where the railroad crossed the Tennessee and Cumberland rivers, including Nashville. To prevent the enemy from using the railroads connecting Bowling Green and Columbus to transfer troops relatively quickly to the threatened position Buell suggested they make a "combined attack on its center and flanks, or at least demonstrations which may be converted into real attacks, and fully occupy the enemy on the whole front." Part of this plan included expeditions up both the Tennessee and Cumberland.[23]

On January 6 Halleck wired a detailed response to President Lincoln's note of December 31. In this message Halleck tried to explain the challenges he faced. With reference to a campaign against the Confederate stronghold at Columbus, he stated that the garrison there numbered about twenty-two thousand men behind strong fortifications. Halleck reported that he had "at Cairo, Fort Holt, and Paducah only about 15,000, which, after leaving guards at these places, would give me but little over 10,000 men with which to assist General Buell." Halleck continued by emphasizing that he believed: "It would be madness to attempt anything serious with such a force and I cannot at the present time withdraw any from Missouri without risking the loss of this State."[24]

Halleck continued his message by stating that he was "satisfied that the authorities at Washington do not appreciate the difficulties with which we have to contend here." Since the beginning of the rebellion Confederate sympathizers had been hard at work stirring up anger against the Federal Government and had succeeded to the point where they had "so enraged the people of Missouri, that it is estimated that there is a majority of 80,000 against the Government." Convinced that he was "virtually in an enemy's country," Halleck also had to deal with thousands of unruly troops who lacked even the basics of military discipline, compounded by the fact that there was an acute shortage of experienced officers who could provide the troops with the training they desperately needed before facing the enemy. Commenting on the situation he inherited from General Frémont, the frustrated general stated, "I assure you, Mr. President, it is very difficult to accomplish much with such means. I am in the condition of a carpenter who is required to build a bridge with a dull ax, a broken saw, and rotten timber."[25]

In regard to the president's continued pressure for him and Buell to work together Halleck admitted that he knew "nothing of General Buell's intended operations, never having received any information in regard to the general plan of campaign." As the most talked-about plan for a joint movement was for Buell to advance against Bowling Green while he moved on Columbus, Halleck emphatically stated that a plan of this nature was certain to fail: "To operate on exterior lines against an enemy occupying a central position will fail, as it always has failed, in ninety-nine cases out of a hundred. It is condemned by every military authority I have ever read." Dismayed by the seemingly endless roadblocks in the way of progress, real and imagined, President Lincoln added a personal note to Halleck's dispatch: "It is exceedingly discouraging. As everywhere else, nothing can be done."[26]

Back in Washington, President Lincoln was becoming more impatient by the day with the lack of movement in the West. In a message sent on January 7, the president insisted that Buell "name as early a day as you safely can on or before which you can be ready to move southward in concert with Major-General Halleck. Delay is ruining us, and it is indispensable for me to have something definite." Trying any means to get either Halleck or Buell to take some action even if he had to use their rivalry against them, the president noted that he had sent a similar wire to Halleck.[27]

3

The Opening Moves

The early idea of the strategy that would eventually produce a string of Union victories in the West began one December evening when General Halleck invited his chief of staff, General George Cullum, and Brigadier General William T. Sherman to join him for dinner at headquarters in St. Louis. After a pleasant meal the generals were relaxing and enjoying their cigars while studying a map on which General Cullum had marked the Confederate defensive line from Bowling Green through Forts Henry and Donelson to Columbus. After briefly examining the map, Halleck asked his guests where they believed would be the best place to try to pierce the Confederate line. Both officers quickly replied, "In the center." The accepted basic strategy to use against an enemy that had the great advantage of operating on interior lines that could not be flanked was to concentrate a large force to offset their ability to move troops quickly from place to place. Sherman noted that Halleck drew a perpendicular line through the Confederate defenses that closely followed the route of the Tennessee River near Fort Henry. "That's the true line of operations," Halleck announced. If a Federal base could be established near the center of the enemy's defensive line, troops could move in all directions against any part of the enemy defenses. A large force inserted into the heart of enemy territory could easily be supplied by the Union-controlled Tennessee and Cumberland rivers, which would also offer a relatively safe route to bring up reinforcements or pull back if necessary. At this time, however, Halleck's observations were just that; he felt that no movement could be made in Tennessee until he had Missouri under control and, as always, there were not enough troops available to begin a major campaign in Tennessee. Halleck was the type of soldier who followed the rules and tried to put everything in its proper order, which inevitably meant that he did things slowly, like making war.[1]

One of General Halleck's officers who was in a hurry to get on with the war was Ulysses S. Grant. In January Grant developed a strategic plan that just happened to coincide with Halleck's observation of where to strike the Confederate defenses. Looking at the map, any campaign down the Mississippi River would have to get by the Confederate fortress at Columbus, which was unlikely. In Eastern Tennessee the mountainous terrain and lack of supply routes made any advance by large numbers of troops through that area very risky. It was on the Tennessee and Cumberland rivers that a thrust into Confederate territory could be successful. The opening of the Tennessee River would not only isolate the western part of the state but also give Union warships access as far south as Florence, Alabama. The enemy stronghold at Columbus would have to be abandoned, opening the upper Mississippi to Union warships and giving them access to Confederate forts downriver. If these forts could be taken, then Memphis could be approached from the river and the rail center at Corinth, Mississippi, would be threatened. By an expedition launched up the Cumberland River the vital manufacturing center of Nashville could be taken and the main Confederate field army at Bowling Green would be cut off. Altogether, a campaign up the two rivers could produce a potentially huge breakthrough for the Union war effort.[2]

The first and only Confederate position defending the mouth of the Tennessee River against Federal incursion was Fort Henry, a small, poorly placed fortification on the eastern side of the river near the border with Kentucky. About a dozen miles east was the main Confederate defensive work on the Cumberland River, Fort Donelson, a much larger and more formidable fortification than Fort Henry. If General Grant could gain the cooperation of the powerful Federal naval forces and seize control of both of these river forts two quick strikes could end up forcing the enemy out of Kentucky and give the Union control of nearly half of Tennessee.[3]

On January 6, following a series of telegrams between Halleck, Buell and McClellan, orders were sent to Grant to make a reconnaissance toward Mayfield, Kentucky, about thirty miles south of Paducah. This movement was made mostly to aid General Buell by preventing reinforcements from being sent to bolster General Buckner's Confederate forces at Bowling Green. Halleck wanted Grant to "make a great fuss about moving all your forces towards Nashville, and let it be so reported by the newspapers," without revealing the true reason for the movement. Doing his best not to start anything he was not yet prepared for, Halleck instructed Grant, "Be very careful, however, to avoid a battle; we are not ready for that; but cut off detached parties and give your men a little experience in skirmishing." General Halleck specifically told Grant not to "advance far enough to expose your flank and rear to an attack from Columbus, and by all means avoid a serious engagement." In other words, Grant was to send his troops into enemy territory but not do anything that they might take offense at and actually bring on a fight.[4]

Pleased that movement of any kind was finally happening, Grant planned a multiple-part movement. Brigadier General Charles F. Smith led two brigades toward Fort Henry while at the same time Union gunboats patrolled the river. General Smith was a tough as leather, an old-school soldier who was itching to get at the enemy. Smith boarded the gunboat *Lexington* as she approached Fort Henry to get a closer look at the layout of the fort and another defensive position still under construction on the opposite riverbank, known as Fort Heiman. Smith got a good look at both Confederate fortifications and discovered what the Confederates already knew, which was why they were building a second installation, that Fort Henry had been built in the wrong place and was open to assault from land and the river. After the *Lexington* exchanged a few shots with the fort she headed back downriver.[5]

Union general Ulysses S. Grant. Less than successful in civilian life, in two years he would become the only lieutenant general in the army and general-in-chief (Library of Congress).

While General Smith was heading in the direction of Fort Henry, Grant took a force of about six thousand men a little farther west than Smith's column in the direction of Columbus. Most of what Grant remembered about that march was not pleasant: "The weather was very bad; snow and rain fell, the roads, never good in that section, were intolerable. We were out more than a week splashing through the mud, snow and rain, the men suffering much." Despite the difficulties, the dual demonstrations served their purpose by keeping Confederate troops destined for Bowling Green at Columbus, which was the original objective. General Smith's discovery of the vulnerability of Fort Henry was an unexpected bonus. When he reported on January 22 Smith wrote that "I think two iron-clad gunboats would make short work of Fort Henry. There is no masked battery at the foot of the island, as we supposed, or, if so, it is now under water." Grant immediately realized that this could be the opening he was looking for to begin a campaign into Tennessee.[6]

Already aware of the advantages of putting together a campaign using the Tennessee and Cumberland rivers to advance into Tennessee, even General Halleck, who was usually almost too cautious and slow to make a move where there was more than minimal risk involved, could not ignore the fact that such a campaign offered the opportunity of gaining extraordinary results. In a message to General McClellan on January 20 Halleck put forth some of his thoughts on a new strategy in the West. Halleck was convinced that trying to force his way down the Mississippi River was, at least at this time, totally unrealistic. He was, however, just as sure that "a much more feasible plan is to move up the Cumberland and Tennessee, making Nashville the first objective point." Besides the capture of the capital of the state and the largest manufacturing center in the West, a movement up the Cumberland would have the added benefit of cutting off Bowling Green and forcing the retreat of the army stationed there. To the west the opening of the Tennessee and the cutting of the railroads that supplied Columbus would render that strategic fortress impotent, and the Confederate forces stationed there would be subject to the choice between starvation and retreat. This plan would also avoid what was sure to be immense loss of life if the Union army was forced to lay siege to the heavily fortified position. After putting forth what was really a very good argument for the river campaign approach, Halleck, always the careful warrior, stated that he could not recommend implementing any movement up the rivers with fewer than sixty thousand men, well above what was realistically available.[7]

General Halleck had put forth a sound plan for what could be a very advantageous campaign, but in addition to the obvious military benefits his sudden urge to take action was at least partly the result of events that occurred outside his department. On January 18 one of Buell's subordinates, General George H. Thomas, won a small but significant battle at Mill Springs in Eastern Kentucky. This victory improved General Buell's standing back in Washington, something that Halleck certainly did not like, as he was obviously in competition with Buell. Another, and significantly more important, issue that came up was that Halleck received news that Confederate general Pierre G. T. Beauregard was heading west with as many as fifteen regiments of Confederate reinforcements for Albert Sidney Johnston's army. If any action up the rivers was going to be taken it obviously would be best to move before these reinforcements arrived.[8]

General Grant had been trying to get a meeting with Halleck to discuss potential plans since early in January, with little success. Grant could be persistent when he had something he believed in, and after receiving General Smith's report on the weakness of Fort Henry he again requested to be allowed to go to St. Louis and meet Halleck at his headquarters. Halleck finally relented and on January 23 Grant got his opportunity to sell his commanding officer on his plan to begin a campaign along the rivers. The meeting Grant had worked so hard to obtain quickly turned into an embarrassing failure, as Grant later wrote that he was received "with so little cordiality that I perhaps stated the object of my visit with less clearness than I might have done, and I had not uttered many sentences before I was cut short as if my plan was preposterous." Whether Halleck was especially rude to Grant because of a personal dislike is debatable, but it is definitely safe to say that Halleck was skeptical of Grant's ability to plan, let alone carry out, a major campaign.[9]

Not one to give in after just one setback, General Grant returned to Cairo and tried again to convince Halleck to act; this time, however, Grant decided that he could use some assistance from Flag Officer Foote. On January 28 Grant wrote to Halleck that with his permission "I will take Fort Henry, on the Tennessee, and establish and hold a large camp there." That same day Foote sent his own message to Halleck stating, "Commanding General Grant and myself are of opinion the Fort Henry, on the Tennessee River, can be carried with four iron-clad gunboats and troops to permanently occupy. Have we your authority to move for that purpose when ready?"[10]

Trying to subtly and respectfully keep the pressure on General Halleck, Grant sent another message the very next day, elaborating on the plan and noting, "In view of the large force now concentrating in this district and the present feasibility of the plan I would respectfully suggest the propriety of subduing Fort Henry, near the Kentucky and Tennessee line." With Confederate reinforcements headed west there was a very real possibility that their defensive positions on both rivers could soon be significantly stronger and that the window of opportunity to launch a successful attack on the enemy defenses along the rivers might soon be closed. Grant also tactfully pointed out that "the advantages of this move are as perceptible to the general commanding as to myself, therefore further statements are unnecessary."[11]

Moving at his own speed, General Halleck was slowly nearing a decision. He didn't really trust Grant to plan, let alone command, what would be the first major campaign under Halleck's authority. Grant was a little too aggressive for Halleck's taste and he was concerned that once Grant had an independent command he would be difficult to control. On the one hand, in addition to the reservations about the campaign's commander, it was the middle of winter and there was the likelihood that poor weather would have a negative impact on any troop movements. Of course, on the other hand, there were several good reasons for implementing Grant's plan, or at least something similar. The rumors of Confederate reinforcements coming from the East were confirmed when McClellan wired both Halleck and Buell that Beauregard was indeed heading west with fifteen regiments. If any major action was to take place, obviously it would be best to begin before these additional enemy troops arrived. In addition, if Fort Henry could be taken the railroad that ran between Bowling Green and Columbus could be broken, seriously damaging enemy communications. Finally, the fact that Flag Officer Foote approved the move and that General Buell had already suggested a similar project convinced Halleck that it was time to make a decision.[12]

On January 30 Halleck wired Grant instructing him: "Make your preparations to take and hold Fort Henry. I will send you written instructions by mail." Also on the thirtieth Halleck sent a message to McClellan to acknowledge receiving the information about Beauregard and informing him that "General Grant and Commodore Foote will be ordered to immediately advance, and to reduce and hold Fort Henry, on the Tennessee river." Halleck also noted that an additional objective of the movement was the cutting of the railroad between Bowling Green and Columbus.[13]

General Grant replied to Halleck's orders that he would immediately begin organizing the forces that would be going on the expedition, drawing as little attention as possible for security reasons, saying that he was "[a]waiting your instructions, which we expect in the morning, I have not made definite plans as to my movements, but expect to start Sunday evening, taking 15,000 men." The troops would be transported by ships as far upriver as possible, and since the movement was still limited in scope to taking Fort Henry, once that place was under Union control a modest-size force commanded by either Brigadier General John A. McClernand or General Smith would be left behind to man the fort and the rest of the army would return.[14]

On the thirty-first General Halleck sent more detailed instructions concerning the size of the expedition, promising to send reinforcements to augment the original fifteen thousand men allocated to the campaign. In addition to the capture of Fort Henry, Halleck confirmed that the railroads linking Bowling Green and Columbus were to be destroyed if at all possible, noting that because of the approach of Beauregard's force "[i]t is therefore of the greatest importance that we cut that line before he arrives. You will move with the least delay possible." The very next day Henry Halleck, who generally took his time in almost everything, was again pushing for Grant to get going as soon as possible: "The object is to move rapidly and promptly by steamers, and to reduce the place before any large reinforcements can arrive."[15]

Since the roads were a mess that time of year, troops and supplies would have to travel by water, escorted by Flag Officer Foote's warships. When Foote was informed that he would be responsible for the safe transportation of the army to Fort Henry he was less than pleased. There were not nearly enough transports to carry all Grant's troops and there were not nearly enough sailors to man the ships they did have. Once again General Halleck moved quickly concerning this potential problem, writing to Foote on the third that he had authorized Grant to furnish men for temporary duty aboard Foote's ships and instructing Foote: "Arrange with General Grant for temporary crews, so that there may be no delay." As it turned out, however, in the end the transports would still have to make two trips to bring up the entire army.[16]

General Grant sent out orders for the movement to his division commanders on February 1. Brigadier General John A. McClernand was in command of the First Division. An energetic former congressman from Illinois, he was an excellent organizer and recruiter, owing his rank to political influence. McClernand's only military experience was in the Black Hawk War and commanding a brigade under Grant at Belmont. The First Division consisted of brigades commanded by Colonels Richard Oglesby and W. H. L. Wallace. McClernand was to have his division ready to move by the next evening with three day's supply of provisions for the troops and forage for his animals.[17]

In Grant's instructions to General Smith he was to join the First Division with all the troops that could be spared from Paducah and Smithland with Monday, February 3, as the date the advance would begin. Trying to keep the Confederates guessing as to the destination of the expedition, Grant suggested, "But very little preparation is necessary for this move; and, if possible, the troops and community should be kept from knowing anything of the design." Grant must have felt a little uneasy giving orders to General Smith. The old soldier had been commandant of cadets when Grant was a student at West Point and had performed with conspicuous gallantry in the Mexican War. Smith had been in the army for thirty-five years and looked the part of a soldier; tall and lean, with a long white mustache, he was the embodiment of discipline and courage. Clearly, with Smith the most experienced of the senior officers assigned to the expedition, politics had played a large part in putting Grant in command over the veteran.[18]

On the last day of January General Halleck finally informed Buell of the expedition to Fort Henry. More information was forthcoming the next few days as Halleck gave Buell more specifics of the expedition and its goals. Buell belatedly offered assistance, to which Halleck replied that none was needed and "at present it is only proposed to take and occupy Fort Henry and Dover [including nearby Fort Donelson], and, if possible, cut the railroad from Columbus to Bowling Green." Halleck admitted that once the Tennessee was open he was not sure how far gunboats should try to penetrate into Confederate territory, leaving that decision to be made at a later time. The longer-term objective of taking Fort Henry was also mentioned, as Halleck noted that a strong force at the fort would almost certainly compel Confederate troops to be "withdrawn either from Bowling Green or Columbus to protect the railroads. If the former, you can advance; if the latter, we can take New Madrid and cut off the river communication with Columbus." Clearly, if the expedition to Fort Henry was handled properly and followed up as Halleck envisioned, large areas of Kentucky and Tennessee would fall under Federal control. In addition to a great military success, this would also very likely be a major factor in Halleck obtaining one of his personal objectives, overall command in the West.[19]

For months President Lincoln had asked, demanded, and finally used threats trying to get the commanders in the West to do something. For months those commanders, especially Halleck and Buell, had done little other than argue with one another, debate conflicting strategies and mostly do and say whatever they could that might give one of them an advantage over the other. It had taken much too long, but finally Union forces were advancing against the enemy. The seemingly modest goals of Grant's expedition would end up having a major impact on the war effort. Seldom during a conflict does everything come together with the right man in the right place at the right time; fortunately for the Union, this was one of those times. General Grant left Cairo on February 2 to rendezvous with General Smith's troops at Paducah. It was dark during the early hours of February 3 as the regiments that would be heading up the Tennessee began filing aboard the transports docked along Paducah's waterfront. Once all the men, equipment and animals had been loaded the expedition was ready to go and Grant did not hesitate; probably he was anxious to finally be on the way. He had sent a short message to General Halleck back in St. Louis that signaled the start of a campaign that began Grant's rise to heights it is doubtful that he ever imagined he would achieve: "Will be off up the Tennessee at 6 o'clock. Command, twenty-three regiments in all."[20]

4

Taking Fort Henry

On the morning of February 3 the transports carrying General Grant's troops gradually pulled away from the docks into the Ohio River and soon after rounding the first bend were moving up the Tennessee River with their escort of seven warships. The fighting vessels and their commanders in Flag Officer Foote's fleet were the ironclads *Carondelet*, Commander Henry Walke; the *Essex*, Captain William Porter; the *St. Louis*, Lieutenant-Commander Leonard Paulding; and the *Cincinnati*, Commander Roger Stemble. Three wooden gunboats, the *Conestoga*, *Lexington*, and *Taylor*, under the command of Lieutenant Seth L. Phelps, joined the escort. Though not as formidable as the ironclads, the wooden gunboats were certainly capable of doing serious damage to the enemy. As the ships began their journey General Grant was observed by his chief of staff, John Rawlins, nervously pacing the deck and looking back toward Paducah. Rawlins believed that even at this late date Grant was worried that General Halleck might cancel the expedition.[1]

The trip up the Tennessee was quiet and uneventful and the fleet arrived in the vicinity of Fort Henry during the morning of February 4. Rain had been falling steadily and the river was running high and fast as the ships approached the fort, requiring strenuous effort to control the ungainly ironclads. As it turned out, however, the swift current had a positive effect by breaking loose many of the mines, or torpedoes, the Confederates had set in the water. Instead of lying in wait for the ships to close on the fort or to be run into at night, these dangerous objects floated harmlessly past the ships in broad daylight.[2]

During the afternoon the transports arrived about three miles below Fort Henry and McClernand's troops began disembarking on the eastern shore. Leaving the three wooden gunboats behind, Foote, accompanied by Grant aboard the flagship *Cincinnati*, led the four ironclads closer to the fort to get a better look at the enemy fortifications and exchange a few cannon shots to test the range before beginning the main attack.[3]

There were not a sufficient number of transports available to bring Grant's entire force to Fort Henry at the same time, so he ordered McClernand to remain in place while the transports returned to Paducah for General Smith's troops. During the wait Grant was able to view the terrain firsthand and began to see that his original plan to use siege warfare could be compromised by the lay of the land and the fact that the heavy rains had turned the fields and roads into quagmires that would prevent any speedy movement of his troops.[4]

The target of General Grant's expedition, Fort Henry, had been built on low ground in a bend of the river where it was prone to flooding when the river was high, like it was now. Captain Jesse Taylor, one of the Confederate artillery officers stationed in the fort, had little positive to say about the position: "Arriving at the fort, I was convinced by a glance at its surroundings that extraordinarily bad judgment, or worse, had selected the site for its erection. I found it placed on the east bank of the river in a bottom commanded by high hills rising on either side of the river, and within good rifle range." Within the fortifications the Confederates' had assembled seventeen heavy guns of various sizes, the largest of which were able to fire straight down the river at attacking ships. Outside the fortifications rifle pits and other entrenchments and obstacles had been built to defend against a land-based assault. This time of year, however, the Confederates' best defenses were the swamp-like flooded fields and heavy woods making it difficult, if not impossible, for large numbers of infantry to approach the fort.[5]

To man the defenses of Fort Henry the commander of the fort, Brigadier General Lloyd Tilghman, could muster a total garrison of a little less than three thousand men. Descended from a prominent Maryland family that had sent its men to fight for the nation since the Revolutionary War, Tilghman was a West Point graduate who had served with distinction in the Mexican War. The size of Fort Henry's garrison did not reflect the importance of its position as the first Confederate installation on the Tennessee River, but if the situation demanded, reinforcements could be quickly brought up from Fort Donelson on the Cumberland River, just eleven miles away and connected by two good roads.[6]

Grant firmly believed that together both forts were so important to the defense of the rivers that he had every right to be concerned that Confederate "reinforcements would come from every quarter from which they could be got. Prompt action on our part was imperative." Despite these concerns, Grant felt good enough about his position that shortly after taking in the situation he was able to write his wife, Julia, "All the troops will be up by noon tomorrow, and Friday morning, if we are not attacked before, the fight will commence. The enemy are well fortified and have a strong force. I do not want to boast but I have a confident feeling of success."[7]

The transports sent back to Paducah to pick up the rest of Grant's force wasted little time in making the round-trip, and the very next day General Smith's troops began arriving and disembarked on the western side of the river, increasing Grant's entire force to about fifteen thousand men. On the fifth Grant issued Field Orders No. 1 spelling out his plan for the coming attack. On the landward side of Fort Henry, General McClernand and the nine thousand men of his First Division were to advance east of the fort and cut off the roads between Fort Henry and Fort Donelson. Grant's orders read: "It will be the special duty of this command to prevent all re-enforcements to Fort Henry or escape from it, also to be held in readiness to charge and take Fort Henry by storm promptly on the receipt of orders."[8]

Union flag officer Andrew Foote. Fervent opponent of slavery and speaker at abolitionist meetings (Library of Congress).

As McClernand advanced against the fort's outer works newly arrived General Smith was to take two of his brigades commanded by Colonels John Cook and Morgan Smith and seize the unfinished Fort Heiman opposite Fort Henry in the hills above the western shore, setting up artillery to fire on Fort Henry. Once Fort Heiman was secure Smith's third brigade and other troops not needed at Fort Heiman were to be transferred to the eastern side of the river to join McClernand's force in the assault on the earthworks outside the fort. While these infantry movements were taking place Flag Officer Foote's gunboats were to move upriver and begin a bombardment of the main Confederate river fortifications.[9]

While the Federal forces were getting into position, inside the fort General Tilghman was well aware of the desperate situation he was faced with. Both the fort itself and virtually all the outer works were within range of Federal artillery on both sides of the river, not to mention the heavy guns of the gunboats. It was clear to Tilghman that his waterlogged defenses would soon be pounded into submission when three Federal gunboats opened fire late in the afternoon of the fifth. After dark Tilghman convened a meeting of his senior officers, who quickly came to the conclusion that the fort could not be held and the best thing to do was evacuate most of the troops to Fort Donelson. Tilghman reported that he clearly saw that "Fort Donelson might possibly be held, if properly re-enforced, even though Fort Henry should fall; but the reverse of this proposition was not true." General Tilghman and about eighty men, including fifty-five members of the 1st Tennessee Artillery, would remain in the fort to man the guns while the remainder of the garrison escaped to Fort Donelson.[10]

The early-morning hours of February 6 were clear with a slight breeze, excellent weather for the assault that was scheduled to take place. Out on the Tennessee River the gunboat's crews began preparing for action, and on the eastern side of the river General McClernand's troops made ready to move forward and cut the roads leading out of Fort Henry, trapping the garrison in the doomed fort. As frequently happens, however, little went as planned, due to the poor condition of the terrain from the recent rain. The roads had been turned into muddy lines on the landscape and every little stream was swollen so high that bridges had to be built for the artillery. It took hours for the infantry to make any appreciable movement toward their assigned positions. Wilbur F. Crummer of the 45th Illinois later wrote that "many times we had to stop, stack arms, throw off knapsacks and put our shoulders to the wheels of the artillery and help them out of the mud holes."[11]

The gunboats got under way just before eleven o'clock in the morning, moving up to Panther Island, situated about two miles below the fort. The four ironclads formed the first line with the *Essex* on the right, then the *Cincinnati*, *Carondelet*, and *St. Louis*. Behind the ironclads, where they would be subject to less danger but still able to add their fire to the coming battle, the wooden gunboats formed a second line consisting of the *Tyler*, *Conestoga*, and *Lexington*. General Grant was on board the flagship with Foote, both of whom were aware of the slow movement of the infantry. Foote half-jokingly commented that his ships would probably force the fort to surrender before the infantry could make its presence felt.[12]

The gunboats came out from behind the island about noon and the *Essex* fired the first shot when she was still well over a mile from the fort. The other ships quickly joined in and they had closed to about a mile of the fort when the Confederate guns opened on the fleet. The ships continued to close the range until they were within about six hundred yards of the fort. As would be expected, as the range decreased the accuracy of fire from both side increased. Commander Walke later wrote, "The firing from the armored vessels was rapid and well sustained from the beginning of the attack, and seemingly accurate, as we could occasionally see the earth thrown in great heaps over the enemy's guns." But the damage was not one-sided, as Confederate shot began striking the Federal ships; as Walke noted, "their heavy shot broke and scattered our iron-plating as if it had been putty, and often passed completely through the casemates."[13]

The Federal ironclads were hit time after time by Confederate shot. The *Carondelet* was struck about thirty times; the *Cincinnati* was hit thirty-two times, although the *St. Louis* received only seven hits. Aboard the *Essex*, however, one of the many hits she received caused more damage and casualties than were suffered by the rest of the fleet combined. A heavy shot pierced the armor and blew up a boiler, causing over thirty casualties, including Captain Porter, who was wounded, and both pilots, who were killed. One of the crew, Second Master James Laning, described the terrible scene, "The steam and hot water in the forward gun-deck had driven all who were able to get out of the ports overboard, except a few who were fortunate enough to cling to the casemate outside." The *Essex* was disabled, and helplessly adrift, she soon fell out of line. The result of this disaster was, as Laning wrote, "in a very few minutes after the explosion our gallant ship was drifting slowly away from the scene of action; her commander badly wounded, a number of her officers and crew dead at their post, while many others were writhing in their last agony."[14]

With the *Essex* out of action the three remaining ironclads continued to pound Fort Henry as they moved even closer. The bombardment had been going on for less than an hour and a half, and by now the condition of the inside of the fort was appalling. Dismounted guns and pieces of gun carriages were mixed together with logs and other rubble from buildings that had burst apart when struck by heavy shells. Fires were burning all around the fort and, worst of all, the bloody and mangled bodies of dead and wounded lay everywhere. Most of the largest Confederate guns had been disabled or destroyed by Federal fire and accidents, and there were only four working guns left. Captain Jesse Taylor was a witness to the destruction inside the fort and acknowledged that the heavy shells from the ironclads had "penetrated the earth-works as readily as a ball from a Navy Colt would pierce a pine board."[15]

The Confederate defenders had fought bravely and the fort had held out long enough for the garrison to make good their escape toward Fort Donelson. General Tilghman clearly saw that further resistance would only sacrifice more of his men for no good reason. The Confederate flag was lowered and the firing came to an end. Lieutenant Commander Phelps accepted the surrender of the fort from Captain Taylor, who represented General Tilghman. The Confederates reported the loss of five killed, eleven wounded and five missing, and over seventy defenders were taken prisoner. General Tilghman later reported that "I take occasion to bear testimony to the gallantry of the officers and men under my command. They sustained their position with consummate bravery as long as there was any hope of success."[16]

The Federal ironclads had won a relatively easy victory in their first serious fight, which fostered the idea that earthworks of any kind could be demolished by heavy naval gunfire. As they would soon learn, however, Fort Henry was the exception rather than the rule. The fort was poorly planned and located where it was susceptible to flooding. The day of the battle the lower part of the fort was already taking on water; in fact, the small boat that brought the naval officers to the fort to accept the surrender was able to sail right up between the fort and prepared infantry positions. Captain Taylor noted, "If the attack had been delayed forty-eight hours, there would hardly have been a hostile shot fired; the Tennessee would have accomplished the work by drowning the magazine."[17]

Other than General Smith's men taking the wide-open Fort Heiman, Grant's infantry contributed little to the victory. While the opening of the Tennessee River was the primary goal of the expedition, Grant certainly wanted to capture as much of the garrison as possible. Good soldier that he was, General Tilghman clearly knew that his position could not be held for long and wisely posted his troops on the outer lines of the fortifications to allow them time to escape to Fort Donelson so they could fight another day. The difficulty of moving through the rain-soaked terrain caused enough delays that McClernand's infantry had little chance of cutting off the retreating Confederates and even less of catching them. Shortly after the fort surrendered, Grant sent a wire to General Halleck giving the naval forces all the credit for the victory: "Fort Henry is ours. The gunboats silenced the batteries before the investment was completed. I think the garrison must have commenced the retreat last night. I shall take and destroy Fort Donelson on the 8th and return to Fort Henry."[18]

Later on February 6 General Grant sent a more detailed report to Halleck explaining that at the time he felt it was imperative to begin the assault immediately rather than waiting for the infantry to move up and complete the investment of the fort and the surrounding fortifications. Believing that the Confederate garrison was already gone by early morning, he informed Halleck that even had he delayed the attack "I do not now believe, however, that the result would have been any more satisfactory." Grant also repeated his relatively casual comment that he would attack and take Fort Donelson on the eighth, possibly leaving a small force behind to occupy the fort and return to Fort Henry with the bulk of the army. He also noted, "Owing to the intolerable state of the roads no transportation will be taken to Fort Donelson and but little artillery, and that with double teams." As it turned out, Grant was being overly optimistic about his ability to march to Fort Donelson and capture that place in two days.[19]

General Grant's confidence that he could take Fort Donelson so easily did not extend to his commanding officer, General Halleck, who made it very clear that he wanted Grant to take a more defensive posture. On February 8 Halleck telegraphed to Grant that the only offensive moves he approved of were to destroy the bridges at Clarksville, if possible. Otherwise, Grant was to dig in at Fort Henry, improve the fortifications to resist an attack by land and wait for reinforcements, which would be arriving soon. Halleck emphasized the importance of keeping hold of what Grant had just won: "Hold on to Fort Henry at all hazards. Impress slaves, if necessary, to strengthen your position as rapidly as possible. It is of vital importance to strengthen your position as rapidly as possible."[20]

Although General Grant was confident that he would quickly take Fort Donelson, he quickly discovered that was not going to happen as soon as he had hoped. Grant with a small escort rode out to take a look at Fort Donelson on the seventh, wanting to see for himself the defenses of his next target. From this quick reconnaissance Grant learned that the fort itself was on a hill overlooking a relatively straight stretch of the Cumberland River. Flooding prevented any approach from the right and the Confederates were actively improving the outer defenses by building up earthworks and cutting trees with sharpened branches facing outward toward the direction of an enemy attack. One of the reasons that Grant was optimistic that he could take Fort Donelson was the officers in command of the fort. Grant later wrote, "I had known General Pillow in Mexico, and judged that with any force, no matter how small, I could march up to within gunshot of any intrenchments he was given to hold. I said this to the officers of my staff at the time. I knew that Floyd was in command, but he was no soldier, and I judged that he would yield to Pillow's pretensions." Grant was proved right, as he approached the fort meeting no scouts or pickets and was able to get a good view of the terrain, also learning that there were two roads he could use to bring his army over to Fort Donelson; one led to the village of Dover, the other to the fort.[21]

Despite Grant's opinion concerning the weakness of the commanders at Fort Donelson, he also learned that it was not going to be as easy as first thought to capture the fort and its garrison. The roads that would have to be used to approach the fort were a mess. The frequent rain and melting snow, not to mention the damage done by the Confederates who had retreated from Fort Henry, had turned the roads into narrow ribbons of mud. The terrain around the fortifications was filled with hills and little gullies that provided numerous places for ambush or the placement of defensive works to delay any approaching troops. Grant would need more men, more artillery, and more time to mount a successful campaign to take Fort Donelson. Extra horses would be needed to pull the wheeled vehicles through the muddy roads and Fort Henry would have to be turned into a supply depot to support the attacking forces. In addition, Grant had been ordered to hold Fort Henry at any cost, so he could not afford to strip that place of defenders. All in all, there simply would be no campaign against Fort Donelson on February 8.[22]

General Halleck was comfortable forming strategy with maps in his office, but when it came to sending men out to fight against forces beyond his control he turned cautious. So right from the start he had been anxious about Grant's expedition and any potential Confederate response, so much so that even before Fort Henry was in Federal hands Halleck asked General Buell to launch a diversionary movement toward Bowling Green to prevent the Confederates from sending troops against Grant's force. As usual, cooperation between the generals was difficult to obtain, as Buell replied on the fifth, "My position does not admit of diversion. My moves must be real ones, and I shall move at once unless I am restrained by orders concerning other plans. Progress will be slow for me. Must repair the railroad as we advance. It must probably be twelve days before we can be in front of Bowling Green." This would clearly be too late to make much difference in the campaign against Fort Henry. Halleck was convinced that as many as ten thousand enemy troops were moving toward Fort Henry and after being rebuffed by Buell he appealed to General-in-Chief McClellan for assistance, but no troops could be spared from the East.[23]

General Halleck became more and more concerned, especially about the thousands of Confederate troops heading west under the command of General P. G. T. Beauregard. It was the warning about these reinforcements that was one of the main reasons Halleck allowed the expedition to Fort Henry to proceed in the first place. Working hard to find more men for Grant, Halleck once again appealed to Buell, trying to show that sending Grant out was not as reckless as he was beginning to fear it appeared to be. Halleck wrote Buell that "I had no idea of commencing the movement before the 15th or 20th instant till I received General McClellan's telegram about the reinforcements sent to Tennessee or Kentucky with Beauregard," adding that although he was not completely ready to begin the campaign Halleck "deemed it important to move instantly" and reminded Buell that "the holding of Fort Henry is of vital importance to both of us." Despite all Halleck's efforts and appeals, General Buell sent no reinforcements to Fort Henry.[24]

While Halleck and Buell were exchanging telegrams Grant was still at Fort Henry and on February 10 wrote to Flag Officer Foote at Cairo, "I have been waiting very patiently for the return of the gunboats under Commander Phelps to go around on the Cumberland whilst I march my land forces across to make a similtanious [sic] attack on Fort Donelson. I feel that there should be no delay in this matter and yet I do not feel justified in going without some of your boats to co-operate." Grant asked for at least two gunboats from

Cairo to head up the Cumberland River and offered to supply artillerymen to supplement the crews if needed.[25]

Except for the *Carondelet*, Flag Officer Foote had taken the ironclads back to Cairo for repairs, and the wooden gunboats were off on an expedition up the Tennessee River. With the fall of Fort Henry the Tennessee was open to Federal ships all the way to Florence, Alabama. Taking advantage of this golden opportunity, Foote sent the three wooden gunboats, under the command of Lieutenant Commander Phelps, on a raid to show the flag and destroy any Confederate property they could find. Near the mouth of Duck River, the gunboats came upon three steamboats carrying military supplies. After a brief chase the crews abandoned their ships and set them on fire, with one of the ships that was carrying ammunition exploding with such force that the upper deck of the *Conestoga* was jarred from its supports. A little farther south the Union ships captured the *Eastport*, a half-finished gunboat that was towed back to Cairo by the *Lexington* and put into Federal service. Continuing all the way to Florence, the Federal flotilla destroyed several more transport ships carrying military stores. With the river cleared of enemy vessels the Federal ships enjoyed an uneventful trip back north after a stunningly successful raid deep into Confederate territory.[26]

Urging Foote to take action, Grant wrote that he was ready "to start as soon as you like, I will be ready to cooperate at any moment." Grant had good reason to urge promptness, as news had arrived that Confederate reinforcements were heading for Fort Donelson. Following Halleck's orders to stay put and make improvements at Fort Henry might give the Confederates enough time to strengthen Fort Donelson to the point that Grant might not be able to take the fort without massive reinforcements and long and costly fighting, if he could take it at all.[27]

While General Grant was planning how to take Fort Donelson, Albert Sidney Johnston was busy trying to find a way to prevent the loss of the fort that protected the Cumberland River and Nashville. No matter how much he asked, begged or threatened, Johnston was unable to materially increase the manpower in his department. The loss of Fort Henry and the opening of the Tennessee River gave the enemy access to the flanks of Western and middle Tennessee, and there was little the Confederate commander could do about it. The Federal raid led by General Smith convinced Johnston that he needed to shore up the defenses along the rivers, so on January 20 he ordered Brigadier General John B. Floyd's small division and a portion of Brigadier General Simon Bolivar Buckner's division, a total of about eight thousand men, to move from Bowling Green to Russellville, where they would be able to move either back to Bowling Green or to the Cumberland as needed. On the same day Grant was taking his first look at Fort Donelson, Johnston was sending orders for General Floyd to start his men toward Clarksville on the Cumberland River.[28]

Even if Grant was aware of how thin the Confederate forces were spread out, he had plenty of other concerns to be taken care of before moving on Fort Donelson. General Halleck was sending reinforcements to Fort Henry, which would normally be a good thing, but the small, poorly designed position was not large enough to house and care for thousands of troops. The immediate area around the fort was becoming overcrowded with men and supplies. There were few tents available to shelter the men from the elements and food was in short supply, forcing the men to subsist mainly on hardtack and coffee. Increasing numbers of the hungry and untrained troops had begun to forage for food by simply plundering the surrounding countryside.[29]

On February 9 General Grant issued General Field Orders No. 5, the main thrust of which was to make the men and their officers accountable for their actions: "The pilfering and marauding disposition shown by some of the men of this command has determined the general commanding to make an example of some one, to fully show his disapprobation of such conduct." The officers would be made responsible for the conduct of their men and if offenders were known but not punished then the officer in charge of that unit would be punished instead. In another portion of the orders Grant tried to get across a larger and more important idea on how the Federal soldiers should act in enemy country, stating that "so much more could be done by a manly and humane policy to advance the cause which we all have so deeply at heart, it is astonishing that men can be found so wanton as to destroy, pillage, and burn indiscriminately, without inquiry." Even at this early period of the war Grant was already thinking about peace and reconciliation.[30]

General Halleck was certainly fearful that the Confederates would make an attempt to retake Fort Henry, although without control of the river that scenario would seem impossible. On the tenth he wrote again to Grant, "If possible, destroy the bridges at Clarksville. Run any risk to accomplish this. Strengthen land side of Fort Henry, and transfer guns to resist a land attack. Picks and shovels are sent. Large re-enforcements will soon join you." The reason Halleck was so adamant about destroying the bridges at Clarksville was that their loss would make it much more difficult for Confederate troops advancing from Bowling Green to reach Forts Henry or Donelson. In addition, with the Federal gunboats controlling the rivers the Confederate forces at Bowling Green would be cut off above the river, where the much larger Union forces could converge on them.[31]

Not wanting to take any action before its time, General Halleck was at first lukewarm on Grant's plan to attack Fort Donelson so soon after Fort Henry had been taken. It was apparent, however, that the capture of Fort Donelson would not only open the Cumberland River to Nashville but also provide an opportunity to move on the town of Clarksville, about thirty miles upriver. Unfortunately, without the gunboats Grant could do nothing against Clarksville and he was convinced that Fort Donelson would have to be taken before advancing any farther.

5

On to Fort Donelson

While Halleck and Grant seemed to have settled on a plan of action regarding Fort Donelson and Clarksville, the overall Confederate commander, Albert Sidney Johnston, was plagued by confusion and indecision. Regarding the loss of Fort Henry and potential future operations Johnston wired to Richmond, "The capture of that fort by the enemy gives them the control of the navigation of the Tennessee River, and their gunboats are now ascending the river to Florence. Operations against Fort Donelson, on the Cumberland, are about to be commenced, and that work will soon be attacked." The ease with which the Federal ironclads had been able to beat Fort Henry into submission caused Johnston to believe that "the best open earthworks are not reliable to meet successfully a vigorous attack of iron-clad gunboats." General Johnston believed that it was quite likely that the Federals would employ the same tactics against Fort Donelson that proved so successful against Fort Henry: "I think the gunboats of the enemy will probably take Fort Donelson with the necessity of employing their land force in cooperation." Johnston knew that if Fort Donelson was lost "it will open the route to the enemy to Nashville, giving them the means of breaking the bridges and destroying the ferry-boats on the river as far as navigable." This would make it very difficult for Confederate forces in the area to cross the river, and Johnston did not have enough troops on either side of the river to stop a serious Federal advance to the Tennessee capital.[1]

General Johnston was not helpless, however, and had several possible options available to counter the Federal advances. He could move troops from Bowling Green to defend Nashville, although there was no really good natural defensive positions in that area and erecting earthworks to defend the city would probably result in the Union forces simply lying back while their gunboats pounded the city to rubble. By using the railroad Hardee's army could speed to Fort Donelson to crush Grant between the fort's defenses and Hardee's men before Grant grew too strong. There was always the possibility, although not a very strong one, that Fort Henry could be retaken, cutting off any advancing Federal force and forcing them to turn around to defend the fort. But one overriding factor that influenced any decision Johnston might make was that the Federal gunboats could always take control of the rivers whenever they wanted, possibly stranding his men on the wrong side.[2]

Part of Johnston's dilemma was that in addition to purely military considerations he also had to take into account the political and economic ramifications that would come to the forefront if Nashville was lost. He finally decided that the significant industrial capacity center around Nashville was too important to lose without at least putting up a serious effort to protect the city, so General Hardee was ordered to move his troops from Bowling

Green to Nashville and prepare to defend the city. It was hoped that if Fort Donelson could hold out long enough to significantly delay the Federal advance the fortifications around Nashville might be made strong enough to withstand the heavy fire of the gunboats, at least long enough to remove the most important equipment and supplies in and around the city. Shortly after issuing the orders for Hardee to head to Nashville, however, Johnston changed his mind and sent twelve thousand men from the garrison at Bowling Green to reinforce Fort Donelson, the concept being that if the Federals could not be turned back at Fort Donelson the troops could always evacuate the fort and still participate in the defense of Nashville.[3]

All through the preparations for the advance on Fort Donelson, General Halleck had been writing to General McClellan in an effort to get reinforcements and, of course, promote his personal agenda. On February 8 Halleck wrote that he was "decidedly of opinion that if General Buell cannot move on Bowling Green, all his available forces not required to guard Green River should be transferred to the Cumberland, to move by water on Nashville." Halleck did not want to send his forces east toward Nashville until he was certain they could not be cut off by a quick strike from the enemy garrison at Bowling Green. Halleck wrote to McClellan again on the tenth warning of the danger facing his command, "It is the crisis of the war in the West. Have you fully considered the advantage which the Cumberland affords to the enemy at Nashville? ... The whole Bowling Green force can come down in a day, attack Grant in the rear, and return to Nashville before Buell can get half way there.... We are certainly in peril." A few hours later that same day Halleck again wrote to McClellan requesting reinforcements, noting that because of the poor weather it was usually difficult to move troops overland in Kentucky until April, which would slow down any enemy response. Practically pleading now, Halleck wrote, "If sufficient forces are sent to the Cumberland, we can by that time be in the heart of Tennessee. Give us the means and we are certain to give the enemy a telling blow."[4]

General Halleck was already well known for usually thinking long and hard when it came to making decisions or taking actions that involved any significant amount of risk. It was probably at least a little surprising then to his chief of staff, General Cullum, and Flag Officer Foote when they both received a message from Halleck on February 11 urging them to "push forward the Cumberland expedition with all possible dispatch. Push ahead boldly and quickly. I will give you plenty of support in a few days. Time now is everything for us. Don't delay one instant." Halleck also sent a separate message to Foote noting that he had "gained great distinction by your capture of Fort Henry. Everybody recognizes your services. Make your name famous in history by the capture of Fort Donelson and Clarksville. The taking of these places is a military necessity." Referring specifically to Fort Donelson, Halleck emphasized how important it was to begin the advance as quickly as possible: "Delays add strength to them more than to us. Act quickly, even though only half ready. Troops will soon be ready to support you."[5]

Everything to set the expedition to Fort Donelson in motion seemed to fall into place on February 11. From Cairo, Foote informed Halleck that he was "ready with three gunboats to proceed up the Cumberland River, and shall leave here for that purpose in two hours — 8:30 P.M." Foote set sail that evening with the *St. Louis, Louisville* and *Pittsburgh*. The three wooden gunboats that had been on the raid up the Tennessee and the ironclad *Carondlet* would rendezvous with Foote near Fort Donelson. Also on the river that day were transport ships carrying six new regiments to reinforce Grant's army. Responding to General Halleck's previous message about Clarksville, Grant wrote him promising that "every effort will be put forth to have Clarksville within a few days." Grant had been anxious to get going to Fort Donelson because, as he later wrote, "I knew the importance of the place to the enemy and supposed he would reinforce it rapidly. I felt that 15,000 men on the 8th would be more effective that 50,000 a month later."[6]

The force that Grant was going to lead against Fort Donelson consisted of over fifteen thousand men in three divisions. General McClernand commanded the First Division with brigades commanded by Colonel Richard J. Oglesby of the 8th Illinois, Colonel William H. L. Wallace of the 11th Illinois and Colonel William R. Morrison of the 49th Illinois. General Smith's Second Division was made up of brigades commanded by Colonel John McArthur of the 12th Illinois, Colonel John Cook of the 7th Illinois, Colonel Jacob G. Lauman of the 7th Iowa and Colonel Morgan L. Smith of the 8th Missouri. General Lew Wallace commanded the Third Division with one brigade commanded by Colonel Charles Cruft of the 31st Indiana and two brigades under Colonel John M. Thayer of the 1st Nebraska.[7]

By land and by water the movement to Fort Donelson began on February 11. Flag Officer Foote was as good as his word, and the fleet started out on the Ohio River that evening. The transports carrying the reinforcements followed and would be landed as close to Fort Donelson as possible to cooperate with the troops moving by land. General McClernand started his troops on the eleventh also and marched out a few miles from Fort Henry using both roads. Leaving a garrison of about twenty-five hundred men at the fort, the rest of Grant's force marched out from their camps on the morning of the twelfth. W. S. Morris of the 31st Illinois remembered that on leaving Fort Henry the road was still muddy and soft from the recent rains and "[t]he column was frequently halted and soldiers were detailed to assist in pulling the cannon out of the mud, and in moving obstructions out of the road." Once they were through the low, flooded area around Fort Henry the troops were able to move ahead with little delay and made good time as they marched toward Fort Donelson. The weather was unusually warm for this time of year and many of the inexperienced soldiers decided they would not need blankets or overcoats and soon the road was littered with these items that would soon be missed. Fort Donelson was not quite twelve miles from Fort Henry, and a little after noon the head of McClernand's column came within two miles of the fort's outer defenses and made contact with Confederate advance pickets, easily driving them back.[8]

One reason that Grant's troops were able to reach the Confederate positions quickly and easily was that there was no enemy opposition on the march. Much of the timber in the area had been cut down for fuel, but there was still dense undergrowth covering much of the hilly terrain the troops had to pass through. The Confederates knew full well that Grant was coming, and it would have been a simple matter to set up at least modest defensive positions among these hills that could have been used to harass and delay the advancing Union forces, causing serious casualties and affecting their confidence. That this was not done gives proof to Grant's belief that he "could march up to within gunshot of any intrenchments" Gideon Pillow was in command of.[9]

During the remainder of the day the Federal troops fanned out around Fort Donelson. McClernand took his men around to the right with his flank near the flooded area south of Dover. It was his job to take control of the routes south that the garrison might use to escape. General Smith's division covered the area from McClernand's left around to the northwest of the fort to near a swampy area along a tributary of the river called Hickman

Creek. It was on the left past Smith's troops that the transports would be landing the reinforcements coming with the gunboats. Pleased with the positions his men occupied, Grant later wrote, "The troops were not intrenched, but the nature of the ground was such that they were just as well protected from the fire of the enemy as if rifle-pits had been thrown up. Our line was generally along the crest of ridges." As a precaution, however, Grant sent word for General Wallace to bring his troops up. Once the entire army was present and the gunboats arrived Grant was going to begin the assault.[10]

Grant had already decided to use the same basic plan of attack that he planned on using against Fort Henry but was unable to implement. The Federal infantry would be spread out all along the Confederate works to prevent any reinforcements from reaching the garrison, essentially trapping the Confederates within their own fortifications. This ring of men would also prevent the garrison from retreating, as had happened at Fort Henry. This time Grant wanted more than just the fort; he wanted the enemy army as well. With the fort cut off from the rest of the Confederacy the Federal gunboats would hammer the fort with their heavy guns while the artillery that accompanied the army would bombard the extensive land fortifications. With no chance of relief or escape and being pounded by artillery from all sides, it would appear that Confederate resistance would be brief, as it had been at Fort Henry. Grant's plan was sound enough, but he was not facing another Fort Henry. It should have been obvious to the senior Federal officers right from the start that Fort Donelson was much larger, better built and better armed than Fort Henry. In addition, the garrison had already been reinforced by thousands of fresh troops. Captain Charles C. Nott wrote that "we had taken for granted all the time, and indeed, up to the last minute, that the gunboats would dismantle the fort, and that all we should have to do would be to prevent the escape of the rebels." Unfortunately for Captain Nott and most of the rest of Grant's army, this was not going to be as easy as they thought it would be.[11]

General Grant, who knew as well as anyone how much success in war depended in large part on timing, was luckily unaware when he arrived outside Fort Donelson of how much the delay at Fort Henry had cost. Shortly before the Federal troops made their appearance the reinforcements General Johnston had sent from Bowling Green and a few other locations, commanded by Generals Pillow, Floyd and Buckner, had arrived to swell the number of troops inside the fortifications to over seventeen thousand men. The addition of these men allowed the Confederates to extend and improve the earthworks that spread out from the fort in all directions. Numerous and well-built, the fortifications around Fort Donelson were now well manned by a force that almost certainly outnumbered the Federal troops outside those fortifications.[12]

While the infantry was advancing from Fort Henry and taking up their positions around Fort Donelson, Flag Officer Foote was kept very busy getting his ships ready to join the assault. The enthusiasm he exhibited before the Fort Henry expedition was gone and had been replaced by caution and reservations about the success of the mission. In a message to Secretary of the Navy Gideon Welles he wrote, "I go reluctantly, as we are very short of men; and transferring men from vessel to vessel, as we have to do, is having a very demoralizing effect upon them. Twenty-eight men ran off to-day.... I shall do all in my power to render the gunboats effective in the fight, although they are not properly manned, but I must go, as General Halleck wishes it." Foote ended his message by commenting, "If we could wait ten days, and I had more men, I would go with eight mortar boats and six armored boats and conquer." Even though Foote did not believe his ships were ready for a fight, he sailed on the eleventh on the flagship *St. Louis*, commanded by Lieutenant Commander Paulding, the *Louisville*, under Commander Benjamin Dove, and the *Pittsburg*, commanded by Lieutenant Egbert Thompson. Both the *Essex* and *Cincinnati* could not be repaired in time to join the fleet. On the twelfth the ironclads were joined by the wooden gunboats *Conestoga* and *Lexington*. The *Conestoga* stayed with the flotilla, but the *Lexington* was seriously damaged in an accident and had to go back to Cairo for repairs.[13]

The objective of all these mighty warships and thousands of soldiers was one of the most important positions in the Confederacy at the time. Fort Donelson commanded about two miles of the Cumberland River, with bluffs above the river nearing one hundred feet high in some areas. The fort itself had artillery positions on three levels overlooking the river, with many batteries dug into the hillside for greater protection. The lowest level, or the water battery, consisted of fifteen heavy guns built into well-protected earthworks about twenty feet above the water and pointed straight down the river. The second and third levels, about fifty feet above the water and on the summit respectively, held about fifty smaller pieces of artillery. Although the guns located on the summit were lighter, with shorter range than the water batteries below them, because of their height they would be able to fire down onto the lightly protected upper decks of Federal warships. The position of the fort on the riverbank meant that approaching ships would have to sail straight into their line of fire with little room to maneuver.[14]

Fort Donelson was just as well protected on the land side as it was on the river. Around the main fortifications of the fort itself the Confederates had built a large entrenched camp. There was a large area consisting mostly of swamp and flooded terrain to the north along Hickman Creek that was basically impassable by any large body of men, eliminating any assault from that direction. Around the perimeter of the Confederate position were trenches and rifle pits dug in along the high ground of the many hills that surrounded the fort. Much of the ground in front of the Confederate works had been cleared of trees and brush to give them an open field of fire. In addition, out in front of many positions small trees had been cut down with their sharpened branches facing outward to slow down attacking soldiers and keep them in the killing zone longer. The terrain in general around the fort was broken up with dense pockets of woods and small but steep ravines that made it difficult for large formations of soldiers to approach the Confederate works, even if no one was shooting at them.[15]

Within the outer fortifications were several secondary lines of rifle pits and separate entrenched positions, again mostly on high ground, that covered the main lines in case of a breakthrough. Scattered throughout the fortifications were well-placed field artillery pieces covering almost the entire line. The fortifications around Fort Donelson extended from the swampy area in the north well over two miles around to the south, where they protected the town of Dover and met another flooded area to the south. The Confederate fortifications were difficult just to approach through the broken terrain. With the recently arrived reinforcements those rifle pits and trenches would be holding enough Confederate troops that breaking through their lines would take a maximum effort from Grant's troops, with the corresponding heavy loss of life.[16]

The strength of Fort Donelson's guns and fortifications was somewhat neutralized by the weakness of the top two officers in charge of those guns and fortifications. General Johnston had decided to place Brigadier General John B. Floyd in overall command of the fort and the surrounding defenses. Floyd was a Virginia politician with little military experience or knowledge who had been secretary of war under President James Buchanan. Many in the North believed that Floyd had used his position to strengthen the military facilities of southern states in anticipation of the coming conflict, and while feelings generally were running high against Southerners who were now taking up arms against the Union, John Floyd was one of the few who were actually being called traitors. Second in command of the fort was Brigadier General Gideon Pillow. We already know what General Grant thought of Pillow's effectiveness as a commanding officer. Pillow at least had some military experience in the Mexican War, but his usefulness as a military leader was just above that of Floyd. The only real soldier among the three senior officers at the fort was Brigadier General Simon Bolivar Buckner, who commanded an infantry division and oversaw the right of the Confederate defenses. A graduate of West Point, Buckner was an intelligent and courageous soldier, as he soon proved. Another officer who would soon show his worth was Brigadier General Bushrod R. Johnson, who was in command of the Confederate left. There was one more man, just a colonel of cavalry at this stage of the war, who would soon be well known across North and South, Nathan Bedford Forrest, who was in charge of defending the far left at Dover with his cavalrymen.[17]

At first light on February 13 General Grant was still waiting for the arrival of Flag Officer Foote's gunboats and General Wallace's troops. Once the reinforcements were put into position, and the gunboats were ready to begin their bombardment Grant could launch his assault. In the meantime, however, he was getting nervous and anxious to do something positive so he contacted Commander Walke on the *Carondelet*, the only gunboat that that had come up from Fort Henry with the main army, advising Walke, "Most of our batteries are established, and the remainder soon will be. If you will advance with your gun-boat at ten o'clock in the morning, we will be ready to take advantage of any diversion in our favor."[18]

The commander was prepared to do what he could to assist the land forces, although it is difficult to understand how much of an impression one gunboat could make against the fort's well-protected batteries. The *Carondelet* moved forward shortly after nine o'clock, taking shelter behind a wooded point of land that stuck out into the river, and opened fire. For much of the day the ship and the fort exchanged fire, as Walke later wrote that he "bombarded the fort until dusk, when nearly all our ten-inch and fifteen-inch shells were expended. The firing from the shore having ceased, we retired." The *Carondelet* sustained some damage and about a dozen wounded from two Confederate shells that struck the ship, but in general both the ship and the fort suffered little damage. The shelling produced a lot of noise but accomplished little other than both sides wasting a great deal of powder and shot.[19]

In addition to the naval diversion on the morning of the thirteenth Grant was also moving his land forces around to try to tighten the ring around Fort Donelson. General McClernand's troops had originally been placed in a relatively poor location for attack or defense. If they were to assault the Confederate lines in their immediate front the men would have to advance a good distance over open ground in the face of enemy artillery fire. Defensively McClernand's men were spread out along the route of the Wynn's Ferry road south and east of Dover and were trying to cover too much territory for the available manpower. The lines were too thin to stop a determined attack if the garrison tried to break out, and there were no reserves available to go to the aid of any trouble spot. McClernand could clearly see the precarious position his division was in and informed Grant, who also understood the situation but could do little to bolster the lines until General Wallace's division arrived the next morning. The best thing for the Federal army to do on February 13 was try to make minor improvements to their positions and just sit and wait for reinforcements before any serious fighting occurred. Unfortunately, sometimes the simplest of tasks were the most difficult to accomplish.[20]

6

Two Attacks and Two Defeats

There was little action taking place on the morning of February 13. The Federal troops were making minor adjustments here and there to more advantageous positions while the Confederates worked to improve their fortifications wherever possible in preparation for the coming storm. Each side threw an occasional shell across the lines, but no one was ready for battle just yet. In the early afternoon, however, General McClernand began a real fight along a portion of his front. For most of the morning his troops had been shelled periodically by Confederate artillery in their main fortifications in front of Colonel Morrison's brigade. General McClernand decided, for some reason, that he saw a "favorable opportunity for storming redan No 2, which lay in front of the Second brigade, and in a position to annoy our forces yet advancing, and which afforded a cover from which to dash upon my line at an exposed and comparatively weak point." McClernand subsequently ordered Colonel Isham Haynie to lead an assault against this enemy position. Colonel Haynie was to be in command of Morrison's two regiments, the 17th and 49th Illinois, and his own 48th Illinois. The troops formed ranks with the 49th on the right with the 17th and 49th to the left about a quarter mile from their target. While the men were getting ready to move out, a question of seniority came up between Haynie and Morrison. It was customary for the senior officer to be in command, and as the colonels were discussing who would lead the assault an exasperated Haynie finally said to Morrison, "then 'Colonel, let us take it (meaning the enemy's redoubt),' 'together,'" and the troops moved out.[1]

When all was ready the two colonels led their men forward through the underbrush and down the hillside in front of their lines toward the enemy line that lay at the top of another hill in their front. As they got closer to the Confederate lines artillery fire increased, as did the number of killed and wounded who lay behind the advancing blue line. About fifty yards from the first line of defenses the Federal troops walked into a thick concentration of abatis, which are trees that have been cut down with sharpened branches to impede the progress of assaulting troops. Once they made their way through the obstructions the men came out into the open and were met with a volley of musket and artillery fire that seemed like a storm of death and destruction. Colonel Haynie reported, "As near as I can judge, we maintained our position under this most galling fire of rifle, shot, and shell for an hour." The casualties mounted and soon Colonel Morrison was among the wounded. With the attack stalled, General McClernand sent the 45th Illinois forward to join the assault, hoping that with more weight his men could punch through the Confederate line. These extra men only gave the Confederates more targets to shoot at, increasing the Federal casualties but having no effect on the result. Colonel Haynie, finally acknowledging that the assault had

6. Two Attacks and Two Defeats

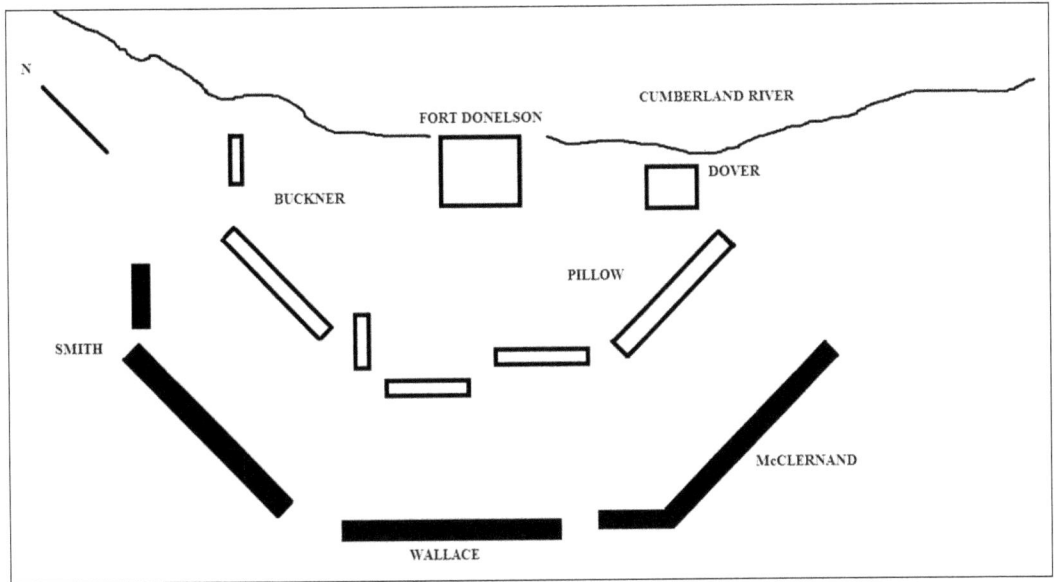

Fort Donelson

failed, decided there was no reason for his men to continue taking casualties and ordered them to fall back down the hillside and return to their own lines. One of the Confederate defenders, Flavel Barber of the 3rd Tennessee, remembered later that as the Union troops fell back the casualties they left behind on the ground in front of the works reminded him of "a flock of sheep, leaving their track in mangled corpses."[2]

Not only was McClernand's attack an abject failure, but he also had sent his men forward without getting approval from General Grant, who was none too happy about the event, writing, "The battery was in the main line of the enemy, which was defended by his whole army present. Of course the assault was a failure, and of course the loss on our side was great for the number of men engaged." Even if McClernand had captured the battery or even punched a hole in the Confederate lines, the rest of the army was unprepared to move forward to take advantage of such a limited success. General Grant's distrust of McClernand, which would eventually led to Grant relieving him from his command of an army corps in front of Vicksburg, probably began from this incident.[3]

With the fighting on McClernand's front over, the troops settled in and tried to get some rest but would be greatly disappointed. The weather had been nice enough for February for much of the day, but that afternoon a winter storm suddenly came up and rain quickly changed to sleet, which soon became snow. After dark the temperature quickly dropped to below zero, which was definitely not usual for this region. As was customary, fires were not allowed anywhere near the front lines, so the men could not even make hot coffee to counteract the freezing cold. To make matters even worse, many of the troops had thrown away their coats and blankets on the march from Fort Henry and about the best they could do was just try to stay awake till morning by moving around and doing anything to warm up even a little. Colonel Richard Oglesby wrote that "on the morning of the 14th the sun rose upon our forces, who were nearly torpid from the intense cold of the night." Once it began getting light it was safe to light fires and as many men as possible tried to get warm by squeezing together around small campfires as they made their coffee.[4]

Over in the Confederate fortifications it was just as cold, but at least they had some little shelter from the wind and snow. It also must have helped them get through the night knowing that they had won the first fight. On the other hand, many of the defenders were beginning to realize how much danger they were in. Tennessean Flavel Barber was one of those who were able to see the reality of the situation: "For the first time we began to realize that we were surrounded and actually besieged by the enemy." With control of the river Grant's army would be able to receive reinforcements and supplies as needed and could establish a tight siege that would eventually force the Confederates to surrender from hunger and lack of ammunition. Barber could see the obvious truth that "[h]ereafter our contest was to be not an effort for victory, but a desperate struggle to escape."[5]

The early-morning hours of February 14 not only brought continued freezing temperatures and misery to the men in both armies, but Flag Officer Foote arrived with his gunboats and transports loaded with reinforcements also. The newly arrived troops from Fort Henry commanded by General Lew Wallace were formed into the Third Division and positioned in the center of the Federal lines. The addition of these troops allowed General McClernand to slide his troops farther toward the river on the right. The road from Dover to Nashville, the last possible escape route for the Confederate garrison, was now under McClernand's control and Fort Donelson was all but cut off from the outside.[6]

With the arrival of the gunboats and the additional troops Grant's confidence was bolstered enough that he sent several messages, including one to General Halleck: "Our troops now invest the works at Fort Donelson. The enemy have been driven into their works at every point. A heavy abatis all around prevents carrying the works by storm at present. I feel every confidence of success." In a letter to his wife, Julia, Grant predicted, "The taking of Fort Donelson bids fair to be a long job. The rebels are strongly fortified and are in very heavy force. When this is to end is hard to surmise but I feel confident of ultimate success."[7]

In a report to Halleck's chief of staff, General Cullum, back in Cairo, Grant wrote that it appeared to him that it was probably going to require a long-drawn-out siege before Fort Donelson could be taken. The terrain surrounding the fort was very rough and filled with ravines, and trees had been cut down far in advance of the actual fortifications to delay advancing troops and keep them under fire longer. Grant added, "I fear the result of an attempt to carry the place by storm with raw troops. I feel great confidence, however, of ultimately reducing the place."[8]

Now that the gunboats had arrived and the reinforcements had allowed the Federal lines to be extended enough to cut off the enemy's escape route, General Grant decided it was time to begin putting pressure on the garrison in hopes of forcing them to surrender without making an all-out attack. The best way to achieve this was to bombard the fort with the heavy naval guns of the ironclads as had been done at Fort Henry, but this time the firepower of the land-based artillery would be added. Grant proposed that Flag Officer Foote begin his attack on the afternoon of the fourteenth, and although Foote believed his ships were not yet ready for a serious fight, he agreed to the plan and began making preparations for battle. Considering the poor results from the long-range firing of the *Carondelet* the previous morning and the relatively easy way in which Fort Henry was taken, Foote decided to bring his ships in close to Fort Donelson and pound the place apart, just like they had done at Fort Henry. Much of the day was spent preparing the ships for battle, including the piling of lumber and bags of coal on the upper decks to provide at least a

U.S. ironclad *Essex*. Later served on the Mississippi River at Vicksburg and Port Hudson (Library of Congress).

little protection from enemy fire that the crews knew would be coming down on top of the ships from the bluffs around Fort Donelson.[9]

The ships were ready for action about three o'clock in the afternoon and they began to move slowly toward the fort. The ironclads were in line in front with the *Louisville* on the right, then to her left the *St. Louis* and the *Pittsburg* with the *Carondelet* on the far left. The more vulnerable wooden ships *Tyler* and *Conestoga* followed the ironclads about one thousand yards behind, hopping to stay out of range of the enemy's guns. When the ironclads had approached to about a mile and a half of the fort the Confederates began testing the range by firing two shots from one of their largest guns, a 10-inch Columbiad that fell short of the ships. The Union gunboats were about a mile from Fort Donelson when the *St. Louis* opened fire and the other ships quickly joined in and the battle was on.[10]

Unlike at Fort Henry, the Confederate gunners had plenty of time to get ready for the Union fleet. The ships had to approach the fort out in the open, moving down a long, straight stretch of water, allowing the Confederates manning their guns to just point and shoot. At the same time, the earthworks that protected the fort were difficult to make out from the water against the dark background from long distance. As the ships closed the distance to the fort the firing from the fortifications grew heavier and more accurate. One of the major problems the Federal ships had to deal with was that as they got closer to the fort the smaller-caliber guns mostly located in the upper fortifications were able to reach the ships. The shot from these smaller guns came down upon the ships from above, in effect dropping onto the upper decks where the ships had the least amount of protection. To make matters worse, the ironclads were unable to elevate their guns high enough to hit these guns, which were located high above the fort's main water batteries.[11]

Getting closer and closer to the fort, Flag Officer Foote tried to throw off the Confederate fire by changing speed several times as the Union gunboats closed to less than five hundred yards of the fort, almost point-blank for the heavier guns. Being this near to the fort aided the inexperienced Confederate gunners more than it helped the accuracy of the ship's guns. Naturally, the land-based Confederate batteries had a much more stable platform from which to aim and shoot, using virtually all their guns facing the river, while the ironclads could only bring at most half their guns to bear on the fortifications while their accuracy suffered from the movement of the ships. Having fixed positions to aim at would usually be a benefit to the ship's gunners, but in fact even when they hit the Confederate earthworks all that really happened was a lot of dirt was thrown into the air. It generally needed a direct hit, or very nearly so, to actually disable a gun or the gun crew within earthworks, and even though the lower works were heavily damaged the majority of the guns were still able to be fired in the midst of the damage and debris.[12]

By the time the ironclads had closed to less than four hundred yards they were being pounded by heavy fire from both the large-caliber Confederate water batteries and the smaller-size guns placed higher up. Aboard the *Carondelet*, Commander Henry Walke later wrote, the Confederate shot "knocked the plating to pieces, and sent fragments of iron and splinter into the pilots, one of whom fell mortally wounded." One of the *Carondelet*'s rifled guns was reloaded too quickly and blew up when fired, wounding over a dozen of her crew. In rapid succession two different hits by heavy shot killed four other crewmen. Luckily for the crew of the *Carondelet*, lookouts were able to actually see much of the large Confederate shot heading for the ship and shouted a warning when it appeared as if the ship would be hit. Even so, the ship was hit repeatedly. As Walke reported, "our pilot-house was struck again and another pilot wounded, our wheel was broken, and shells from the rear boats were bursting over us. All four of our boats were shot away and dragging in the water." After about an hour and a half the casualties were mounting and Walke reported that the decks had so much blood on them "that our men could not work the guns without slipping."[13]

All the Federal ships were suffering from numerous hits by the heavy Confederate guns. Multiple hits on the armored side had loosened some of the iron plates and in some instances the armor had been pierced. Holes opened along the waterline and fires began igniting on the wooden decks. Worst of all, like on the *Carondelet*, blood from the killed and wounded coated decks, making it even more difficult for the crews to work the ship and guns. The *St. Louis* was hit fifty-nine times; one of these shots hit the pilothouse, destroying the wheel and killing pilot F. A. Riley when he was hit by a large wooden splinter. The same shell wounded Flag Officer Foote in the leg. On the *Louisville* her pilot was wounded, and both she and the *St. Louis* had their steering ropes shot away. The crews of both ships tried to steer them with the tiller ropes at the stern, but it was too dangerous, as sometimes the shells fired by the wooden ships in the rear had their fuses cut too short and burst over the ironclads instead of the fort. Both the *St. Louis* and the *Louisville* were eventually forced to withdraw from the battle and let the current carry them downstream to safety.[14]

The *Pittsburg* was hit at least thirty times, suffering heavy damage, and also lost her ability to steer properly but remained under control enough to join the heavily damaged *Carondelet* in covering the *St. Louis* and *Louisville* as they drifted downstream until they were out of range. In just over an hour and a half three of the four Union ironclads had been severely damaged and were drifting downstream unable to continue the fight. Only the *Carondelet*, which had taken the worst punishment, was still under control and able to continue firing until the rest of the fleet had reached safety. In the entire Federal fleet eleven men were killed and forty-three wounded; almost half of these casualties were on the *Carondelet*.[15]

Clearly the attack was a failure. All four ironclads were damaged badly enough that they were barely fit for further service in front of Fort Donelson. The *Carondelet* was in such bad shape that she spent a lengthy period of time back in Mound City being repaired. The battle was the first time the ironclads faced serious opposition, and Foote and his captains learned that while heavy guns at water level were dangerous enough, the real problem for the ironclads was the plunging fire from smaller guns mounted on bluffs above the river. As if the damage and casualties suffered by the fleet were not bad enough, as it turned out the fortifications at Fort Donelson had not been damaged as severely as it first appeared. Mostly the Federal fire had moved around a lot of dirt, but there were few casualties and little permanent damage done to the fort.[16]

With the gunboats unable to force Fort Donelson to surrender as they did at Fort Henry or even cause enough appreciable damage to make an infantry assault feasible, General Grant decided the smartest thing he could do was stay put and wait for more reinforcements. His next step was to "make the investment of Fort Donelson as perfect as possible, and partially fortify and await repairs to the gunboats." With the newly arrived troops under General Wallace filling in the center of the lines and McClernand shifted over more to the right, covering the mostly flooded area south of Dover and the main road to Nashville, the Confederate garrison was pretty much surrounded. Over on the far right, however, the Federal troops were stretched especially thin near the Clarksville road. Grant had moved one of General Smith's brigades commanded by Colonel McArthur over past McClernand's position to the far right of the line to close up the gaps in that area, but even with the addition of these troops the far right remained the weakest portion of the Federal lines. If the Confederates learned how light those defenses really were they might have an opportunity to launch their own attack and break out of what was quickly becoming a trap. For some reason, Grant did not consider an enemy advance out of their fortifications a real possibility, later writing that he "had no idea that there would be any engagement on land unless I brought it on myself."[17]

In the Confederate camp, while the repulse of the Federal gunboats was a clear victory and gave the garrison a much-needed boost to morale, it was obvious to the senior officers that they were still in serious trouble. There would be no reinforcements heading to the fort and there was no Confederate force close enough to force Grant to give up the siege he was clearly planning to conduct. The simple fact was that Fort Donelson had become a trap for the thousands of men inside the fortifications and it was only a matter of time before they were starved into submission. The Federal fleet still had control of the river, so there would be no escaping that way. The only way to save even part of the garrison was to attack the Federal line where it was thinnest and basically make a run for it. General Floyd put the situation clearly, saying, "I had already seen the impossibility of holding out for any length of time with our inadequate numbers and indefensible position. There was no place within our intrenchments but could be reached by the enemy's artillery from their boats or their batteries."[18]

On the morning of the fourteenth as the Federal lines were being strengthened and expanded farther to their right the senior Confederate officers held a council of war to decide what action they could and should take. General Buckner reported that "it was decided unanimously, in view of the arrival of heavy reinforcements of the enemy below, to make an immediate attack upon their right." The plan was for General Pillow to launch an attack upon the weakest point of the Federal lines, General McClernand's far right flank. Once the lines were broken the troops would continue on toward Nashville with Buckner's men covering the retreat until as many men as possible could escape. The Confederates began making preparations for the move, but Buckner reported that "early in the afternoon the order was countermanded by General Floyd, at the instance, as I afterwards learned, of General Pillow, who, after drawing out his troops for the attack, thought it too late for the attempt."[19]

Even though the first attempt to break through the Federal lines did not get off the ground, another attempt was, as Buckner later wrote, "imperatively necessary in consequence of the vastly superior and constantly increasing force of the enemy, who had already completely enveloped our position." That night the senior officers met at the Dover Hotel and again unanimously approved a plan to break through the Federal lines, this time early the next morning. With Grant's advantage over the Confederates improving by the hour they could not afford to wait any longer.[20]

The Confederate plan consisted of two parts; both had to succeed for the troops to have any chance of escaping. General Pillow's division, about ten thousand men strong, with cavalry support, would attack McClernand's men on the far right of the Federal lines, pushing them out of the way to the west into the center of the Union lines. General Buckner would take his force out and attack the right of the Federal center, manned by Wallace's green troops, which would support Pillow's men in creating an opening through which the Confederates could escape down the Clarksville road. General Pillow reported that if all went as planned, "My success would roll the enemy's force to retreat over upon General Buckner, when by his attack in flank and rear we could cut up the enemy and put him completely to rout." Once the Federal line had been opened Buckner would "take up a position in advance of our work on the Wynn's Ferry road, to cover the retreat of the whole army, after which my division was to act as the rear guard." Once the Confederates got past the Federal lines they would march to Charlotte, Tennessee, and then toward Nashville. This plan was very feasible if Pillow could surprise and overwhelm the thin Federal forces on their right and if Buckner could keep the avenue of escape open long enough.[21]

The night was bitter cold, with rain changing to sleet and snow, but despite their discomfort the already tired and hungry Confederate troops had to spend much of the night preparing for the morning assault. Over in the Federal camps the men who were without tents and unable to build fires tried to keep from freezing rolled in overcoats and blankets or just kept moving around in the wet snow in a vain effort to deal with the cold. For most of the night noise could be heard from the Confederate lines indicating something was going on, but nobody in the Federal lines seemed to notice, or if they did they were too busy trying to fight the cold to pay much attention.[22]

7

The Confederates Strike First

The early-morning hours of February 15 were just as cold and wet as the night before and the men in the Federal lines were just as miserable as they had been the night before. Thomas Durham, of the 11th Indiana Volunteers, wrote, "We had no tents and were not allowed any fire; we lay on the snow and frozen ground with our wet and frozen clothes that night. With our suffering from the cold and the bombardment which was kept up all night, there was no sleep for us."[1]

Colonel W. E. Baldwin, commander of the advance troops for the Confederate assault, reported, "My command, to which the 20th Mississippi, Major Brown, was temporarily attached, constituted the advance in the following order: first, the 26th Mississippi, second, the 26th Tennessee, third, the 20th Mississippi." Just after four o'clock in the morning General Pillow arrived on the ground to find Baldwin's troops formed up and ready to march, but there was some delay in getting other troops organized and it was 5:45 A.M. before Colonel Baldwin led his brigade out of the embrasures of the rifle pits and formed in line of battle. On the far right of the Federal lines Colonel Oglesby's brigade held the right flank of McClernand's division and was supported by three regiments commanded by Colonel John McArthur that had been transferred from General Smith's division to strengthen the right. The Confederates hit the right side of the Federal line like a sledgehammer, but Oglesby got his men formed quickly and was able to hold his position, at least for the moment. One of Oglesby's men, W. S. Morris of the 31st Illinois Volunteers, remembered that before the men in his unit even had a chance to make their morning coffee or cook their bacon the Confederates came charging out of their works and, "deploying rapidly to our right, burst upon McClernand's division with loud and defiant yells."[2]

Field artillery that followed the infantry out from the fortifications to support the Confederate assault poured out a heavy fire of grape and canister that produced a most deadly effect on the Federal troops when combined with the continuous musket fire from the attacking infantry. The continuous roar of the battle made it difficult for the troops to hear or understand the orders their officers shouted out, and the smoke got so thick that the men could see only a short distance to their front, so much so that not long after the firing began it became impossible for regimental commanders to see from one end of their line to the other. Casualties were growing rapidly with many of the wounded lying where they fell, too injured to drag themselves out of the line of fire, and few men could be spared from the firing line to remove them to safety.[3]

As General Pillow's troops continued to swarm out from behind their works they moved forward as quickly as the units could form their lines. The 26th Mississippi and the

26th Tennessee made for the Forge road on the right of Colonel Oglesby's front, hammering the 8th and 18th Illinois regiments, who gave as good as they got. Three times the men of the 26th Mississippi launched themselves at Oglesby's men but were thrown back in confusion by rapid fire from the Federal ranks hitting them in the flank, but each time the men from Mississippi rallied and moved forward again. The Confederate brigade of Colonel Gabriel Wharton consisting of the 51st and 56th Virginia regiments followed Colonel Baldwin's troops out of the fortifications. As more and more Confederates came out of the fortifications the fighting spread down the Federal line. On Oglesby's left was the brigade of Colonel W. H. L. Wallace and they were hit next with just as much fury as the far right had endured. They were able to beat back the first charge, but the Confederates came right back only to be repelled again. Over on the far right Colonel McArthur first brought his 9th Illinois up to the front to support Oglesby, but as the field of battle spread out his entire command quickly found themselves engaged in the desperate fighting along with the brigades of Oglesby and W. H. L. Wallace.[4]

Union general John A. McClernand. Former congressman from Illinois who hoped to use military success to further his political career (Library of Congress).

The fighting on General McClernand's front went back and forth but never stopped, as the Confederates continued to press forward regardless of the heavy Federal fire and the number of casualties they were taking. Dismounted cavalry from Nathan Bedford Forrest's command joined in the attack from the flank and rear and soon the Federals were in trouble. Heavy smoke began to obscure the fields; the snow was stained red from the dead and wounded. The Union troops were not prepared for such heavy and continuous fighting and began to run low on ammunition. Lieutenant Colonel Frank L. Rhoads, of the 8th Illinois, reported, "We were enfilated at turns by a battery on the left, which never ceased to pour grape and canister into our ranks, the fire was murderous, as the long list of the dead and wounded sadly shows." Gradually the weight of the Confederate attack forced Oglesby and McArthur back.[5]

After less than two hours of heavy fighting the Federal right was gradually breaking down. The 8th and 18th Illinois were running out of ammunition and the commander of the 18th, Michael Lawler, and his replacement were both wounded. Of Oglesby's original five regiments only the 11th and 31st Illinois, which had been on the brigade's left, were able to maintain their front against the growing mass of enemy troops coming at them. Colonel John Logan, commanding the 31st Illinois, held his men together as long as possible, but he was wounded and with ammunition running out his men gave way. As the survivors of Colonel Oglesby's brigade were in the process of falling back to the left and rear, reinforcements from General Wallace's division began to arrive.[6]

It did not take General McClernand long to see his men were being overwhelmed and the situation was quickly becoming desperate, so he sent a message to General Lew Wallace, commanding in the center of the Union line, asking for assistance. General Wallace was hesitant to transfer any of his troops, considering that Grant had sent out orders not to move any troops without express orders from him and refused McClernand's first appeal for assistance but sent an officer to Grant's headquarters for instructions. With the commanding general currently absent from headquarters none of the staff had the authority, nor was anyone willing to act on their own initiative, to approve transferring any of Wallace's units. Growing more desperate, McClernand repeated his appeal for assistance, after which Wallace took the responsibility on himself and sent a brigade commanded by Colonel Charles Cruft to reinforce the right of the line.[7]

Colonel Cruft reported that he received orders from General Wallace about 8:30 A.M. to "put the brigade in rapid motion to the extreme right of our line, for the purpose of reenforcing General McClernand's division." Cruft quickly moved to the right with the 17th and 25th Kentucky and the 31st and 44th Indiana regiments. When the reinforcements arrived at their designated position on the right, replacing the brigades of Oglesby and McArthur, who were trying to regroup and get more ammunition, Cruft reported, "the head of the column became suddenly engaged with a superior force of the enemy in front and to the right. This appeared to be a force that was endeavoring to outflank the battery and the line of infantry supporting it, and pass into the ravine behind." The two lead regiments, the 25th Kentucky and the 31st Indiana, ran into this heavy enemy fire before they could even form their lines properly, but when the 17th Kentucky and 44th Indiana arrived on the scene Cruft's men were able to deploy in line despite the continued fire they had to endure. The firing grew even heavier as the Confederate assault from the right continued and, as Cruft noted, "the enemy's fire upon the right continued to be very severe, and this assault was pressed up to within 20 feet of our lines. It continued for some minutes with much fury, and was replied to with effect by our men."[8]

When the remainder of McClernand's troops on the far right fell back Colonel Cruft soon found himself "left without support, occupying the extreme right of the line of investment." He fell back a few hundred feet to a new line on a hillside where his men withstood another assault. With the Confederates continually working their way around the right Cruft had to thin out his line to meet them or be flanked and attacked from front and flank by the more numerous enemy. After holding this line against attacks from both right and left Cruft was able to take advantage of a brief lull and move his brigade farther back to a ridge where another Confederate attack was beaten off. At this point the Confederates pulled back a short distance to regroup and only light firing by skirmishers continued for a while. While Cruft's men enjoyed the relative peace and quiet it was learned that a new line was being formed to his rear, and he pulled the brigade back to join with the main lines on some high ground and remained there on the far right for the rest of the morning.[9]

Over in the Confederate works about nine o'clock General Pillow sent word to General Buckner that now was the time for him to advance his troops against the left of the Federal troops already engaged with Pillow's men on the right. Sending the 14th Mississippi forward supported by the 3rd and 18th Tennessee regiments, Buckner reported, "Their line of march unfortunately masked the fire of my artillery upon the Wynn's Ferry road, but it continued to play with effect upon the force which was opposing General Pillow's advance. The combined attack compelled the enemy to retire, not, however, without inflicting upon my troops considerable loss." For some reason — Buckner called it a "misapprehension of instructions"— his troops fell back "to the trenches, after the enemy's infantry had been driven a considerable distance from their position."[10]

One of Buckner's men who made this advance was Flavel Barber of the 3rd Tennessee. With the assault on the Federal right so successful up to this point Barber and his comrades confidently moved forward through a wooded area, "the bushes in many places being so thick that the men could not keep their ranks, believing that before us lay an easy task and that the enemy were in full retreat, not knowing that before us lay the main force of the Federal army." As they advanced toward what would now be the left of the Federal lines manned by Colonel W. H. L. Wallace's men there was surprisingly little fire coming at them until they halted along the side of the hill on the crest of which the Federal troops were waiting. Suddenly a tremendous fire opened up on the advancing Confederates: "Grape and canister, shot and shell and rifle balls, fell like hail upon us. Scarcely three seconds seemed to intervene between the discharge of the cannons, while the balls fell like a driving rainstorm into our crowded ranks." Colonel John C. Brown of the 3rd Tennessee reported that as his men moved up the hill "and through comparatively open ground, and especially on reaching the summit of the hill, they were met by a murderous fire. Some confusion enued, but they returned a steady fire, until the enemy retired, under cover of dense timber and undergrowth, withdrawing his battery, which had been pouring a heavy fire into our reserves." Colonel Brown's exhausted men were now scattered all over the terrain and he decided that "further pursuit being impracticable in that direction, and companies having become separated and somewhat intermixed, on account of the obstacles over which they had marched, the command retired within the intrenchments, and immediately reformed, to renew the attack still farther to the right, whither the enemy were retiring."[11]

By late morning the majority of General McClernand's original position was in enemy hands, with the victorious Confederates continuing to press forward toward the Union center. About ten o'clock, in answer to urgent requests for assistance from McClernand, General Wallace ordered forward his last remaining brigade commanded by Colonel John A. Thayer, sending him to cover the right side of Wallace's assigned area to stem the enemy tide before his position was also overrun. Colonel Thayer's force was actually a combination of two brigades made up of the 1st Nebraska, the 58th, 68th, and 76th Ohio, and the 46th, 57th, and 58th Illinois. Time was of the essence, and time was what the arrival of Wallace's troops gave to the hard-pressed Union right. Colonel Thayer found a good defensive position that was protected by heavy woods on each side and established his lines across the Wynn's Ferry road, waiting for the enemy to arrive. While this new line was being formed General Wallace reported that "the new front thus formed covered the retiring regiments, helpless from lack of ammunition, but which coolly halted not far off, some of them actually within reach of the enemy's musketry, to refill their cartridge boxes." This was the final main line for the Federal forces that Colonel Cruft had joined on the right. They had only a brief rest, however, as the Confederates continued to advance to their right, hitting this new line with the same ferocity as they had exhibited earlier in the morning.[12]

The 58th Ohio was stationed on the left of the road with the 58th Illinois and the 1st Nebraska on the right of the road next to the Chicago battery. General Wallace reported, "Scarcely had this formation been made when the enemy attacked, coming up the road and through the shrubs and trees on both sides of it, and making the battery and the First

Nebraska the principal points of attack. They met the storm, no man flinching, and their fire was terrible. To say they did well is not enough, their conduct was splendid." Colonel Thayer also noted the Nebraskans in his report: "This regiment continued an almost incessant discharge of musketry for three-quarters of an hour, the battery continuing its firing at the same time." The fighting was just as desperate along most of the Federal line as "[t]he enemy made an effort three times to push forward through our lines, but were as often driven back." General Wallace later wrote about the severity of the fighting along the Wynn's Ferry road, "The woods rang with musketry and artillery. The brush on the slope of the hill was mowed away with bullets. A great cloud arose and shut out the woods and narrow valley below. Colonel Thayer and his regiments behaved with great gallantry, and the contest was over." Finally there was a halt to the fighting around 1:00 P.M. Colonel Cruft noticed that the Confederates began falling back through the woods to the right "to a ridge across a large ravine about a half mile to our right, and establishing himself there in force."[13]

One of Colonel Thayer's men, Charles Dana Miller of the 76th Ohio, later wrote about how the men in his regiment handled their initiation to combat. The Ohioans were just getting into position as the reserve behind the 1st Nebraska when "the Rebels opened fire on our lines with artillery and musketry. The front line returned the fire and stood firmly in line. The trees and underbrush were so thick, we could see nothing of the enemy, but his lead whistled over our heads and the shot from a battery shattered the timber around us." As the reserve, Miller's regiment was supposed to stay in their position behind the front line and hold their fire unless the front line gave way. The excitement of being in their first battle, combined with the noise and confusion that are present during every battle, caused a few of the new soldiers to discharge their weapons, which caused most of the regiment to let loose with a full volley. Luckily, the Ohioans were positioned on higher ground than the frontline troops and the bullets went over the heads of the regiment from Nebraska.[14]

General Buckner had sent the 3rd, 18th and 32nd Tennessee regiments against the Federal line defending the Wynn's Ferry road. Under the command of Colonel Brown the Confederates hit the Union line hard, but after a brief and violent struggle they were unable to force the defenders back any farther, so Buckner decided to consolidate his position and wait for his artillery and reserves to join the advance troops so that he could "defend the position I now held, in order that the army might pass out on the Forge road, which was now completely covered by the position occupied by my division." Buckner soon learned, however, that General Pillow had ordered his artillery to remain in the works, and Buckner was also ordered to return to the trenches on the right. In the process of returning to the fortifications that his men had fought so hard to escape from, Buckner met General Floyd, who wondered why Buckner was heading back to their lines. Replying to Floyd's inquiry, Buckner told him "that nothing had occurred to change my views of the necessity of the evacuation of the post, that the road was open, that the first part of our purpose was fully accomplished, and I thought we should at once avail ourselves of the existing opportunity to regain our communications." Floyd told Buckner to remain in his position until he had the opportunity to consult with General Pillow about the withdrawal. Not long after, Buckner received instructions from Floyd to "retire within the lines and repair as rapidly as possible to my former position on the extreme right, which was in danger of attack."[15]

By early afternoon the Confederates had a clear road ahead with no Federal force close enough or large enough to prevent Fort Donelson's garrison from making their escape. Pillow's plan to break through the Federal right had succeeded brilliantly, and as Flavel Barber of the 3rd Tennessee wrote, "now was the time to save ourselves." Unfortunately, General

Pillow appears to have spent too much time enjoying the victory instead of taking advantage of the opening that had been created to get his troops to safety. Barber bitterly remembered, "Now was the time to take up our march for Nashville, we had found the enemy too strong in numbers for us, but his lines were broken and there was no hindrance to our retreat. But the golden opportunity passed away, never to return: we were doomed."[16]

Why Pillow made the decision to bring the Confederate troops back to their fortifications is not clear. In his report Pillow stated that he decided to end the fighting "after seven and a half hours of continuous and bloody conflict." Orders were issued to the various commanders to return their men to their original positions within the fortifications. It is true that the Confederates must have been exhausted after suffering through several days of extreme cold, low rations and hard fighting and probably needed a rest before starting off on what was sure to be a long and difficult march to escape from the fort, but why not just stay where they were for a brief rest, then move out? The threat of an attack on their right was real enough and perhaps the Confederate commanders thought they could begin the evacuation after that attack was beaten off, if it even took place. The real mystery was why anyone would believe that a commander as aggressive as General Grant would not do everything in his power to close the escape route as quickly as possible and take advantage of any confusion in the Confederate ranks as they returned from their assault.[17]

8

The Battle for Fort Donelson

It was not just the ferocity of the attack or the fact that none of the senior Federal officers had any idea that the Fort Donelson garrison was going to attempt a breakout that accounted for the success of the Confederate attack; another contributing factor was that the commander of the Union army was nowhere near the scene when the fighting broke out that morning.

About two o'clock on the morning of the fifteenth Flag Officer Foote had sent a message to army headquarters requesting a meeting with General Grant. The wound Foote received in the previous day's failed bombardment of the fort prevented him from traveling, and he asked Grant to meet him on board the *St. Louis* about four miles downriver. Before leaving headquarters Grant issued orders for the division commanders to hold their current positions and not launch any attacks without his express order. No doubt this was a reaction to McClernand's failed attack of the day before. Unfortunately, this order also produced some confusion and delay in moving troops around to where they were needed most during the fighting on the Federal right.[1]

Leaving headquarters as soon as it was light enough to see, Grant rode out to the landing where a small boat was waiting to carry him to the *St. Louis*. On board the flagship Foote informed Grant that his ironclads had been too badly damaged during the bombardment and that the ships would have to return to Cairo for repairs before they could go up against the fort again. This was news that Grant did not want to hear, since in addition to providing protection for the transports and supply ships that filled the Cumberland, losing the support of the ironclads would be a major setback for several reasons. Despite their lack of success during the bombardment the day before, Grant knew that the big guns of the ships could wreck havoc on fortifications from long range and would be indispensable if he had to settle down for a long siege. In addition, Grant was concerned that seeing the ships sail away could affect the moral of the infantry, who felt a little more secure just from hearing the booming of the ship's big guns. Grant was able to convince Foote to leave the two least damaged ships to support the land operations while he took the other two back for repairs. Foote thought he would be able to return in ten days, possibly with the powerful gunboat *Benton* and several mortar boats, and renew the attack with an even stronger naval force. Grant left about noon with the understanding that they would follow Foote's plan, but as the general later wrote, "the enemy relieved me from that necessity."[2]

On the ride back to his headquarters Grant could faintly hear the sound of gunfire in the distance but at first took it to be just the everyday skirmishing that had been going on since his army arrived in front of Fort Donelson. Grant believed that his army would be the side to initiate any fighting, since the Confederates had been content to stay secure within their fortifications and had shown no hint of making any aggressive moves. Now that the Federal army was much stronger than it had been just two days ago the possibility of an enemy attack seemed less likely than ever. While making an unhurried ride back to the army Grant received the shocking news that it was not skirmishing that he was hearing but that the whole right side of his army was being pushed back by a fierce enemy assault.[3]

Once he learned of the heavy fighting that had been taking place in his absence, Grant wasted no time riding as quickly as the bad roads allowed to return to the army. About one o'clock in the afternoon Grant found both McClernand and Wallace meeting behind Colonel Thayer's line, trying to put together a plan of action to hold the current positions. After receiving a quick briefing from these officers, Grant learned just how close the army had come to disaster. McClernand's division had lost almost fifteen hundred men, and what was left of the Federal forces that had been on the right had been pushed back into General Wallace's area in the center of the original Federal lines. Over on the left General Smith's troops were too far away to provide any immediate assistance. Perhaps most important, the Confederate garrison that just a few hours ago was trapped inside their fortifications now had a wide-open escape route.[4]

It must have been difficult for Grant to keep his composure after hearing the news that his army was facing a disastrous and for him personally embarrassing defeat, but he did. General Wallace later wrote about how Grant took the bad news and his reaction:

> In every great man's career there is a crisis exactly similar to that which now overtook General Grant, and it cannot be better described than as a crucial test of his nature. It cannot be doubted that he saw with painful distinctness the effect of the disaster to his right wing. His face flushed slightly. With a sudden grip he crushed the papers in his hand. But in an instant these signs of disappointment or hesitation cleared away. In his ordinary quiet voice he said, addressing himself to both officers, "Gentlemen, the position on the right must be retaken."[5]

In addition to ordering the troops on the right to regroup and prepare to take back the ground that had been lost that morning, Grant suspected that in order for the Confederates to launch such a massive attack on his right they would have had to weaken their lines elsewhere. The Federal commanders could only guess at the reasons the Confederates had ceased their attacks — presumably they were gathering forces for another major attack on the new line — but the lull in the battle gave time for the Union soldiers to rejoin their scattered units and search for food and ammunition, both of which were in short supply. It also gave Grant time to consider several aspects of the battle after hearing some of his men comment that the Confederates had entered the fight carrying knapsacks filled with rations, not something that soldiers would normally be burdened with during a battle. This fact told Grant that the Confederates were not just fighting to save Fort Donelson, but they were preparing to abandon the fort and were carrying rations so they could stay out of their works as long as it took to break out past the Union lines and escape to safety. Grant said to one of his staff officers, Colonel J. D. Webster, that "some of our men are pretty badly demoralized, but the enemy must be more so, for he has attempted to force his way out, but has fallen back; the one who attacks first now will be victorious and the enemy will have to be in a hurry if he gets ahead of me."[6]

One of Ulysses Grant's most important personality traits, and one that would be most useful throughout the war, was that he simply refused to allow himself or his troops to admit that they had lost a fight. He truly believed that in every hard-fought contest at some point both sides would be near exhaustion and feel that they could not continue the struggle.

It was at this point in the battle that the side that mustered up enough courage and energy for one more effort would be victorious. The individual or army that does the unexpected will succeed. Now was that time and Grant was determined not to let it slip through his fingers for lack of effort.[7]

Grant decided that in order to reclaim the lost ground on the right it would be necessary to attack not just that side of the lines but also the presumably weakened Confederate right where General Smith's fresh troops were stationed. Grant wanted General Wallace and as many men as McClernand could regroup to advance against the enemy in their front and force them back to the fortifications. On the Union left General Smith was to launch his division against what were assumed to be lightly manned trenches in his front. Not wanting to leave any advantage unused, Grant also wrote to Foote explaining the situation and asking for as much help as he could possibly give, even if it was just a token appearance: "If all the gunboats that can will immediately make their appearance to the enemy it may secure us a victory. Otherwise all may be defeated. A terrible conflict ensued in my absence, which has demoralized a portion of my command, and I think the enemy is much more so." Grant knew the frightening effect the heavy shells of the gunboats would have on the Confederate troops occupying open trenches and that hearing the booming of the ship's guns would have a reassuring effect on his own troops. He was also aware that the reverse was true and was looking more for moral support from Foote's ships rather than for a real contribution to the fighting that lay ahead: "If the gunboats do not show themselves, it will reassure the enemy and still further demoralize our troops. I must order a charge to save appearances. I do not expect the gunboats to go into action, but to make appearance and throw a few shells at long range."[8]

On the right the orders went out to form regiments and prepare to advance and reclaim the former positions. As late afternoon approached, General Wallace formed three brigades to make the assault. Most of McClernand's command had fallen back to re-form and were available for support but did not really play a significant part in the afternoon fighting. On the far right of the new Union line Colonel Morgan L. Smith commanding a brigade made up of his 8th Missouri and the 11th Indiana that had been moved from General Smith's right during the lull in the fighting joined Colonel Cruft's brigade on the front line preparing to lead the assault. Colonel Leonard F. Ross took over command of McClernand's third brigade consisting of the 17th and 49th Illinois to support the attack on the left and act as a reserve. The assault began about four o'clock with Colonel Smith moving toward a hill occupied by the Confederates with the 8th Missouri in the lead. The Confederate position was covered by woods on both sides of the only road leading up in the direction of the works. The Federal troops had to pass over an open space of several hundred feet, exposed to the enemy's fire, before reaching the foot of the hill. As the troops were moving forward toward the enemy Thomas Durham of the 11th Indiana saw Colonel Smith casually riding his horse smoking a cigar. Out of nowhere a bullet hit Smith's cigar, cutting it off near his face. Smith calmly "spit the stub out, took another cigar from his pocket and called to one of the boys to give him a match. He lit it with such coolness that it had a very quieting effect on the high-strung nerves of the boys."[9]

As Colonel Smith led his men up the hillside, Colonel Cruft formed his brigade at the foot of the hill and advanced around to the right. The slope of the hillside was broken up by rock ledges and mostly covered with underbrush, and in their respective fronts Smith's men had to negotiate the rough and stony areas while Cruft's men faced mostly the wooded terrain. Smith ascertained that facing his men were the 1st and 3rd Mississippi, the 1st Texas, and the 8th Kentucky. As Smith's men started up the slope they ran into enemy skirmishers who stubbornly defended their ground until the weight of numbers forced them back. Moving up the slope toward the Confederate lines, the men in blue began receiving heavy volleys of musket fire from the defenders. When the first volley was fired Smith ordered both his regiments to lie down and, as General Wallace witnessed, "[s]oon as the fury of the fire abated both regiments rose up and rushed on, and in that way they at length closed upon the enemy, falling when the volleys grew hottest, dashing on when they slackened or ceased."[10]

As Colonel Smith's brigade moved up the main portion of the hill Colonel Cruft's troops were moving up the hill on the right and also around the right of the enemy position that was manned primarily by the 4th Mississippi and 15th Arkansas. The 44th Indiana followed the 8th Missouri more toward the center of the line while Cruft sent most of the rest of his brigade around the right to attack from that flank and rear. As Colonel Cruft reported, "The assault was a complete success.... In a sharp and desperate fight of a few minutes' duration the hill was carried by storm, and the enemy, with tremendous cheers, driven up to and within his breastworks. The flank attack of the portion of my brigade up the hill, in a line at a right angle to the main advance, was gallantly conducted, and contributed no doubt largely to the rout of the enemy." The fleeing Confederates were pursued over the hillside and up to the open ground in front of their fortifications, about half a mile, before the Union troops were recalled. The victorious Federal troops pulled up about 150 yards from the main Confederate works with both sides in about the same positions they were in before the fighting began that morning.[11]

Considering how fiercely and stubbornly the Confederates had fought for hours earlier in the day, retaking the lost ground and pushing them back into their works seemed to go perhaps a little too easily, and there was a good reason for that impression. There is little doubt many of the Confederate units, complying with General Pillow's orders to return to the fortifications, were already either on their way back or getting ready to pull out when they were hit by the Federal assault and the Union troops probably faced much less resistance than they would have if the Confederates had really wanted to hold on to their hard-won positions on the Union right.[12]

Confederate general Gideon J. Pillow. Commanded a brigade at Stones River where he was found taking cover behind a tree (Library of Congress).

Around four o'clock in the afternoon over on the Union left General Smith sent his two remaining brigades forward. Colonel John Cook's brigade was sent on the right to make the Confederates think the attack was coming head-on, while General Smith personally led Colonel Jacob Lauman's brigade forward against the enemy works facing the Union far left. Although the Confederate line was thinly manned in this sector, the Federal troops found it slow going as they made their way through felled trees in front of the works under a heavy fire from the stubborn defenders who were putting up quite a fight. One of the sights that many of the Federal soldiers remembered long after the battle was that of General Smith astride his horse, waving his sword above his head and yelling, to be heard over the din of the firing, for the men to follow him. Seeing some of the soldiers begin to hesitate, Smith rode over shouting to them, "Damn you gentlemen, I see skulkers, I'll have none here. Come on, you volunteers, come on. This is your chance. You volunteered to be killed for love of country, and now you can be."[13]

One of Cook's men who followed him toward the Confederate lines was Charles F. Hubert of the 50th Illinois, who later wrote that the direction followed by the assaulting troops "led us over two steep ridges and across two deep ravines, the timber had been cut low and the limbs trimmed so as to impede our progress. The enemy covered this portion of the field with a six gun battery which swept the ground, in many places with terrible effect." The going was no easier for Lauman's men on the left. On the way to the first line of enemy works the 2nd Iowa accompanied by the 14th Iowa and supported by Lauman's two other regiments had to struggle up a steep hill made slippery by melted snow that turned the ground to mud. From the top, musket fire poured down on Lauman's troops while artillery fire came in from the sides. The fighting was desperate and there was a trail of dead and wounded behind the Federal lines as the troops continued to bravely advance up the side of that hill closer and closer to the enemy breastworks. One of the men who experienced that attack was Charles Nott, who wrote home that he especially remembered that the artillery fire "came with the rushing, clashing of a locomotive on a railroad. You heard the boom of the cannon up the ravine — then the sound of the shell — and then *felt* it rushing at you. There was a loud bang — fragments flew about, and all was over. It was so quickly done, that you had no time to anticipate or think — you were killed or you were safe, and it was over." The real question facing those men as they continued to move up the hill was if enough of them would survive to be able to take the Confederate works once they got there.[14]

Inside the Confederate works that were being attacked the situation was just as desperate as it was for the men coming toward them. The defenders were from Colonel John Head's 30th Tennessee, who had relieved General Buckner's men when they moved out for the morning assault on the Federal right. Colonel Head had fewer than five hundred men to cover about three-quarters of a mile of entrenchments, so his men were spread out precariously thin. When the exhausted Confederate soldiers began returning to the trenches during the late afternoon Colonel Roger Hanson's 2nd Kentucky was just beginning to file into their trenches on the right when General Smith began his assault. Outnumbered and not yet fully organized to defend the rifle pits in the outer works on the far right, the defenders put up a gallant struggle, holding off the Federal attack long enough for more of Buckner's men to return to the main lines. Colonel Head reported, "About 4 P.M., and before the regiment of Colonel Hanson could be arranged in the pits, the enemy, in heavy force, attacked the three companies under Major Turner on the extreme right. They held their position with great gallantry, pouring a destructive fire into the ranks of the enemy until he passed between the pits and overpowered them." The survivors of the fight for the rifle pits were able to get away to the hills in their rear and join the Confederate troops who were just now arriving to man the main line of works.[15]

General Buckner reported that after he received orders to return to the fortifications his exhausted troops had to march back almost two miles to their original positions, which they did as rapidly as possible. As it turned out, however, Buckner reported, "But a small portion of my division had reached their position when a division of the enemy, under command of General C. F. Smith, assaulted the extreme right of my position, falling upon Hanson's regiment before it had reached its rifle pits. This gallant regiment was necessarily thrown back in confusion upon the position of the Eighteenth Tennessee." When Buckner reached the scene he was able to build up the defenses on the hill overlooking the outer works that had just been taken by General Smith's men. Reinforcing this position as his men continued to return, Buckner built up a solid line to resist the next Federal assault.[16]

General Smith now had control of one of the outer defensive works of the Confederate line, but he wanted to break through the main line before they had time to reinforce and stabilize their defenses. Charles Nott noted that once the 2nd Iowa had "reached the top and scrambled over the breastwork. I saw a second hill rising gradually before us, and on the top of it a second breastwork — between us and it about four hundred yards of broken ground. A second fire opened upon us from these inner works. We were ordered back, and, recrossing those we had taken, lay down upon the outer side of the embankment."[17]

Working as quickly as possible, Buckner had been able to strengthen the inner defensive line just before the Federal assault began. At this time there began a series of attacks and counterattacks that lasted until after dark. Buckner reported, "During a contest of more than two hours the enemy threatened my left with a heavy column and made repeated attempts to storm my line on the right, but the well-directed fire of Porter's and Graves' artillery and the musketry fire of the infantry repelled the attempts, and finally drove him to seek shelter behind the works he had taken." Buckner estimated that during the fighting the Federals had thrown three to five times his own number of men against their lines.[18]

Exhausted, hungry and freezing, Flavel Barber and his comrades in the 3rd Tennessee had just returned to their camp from the fighting on the Union right when they were called on to reinforce the trenches being attacked by General Smith's men. Bullets swept the position they were assigned to and almost at once the Tennesseans were thrust into the thick of the fighting. Barber remembered that they "leaped out of the trenches and rushed to the spot where the battle raged most fiercely. Everything was in wild confusion.... The enemy kept advancing up the hill and we met them at the crest with bayonets fixed ready for a charge. A perfect tornado of balls swept our ranks. Buckner called to us not to cross the hill and expose ourselves to certain destruction." But a final charge never came, as General Smith pulled his men back to the outer works they had captured earlier and the firing ended at last.[19]

The night of February 15 found the garrison of Fort Donelson manning the same trenches they had left that morning. Cold and worn-out from hours of marching and fighting, they had opened a clear path to freedom by gaining possession of the Charlotte and Forge roads but were unable to take advantage of their early success. General Floyd made the unfortunate decision to prematurely telegraph to General Johnston that an attack had been launched against the Federal right flank and, "after a most obstinate and sanguinary conflict, succeeded in driving the enemy from his position and forcing him back towards his left flank. The enemy maintained a successful struggle, which continued for nine hours, and resulted in driving him from the field with a loss on his part of 1,240-odd killed and wounded." The obvious implication was that a great victory had been won, but Floyd forgot to mention that he had subsequently withdrawn his men from the positions they had won and was now threatened by Union possession of part of his lines on the far right of the Confederate positions.[20]

Even at this late moment and well into the night there was still time for at least most of the Confederate garrison to escape from the fort and its surrounding fortifications. The Federal troops had been fighting just as long as had the Confederates and were just as cold and exhausted, which delayed the movement of men to regain control of much of the area they had lost that morning. The area adjacent to the Forge road was still unoccupied and the Charlotte road was wide open, although Smith's Ford was flooded, making passage by that route difficult but certainly not impossible. Unfortunately for their men, many of the senior Confederate commanders spent much of the evening debating what actions they should take next rather than actually doing something.[21]

The most distressing problem facing the Confederate leaders was General Smith's capture of the works on the far right. In his report Pillow wrote that this was a commanding location, "being immediately in rear of our river batteries and field work for its protection. From it he could readily turn the intrenched work occupied by General Buckner and attack him in reverse, or he could advance, under cover of an intervening ridge, directly upon our battery and field work. While the enemy held the position it was manifest we could not hold the main work or battery."[22]

Out in the Confederate trenches the night was cold and dismal as the men tried to get some rest. They had to remain alert since the Federal troops were only a short distance away. Flavel Barber got no sleep that night, knowing that the fighting was sure to begin again when it grew light enough to see what you were shooting at and "if we should escape it would only be by cutting our way through with fearful loss, leaving behind our sick and wounded and the unburied bodies of the dead. The word 'surrender' had not been mentioned nor even thought of."[23]

Over in the Union lines the soldiers suffered from the same cold and exhaustion as their enemies. On General Smith's front where his men had been able to take control of a key position in the enemy lines they also had to prepare for the inevitable counterattack that would come in the morning. About the only real difference between the two groups of soldiers was that the Confederates had won a victory during the day and then given it away, missing their opportunity for escape, and the Federal troops were looking forward to completing the victory they had begun at the end of a long day of fighting.

9

A Most Important Victory

With General Smith's troops already holding part of the Confederate line and most of the defenders exhausted from fighting and marching all day, it was quite clear that Fort Donelson's destiny had already been decided. Still left open, however, was what would be the fate of the garrison: freedom, prison camps, or death. About 1:00 A.M. General Floyd called a council of all the general officers and the brigade and regimental commanders at the Rice house. Floyd informed them that he had information from scouts on the ground that at least a dozen more Federal transports were in the process of landing reinforcements for Grant's army. Pointing out the foolishness of trying to continue the fight against the overwhelming strength of the Federal army, Floyd instructed the officers present to prepare their men to abandon the fort by four o'clock that morning. Floyd wanted to try making a dash for freedom along the Charlotte road on the far left of the fortifications.[1]

General Pillow reported that while preparations were in progress to evacuate Fort Donelson scouts sent out to reconnoiter the escape route returned to report that the "overflowed valley was not practicable for infantry; that the soft mud was about half-leg deep, and that the water was about saddle-skirt deep to the horses, and that there was a good deal of drift in the way." It was also discovered that the Federal troops were moving back into the positions they had occupied before being driven off during the Confederate assault. Considering how difficult it would be for the already-exhausted infantry to wade through the freezing water with any kind of speed it was decided to abandon the idea of evacuating down the Charlotte road and look for another solution to save the garrison troops.[2]

Realistically there were precious few options left for the Confederates. General Pillow stated that he was in favor of fighting their way out. Being a more practical soldier, General Buckner stated in his report, "I regarded the position of the army as desperate, and that an attempt to extricate it by another battle, in the suffering and exhausted condition of the troops, was almost hopeless." Buckner noted that his men "had been worn down with watching, with labor, with fighting. Many of them were frosted by the intensity of the cold; all of them were suffering and exhausted by their incessant labors. There had been no regular issue of rations for a number of days and scarcely any means of cooking. Their ammunition was nearly expended." Considering the number of Federal troops available, he felt, "An attempt to make a sortie would have been resisted by a superior force of fresh troops." Buckner went on to say that once the water batteries were abandoned the Federal gunboats could approach the fort and fire on the retreating Confederates from close range, resulting in the troops being fired upon from nearly all directions when the Federal field artillery joined in, and "the result would have been a virtual massacre of the troops, more disheartening in its effects than a surrender." Even if the retreating Confederates were able to break out of the Fort Donelson perimeter, Buckner believed, they would be followed by the fresher and more numerous Federal troops and cut to pieces, and he flatly stated that "it would cost the command three-fourths its present numbers to cut its way out; that it was wrong to sacrifice three-fourths of a command to save one-fourth, and that no officer had a right to cause such a sacrifice."³

Pillow then proposed that they hold the lines one more day to allow as many men as possible to escape on the river using ferries and small boats that were still available. Stating the grim reality of the situation, Buckner replied that the Federals had already taken possession of a portion of the lines on his right and that he was convinced that what would be the final assault would begin at first light and "they were in position successfully to assail my position and the water batteries — and that, with my weakened and exhausted force, I could not successfully resist the assault which would be made at daylight by a vastly superior force." Buckner noted that the troops

Confederate general Simon B. Buckner. Commanded Kentucky state militia when war broke out and later became governor (Library of Congress).

were suffering from the intense cold and exhausted by constant labor. They had not been issued regular rations for several days and the supply of ammunition was dangerously low. He admitted that when the Federal assault came "I cannot hold my position half an hour."⁴

Still looking for any possible way to delay the inevitable, Pillow asked Buckner why he could not hold out longer, saying, "I think you can hold your position; I think you can, sir." In reply Buckner immediately stated, "I know my position; I can only bring to bear against the enemy about 4,000 men, while he can oppose me with any given number." Looking at the bigger picture, Buckner continued by commenting that he was under the impression that the most important reason for trying to hold Fort Donelson was to cover the retreat of the main army from Bowling Green to Nashville and until that was accomplished it was important to try to hold their position "even at the risk of the destruction of our entire force, as the delay even of a few hours might gain the safety of General Johnston's force." At that point General Floyd informed the gathered officers that Johnston had reached Nashville. As far as Buckner was concerned, this news eliminated any rationale for continuing to hold the fort, and he finally stated what all the officers present must have been thinking, that "it would be wrong to subject the army to a virtual massacre when no good could result from the sacrifice, and that the general officers owed it to their men, when further resistance was unavailing, to obtain the best terms of capitulation possible for them."⁵

General Buckner related parts of the conversation in his report. Finally convinced that there was no hope of saving the fort, Buckner remembered that Pillow said, "Gentlemen, if we cannot cut our way out nor fight on there is no alternative left us but capitulation, and I am determined that I will never surrender the command nor will I ever surrender myself a prisoner. I will die first." Relatively quiet through most of the discussion, General Floyd declared that "we will have to capitulate; but, gentlemen, I can not surrender, you know my position with the Federals; it wouldn't do, it wouldn't do." Speaking to Floyd, Pillow commented that he believed "there were no two persons in the Confederacy whom the Yankees would prefer to capture than himself and General Floyd." Both officers then announced that they were going to attempt to escape from Fort Donelson if possible. In contrast, General Buckner, the only real soldier of the three top officers, declared that he "regarded it as my duty to remain with my men and share their fate, whatever it might be."[6]

Looking to pass the responsibility of defeat to someone else, Floyd asked Buckner if he would be willing to take over command of Fort Donelson and arrange for the surrender of the fort and garrison. Buckner replied that "a capitulation would be as bitter to me as it could be to any one, but I regarded it as a necessity of our position, and I could not reconcile it with my sense of duty to separate my fortune from those of my command." Floyd then inquired of Buckner that if he were the commanding officer of Fort Donelson would he allow Floyd to withdraw his brigade to escape from the fort, to which Buckner replied, "Yes, sir, if you move your command before the enemy act upon my communication, offering to capitulate." General Floyd then informed Pillow that he was now the commander of Fort Donelson. General Pillow immediately turned the command over to Buckner and just that quickly the transfer of power was done. Colonel Nathan Bedford Forrest, the cavalry commander, was also in the room during the discussions about surrender, and he commented that "I think there is more fight in these men than you all suppose, and if you will let me, I will take my command." After General Buckner gave his assent to Forrest's request there was a brief general discussion of the various possible ways for the garrison to escape from the fort and get through the Federal lines to safety.[7]

While the generals were debating the merits of surrender or escape most of their men were still in ranks awaiting orders to begin the evacuation. During the early-morning hours most of the garrison received orders to return to their assigned positions in the works. All except Bushrod Johnson's command over on the Confederate left, that is. General Johnson realized that something was going on when Floyd's Virginia regiments began moving back to the landing. An aide sent back to headquarters to inform the senior commanders that Johnson's men were formed and ready to move out soon returned with a note from Buckner advising Johnson to hold his division until new orders were received. This was the first notice Johnson had of the change in commanders. Riding over to the Dover Hotel to consult with Buckner, Johnson learned that the new commanding officer was away from headquarters, but a staff officer advised Johnson to try to make contact with the Federal officers in his area and ask them not to fire on his troops as they returned to camp. This was also the first news Johnson received of plans to surrender the fort that morning.[8]

The formal process of surrendering Fort Donelson to the surrounding Federal forces began at about three o'clock on the morning of February 16 when a Confederate staff officer was brought to General Smith's camp with a letter for General Grant. The letter was from Buckner, who proposed to Grant the "appointment of commissioners to agree upon terms of capitulation of the forces and post under my command, and in that view suggest an armistice until 12 o'clock to-day." When Grant asked General Smith to give his opinion of

Buckner's request the crusty old general replied emphatically, "No terms to the damned rebels." Grant was amused by Smith's answer, then wrote out one of the most well-known and important messages in American history: "Yours of this date, proposing armistice and appointment of commissioners to settle terms of capitulation, is just received. No terms except unconditional and immediate surrender can be accepted. I propose to move immediately upon your works." Smith grumbled that Grant's reply was "the same thing in smoother words."[9]

When General Buckner received Grant's message demanding unconditional surrender the Confederates were in no position to put up much of a resistance. Few of the troops had been able to return to the defenses, and there wasn't enough ammunition for more than a brief engagement if the Federals did launch another assault in the morning. More important, however, was the condition of the troops. The garrison had been under almost continuous fire for nearly four days and "had suffered intensely in a heavy snow-storm and from intense cold, almost without shelter, with insufficient food, and almost without sleep." Buckner believed that the combination of all these factors was beginning to weaken the men's will to fight. General Smith's division already occupied a portion of the defenses and was preparing to renew the assault. The Confederates did not have nearly enough men in position to do more than just slow down the massive attack that was about to begin. There was only one realistic choice for Buckner to make.[10]

Grant's threat of moving on the Confederate lines was not just words on paper. He had already sent out orders to the division commanders to launch their men against the weakened Confederate lines at first light. Buckner's answer to Grant's ultimatum arrived at Union headquarters shortly before the attacks were to commence: "The distribution of the forces under my command incident to an unexpected change of commanders and the overwhelming force under your command compel me, notwithstanding the brilliant success of the Confederate arms yesterday, to accept the ungenerous and unchivalrous terms which you propose. " It was done. Ulysses S. Grant had just won the most significant Union victory of the war to date and one of the most strategically important victories of the entire war.[11]

While Grant and Buckner were sending messages back and forth, Floyd, Pillow and Forrest were making their escape. As one might expect, Colonel Forrest was the only one of the three who exhibited much courage or determination. Informing his men that he was not going to surrender, Forrest stated that he would take anyone willing to join him in escaping from the doomed fort. By 4:00 A.M. Forrest moved out from Dover heading east with about five hundred of his own men and two hundred men from other units who followed behind on horseback or on foot desperate to get away. They slowly made their way through the swampy landscape and by the time it was dark were nearly twenty miles from the fort and well on the way to Nashville, and safety.[12]

As for Floyd and Pillow, their route to safety was significantly less impressive. General Floyd had originally planned on leaving with Forrest but then changed his mind and decided to cut through the Federal lines with his own troops along the Charlotte road in the same area where they broke through the day before. While making preparations for the attack Floyd learned that two steamboats were headed to Dover. Changing his mind again, Floyd decided to use these ships to carry as many of his men across the river as possible, rather than risk losing them all trying to break through the Union lines and, if successful, moving through the flooded terrain. When the ships docked, Floyd had his men board in order of the seniority of their commanders, with Colonel John McCausland's men the first to board, and after a quick trip across the river to deposit the men on the opposite side the boats returned for Colonel Gabriel Wharton's troops. While Major William Brown was waiting for his turn he saw that the news of the surrender was spreading through the camps and many men had naturally run "to the river, almost panic-stricken and frantic, to make good their escape by getting aboard" one of the ships or anything else that might carry them across the river to safety. Some men tried to swim across the icy river using logs or wooden planks for support; many did not make it.[13]

As the last of Wharton's men were boarding the ships, General Buckner sent for Major Brown and informed him that the boats must leave the landing immediately. Major Brown reported that Buckner informed him "that we were in danger of being shelled by the gunboats of the enemy, as he had surrendered the place, and the gunboats were or may be at the fort; that his honor as an officer, and the honor and good faith of the Confederacy, required that at daylight, he should turn over everything under his command, agreeably to the terms of capitulation." The ships did not return for another trip across the river and Brown and the troops of the 20th Mississippi who were guarding the docks were left behind to their fate. While the troops were being loaded onto the ships General Pillow and his staff were able to locate a small flatboat and used that to cross to the opposite shore, where they waited for the steamboats to bring the troops across. Pillow and a small group of his officers and men made their way to Clarksville, where they joined Floyd and the troops aboard the steamships, reaching Nashville the next morning.[14]

Just as Grant had informed Buckner in his surrender note, the Federal army was preparing to assault the Confederate lines early on the sixteenth. In the center General Lew Wallace had his men ready to attack the enemy rifle pits along the Wynn's Ferry road well before dawn. Colonel Thayer's brigade was on the right, with Colonels Cruft and Morgan L. Smith forming their men on the ridge above the road so that Wallace could attack the left flank of the defenses "about breakfast time." During the time it took to organize the troops they were within range of the Confederate artillery, and Wallace was pleasantly surprised that they did not open fire to disrupt his ranks. On the Union right General McClernand had received instructions from Grant to support the attacks of the other two divisions, and his men were also ready to go before daybreak.[15]

General Wallace was ready to launch his assault and was just waiting for word from Grant to send his men forward. There had been no artillery firing that morning and the officers could see no signs that the Confederates were preparing to resist the attack that everyone knew was coming, but the enemy battle flags still flew defiantly above the works, so the men steeled themselves for the coming battle. Suddenly two Confederate horsemen rode out from the fortifications with one of them carrying a white flag. They carried a message asking Wallace to hold off on his assault because the fort had been surrendered. Wallace quickly sent the couriers to headquarters and informed Grant that he was moving forward to take possession of the defenses in his front.[16]

As the sun came up on February 16 most of the Federal soldiers had no idea what was going on. All they knew for sure was that the guns were silent for the first time since they arrived in front of Fort Donelson. Gradually news of the surrender began to spread and the sounds of cheering and celebration followed. For the rest of his life Ira Blanchard, of the 20th Illinois, remembered the moment he and his comrades learned of the surrender: "Soldiers threw up their hats, pulled off their coats and fell to whipping one another until their wind gave out, or their coats went to pieces. This was the first great victory of the war, and the greatest day of rejoicing I ever saw."[17]

On the other side of the lines Flavel Barber was just as surprised when word of the surrender passed among the Confederate troops. He remembered that he and the men of the 3rd Tennessee "were thunderstruck. We had expected a desperate fight at break of day, but no one had dreamed of a surrender. We thought even yet there must be some mistake about it, that the white flag was but a pretext to gain time and to give us a chance for escape." Once the men learned that they had really been surrendered many decided to take it upon themselves to escape and soon hundreds of men, some of whom had discarded their uniforms and donned disguises, were heading to Clarksville by any route they could find.[18]

Over on the Federal left, Colonel Lauman's brigade of Smith's division that had spearheaded the attack on the rifle pits along the Eddyville road was awarded the honor of being the first unit to enter the enemy works, with the 2nd Iowa taking the post of honor in front. With drums beating and their colors waving in the breeze Lauman's brigade proudly headed toward the Confederate lines down the Eddyville road. When the victorious Union soldiers passed through the first line of trenches they saw the Confederate troops "drawn up in line, with their arms in great heaps." Colonel Lauman thought the grey-clads looked "quite woebegone" as his men smartly marched into the interior of the defenses. When the 2nd Iowa reached the fort, they set their "colors upon the battlements beside the white of the enemy." Colonel Lauman's brigade was assigned to take charge of the fort, acting as the new garrison. General Smith's other two brigades commanded by Colonels Cook and McArthur had followed Lauman's troops into the fort and were assigned to guard prisoners and protect captured public property.[19]

Upon encountering the Confederates who had just the day before been trying to kill them, the Federal soldiers generally behaved with courtesy and respect to their defeated foe. Flavel Barber noted that few insults were traded between the men and that the Union troops "seemed anxious to converse with us and tried to persuade us that they were our friends, but they met with but little success. Candor compels me to say that their officers acted toward us as gentlemen and in their conversation with us carefully avoided saying anything which might irritate our feelings already so sore from defeat and surrender."[20]

A little later in the morning General Grant rode over to the Dover Hotel to meet in person with General Buckner. Years before the war the two men had been friends in the army, and in 1854 it was Buckner who loaned Grant enough money to get back home when he resigned his commission. By the customs of the time Grant had been rather harsh in his demand for unconditional surrender, but now that the fighting was over he was more than ready to repay Buckner's earlier kindness and offered him any assistance he might need to get through his captivity. During what was a relatively friendly conversation Buckner told Grant that if he had been in command of the Confederate forces from the beginning Grant's men would not have been allowed to march unopposed right up to the Confederate fortifications. Knowing Buckner's qualities as a soldier, Grant replied that if Buckner had been in command he would not have tried to approach the fort in the way that he did.[21]

Arrangements were quickly made for the Confederate prisoners to be disarmed as soon as possible and assembled in camps near the Dover landing. The officers would remain in command of their units and were allowed to retain their sidearms to assist in keeping the prisoners under control. Once ships became available the prisoners would be given enough rations for two days and taken to Cairo. The men would be allowed to keep their clothing, blankets, and any private items they could carry on their person.[22]

Once everything was settled, Grant sent a telegram to General Halleck announcing the victory and informing him that his army had taken "from 12,000 to 15,000 prisoners, including Generals Buckner and Bushrod [R.] Johnson; also about 20,000 stand of arms, 48 pieces of artillery, 17 heavy guns, from 2,000 to 4,000 horses, and large quantities of commissary stores." Acknowledging the significant part that General Smith had played in the victory in a later telegram, Grant noted that he "ordered a charge upon the left (enemy's right) with the division under General C. F. Smith, which was most brilliantly executed, and gave to our arms full assurance of victory."[23]

The day after the surrender Grant issued a formal order of congratulations to the men of his army:

> For four successive nights, without shelter, during the most inclement weather known in this latitude, they faced an enemy in large force in a position chosen by himself. Though strongly fortified by nature, all the safeguards suggested by science were added. Without murmur this was borne, prepared at all times to receive an attack, and with continuous skirmishing by day, resulting ultimately in forcing the enemy to surrender without conditions.
>
> The victory achieved is not only great in breaking down rebellion, but has secured the greatest number of prisoners of war ever taken in one battle on this continent.[24]

Right after the surrender General Wallace was sent back to Fort Henry with two brigades to secure that position against a possible Confederate attack, although considering the reality of the strategic situation now facing General Albert Sidney Johnston, this was most unlikely. At Fort Donelson chaos reigned. No one in the army had any experience dealing with the number of prisoners who had to be processed, fed, and sent to prison camps in the North. There were bodies of fallen soldiers of both sides everywhere and they needed to be identified, if possible, and laid to rest. There were literally thousands of items of a military nature that had to be gathered up and sorted through to see what could be salvaged for use by the victors. On the waterfront several large piles of food had been just left to rot, and this had to be destroyed. Adding to the confusion, hundreds of civilians began arriving at Fort Donelson. Most were searching for family members or wanted to volunteer to assist the hundreds of wounded men who needed care. Unfortunately, there were others who were looking for souvenirs or ways they might turn a profit from the tragedy of battle and the disorder left over after the fighting was done.[25]

Throughout the North the twin victories at Fort Henry and then Fort Donelson were celebrated with nearly unbounded joy. The captures of the forts were the first significant Union victories since the discouraging defeat at Bull Run. When news of the capture of Fort Donelson reached Chicago during the day of the sixteenth, Mary A. Livermore wrote, "the delight of the West was boundless. It was a great victory, and the first of any importance since the beginning of the war. Great as were its military results, its happy effect on the spirits of the soldiers and the people was even greater." Few later Union victories brought as much delight to the citizens of the Northwest as did the fall of Fort Donelson. Spontaneous celebrations occurred throughout the nation, church bells were rung, bands struck up patriotic tunes, and excited crowds thronged the streets. Meetings were held to raise money to assist the wounded soldiers and many streets were lit with bonfires, turning night into day.[26]

Much of the attention of the public became focused on the up-to-now-unknown little general who had produced these victories, Ulysses S. Grant. Here was a man who knew how to win battles, and his demand for unconditional surrender became famous across the nation. Secretary of War Stanton recommended Grant be promoted to major general of volunteers and President Lincoln nominated Grant that same day. The United States Senate happened to be in session at this time, and Grant was quickly confirmed in his new rank. In a letter written for public consumption and printed on February 20 Secretary Stanton wrote, "We may well rejoice at the recent victories, for they teach us that battles are to be won now, and by us, in the same and only manner that they were ever won by any people, or in any age, since the days of Joshua — by boldly pursuing and striking the foe."[27]

The capture of Forts Henry and Donelson and the subsequent opening of the Tennessee and Cumberland rivers immediately changed the entire military situation in the West. As General Halleck had foreseen, once the center of the Confederate defenses was broken the ends could not sustain themselves. The whole of Kentucky and most of Tennessee quickly fell under Federal control; the Tennessee and Cumberland rivers were opened to national vessels for hundreds of miles. The large Confederate camp at Bowling Green had become untenable as soon as Grant's army arrived in front of Fort Donelson and was abandoned and the great industrial center and state capital of Nashville was exposed to capture. On the other end of the Confederate line the fortress at Columbus was practically cut off from support and would soon be evacuated. General Johnston could do little more than pull his badly outnumbered troops south and try to find a place to make a stand near the border with Mississippi.[28]

Before the capture of Forts Henry and Donelson the Federal armies had achieved very few victories and those were of little consequence. Generals had made promises and campaigns had started with high hopes, but none accomplished nearly as much as Grant had in two weeks. This short, generally unkempt man, unknown outside his immediate circles, with few accomplishments to show for his previous time in the army, an army he left under a cloud, had achieved victories that brought joy and hope to the nation and showed the troops what victory was like, giving them a taste for more.[29]

10

Johnston Saves What He Can

The capture of Fort Henry and Grant's investment of Fort Donelson on February 12 had serious repercussions on the Confederate strategic plans in the West. Gone was the idea of holding a line through Southern Kentucky and Northern Tennessee to Columbus on the Mississippi River. Kentucky was lost as far as the Confederacy was concerned and could not be retrieved. Instead of planning the protection of Nashville and closing the Tennessee and Cumberland rivers to Union ships, now General Johnston was concerned with saving as much of Southern and Western Tennessee as possible and avoiding getting his small army destroyed by one or both of the much larger Union armies he had to contend with in the process. As soon as Grant's army showed up in front of Fort Donelson, General Johnston knew that his most important job was to save as much of the army as he could, and the evacuation of Bowling Green was ordered immediately.[1]

It is quite possible that General Johnston was caught off guard by the quickness of Grant's advance, or that he devoted too much attention to General Buell's army moving down from the north, or that he just couldn't decide which force to concentrate against. From his vantage point at Bowling Green it would certainly appear to Johnston that Buell's army was more of a threat to the Confederate troops stationed there than was Grant, who was just coming up to Fort Donelson. The fact is, however, that if Fort Donelson fell after putting up only a brief fight, which is what happened, Johnston's men could find themselves cut off from Nashville and points farther south if the Federals sent their gunboats up the Cumberland River destroying the bridges as they went. General Johnston did not have enough available troops to concentrate and attempt to stall their advance by taking the offense against either Grant or Buell, and if they were to combine Johnston could only offer a brief and ineffectual resistance before falling back as quickly as possible to save the remnant of his forces. The last thing Johnston wanted was to be caught between the two Federal armies, each of which was larger than any force he could currently put together, with little chance to escape with the troops he had left after sending nearly sixteen thousand men to Fort Donelson.[2]

To be fair to Albert Sidney Johnston, it had been obvious since the day he took command in the West that he had been given too few men and resources to properly defend the huge area he was responsible for. Everything was in short supply, including weapons, ammunition, uniforms and, most of all, men. Right from the opening of hostilities the only impediments to Federal ships on the Tennessee and Cumberland rivers were the two forts, Henry and Donelson. There were no Confederate warships available to confront the Union gunboats even though there had been two acts passed by the Confederate Congress to purchase civilian steamships and rebuild them as gunboats. The main supply lines for Confederate troops were the rivers, which easily fell under Federal control, or long, undependable rail lines running back to supply centers such as Nashville and Memphis. Despite his constant pleas for reinforcements and more of the basic necessities needed to outfit an army and fight a war, Johnston received little assistance from the Confederate government.[3]

Even before General Grant arrived at Fort Donelson, General Johnston had ordered the construction of defensive works at Clarksville and Nashville. That little had been done to construct defenses at these two important locations by the time Fort Donelson was lost is primarily due to the relatively short time between the loss of Fort Henry and Grant's taking of Fort Donelson and a decided lack of cooperation by local officials and citizens. Most of the citizens living up the Cumberland River from Fort Donelson and in Nashville were confident that the strong fort would hold back any enemy invaders, which it probably would have, at least for a much longer time period, if the fort had been commanded by more competent officers. Many of the civilian leaders had become complacent due to the lack of military activity since seceding from the Union the previous summer. It was also possible that the lucrative military contracts received by the numerous industries located around Nashville contributed to the lack of available labor to construct defensive works for the protection of the city.[4]

The Confederate troops began marching out of their camps at Bowling Green on February 12. One of the units that participated in that miserable retreat was Kentucky's Orphan Brigade. After leaving camp they marched to the vicinity of Franklin, Kentucky, a few miles above the Tennessee border, where they stopped for the night. The same cold weather that hit Fort Donelson also hit the retreating troops, and the morning of February 14 came in cold and windy, with the ground covered with snow. The troops, most of whom were unprepared for the severe weather, suffered terribly, with some of them making their way into the town looking for shelter and provisions. Once the column was past Franklin, every time they halted the fences of local farmers were quickly turned into blazing fires, providing at least some relief from the intense cold. Camping just inside Tennessee, the men spent a sleepless night just trying to avoid freezing and on the fifteenth the march south was continued under the same conditions. On the afternoon of February 16 the troops passed through Nashville without stopping and continued several miles down the Murfreesboro Pike, where they made camp.[5]

As the army passed through Nashville, news of the fall of Fort Donelson had just been received and in the city fear and alarm were everywhere. Soldiers assigned to keep order were overwhelmed by the hordes of distraught citizens and confusion was the order of the day, with both public and private property destroyed or taken for personal use. Civilians who had the means were deserting the city in droves using any type of transportation they could get their hands on. With no possibility of successfully defending Nashville, General Johnston ordered all the troops from Bowling Green, Clarksville, Nashville, and those who had escaped from Fort Donelson to concentrate at Murfreesboro, about thirty miles southeast of Nashville.[6]

Many people expected the Confederates to make a stand near Murfreesboro, but Johnston was never in favor of fighting there. Back on February 7 during a conference of senior officers at Bowling Green it had been decided that if Nashville had to be abandoned the army would move south to Stevenson, Alabama, where it would be in position to protect the transportation center of Chattanooga. A week later Johnston met with General Beauregard in Nashville, where the generals discussed possible scenarios to respond to the Union victories, but Johnston made it clear there would be no stand made at the present time and he was still planning to fall back along the line of the Nashville and Chattanooga rail line to the vicinity of Stevenson.[7]

While the army rested and regrouped at Murfreesboro they were joined by General George B. Crittenden and his troops who came down from Kentucky. General Johnston now organized his troops into three divisions commanded by Generals Hardee, Pillow and Crittenden. General Beauregard had written to Johnston that he was gathering troops in Northern Mississippi and suggested that they join forces. There were several routes the army could take depending on what Johnston wanted to accomplish in addition to saving the men he had left to fight another day. Johnston considered marching the army to Stevenson, Alabama, which was on the railroad running east to Chattanooga, and taking the railroad to Decatur. In addition to being faster than moving on foot, this route might temporarily mislead the Union commanders into thinking that Johnston was heading for Chattanooga and delaying any pursuit at least for a little while. The problem with this plan was that there was such an immense amount of supplies and military equipment that had to be moved that only by using the railroad could this invaluable material be saved for later use. There were not enough railroad cars available to transport both supplies and equipment and troops at the same time, so the men would have to walk. Considering the situation, Johnston had to change his original plans and decided instead to head for Decatur through Shelbyville and Huntsville, Alabama. This route would take the army between Chattanooga and the direct road from Nashville to Decatur, offering Johnston the opportunity to meet Buell if he should advance on either route. So early on the morning of February 28 the troops began moving out of the Murfreesboro area heading southwest under orders to "continue day to day, by Shelbyville, Fayetteville and Decatur, Alabama. The march so arranged as to make about fifteen miles a day, so long as the roads permit."[8]

Over the next two weeks the Confederates slowly made their way over muddy roads through Central Tennessee and Northern Alabama. There was no fighting or even any pursuit by Federal forces, but still the march was miserable. It rained almost constantly, and frequently the unseasonably cold temperatures turned the rain to snow and sleet. The suffering troops had to spend nights sleeping sitting up with their backs against trees to avoid being assailed by the wind-driven rain. The few men who had tents frequently had to try to hold them down while they slept to keep the tents from being blown away.[9]

Despite the terrible weather and atrocious roads, the troops made reasonably good time. On March 2 they arrived in a light snowstorm, at Shelbyville where they rested for two days before moving on. The troops reached Fayetteville on March 5, where the army divided, with some men heading southwest to Athens, Alabama, and the rest straight south to join General Johnston at Huntsville. After another brief rest the army pushed on, with Johnston arriving at Decatur on March 10 and the rest of the army trickling in over the next few days. The troops spent several days in the vicinity of Decatur while crossing to the south side of the Tennessee River.[10]

The army would be relatively safe now that the Tennessee River was between them and any Union forces, but as W. J. Worsham of the 19th Tennessee later wrote, after crossing the river they went into camp for a couple of days, then "[p]ush now became the order of the day, everything and everybody seemed to be in a hurry. On the 15th of March we moved out for Corinth, Mississippi, where we pitched our tents on the 20th." The apparent reason for the haste was that General Johnston was building up an army to strike back at the victorious Federals before Grant and Buell could join forces, so time was of the essence. While Johnston's men were marching toward Corinth from the east Confederate troops were also heading there from all over the South. General Beauregard was bringing his troops down to Corinth from Jackson, Tennessee. General Braxton Bragg was bringing reinforcements from the Gulf Coast with about ten thousand trained troops. With Fort Donelson gone and the Confederate army abandoning Central Tennessee, General Polk at Columbus could see that the continued occupation of that place was inviting a siege and eventual surrender of his troops, so he had already abandoned the fortress and also headed toward Corinth.[11]

With his exhausted army safely behind the Tennessee River, General Johnston now had time to turn his attention to another important situation that had been a cause for concern not only for Johnston but also for his friend Jefferson Davis: convincing the people in power and the general public that Johnston should keep his command. While it is true that the army had been saved, the cost had been high in loss of morale by the troops, and the great deal of military and civilian equipment and supplies that had been abandoned or destroyed. The route of the march from Nashville to Alabama could easily be followed by the trail of destroyed road and railroad bridges left in the army's wake. The lack of any kind of defensive effort and the subsequent evacuation of Nashville surprised and shocked not only Tennesseans but much of the Confederacy. Another factor that was frequently mentioned was that the long and miserable retreat probably cost the army many hundreds of men who lived in the area and just went home and other men who might have been willing to join up and fight for the Confederacy but decided not to after hearing nothing but negative news with the loss of Forts Henry and Donelson, the abandonment of Nashville and the decision to run away rather than put up some kind of fight.[12]

Since the fall of Fort Henry the problems did nothing but increase for the Confederacy in the West. With both the Tennessee and Cumberland rivers open to Union warships, with the great fortress at Columbus cut off from its main supply line and abandoned without a fight and the loss of the city of Nashville and all its industry, about all that stood between the heart of the Confederacy and the Union armies of Generals Grant and Buell was what was left of General Johnston's army, and this army was in trouble. The men were exhausted, hungry, many of them lacked proper weapons, supplies and equipment of all types were in short supply or nonexistent and, worst of all, their morale was at a new low. Naturally the commander of the army was blamed for these reverses. Not long after the loss of Fort Donelson the criticism began, and it continued throughout the long march to Corinth. Newspapers called for the removal of General Johnston. President Davis was flooded with calls to name a new commander in the West but responded by stating flatly, "I know Sidney Johnston well. If he is not a general, we had better give up the war, for we have no general."[13]

President Davis received a letter signed by most of the Tennessee congressional delegation dated March 8 that was highly critical of General Johnston's performance to date and strongly suggested that a change in command might be in order. Citing information received from one of the Tennessee representatives, the letter stated, "from him, as well as from other sources of information so varies and so numerous, that we cannot doubt the melancholy fact, we learn that the public sentiment in Tennessee is strangely dispirited and demoralized, on account of our recent disasters, and that this deplorable feeling is daily increasing." The representatives state that, right or wrong, "confidence is no longer felt in the military skill of Gen. A. S. Johnston. This may be all wrong; foolishly wrong; but still the stubborn fact remains, that his command have lost confidence; will not fight under him with that alacrity which is necessary to secure success; and what is even worse, if possible — that the people of Tennessee, from whom our new levies must come, partake in the same feeling."[14]

The letter from the Tennessee delegation continues by suggesting that if President Davis personally visited Tennessee "the enthusiasm which such presence would excite, would, of itself, be worth to us legions of armed men." If Davis is unable to make a visit to Tennessee in person, the representatives asked "whether some other leader, possessing more of the confidence of the command /of Gen Johnson/ and of the country, should not be assigned to that most important post."[15]

President Davis was facing a serious problem. This was not the first, nor would it be the last, correspondence he received from people he knew and respected suggesting, and in some cases demanding, that General Johnston be replaced. If Johnston was relieved the most obvious choice for his replacement would be General Beauregard, second-in-command of the department. While this might be a popular move with the public in the West, Davis had major personal and professional reasons why he absolutely did not want to elevate Beauregard to the top command in the West. There is, however, no real evidence that Davis' personal feelings toward Beauregard prevented him from making the change; in addition, apparently none of the other top Confederate generals — Polk, Bragg, or Hardee — were considered for the position. Davis's loyalty to Johnston never wavered and his confidence in Johnston's ability remained strong.[16]

Jefferson Davis wrote to General Johnston on March 12, beginning a series of communications between them. In commenting on the recent reverses in Kentucky and Tennessee and on the growing number and volume of the attacks against Johnston, Davis wrote, "I expected you to have made a full report of events precedent and consequent to the fall of Fort Donelson. In the mean time, I made for you such defense as friendship prompted, and many years of acquaintance justified; but I needed facts to rebut the wholesale assertions made against you to cover others, and to condemn my administration." As a former army officer and United States secretary of war, Davis knew that the general public "have no correct measure for military operations; and the journals are very reckless in their statements."[17]

Davis noted that, as frequently happens after a military disappointment, the size of Johnston's army "has been magnified, and the movements of an army have been measured by the capacity for locomotion of an individual." Among the factors causing the public disappointment is that "the readiness of the people, among whom you are operating, to aid you in every method had been constantly asserted; the purpose of your army at Bowling Green wholly misunderstood; and the absence of an effective force at Nashville, ignored." Davis also stated that many people believed that the capture of Fort Donelson and the subsequent loss of Nashville should be laid at Johnston's feet, "T'is charged that no effort was made to save the stores at Nashville, and that the panic of the people was caused by the army."[18]

President Davis also added that while the complaints he had been receiving against his old friend were personally painful and could cause difficulties for both president and general, the most important consideration was: "They have undermined public confidence, and damaged our cause. A full development of the truth is necessary for future success." On a more personal note, Davis wrote that "I respect the generosity which had kept you silent, but would impress upon you that the question is not personal, but public in its nature. That you and I might be content to suffer, but neither of us can willingly permit detriment to the country." Davis also wrote that he would like to visit with Johnston in person: "As soon as circumstances will permit it is my purpose to visit the field of your present operations; not that I should expect to give you any aid in the discharge of your duties as a commander, but with the hope that my position would enable me to effect something in bringing men to your standard." President Davis was also realistic enough to acknowledge some of the problems facing not only General Johnston but the Confederacy in general and suggesting some possible ways to overcome those very real problems: "We are deficient in arms, wanting in discipline, and inferior in numbers. Private arms must supply the first want; time and the presence of an enemy, with diligence on the part of commanders, will remove the second, and public confidence will overcome the third."[19]

On March 18 General Johnston responded to President Davis in a long letter to explain his actions and why he took those actions, saying that he was expecting to be roundly criticized after the loss of Fort Donelson and Nashville, "but it was impossible for me to gather the facts for a detailed report, or to spare time which was required to extricate the remainder of my troops, and save the large accumulation of stores and provisions after that disheartening disaster." Johnston also mentioned that to gain time to build up his forces and train the new recruits "I magnified my forces to the enemy, but made known my true strength to the Department and the Governors of States. The aid given was small. At length when General Beauregard came out in February, he expressed his surprise at the smallness of my force, and was impressed with the danger of my position." The general explained that he and Beauregard discussed the situation facing the Confederates in the West and that Beauregard supported Johnston's proposed future actions.[20]

As far as Fort Donelson was concerned and what might have been done to save that important position, Johnston stated, "I determined to fight for Nashville at Donelson and gave the best part of my army to do it, retaining only 14,000 men to cover my front, and giving 16,000 to defend Donelson.... Had I wholly uncovered my front to defend Donelson, Buell would have known it and marched directly on Nashville." The evacuation of Bowling Green was imperative after the Union took Fort Henry and invested Fort Donelson, and the garrison there was already on the way south when the fort surrendered. Johnston told Davis that he had done everything within his power to bolster the defenses of Fort Donelson and that the troops he sent to reinforce that place were among the best he had available. Defending the senior officers at the fort, Johnston wrote that Generals, Floyd, Pillow and Buckner "were high in the opinion of officers and men for skill and courage, and among the best officers of my command. They were popular with the volunteers, and all had seen much service. No reinforcements were asked. I awaited the event opposite Nashville. The result of the conflict each day was favorable. At midnight on the 15th, I received news of a glorious victory—at dawn of a defeat."[21]

Commenting on the evacuation of Nashville, he noted that "Nashville was incapable of defence from its position, and from the forces advancing from Bowling Green and up the Cumberland." A rear guard commanded by Floyd was left to secure the stores and provisions, and although they were able to remove most of the food and supplies stored in the city, much was lost. "The people were terrified, and some of the troops were disheartened. The discouragement was spreading, and I ordered the command to Murfreesboro, where I managed, by assembling Crittenden's division and the fugitives from Donelson, to collect an army able to offer battle." On a positive note Johnston could point out that although the march south had been difficult due to inclement weather turning roads into streams and washing away bridges, most of the stores and provisions were saved and transported to new depots.[22]

General Johnston confirmed that the retreat was almost over and he planned on cooperating with General Beauregard to defend the Mississippi Valley, "The passage is almost completed, and the head of my column is already with General Bragg at Corinth. The movement was deemed too hazardous by the most experienced members of my staff, but the object warranted the risk.... Day after to-morrow, unless the enemy intercepts me, my force will be with Bragg, and my army nearly fifty thousand strong. This must be destroyed before the enemy can attain his object."[23]

Johnston went on to say that when he sent the reinforcements to Fort Donelson he expected that if the fort could not be defended the army would be withdrawn and saved as had been done at Fort Henry: "On the 14th, I ordered General Floyd by telegraph, 'if he lost the fort to get his troops to Nashville.' It is possible this might have been done, but justice requires to look at events as they appeared at the time, and not alone by the light of subsequent information." The facts of the surrender were still being collected, but it was already clear that "General Buckner, being the junior officer, took the lead in advising the surrender, and that General Floyd acquiesced, and they all concurred in the belief that their force could not maintain its position — all concurred that it would require a great sacrifice of life to extricate the command."[24]

Although General Johnston admitted that the loss of Fort Donelson "was most disastrous and almost without remedy," he decided to remain silent, not because of any generosity to the commanders involved but because "it seemed to be the best way to serve the cause and the country. The facts were not fully known — discontent prevailed, and criticism or condemnation, were more likely to augment than to cure the evil." Johnston knew full well that he would bear the brunt of the criticisms but was "convinced that it was better to endure them for the present and defer to a more propitious time, an investigation of the conduct of the generals; for in the meantime their services were required and their influence useful."[25]

Adding a more personal note to his report, Johnston wrote, "I have thus recurred to the motives by which I have been governed from a deep personal sense of the friendship and confidence you have always shown me and from the conviction that they have not been withdrawn from me in adversity." Commenting on Davis' proposed visit, Johnston wrote that the president would be more than welcome, "You mention that you intend to visit the field of operations here. I hope to see you, for your presence would encourage my troops, inspire the people, and augment the army. To me personally it would give the greatest satisfaction." Johnston closed his letter saying, "The test of merit in my profession, with the people, is success. It is a hard rule, but I think it right."[26]

In reply to General Johnston's letter explaining the actions he took concerning Fort Donelson, Nashville and the army's march south President Davis sent a note expressing his confidence in the general: "So far as the past is concerned it but confirms the conclusions at which I had already arrived. My confidence in you has never wavered and I hope the public will soon give me credit for judgement rather than continue to arraign me for obstinacy." Davis stated that he was quite pleased with the actions Johnston had taken so far and that "I breathe easier in the assurance that you will be able to make a junction of your two armies. If you can meet the division of the enemy moving from the Tenn. before it can make a junction with that advancing from Nashville the future will be brighter." Davis did caution, however, that if the Federal columns could not be beaten separately, "our only hope is that the people of the South West will rally en masse with their private arms and thus enable you to oppose the vast army which will threaten the destruction of our country."[27]

Writing later about the loss of Forts Henry and Donelson, General Beauregard defended his former commanding officer, saying that the loss of the forts caused "a feeling of consternation, anxiety and distrust that spread over the entire section of country comprised within the bounds of General Johnston's department." The civilian population was panic stricken at the thought of hordes of Yankees ravishing the countryside, and many of the soldiers whom the people were depending on to defend them were as demoralized as those civilians were. General Johnston was criticized from every side: "A clamor, as loud as it was unfair, arose from almost every neighboring city, town or hamlet, against the general commanding our forces in the West." Despite the attacks made on the general's abilities as a soldier and leader of the army, he "withstood the storm with firmness and manliness, and was uncomplaining."[28]

11

On to Nashville

Just after the capture of Fort Donelson, General Halleck decided to give General Grant more responsibility and named him the commander of the newly created District of West Tennessee that encompassed the area from Cairo to the Mississippi border between the Cumberland and Mississippi rivers. The fact that the Cumberland ran mostly east to west and did not provide a distinct boundary on the eastern side of Grant's new command left the limit of the district to the east open to dispute. In Halleck's original orders Grant had been authorized to advance to Clarksville and destroy the railroad bridge at that location. With the Confederate army from Bowling Green in full retreat there was little to oppose such a move, and on February 18 Flag Officer Foote sailed up the Cumberland with the gunboats *Conestoga* and *Cairo*.[1]

Flag Officer Foote halted the ships just six miles out of Dover to burn the Tennessee Iron Works before continuing on toward Clarksville, which they reached the next day. Foote reported back on the twentieth that he had taken possession of Clarksville, the military fortifications had been abandoned, and most of the civilian residents had fled and he had issued a proclamation: "I hearby announce to all peaceably-disposed persons that neither in their persons nor in their property shall they suffer molestation by me or the naval force under my command, and that they may in safety resume their business avocations with the assurance of my protection." In addition, Foote also required that "all military stores and army equipments shall be surrendered, no part of them being withheld or destroyed." Foote informed Grant that there was no opposition in sight and that with a few more gunboats he could probably sail right up to Nashville with little difficulty.[2]

After hearing from Foote that Nashville was ready to be taken whenever it was convenient Grant wrote to General Cullum in Cairo on the twenty-first, "It is my impression that by following up our success Nashville would be an easy conquest; but I only throw this out as a suggestion.... White flags are flying from here to Clarksville, and rumor says the same thing extends to Nashville." Grant also stated that he would not to take any action against Nashville without express orders to do so. Flag Officer Foote also requested permission to take his gunboats to Nashville or to have the army send troops to occupy the undefended city. But, instead of moving forward, Foote wrote that "[w]e were about moving for this purpose when General Grant, to my astonishment, received a telegram from General Halleck not to let the gunboats go higher than Clarksville."[3]

Foote could have easily taken control of Nashville on February 22. It was known that the Confederate troops had fallen back out of the city and the civilian population was in a panic, so there would be no resistance offered to any Federal force that made an appearance.

But, despite the urging of both Grant and Foote, General Halleck refused to let the gunboats advance past Clarksville. The main reason for Halleck's refusal was that Nashville was in General Buell's jurisdiction and rather than have a conflict with that officer Halleck was waiting for permission to take Nashville from Washington. The only result of this delay was that it allowed the Confederates several more days to remove tons of provisions and an immense amount of military equipment.[4]

General Halleck's refusal to allow his subordinates to advance on the undefended capital of Tennessee and industrial center and capture one of the biggest prizes of the war appeared to be a monumental error in judgment. There were, however, other factors that were being considered and almost from the start of Grant's campaign Generals McClellan, Halleck and Buell were in constant communication. These three officers were generally considered, among the best strategic planners in the army. Unfortunately, what they were best at was planning campaigns, making sure every detail was perfectly worked out before taking action, and striving to promote their personal agendas. Another factor that affected Halleck's actions was that he just did not have much confidence in Grant's ability to command. Even after the surrender of Fort Henry, which really was a naval victory, Halleck was working to demote Grant. On February 8 Halleck requested that Brigadier General Ethan Allen Hitchcock be promoted to major general and assigned to Halleck's command. This would result in Hitchcock replacing Grant as commander of the army in the field. Hitchcock's promotion was approved, but he would eventually turn down the offer due to poor health.[5]

The high-stakes political maneuvering between McClellan, Halleck and Buell continued even as Grant was preparing to move on Fort Donelson. General McClellan was convinced that the weather and poor roads made a winter campaign against Bowling Green unlikely to succeed. On February 6 the general-in-chief, who had not yet learned of the capture of Fort Henry, suggested to both Halleck and Buell that they halt all other operations and concentrate on a combined move up the Tennessee and Cumberland rivers. General Buell liked the idea but as usual found problems in its implementation: "This whole move, right in its strategical bearing, but commenced by General Halleck without appreciation, preparative or concert, has now become of vast magnitude. I was myself thinking of a change of the line to support it when I received your dispatch. It will have to be made in the face of 50,000, if not 60,000 men and is hazardous. I will answer definitely in the morning." Once again Buell was grossly overestimating the size of his opposition.[6]

General Halleck replied to McClellan on the same day and was more positive about the possible campaign but still found a way to promote his agenda to Buell's detriment. "If you can give me, in addition to what I have in this department, 10,000 men, I will take Fort Henry, cut the enemy's line, and paralyze Columbus. Give me 25,000, and I will threaten Nashville and cut off railroad communications, so as to force the enemy to abandon Bowling Green without a battle." As it turned out this is pretty much what Grant did with the troops he already had.[7]

After learning of the capture of Fort Henry, McClellan telegraphed Halleck the next day, "Either Buell or yourself should soon go to the scene of operations. Why not have Buell take the line of [the] Tennessee and operate on Nashville, while your troops turn Columbus? These two points gained, a combined movement on Memphis will be next in order." McClellan sent basically the same dispatch to Buell, who quickly replied, "I cannot on reflection, think a change of my line would be advisable.... I hope General Grant will not require further re-enforcements. I will go if necessary."[8]

After thinking further on the situation and the part he might be willing to play, Buell wired McClellan on the morning of February 8, "I am concentrating and preparing, but will not decide definitely yet." General Halleck had fewer doubts about what part he wanted to play in any upcoming campaign, and at noon on the same day he again suggested that Buell shift the majority of his force to the Cumberland River and advance to Nashville by water. Always trying to work events to his advantage, Halleck also suggested shifting the department lines, giving Buell command on the Cumberland and another officer such as William T. Sherman command over the Tennessee movement, with himself in overall command of both movements.[9]

After waiting three days for a response from Washington, Halleck wrote to Buell directly, asking, "[C]an't you come with all your available forces and command the column up the Cumberland? I shall go to the Tennessee this week." General Buell, seeing two dazzling opportunities in front of him, has only to pick one, but again he hesitates, telling Halleck that he will go to either the Cumberland or the Tennessee and that he needs at least ten days to redirect his troops, and as Buell is trying to make up his mind events pass him by once more. Grant moved on Fort Donelson without any assistance from Buell, and when Buell learned that General Johnston has pulled his troops out of Bowling Green he announced, "The evacuation of Bowling Green, leaving the way open to Nashville, makes it proper to resume my original plan. I shall advance on Nashville with all the speed I can."[10]

When he learned of Buell's latest plan Halleck wrote to McClellan informing him that Grant had fully invested Fort Donelson and that there was little doubt of the outcome but now that the Confederates had abandoned Bowling Green those thousands of enemy soldiers would be moving against Grant to rescue Fort Donelson. Halleck said on the sixteenth, "I am still decidedly of the opinion that Buell should not advance on Nashville, but come to the Cumberland with his available force. United to Grant we can take and hold Fort Donelson and Clarksville, and by another central movement cut off both Columbus and Nashville.... Unless we can take Fort Donelson very soon we shall have the whole force of the enemy on us. Fort Donelson is the turning-point of the war, and we must take it, at whatever sacrifice." Halleck could not know it, but General Johnston never had any intention of trying to rescue Fort Donelson and on the day he wrote this the fort surrendered.[11]

General McClellan pretty much ignored Halleck's appeals for more troops and more authority and decided to back General Buell's proposals asserting that the occupation of Nashville was most important. Buell finally did decide to send assistance to Grant at Fort Donelson by ordering General William Nelson's division there, but he took so long to make that decision that the fort surrendered as Nelson's men were just beginning their journey by river. Two of President Lincoln's assistants, John G. Nicolay and John Hay, who witnessed the frustration caused by trying to get the generals in the West to do something other than maneuvering to score political points and advancing their personal agendas during this early period of the war, later wrote that this state of affairs "show[s] both Buell and McClellan incapable, even under continued pressure, of seizing and utilizing the fleeting chances of war which so often turn the scale of success, and which so distinctly call out the higher quality of military leadership." They might have added Henry Halleck's name to the list of those who hesitated to act and seize opportunities.[12]

In his ever-continuing efforts to expand the size of his command and authority, which really meant power and political influence, General Halleck suggested that a Western Division be created made up of the current departments of the Ohio, the Mississippi, and the Missouri. He further suggested that the commanders of these departments would be Buell, Hitchcock or Sherman, and General David Hunter. Naturally, the commander of the Western Division would be Henry Halleck. It is interesting to note that General Grant, the only man in Halleck's command to have won two important victories, was not mentioned as a possible department commander.[13]

Still working to promote his personal agenda, on February 17 Halleck wired General McClellan asking him to "make Buell, Grant, and Pope major-generals of volunteers, and give me command in the West. I ask this in return for Forts Henry and Donelson." Two days later Halleck was again on the wire to Washington: "Brig. Gen. Charles F. Smith, by his coolness and bravery at Fort Donelson when the battle was against us, turned the tide and carried the enemy's outworks. Make him a major-general. You can't get a better one." This was one of Halleck's recommendations that would have been difficult to argue against, but once again he seemed to forget who ordered Smith to make that gallant attack that brought about the Confederate surrender.[14]

Getting more and more desperate, Halleck wrote to McClellan on the twentieth practically demanding that he be given overall authority in the West: "I must have command of the armies in the West. Hesitation and delay are losing us the golden opportunity. Lay this before the President and Secretary of War. May I assume the command? Answer quickly." After just complaining about "hesitation and delay," the very next day Halleck again wired McClellan informing him that he had not taken action on the Tennessee and Cumberland as soon as he might have because of a perceived threat on his rear from the Confederate fortress at Columbus, but Halleck still insisted, "I cannot possibly be mistaken in the strategy of the campaign."[15]

General McClellan wasted little time in replying to Halleck's inappropriate messages, "Buell at Bowling Green knows more of the state of affairs than you at Saint Louis. Until I hear from him I cannot see necessity of giving you entire command. I shall not lay your request before the Secretary until I hear definitely from Buell." McClellan always supported his old friend Don Carlos Buell and suggested to him that it would be a good idea for Buell to report on the situation in his department every day and also advised the slow-moving general that taking Nashville "is of the greatest importance." The general-in-chief also offered to order Halleck to concentrate his forces in the direction of Columbus and Memphis if Buell wanted to advance on the Cumberland, which would be much quicker than slogging through the muddy roads to Nashville.[16]

On February 21 General Halleck continued his shameless self-promotion by contacting Assistant Secretary of War Thomas A. Scott in Louisville. Halleck informed Scott that based on the reports from Grant and Foote requesting permission to advance past Clarksville it looked like the Confederates were planning on continuing their retreat past Nashville and abandoning the city. Halleck asked Scott, "Can't you come down to the Cumberland and divide the responsibility with me? If so, I will immediately prepare to go ahead. I am tired of waiting for action in Washington. They will not understand the case. It is as plain as daylight to me."[17]

Secretary of War Stanton now got involved and wired Halleck that although he was in favor of Halleck's proposals, the president's son had been ill and "on account of the domestic affliction of the President I have not yet been able to submit it to him." Emboldened by what he considered a positive response, Halleck wrote directly to Secretary Stanton, mentioning that too much time had already been wasted. Halleck told Stanton that in order to strike a meaningful blow he would need to use Buell's force in conjunction with his own: "I am perfectly willing to act as General McClellan dictates or to take any amount of responsibility. To succeed we must be prompt. I have explained everything to General McClellan and Assistant Secretary Scott. There is not a moment to be lost. Give me authority and I will be responsible for results."[18]

On February 22 General Halleck finally received an answer to his numerous requests to be named overall commander in the West. Secretary Stanton informed Halleck that the president had reviewed his telegrams and Assistant Secretary Scott's reports and decided that there was no great need to change the current command structure. Stanton also mentioned that President Lincoln "desires and expects you and General Buell to co-operate fully and zealously with each other, and would be glad to know whether there has been any failure of co-operation in any particular." On another subject, Halleck was most likely not happy to learn that of the officers he had submitted for promotion to major general President Lincoln had forwarded only Grant's name to the Senate. He was quickly approved and now Major General Ulysses S. Grant was the second-highest-ranking officer in the West.[19]

While the telegraph lines between St. Louis and Washington were buzzing with messages, devastating destruction and the appalling suffering of thousands of civilians was taking place in and around the capital city of Tennessee. On Sunday morning, February 16, the citizens of Nashville, Tennessee, awoke to the news that the Yankee army outside Fort Donelson had been beaten and the fort was still in Confederate hands, protecting the river approach to the city. Not too many hours later, however, the truth was learned and as news of the fort's surrender spread around the city many people believed that Federal gunboats would be bombarding the city before the day was over and evacuation seemed the only course to take. General Johnston, who had just arrived with the troops evacuated from Bowling Green, joined Mayor R. B. Cheatham in urging the citizens to remain calm; the enemy was not at the gates. Few people actually left Nashville that day, but Governor Isham G. Harris provided a poor example of leadership by fleeing to Memphis with the state archives and issuing a call for the legislature to also leave the capital and meet again in Memphis. The confidence of Nashville's residents was further eroded when beginning late Sunday morning and continuing through Monday night General Johnston's men wearily shuffled into the city. Cold, worn-out and hungry from the forced march in freezing temperatures, many men fell out of ranks and mingled with the civilians as the rest of the army continued through the city and out the Murfreesboro Pike.[20]

Up until this moment it appeared that few private citizens and few in the government had believed that Nashville was in any real danger. The strength of Fort Donelson had already been proved with the defeat of the Union gunboats and there was no reason to expect any change in the ability of the fort to hold out. Unfortunately, the weakness of the fort's commanders offset the strength of its fortifications, as was sadly discovered. Defenses to protect Nashville were almost nonexistent. There were a few minor earthworks in scattered locations around the city, but there was nothing even close to a proper organized defensive line. Now there was not enough time and not enough manpower to construct anything like the type of fortifications that might have a chance to stand up to the heavy guns on Flag Officer Foote's gunboats.[21]

General Floyd and the Virginia troops who escaped from Fort Donelson with him arrived on Monday and Johnston put him in charge of removing the mountains of provisions and military equipment in the city. With help from the 1st Missouri Regiment and Colonel Forrest's cavalry that arrived after their overland escape from Fort Donelson some semblance of order was restored to the streets that had been taken over by mobs of people seeking food and other supplies from the numerous warehouses around the city. From the twentieth to the twenty-second every effort was made by the Confederate rear guard to save what supplies they could before the city was abandoned. General Johnston called thirty-five railroad cars up from Chattanooga and wagons of all sizes were seized throughout the city. Hundreds of wagonloads of meat and other provisions were loaded onto trains that were continuously arriving and departing. Over a thousand wounded and sick soldiers jammed aboard boxcars to make the trip to Chattanooga. Dozens of wagonloads of small arms and ammunition as well as machinery to manufacture these items were loaded onto railcars and saved. But the heroic efforts were not nearly enough to save the majority of supplies that were stored in the city. In addition to the destruction of supplies and military equipment, before the Confederate rear guard left the city several half-finished gunboats were burned and the bridges over the Cumberland were destroyed to inhibit pursuit by Federal troops.[22]

The estimates of the provisions and other supplies that remained in the city when the Confederates finally left is astonishing. Nearly seventy-five thousand pounds of pork was left on the wharfs, not including several warehouses that were never opened. Five hundred barrels of government whiskey were smashed at the railroad depot. A huge amount of quartermaster equipment was abandoned, including ten thousand pairs of shoes and five hundred new tents. Over forty cannon were spiked and left behind. All this and much more was lost despite the fact that many warehouses had been abandoned by their caretakers and left open for the public who did not hesitate to take what they wanted in the way of food and other supplies.[23]

By the end of the week Nashville had changed from a thriving industrial city and state capital to a dark and depressing shell of its former self abandoned by thousands of citizens who were fearful of suffering unspeakable acts of violence and outrage by the coming Yankee hordes. Trains ran almost hourly and anyone who could find room among the military supplies that filled the cars were happy to flee even a few miles out of the city. The narrow roads were clogged with wagons and carts of all kinds carrying families and what meager possessions they could carry with them to imagined safety. Rain fell constantly, making it even more difficult to travel the poor country roads, but the people continued their exodus. Men and women, young and old, healthy and infirm, they all slowly made their way out of the city. Small children were wrapped in blankets to protect them from the cold and rain. Some were headed to the homes of relatives or friends in the country; others were just running with no particular place to go, just away from the enemy.[24]

While General Halleck was doing his best to promote himself General Grant was doing what little he could to take advantage of the victory at Fort Donelson despite being under orders to basically stay put and not make any advance toward Nashville. But there was usually more than one way to achieve a desired goal, and it was General Buell who had kindly supplied the means. General Nelson's division that Buell had sent to reinforce Grant at Fort Donelson did not arrive at that place until February 24, long after they might have been of any use there, but Grant knew exactly what to do with Nelson's troops.[25]

General Buell was slowly marching the rest of his army overland toward Nashville and had just reached the vicinity of Bowling Green on the day Fort Donelson surrendered. Since Nelson's division was under Buell's command it made sense to Grant to let Nelson rejoin Buell's force. It also seemed logical that since Buell's exact location would be difficult to determine it would be best to send Nelson to Buell's known destination, which was Nashville. Grant instructed Nelson to keep his troops on board their transports and head upriver to rendezvous with Buell at Nashville. Grant suggested that if Buell was still more than two days away from the city when Nelson arrived he should play it safe and stay aboard the ships until Buell arrived. Since he was taking the responsibility of changing the orders of troops belonging to another department, Grant made sure to advise his own headquarters. In a dispatch to General Cullum updating him on the situation Grant wrote, "As requested, the gunboats have gone up to Nashville. Johnston, with his army, has fallen back to Murfreesboro.... General Nelson reported to-day with his division. I forwarded them immediately to Nashville."[26]

General Nelson's transports made good time and he landed on the south bank of the river the next morning and met no opposition as his troops entered the city. Not long after this the advance troops from General Ormsby Mitchel's division of Buell's force approached the city from the north side of the city and found that Nelson's men were already in control of Nashville and had raised the national flag over the capitol building. When he arrived with the rest of his troops General Buell was upset and embarrassed that troops from his command had taken Nashville without him. He was also concerned that Nelson's division on the south side of the river, contrary to Buell's orders by the way, was open to a Confederate attack that could overwhelm his six thousand men. Buell quickly sent Nelson's transports back to Clarksville with orders for General Smith's division to immediately board the ships and hurry upriver to reinforce Nelson. General Grant now decided that perhaps he should go to Nashville in person and wired General Cullum, "I shall go to Nashville immediately after the arrival of the next mail, should there be no orders to prevent it." Receiving no reply, General Grant arrived in Clarksville on the twenty-seventh, and as his men were loading onto the ships General Smith showed him Buell's order: "The landing of a portion of our troops, contrary to my intentions, on the south side of the river has compelled me to hold this side at every hazard. If the enemy should assume the offensive ... my force is altogether inadequate." Grant and Smith knew full well that General Johnston's troops were already past Nashville at Murfreesboro and in no condition to launch an attack. General Smith commented to Grant that the order "was nonsense," but "of course I must obey," and set off to Nashville.[27]

General Smith was right of course. The whole idea that Johnston, who had just gotten his worn-out troops to Murfreesboro, had any intention of launching an attack on anyone was ridiculous. In addition, even if Nelson's division was really in any serious danger Buell could have easily used the numerous transport ships available to transfer Mitchel's division over to the south side of the river to assist Nelson in fighting off any attack or, if circumstances warranted, he could have just as easily evacuated Nelson's men to safety on the north side of the river.[28]

General Grant arrived in Nashville expecting to meet with General Buell but learned that he was still in his headquarters on the north side of the river. Grant decided to take a brief tour of the captured city visiting hospitals and paying his respects to the widow of former president James K. Polk. While Grant was still in the city on the evening of the twenty-seventh he sent a note to Buell saying that he could not wait any longer to meet and offered to send him additional reinforcements if Buell deemed it necessary, but Grant did not believe that would be the case, since the only organized Confederate troops "are not far north of the Tennessee line." Grant's note was less than diplomatic in tone, and just to make sure Buell knew that he was now the higher-ranking officer he signed it, "U. S. Grant, Major General."[29]

As luck would have it, Buell had finally decided to enter the city in person and that evening as Grant was heading back to his ship he and Buell met on the docks. The two men exchanged polite greetings and not much more. They had a brief discussion with Grant, mostly repeating what he had written earlier, making sure to point out that he was convinced by all the reports coming to his headquarters that General Johnston was taking his ragged troops away from Nashville with all possible speed. General Buell insisted that large numbers of enemy troops were still in the immediate vicinity and that fighting was taking place less than twelve miles away, putting his divided forces in danger of an enemy assault. Grant commented that he believed that any nearby fighting was probably with the Confederate small rear guard. Buell insisted that "he knew" his information was correct and that his troops were still in danger. Grant snapped back, "Well, I do not know," and both men parted even more irritated than they had been. Grant later wrote that "Smith's troops were returned the same day. The enemy were trying to get away from Nashville and not to return to it." About the only thing Grant accomplished was to get his name in Northern newspapers, further alienate Buell and put even more strain on his relations with General Halleck.[30]

The recent string of victories in the West: the fight at Mill Springs; the capture of Forts Henry and Donelson; the evacuation of Confederate forces from Bowling Green; and now the occupation of the first Confederate state capital at Nashville gave a much-needed boost to the morale of the citizens of the North. Conversely, for the South that had been confident that they would eventually prevail since their victory at Bull Run the defeats in the West indicated that the road to establishing the Confederate States of America as an independent nation would probably be a long and bloody journey with no assurance of success at its end. The importance of these early Union victories should not be measured in terms of numbers involved or casualties and prisoners taken but rather in terms of their effect on the people of both sides and the opportunities that were created for further advancement by Union forces into the heart of the enemy's territory.

12

Problems for Grant

While Ulysses Grant was still basking in the glow of the victories at Forts Henry and Donelson and his recent promotion events were occurring behind the scenes that came very close to costing him his current job and his career in the army and did cause problems for the Union war effort in the West. From the end of February to well into March, General Halleck spent almost as much effort in self-promotion and positioning himself to be appointed to overall command in the West as he did in actually prosecuting the war. One of the problems that plagued commanders during the Civil War was difficulties in communicating between headquarters and commanders in the field. Messages could travel by courier, train or steamship, and telegraph, although a combination of these modes of communication was frequently used. Sending messages over long distances by multiple means was at best slow, and they were frequently delayed and occasionally lost. Shortly after the fall of Fort Donelson the problem took on special significance between Halleck and Grant. Messages between them were first sent to Fort Henry and then forwarded to the appropriate recipient. Unknown at the time, a Confederate sympathizer was working in the telegraph office at Fort Henry and some of the messages he received were not passed along. As a result Halleck had little idea of what Grant was doing and Grant was receiving few instructions about what Halleck wanted him to do, so Grant decided to do what he thought best.[1]

Once Halleck finally accepted the fact that he would not be taking over command in the West and absorbing Buell's command, at least not right now, he decided it was time to move forward with the war and planned to send Grant's army on an expedition up the Tennessee River. Orders were issued for Grant to pull General Smith's troops out of Clarksville, where Halleck supposed them to be, concentrate near Danville, about thirty-five miles upriver from Fort Henry, and make preparations for an advance up the river. The problems began when Grant did not receive these orders and Halleck finally learned that troop movements had been taking place that he did not approve and was totally unaware of. The most important of these was Smith's division being in Nashville instead of Clarksville where Halleck had thought they were.[2]

On March 1, a very displeased Halleck wrote to General Cullum in Cairo demanding to know who had sent Smith's division to Nashville: "I ordered them across to the Tennessee, where they are wanted immediately. Order them back. What is the reason that no one down there can obey my orders? Send all spare transports to General Grant up the Tennessee." Grant was going to need all the transports he could get, because also on the first Halleck issued orders to begin the expedition up the Tennessee. These orders stated, "The main object of this expedition will be to destroy the railroad bridge over Bear Creek, near Eastport,

12. Problems for Grant

Miss., and also the connections at Corinth, Jackson, and Humboldt." After successfully completing this part of the mission Grant was to return to Danville and then advance to the town of Paris, on the west side of the river.[3]

At the same time that Halleck was sending instructions for Grant to move up the Tennessee, Grant, unaware that he was supposed to be leading his army south, was sending his own report to Halleck. Grant reported that many of his men were suffering from a variety of illnesses and stated, "If I am compelled to move suddenly, it will be with a very weak force compared with what the major-general commanding probably expects. The loss in battle and the number who have sickened since reduces my force considerably." Grant also noted that he had been very diligent in sending messages to headquarters almost daily.[4]

There were quite a few military operations taking place in General Halleck's department in March of 1862. In Missouri there was constant skirmishing and guerrilla raids by the several small bodies of Confederates that roamed the state. General John Pope was in the middle of what would turn out to be a very successful campaign to capture enemy strongholds on the Mississippi at New Madrid, Island No. 10, and Fort Pillow. Now, with the addition of Grant's expedition, one objective of which was to aid Pope's campaign by cutting the railroad connections that supplied the enemy forces along the Mississippi, it was very clear that Henry Halleck was going to be a very busy man as he tried to control or at least follow all the operations taking place under his command. In addition to the strictly military undertakings that he was responsible for, Halleck's problems were compounded by General Buell's requests for collaboration in various operations and Washington's unwillingness to give him the overall command in the West that he so desperately wanted. There were also reports coming in from various sources that the troops at Fort Donelson had engaged in looting and that discipline was extremely lax. With all this on his table Halleck now became aware that none of his plans for movements up the Tennessee had been carried out as he had ordered. This last bit of news pushed the easily annoyed Halleck over the edge.[5]

On March 2 Halleck initiated a series of events that would consume much of his time and energy and hindered the war effort in the West. Halleck complained in a message to General McClellan that despite numerous requests for information about his command Grant had not been heard from in over a week and against orders had made an unauthorized trip to Nashville. Since Grant had just won an important victory, Halleck said he was hesitant to condemn him, "but I think he richly deserves it. I can get no returns, no reports, no information of any kind from him. Satisfied with his victory, he sits down and enjoys it without any regard to the future. I am worn-out and tired with this neglect and inefficiency."[6]

Halleck's dispatch to McClellan was clearly an exaggeration and would appear to be an attempt to provide cover in case any real trouble emanated from problems in his command by using the age-old tactic of blaming a subordinate. Of course there was always the possibility that this approach might raise concerns that Halleck could not control some of the officers under his command, so he had to be careful not to spread the blame in too many directions, making it clear that the fault lay specifically with Grant. The reason that complaining about Grant was so unfair was that of all of Halleck's field commanders none were more aggressive than Grant and none wanted to continue pushing the defeated enemy more than he did. One of Halleck's major complaints, that Grant had left his troops and his area of authority to visit Nashville, was, at worst, a minor violation, since the size and boundaries of Grant's command had never been specifically established.

General McClellan gave his full support to whatever action Halleck decided was needed to bring his subordinate in line, saying in his reply to Halleck on March 3, "The future success of our cause demands that proceedings such as Grant's should at once be checked. Generals must observe discipline as well as private soldiers." The general-in-chief also authorized Halleck to place Grant under arrest if necessary and replace him with veteran General C. F. Smith, continuing his message with: "I appreciate the difficulties you have to encounter, and will be glad to relieve you from trouble as far as possible." As a sign of just how seriously this matter was being taken in Washington, McClellan's message was also signed by Secretary of War Stanton.[7]

Halleck followed up with a second, even more damning complaint about Grant, writing to McClellan on the fourth, "A rumor had just reached me that since the taking of Fort Donelson General Grant has resumed his former bad habits. If so, it will account for his neglect of my often-repeated orders." The former habits mentioned were, of course, Grant's propensity to drink a little too much on occasion. Halleck would not go so far as to put Grant under arrest but did remove him from command of the Tennessee River expedition, replacing him with General Smith. In the message informing Grant that he had been replaced, Halleck demanded to know, "Why do you not obey my orders to report strength and positions of your command?" This was Grant's first indication that his commanding general was dissatisfied with his performance and that he might be facing serious trouble.[8]

Dutifully following Halleck's orders, Grant wired Smith the next day informing him that he was now in command of the expedition up the Tennessee. Along with intelligence about the enemy forces that might be encountered Grant wrote that although it was important that the bridges be destroyed, Smith should be cautious and, if at all possible, "a general engagement is to be avoided, while the bridges are to be destroyed, if possible. The idea probably is there must be no defeat, and rather than risk one it would be better to retreat." That same day Halleck expanded on his original orders, saying that if the Corinth and Bear Creek bridges were destroyed the troops should "encamp at Savannah, unless threatened by superior numbers."[9]

Still not fully understanding the seriousness of the situation, Grant wrote to Halleck on March 5 informing him that, per his instructions, General Smith had been put in charge of the expedition and asking if Clarksville should be abandoned. Grant then went on to state, "I am not aware of ever having disobeyed any order from headquarters—certainly never intended such a thing. I have reported almost daily the condition of my command and reported every position occupied." Grant also stated that he had been sending reports to "General Cullum, chief of staff, and it may be that many of them were not thought of sufficient importance to forward more than a telegraphic synopsis of." Grant reported that his command contained "forty-six infantry regiments, three cavalry regiments, and eight independent companies, and ten batteries of light artillery," with an average strength of five hundred men per regiment. Finally, Grant confirmed to Halleck that "you may rely on my carrying out your instructions in every particular to the very best of my ability."[10]

For most people Grant's message would have been enough to put the matter to rest, but not Henry Halleck. Grant had forwarded the information Halleck had been waiting for, promised to carefully follow any future orders and offered a sort of apology for past mistakes. Unfortunately for all concerned, Halleck just had to have the last word and on March 6 he sent Grant another reprimand, repeating the complaint that he had ignored repeated orders to report his troop strength: "Your neglect of repeated orders to report the strength of your command has created great dissatisfaction and seriously interfered with military plans. Your going to Nashville without authority, and when your presence with your troops was of the utmost importance, was a matter of very serious complaint at Washington, so much so that I was advised to arrest you on your return."[11]

Ulysses Grant has the reputation of being a generally mild and quiet man who seldom showed any flashes of temper. The reality was that there was nothing at all meek about Grant; when he felt wronged he could get just as angry as anyone else. In replying to Halleck's latest grievance Grant basically challenged him to prove the allegations and insisted that he had been consistently sending in reports on the strength of his command and that it was not his fault if there was a breakdown in communications between them. Grant emphatically stated, "I have done my very best to obey orders and to carry out the interests of the service. If my course is not satisfactory, remove me at once. I do not wish to impede in any way the success of our arms." Grant also stated that his side trip to Nashville was "strictly intended for the good of the service, and not to gratify any desire of my own." Firm in his conviction that he was being unjustly accused, Grant closed with: "Believing sincerely that I must have enemies between you and myself, who are trying to impair my usefulness. I respectfully ask to be relieved from further duty in the department."[12]

The exchange of messages continued with neither man being willing to back down. On the eighth Halleck wrote to Grant: "You are mistaken. There is no enemy between you and me." Once again Halleck insisted that no information on the number and position of Grant's command had been received at headquarters since the capture of Fort Donelson, informing Grant that "General McClellan has asked for it repeatedly with reference to ulterior movements, but I could not give him the information. He is out of all patience waiting for it." The very next day Grant sent in a report stating that he had 35,147 infantry, 3,169 cavalry, and 12 batteries of artillery in his command, with about twenty-five thousand men heading up the Tennessee with General Smith. In addition, there were about fifty-seven hundred men at Fort Henry in the process of being transported with the remainder of his forces garrisoning Fort Henry, Fort Donelson and Clarksville.[13]

Grant, like his commanding officer, was unable to just let the situation go away on its own and had to write another dispatch to Halleck offering to do everything he could to improve the chances for success of Smith's expedition. Grant also remarked that due to the constant reinforcements coming to the army at Fort Donelson, by Halleck's orders, that headquarters probably knew the strength of the field army better than Grant did. Grant also insisted that he received no orders to send in reports on troop strength until February 28 and then he tried to gather that information as soon as possible. Grant closed once again with a challenge to Halleck to prove the allegations made against him: "I have always been ready to move anywhere, regardless of consequences to myself, but with a disposition to take the best care of the troops under my command. I renew my application to be relieved from further duty."[14]

Wanting to have the last word, Halleck sent another dispatch on March 9 informing Grant that his report on the fifth was the first time headquarters had received any information regarding Grant's troop strength since late February. Halleck mentioned again that "General McClellan had repeatedly ordered me to report to him daily the numbers and positions of your forces." Halleck also stated that not being able to supply the general-in-chief with up-to-date information was personally embarrassing and warned Grant, "Don't let such neglect occur again, for it is equally discreditable to you and to me." Now that he had his final say it appeared that Halleck wanted to put the matter aside and get on with new business, as he instructed that the garrisons manning Forts Henry and Donelson should be no larger than a regiment and that all other available troops be sent to support Smith's expedition. Halleck ended by suggesting that Grant would soon resume his normal duties: "As soon as these things are arranged you will hold yourself in readiness to take the command. There will probably be some desperate fighting in that vicinity, and we must be prepared."[15]

This should have been the end of the matter, except that Grant now received a dispatch from Halleck that had been sent back on the sixth, which contained a copy of an anonymous letter alleging that Grant's troops had engaged in a great deal of looting of civilian property and that there was a continuing flow of military supplies to private businesses, with little being done to stop either illegal activity. In his wire Halleck complained that the "want of order and discipline and the numerous irregularities in your command since the capture of Fort Donelson are matters of general notoriety, and have attracted the serious attention of the authorities at Washington." He added that "unless these things are immediately corrected I am directed to relieve you of the command."[16]

To be fair to General Halleck, it should be acknowledged that there had been a good deal of requisitioning of civilian property done by the Union troops in the vicinity of Fort Donelson. Most of Grant's soldiers were new to military life and had received little training and discipline. They had just been shocked by the sight of hundreds of their fellow soldiers, in many cases friends and neighbors back home, killed and wounded in front of Fort Donelson. Cold, probably hungry, and definitely vindictive, they had little problem taking their anger out on any "Rebel" farms and businesses in the vicinity, caring little about the so-called rules of war. The government would usually offer compensation for items stolen by Union soldiers, but most citizens and especially Confederate sympathizers made frequent and vocal complaints, some of which were reported in newspapers and reached the ears of officials in Washington.

On March 11 Grant escalated the situation to another level. Responding to the accusations of looting and fraud in his command, Grant wrote that orders he issued to end such activity were "the only reply necessary. There is such a disposition to find fault with me that I again ask to be relieved from further duty until I can be placed right in the estimation of those higher in authority." Grant was sick of the constant accusations and complaints about his ability and decided that an official court of inquiry was the only way to settle the situation, one way or another. This was not at all what Halleck wanted, and he made every effort to calm Grant and dissuade him from demanding official action, especially since there was little, if any, actual evidence against him. Halleck replied, "You cannot be relieved from your command. There is no good reason for it." All anyone wanted was for Grant to enforce proper discipline among his troops. The next part of the message revealed why Halleck did not want to push his subordinate too far: "Instead of relieving you, I wish you as soon as your new army is in the field to assume the immediate command and lead it on to new victories." Apparently, this is just what Grant wanted to hear. Replying on March 14, Grant said that considering the seriousness of some of the charges that had been leveled against him, being vindicated by a court of inquiry was the only way he could possibly continue in command. The receipt of Halleck's recent telegram, however, "places such a different phase upon my position that I will again assume command, and give every effort to the success of our cause. Under the worst circumstances I would do the same."[17]

During the weeks that Halleck and Grant were exchanging telegrams important events were taking place back east. President Lincoln, finally tired of McClellan's inactivity and impressed with the successes that were occurring in Halleck's department, had Secretary Stanton inquire of Halleck what areas should be included in a possible new Western Department. Halleck clearly believed it was important to combine all the activity in the West under one commander who could coordinate movements far better than was being done under the current separate command structure. Just as clearly, Henry Halleck believed that he was the one man who could shoulder that burden successfully. Halleck wrote in a message to McClellan that under the current command structure in the West "there never will and never can be any cooperation at the critical moment; all military history proves it." Recalling McClellan's previous refusal to support his efforts to be appointed to overall command because of, as Halleck believed, McClellan's friendship with Buell, he indignantly wrote, "You will regret your decision against me on this point."[18]

It was now that Henry Halleck finally got that for which he had worked so hard. General McClellan's slowness to act in Virginia had finally cost him his job as general-in-chief, and he was reduced to the command of the Army of the Potomac. The new Department of the Mississippi was created by combining the departments of Missouri and Ohio. There was only one man considered for the command of this important new position, the only general with the seniority and an unbroken record of success in the field, Henry Halleck. With the command that he had so desperately wanted finally his and General Buell now under his authority, much of the anxiety that had colored Halleck's relations with Grant was now eliminated.[19]

Grant's position was also helped by the fact that President Lincoln now became involved in resolving the accusations against Grant. The president had no interest in allowing the officer who had won the Union's only major victory thus far in the war to be disgraced and perhaps even forced out of the army without at least the opportunity to present his side of the situation to a court of inquiry. On March 10, Brigadier General Lorenzo Thomas, adjutant general of the army, wrote to Halleck that reports had been received in Washington that shortly after the capture of Fort Donelson Grant had left his command without permission. Thomas further wrote that the president had instructed Secretary of War Stanton to learn from Halleck "whether General Grant left his command at any time without proper authority, and, if so, for how long; whether he has made to you proper reports and returns of his force; whether he has committed any acts which were unauthorized or not in accordance with military subordination or propriety, and, if so, what." This new development put Halleck in the awkward position of having to file formal charges against Grant and prove them or drop the matter altogether. This was not a difficult decision for Halleck to make.[20]

At this point General Halleck was more than happy to just drop the issue and concentrate on running his new command. He had done what was needed to protect himself from reproach by reprimanding Grant, and now that he was no longer subordinate to McClellan things were certainly going in Halleck's favor. This was not the time to start another inquiry. In addition, there was also the fact to consider that proving Grant had done anything wrong through willful disobedience of orders or failure to exercise his authority over his troops would be difficult, if not impossible. In his response to Thomas on March 15, Halleck wrote that although it was true that Grant and several of his officers did indeed travel to Nashville without authorization, he was now convinced that "General Grant did this from good intentions and from a desire to subserve the public interests." The reported problems with discipline that occurred at Fort Donelson should not be held against Grant, as they were in direct violation of published orders and discipline among the troops was being improved. The problems with not receiving Grant's reports at headquarters, which had started this whole mess, were found to be due partly from his subordinates' failure to submit their own reports and "partly from an interruption of telegraphic communication. All these irregularities have now been remedied." Halleck had been satisfied by Grant's explanation of the various charges and he had been ordered to once again return to his command in the field. Halleck wrote that since he believed Grant had "acted from a praiseworthy although mistaken zeal for the public service in going to Nashville and leaving his command, I respectfully recommend that no further notice be taken of it."[21]

Grant's final comments on this unfortunate period came in a message to Halleck on March 24 where he commented, "In regard to the plundering at Fort Donelson, it is very much overestimated by disappointed persons, who failed in getting off the trophies they had gathered." Orders had been issued that forbade looting and the destruction of private property, but trying to control thousands of soldiers and the hundreds of civilians who came to the area to grab souvenirs proved to be impossible. Grant also felt that considering the command situation at the time and the importance of pursuing the beaten enemy, sending Nelson's troops to Nashville and then following up in person to confirm that the enemy had fled and to confer with General Buell was the proper action to take, "My going to Nashville I did not regard particularly as going beyond my district. After the fall of Donelson, from information I had, I knew that the way was clear to Clarksville and Nashville." Grant ended his message by saying that "I do not feel that I have neglected a single duty. My reports to you have averaged at least one a day since leaving Cairo, and there has been scarcely a day that I have not either written or telegraphed to headquarters. I most fully appreciate your justness, general, in the part you have taken, and you may rely upon me to the utmost of my capacity for carrying out all your orders."[22]

There is little doubt that the gratitude Grant expressed to Halleck was genuine based on the facts as he knew them at the time. It was not until years later, after Grant had been general-in-chief, that he had access to the records and learned that Halleck had been the main cause of the problems Grant faced in March of 1862. Normally not one to hold a grudge, Grant had no trouble remembering this when he wrote in his *Memoirs* that shortly after the victory at Fort Donelson "I was virtually in arrest and without a command." Grant exaggerated here, since he was never actually under arrest, but he never let go of his bitterness toward Halleck after learning that "it was his own reports that had created all the trouble."[23]

It was during this period of being out of favor that Grant wrote a personal letter to his friend and sponsor Congressman Elihu B. Washburne concerning his views on the responsibility of soldiers obeying the commands of superior officers whether they approved of the order or not: "So long as I hold a commission in the army I have no views of my own to carry out. Whatever may be the orders of my superiors and law I will execute. No man can be efficient as a commander who sets his own notions above law and those whom he has sworn to obey. When Congress enacts anything too odious for me to execute, I will resign." In the long run, this brief trouble did Grant's career no real harm, but he must have suffered an emotional roller coaster, as the accusations against him had followed so closely upon his first real success after years of mediocrity. Dr. John H. Brinton, a military surgeon and friend of Grant, later wrote, "The treatment received by General Grant from his superior officers at this time cut him bitterly."[24]

The issues of who was in charge in the West had been resolved. Halleck had the command he wanted, and Grant was back in the field where he belonged. There was now a single controlling hand in the West where, it was beginning to be felt in Washington, the war might be won or lost. There would be a decisive shift in the strategy for fighting the war after this point. The first evidence of this was that the Tennessee River expedition was going to be shifted from a being quick raid to destroy some bridges to an invasion that might produce great results and influence the outcome of the war.[25]

13

Pittsburg Landing

General Halleck was eager to continue the success his department had been enjoying, and it now appeared that the best place to strike next was the Confederate center, using the Tennessee River for transportation. Advancing up the waterway would provide an expedition with rapid movement and a secure line of communication. At the beginning of March, Halleck decided it was time to move, with or without assistance from General Buell. The target was the already-suspect Confederate railroad system, specifically the Memphis & Charleston and the Mobile & Ohio Railroads. If these rail lines could be cut, it might be possible to take advantage of the weakened condition of General Johnston's forces and mount an expedition to take Memphis. Federal control of Memphis would cut off the Confederate forts north of the city such as Island No. 10 and Fort Pillow, forcing their abandonment or eventual surrender to Federal forces.[1]

Knowing that General Grant, with the main field army, would probably not have any support, Halleck wanted the first part of the campaign to be little more than a large raid on the railroads. Grant's entire army would take part in the movement, but the actual raid would be a quick dash by cavalry to disrupt the rail service before the Confederates could organize any serious opposition. The always cautious Halleck instructed Grant to "avoid any general engagement with strong forces. It will be better to retreat than to risk a general battle. This should be strongly impressed upon the officers sent with the expedition from the river." A base would be set up on the river at a small town called Savannah several miles downriver and on the opposite bank from the landing that provided access from the Tennessee River to the important Confederate rail center of Corinth, Mississippi. The small and obscure spot along the river was known as Pittsburg Landing.[2]

The first military action involving the location that would soon become the site of one of the bloodiest battles of the war was a brief artillery duel. The commanding officer of the *Tyler*, Lieutenant William Gwin, learned that the Confederates were beginning work on fortifying Pittsburg Landing. On March 1, on his own initiative, Gwin sailed up the Tennessee accompanied by the *Lexington*. The next morning the ships confronted the Confederate position that at that time consisted of only eight pieces of field artillery and a small force of supporting infantry. The large guns of the Federal gunboats clearly had the advantage, and in short order the Confederates had been forced to flee. Troops from the gunboats landed to scout the area but found nothing of interest, and the ships soon left the area.[3]

On March 1 General Grant received orders from General Halleck to bring his entire force back to the Tennessee River around Fort Henry and prepare for an expedition up the river to Eastport and Corinth, Mississippi. On the fourth Grant was relieved of command of the expedition due to problems in communicating with headquarters and Halleck's perception that Grant had disobeyed orders. General Smith was put in command of the expedition with orders to proceed up the Tennessee and break the line of the Memphis & Charleston Railroad near Florence, Alabama. Eventually fifty-eight ships were assembled to transport the expedition escorted by the gunboats *Tyler* and *Lexington*. A total of five divisions were assigned to the expedition. The three divisions that had been at Fort Donelson commanded by Generals McClernand, Lew Wallace and, since General Smith was now in overall command of the expedition, newly promoted W. H. L. Wallace, who now commanded Smith's division. Joining these now veteran troops were two newly formed divisions commanded by Brigadier Generals Sherman and Steven A. Hurlbut. General Smith got under way on March 10, and despite all the delays, change of plans and bickering that had taken place between the commanders in the West a Federal army was finally advancing up the Tennessee deep into the enemy's territory.[4]

On the evening of the twelfth General Smith went aboard the ship carrying General Lew Wallace for a brief meeting during which he instructed Wallace to take his division and continue upriver about four miles to Crump's Landing. From that point Wallace was to support a cavalry raid on the Mobile & Ohio Railroad. As Smith was returning to his own ship he fell while getting into the rowboat and seriously cut his leg. Smith's wound would gradually worsen, at first preventing him from fully participating in the expedition and eventually proving fatal. On March 13, the expedition's advance transports reached Savannah where the troops aboard those ships were landed, work began setting up a base of operations, and word was sent to bring up the remainder of the army.[5]

As some of the transports were unloading men and material at Savannah on the thirteenth, the ships carrying Lew Wallace's troops continued upriver to Crump's Landing, where they disembarked in a heavy rain. Major Charles S. Haynes' battalion of the 5th Ohio Cavalry headed out the Purdy road toward Bethel Station about nineteen miles from the landing site. The rain continued all morning and the Ohio horsemen learned from captured Confederate pickets that a large body of their troops was in the area. Avoiding contact with the enemy infantry, Major Haynes led his troopers around the Confederate troops and was able to locate and destroy the Beach Creek Bridge near Bethel Station. Again going out of their way to avoid any fighting with the enemy infantry, the cavalrymen were able to get back to the landing later evening, and by eleven that night Wallace and his entire force were back aboard the transports heading back to Savannah. The raid was considered a success, but the Confederates quickly rebuilt the bridge and it was in use again in a few days.[6]

Early on the fourteenth General Sherman's division arrived at Savannah, where the injured General Smith instructed him to continue on with his troops up the river to near Eastport for the purpose of breaking the Memphis & Charleston Railroad in that area. Around noon that same day Sherman's division, transported by nineteen steamers and escorted by the *Tyler*, departed on their raid. Sailing past Pittsburg Landing, the *Tyler* fired several shells at the position previously occupied by Confederate artillery, but there was no response and it was assumed the enemy had not returned. Lieutenant Gwin informed Sherman that this was the same position previously occupied by Confederate artillery and that there was a good road from the landing leading directly to Corinth. Sending this information back to General Smith, Sherman requested that support troops be dispatched to Pittsburg Landing in case he ran into trouble during the raid. About thirty-two miles out from Savannah the ships pulled in at Tyler's Landing at seven o'clock that evening. It was raining heavily as Major Elbridge Ricker led about four hundred troopers of the 5th Ohio Cavalry off the ships to begin the raid. At eleven o'clock that night the cavalry headed out for Burnsville, about seventeen miles southwest of the landing. Major Ricker had to carefully lead his troopers around several bodies of Confederate troops stationed in the area. Sherman decided to disembark his infantry to provide support for the cavalry expedition, but he had to be careful not to get too far from the ships, since the main Confederate camp of Corinth was only twenty-two miles away and Sherman certainly did not want to get cut off from his line of retreat to the ships.[7]

The river had been rising steadily and parts of the landing were already underwater, making it difficult to get all the infantry ashore until nearly three o'clock in the morning of March 15. Sherman left two brigades behind to guard the landing and set out with his other two brigades to where the Burnsville and Iuka roads intersected, where he would be in position to provide support for the cavalry if they needed it. Less than two miles from their destination, however, Sherman's troops came up to a bayou nearly a half mile wide and too deep for the men to wade across. While he was deciding what to do a message reached Sherman from Major Ricker saying that the icy rain had made the already-poor roads virtually impassable and that he was returning to the landing. There was nothing for Sherman to do but march his men back through the rain and mud to the ships and wait for the cavalry to arrive and head back to Savannah. As General Sherman's force sailed back down the Tennessee he was looking for another site where he might land his troops and accomplish his task, but every possible landing was totally flooded except for Pittsburg Landing. When Sherman's transports arrived at the landing the division of General Hurlbut was already there on their transports.[8]

Union general William T. Sherman. Considered mentally unbalanced early in the war, he would follow Grant as general-in-chief (Library of Congress).

Since Pittsburg Landing was the only landing site not flooded and it provided plenty of room for the army to camp and also had direct access to Corinth, it seemed natural to consider that place as a forward base for future operations. Leaving his troops at the landing, Sherman returned to Savannah and informed General Smith that Eastport was occupied by Confederate troops and that Pittsburg Landing was the closest landing site to Eastport that was still above water. General Smith could clearly see that Pittsburg Landing was the best place from which to launch an attack on the important Confederate rail center at Corinth, disrupting the enemy's communications throughout the region, and also the best location from which to begin a movement on Memphis by following the railroad to that city. Sherman later wrote that General Smith instructed him to return immediately to Pittsburg Landing and occupy the position with his and Hurlbut's troops, making sure "to take positions well back, and to leave room for his whole army, telling me that he would soon come up in person, and move out in force to make the lodgment on the railroad, contemplated by General Halleck's orders."[9]

General Sherman suggested that since the Confederates were already expecting an attack on Corinth he could use this to his advantage by launching another cavalry raid. Sherman proposed to land his division at Pittsburg Landing and start marching toward Corinth, attracting the attention of any enemy units in the area, while a cavalry raid was made on the Memphis & Charleston Railroad. General Smith approved the plan, and on the night of March 16 Lieutenant Colonel Thomas Heath led a detachment of troopers from the 5th Ohio Cavalry and the 4th Illinois Cavalry down the Corinth road toward the village of Monterey. Sherman began landing his troops that same night with Colonel John A. McDowell's First Brigade the first troops to disembark. McDowell's infantry had moved only about a mile out the road to Corinth when they came upon Union cavalry troopers heading back to the landing. Apparently, Colonel Heath's raiding party ran into a much larger force of Confederate cavalry a few miles down the road and had to turn back. Sherman continued disembarking his troops during the night and moved inland during the day of the seventeenth.[10]

Sherman's troops quickly marched out about eleven miles from the landing to Monterey, where they forced the Confederate cavalry to fall back. During the next two days Sherman brought up his entire division and set up camps about two and a half miles from the river. During this same time General Hurlbut landed his division and made camp about a mile from the landing. General Sherman had been in touch with Grant back at Fort Henry, commenting on how much he liked the idea of establishing the army at Pittsburg Landing since he was "strongly impressed with the importance of this place, both for its land advantages and its strategic position. The ground itself admits of easy defense by a small command, and yet affords admirable camping-ground for a hundred thousand men."[11]

While the Federal troops were making camp near Pittsburg Landing, General Grant had been reinstated as commander of the field army. When he arrived at Savannah on March 17 to take command he found the troops spread out with "about half being on the east bank of the Tennessee at Savannah, while one division was at Crump's Landing on the west bank about four miles higher up, and the remainder at Pittsburg Landing, five miles above Crump's." With Grant came several staff officers who would have important roles to play in the coming weeks and months. Probably his most trusted aide was Captain John A. Rawlins; thirty-one years old, profane, ill-tempered, and extremely loyal, he protected Grant like a mother hen. Rawlins stayed with Grant through the rest of the war, becoming his chief of staff when Grant became general-in-chief. Other aides who would play a part in coming battles were Captain W. S. Hillyer, a former St. Louis real-estate agent who had known Grant before the war, and Captain William R. Rowley, a former neighbor of Grant's in Galena, Illinois. Grant's current chief of staff was fifty-one-year-old Colonel Joseph D. Webster, a native of New Hampshire.[12]

It was as clear to Grant as it had been to Smith and Sherman that capturing the rail center at Corinth would deal a serious blow to the ability of the Confederates to conduct operations in the region. When General Buell's troops arrived from Nashville the combined armies would begin an advance toward Corinth, where it was learned that General Johnston was collecting troops and any advance on that location must obviously begin from the west side of the river. The fact that Federal gunboats had complete control of the Tennessee River in the area made it much easier to transfer the army to the west side of the river, and Pittsburg Landing was the most logical place to assemble the army for the advance on Corinth.[13]

We know that Grant decided to put the army on the western side of the river because he believed that was the best place from which to begin the advance on Corinth. There were, however, several advantages to keeping the troops on the eastern side, at least temporarily. The chance of General Johnston crossing the Tennessee River and attacking Union camps on the eastern side was virtually zero. Even if the Confederates had enough ships to ferry the army across the river, which they didn't, Federal gunboats would have sunk most of them before they reached the opposite shore. Grant could have safely waited at Savannah for Buell's army to arrive then; even if the Confederates had tried to fortify the western side of the river, the gunboats and nearly two hundred pieces of field artillery with the combined armies would almost certainly have been able to drive them away. But Grant was less interested in safety than he was in getting at the enemy as quickly as possible, and to do that he needed the army on the western side of the river. The campsite chosen by General Sherman had many defensive advantages, and since none of the senior Federal officers believed for a moment that Johnston would attack them it certainly seemed safe enough at the time.[14]

Anytime he was within striking distance of the enemy General Grant naturally wanted to advance and attack while General Halleck just as naturally ordered caution. Halleck had sent instructions on the sixteenth that Grant was to absolutely avoid a major battle: "As the enemy is evidently in strong force, my instructions not to advance so as to bring on an engagement must be strictly obeyed." Halleck wanted Smith and then Grant to stay put and not take any aggressive action that might encourage General Johnston to come out from Corinth and attack the Federal camp. It would certainly appear that this was the proper strategy, since Halleck knew that General Buell's army and another ten thousand men from Missouri were on the way to join Grant's army. There was no good reason to provoke a major battle or for an attack to be made on Corinth until these troops arrived and, as Halleck wrote, no advance was to be made until the combined Federal forces were "strong enough to admit no doubt of the result."[15]

Just two days later, however, Halleck provided Grant with an excuse to initiate an advance. Halleck had received information that an enemy force had "moved from Corinth to cut off our transports below Savannah." Realizing that this meant that the number of Confederate troops defending Corinth would be greatly reduced, offering a golden opportunity to strike if the Federals could move quickly enough, Halleck wired to Grant on the eighteenth that if this information was accurate, "General Smith should immediately destroy railroad connection at Corinth." As it turned out, Halleck's information was incorrect and, although Grant knew this, he quickly instructed Generals Smith and Lew Wallace to get their men ready to march on Corinth. This time, however, Grant's eagerness to get at the enemy caused problems when he sent a dispatch to Halleck informing him, "Immediate preparation will be made to execute your perfectly feasible order. I will go in person, leaving General McClernand in command here."[16]

General Halleck had not expected such quick action and his natural caution made him ill prepared to approve such a move before all the circumstances had been studied and then studied again. He quickly wrote back to Grant, "Don't let the enemy draw you into an engagement now. Wait until you are properly fortified and receive orders." For Grant this meant there would be no advance, at least not at this time. Like most generals in the field, he didn't have a problem interpreting orders to his own liking, but in light of his recent problems with Halleck and McClellan in Washington Grant could not bring himself to outright disobey an order. On March 20 he wrote back to Halleck saying that he would not engage in any action unless he was significantly stronger than the enemy and assuring Halleck that "I will take no risk at Corinth under the instructions I now have."[17]

In March of 1862 Pittsburg Landing and the ground immediately inland from the river was a very unimpressive-looking place. The only function of the place, located about eight miles above Savannah, was to provide a location for steamboats to land and unload cargo that was destined for Corinth or the few farms in the area. High bluffs, some near eighty feet above the high-water line, ran along both sides of the river above and below the landing. A small, run-down warehouse was the only building located at the landing. Nearby was a single narrow dirt road that ran through a deep ravine to the top of the bluff. The ground was made up of mostly heavy clay that made moving even moderately heavy cargo up the bluff difficult even in good weather. When it rained, which happened frequently in winter, the road became almost impassable for any cargo and even individuals.[18]

Once you made your way up the bluff the terrain did not improve that much. The few dirt roads in the vicinity turned into mud trails in wet weather and were difficult to negotiate even when it was dry. There was one relatively good road running along a modest ridgeline to the southwest and Corinth. About a mile from the river the Corinth road crossed another road running parallel to the river that connected Savannah with the small town of Hamburg about four miles above Pittsburg Landing. Another of what were called main roads ran to the northwest to a village called Purdy. There was really only one building of any note in the vicinity, a small, dilapidated log building used as a Methodist meetinghouse and known locally as Shiloh Church.[19]

The reason that General Sherman and the other commanders liked the position near Pittsburg Landing so much was that it was an excellent site for large numbers of men to make camp and had natural defenses on three sides. To the east of the campsites flowed the Tennessee River, totally under the control of Federal gunboats, protecting that side of the campground and allowing unlimited access to the landing for supplies and reinforcements. On the north side of the camp ran Snake Creek, which flowed into the Tennessee just below the landing. Northwest of the camps was a tributary of Snake Creek known as Owl Creek. To the southeast of the camps Lick Creek flowed back to the Tennessee above the landing. The spring rains had flooded these streams to such an extent that they provided almost impassable obstacles to any large body of troops that might try to cross them to attack the Federal camps from those directions. About the only open space large enough for an attacking army to advance was to the southwest, along the road from Corinth.[20]

The plateau on which the Federal army camped was divided by numerous little gullies and ravines cut into the terrain by small streams that ran in all directions as they made their way to join the several larger creeks that bordered the campsites. Most of these streams ran through marshy and swamp-like bogs that were difficult for infantry to pass through and nearly impossible for horses and mules pulling artillery and wagons to cross over except at a few scattered bridges. Many of the ravines that littered the landscape were deep cuts in the earth and so thickly filled with briars and underbrush as to prevent passage to any creature much larger than a rabbit. Moving any large number of soldiers through many of these narrow defiles was simply not possible, thereby providing a natural barrier to any attacking troops.[21]

Much of the terrain behind Pittsburg Landing was heavily wooded. Low hills and ridges dotted the countryside mostly covered with trees and underbrush except for a few places where hardy pioneers had cleared the land for small farms. While there were many elevated positions, none were high enough to provide a view of the entire plateau. There was no room for any large body of troops to make an attack from any flank, and the broken ground and frequent woods made cavalry practically useless. In addition to what passed for main roads to Corinth, Purdy and Hamburg, there were numerous narrow farm roads and trails built by the army, all deep with the heavy clay that made moving men and supplies a slow and laborious process. The combination of streams, ravines, ridges and woods gave the Federal troops every opportunity to create a variety of defensive positions. General Sherman later said that "at a later period of the war we could have rendered this position impregnable in one night."[22]

Convinced that the Confederates were gathering their forces at Corinth, which they were, on March 21 Grant informed Halleck, "I have certain information that thirteen trains of cars arrived at Corinth on the 19th, with twenty cars to each train, all loaded with troops." Knowing that the enemy forces in Corinth were being reinforced in such numbers pretty much ended any thought of a quick raid on the railroad center. Grant acknowledged this by conceding that this new information "would indicate that Corinth cannot be taken without a general engagement, which, from your instructions, is to be avoided." Grant then went on to write that he believed that the recent string of defeats suffered by the Confederates had so discouraged most of the common soldiers that "the great mass of the rank and file are heartily tired." This early in the war there were many intelligent and serious people on both sides who simply did not understand how deeply committed their opponents were to the cause they were fighting for. Ulysses Grant was one of those who believed that most Confederate soldiers really did not have it in their hearts to destroy the nation. He would soon learn just how wrong he was.[23]

Unable to take the fight to the enemy and growing restless under the constraints imposed by General Halleck against taking any action that might result in a major engagement, Grant wrote to the injured General Smith on the twenty-third, "I do not hear one word from Saint Louis. I am clearly of the opinion that the enemy are gathering strength at Corinth quite as rapidly as we are here, and the sooner we attack the easier will be the task of taking the place." Even in his deteriorating physical condition, General Smith agreed with Grant: attack now before the enemy grew too strong. At army headquarters in Savannah it appeared that the only thing preventing them from achieving another victory was the string of orders emanating from General Halleck's headquarters in St. Louis advising caution and prohibiting the taking of any aggressive action. Apparently, neither Grant nor any of his senior officers believed that the Confederates were capable of making any offensive move of their own or that General Johnston was even considering launching an attack against the Federal army comfortably ensconced in front of Pittsburg Landing.[24]

One of the main criticisms leveled at Grant after the battle was that he had not built any defensive works to protect the troops. The fact is that this early in the war the value of fieldworks, even the modest protection provided by piles of wood and stones, was not fully appreciated by either side. Grant did look into the possibility of building some defensive works and sent his engineer officer Colonel James B. McPherson to map out a line of works, but the best line that he could come up with was well behind the current camps and would leave the creeks that currently protected the camps in enemy hands. Grant decided that, "besides this, the troops with me, officers and men, needed discipline and drill more than they did experience with the pick, shovel, and axe." The officers and men who had experienced the relatively easy victories at Forts Henry and Donelson were clearly confident in their ability to defeat the enemy under any circumstances, and most of the new soldiers did not know any better. It also appears that they all undervalued the determination of the Southerners to defend their home territory.[25]

Another factor that played a part in the choice of Pittsburg Landing as the site for the army to gather and the absence of defensive works was that General Grant's plan for this campaign, as well as any other, was to attack and crush the enemy wherever they might be. With that enemy on the west side of the Tennessee River, placing his troops on the opposite side of the river made no sense to Grant. If the enemy should occupy the Pittsburg Landing area in any strength, crossing the river under fire, even with the assistance of the gunboats, could be a very costly proposition. There was no doubt in Grant's mind that Pittsburg Landing was the place to be. The position was naturally well protected for defense, and in case a disaster did befall the army, with the gunboats commanding the river there would be sufficient transportation to evacuate to the east side of the river if necessary. The plan was simple: keep the army near Pittsburg Landing until General Buell arrived with his Army of the Ohio; then the combined armies could advance on Corinth and overpower any conceivable force the Confederates could have pulled together at that point.[26]

Over in Corinth the Confederate commander was just grateful to have a bit of breathing room. After the loss of Fort Donelson, the abandonment of Nashville, and the humiliating retreat that followed, Confederate prospects in the West did not look good at all. With his forces scattered and badly outnumbered, what Albert Sidney Johnston needed most of all in late February and March of 1862 was time. Johnston needed time to pull his forces together, restore morale and instill confidence in his dejected troops, and, most important, draw reinforcements from other areas of the South to build a new army that could strike back and regain what had been lost in Tennessee and Kentucky. As it turned out, the Federal commanders gave Johnston exactly what he needed; with the senior Federal officers devoting most of their efforts to promoting their own agendas and the two most aggressive Union commanders, Grant and Foote, being held back by orders or other problems, the Union war effort in the West came to a grinding halt during this time period. Basically the Federal authorities gave General Johnston and his troops the opportunity to live to fight another day, an opportunity that Johnston would take full advantage of.

14

The Forces Gather

The transfer of the Federal army to Pittsburg Landing was an impressive display of the strength of the Union and illustrated just how overmatched the Confederates in the West really were. Marion Morrison, chaplain of the 9th Illinois, later wrote about what he saw during the move, "The trip up the Tennessee River, with this great army, is described by the boys, as grand beyond all description. There were, I believe, ninety-five steamboats loaded with soldiers. The weather was beautiful and pleasant. Bands of music were playing. Everything that was calculated to charm was there." By the time General Grant arrived to take over command on the seventeenth of March most of the spectacle of the huge fleet of ships had faded and the troops were faced with all the normal mundane work of setting up camps and drilling and more drilling.[1]

When Grant arrived at Savannah he wrote to Sherman that "I have just arrived, and although sick for the last two weeks, begin to feel better at the thought of being again with the troops." At that time the army consisted of five divisions commanded by Major Generals Smith and McClernand and Brigadier Generals Sherman, Hurlbut and Lou Wallace. Sherman and Hurlbut were already camping on the west side of the river inland from Pittsburg Landing. The divisions of Smith and McClernand were still at Savannah, and Wallace's division had been sent to Crump's Landing, about five miles below, to guard the Purdy road but still within supporting distance of the main army. One of the first orders Grant issued when he arrived was for Smith and McClernand to move their troops across the river to join Sherman and Hurlbut. Grant remained at Savannah to supervise the organizing of the new troops who were continually arriving, forming them into a sixth division commanded by Brigadier General Benjamin M. Prentiss, which was then sent across the river to join the rest of the army. Another reason why Grant decided to make his headquarters at Savannah was that it provided quicker communications with General Buell, who had finally begun his march from Nashville to join Grant.[2]

The Union army camped near Pittsburg Landing was a mixture of veterans of the Henry and Donelson campaigns and raw recruits, most of them just barely getting used to wearing a blue uniform and many of whom had never fired a weapon in anger; in fact, more than a few of them did not even have weapons at first. The division commanders whom Grant had to deal with were also a varied group of men with vastly different personalities. The man who caused Grant the most concern was the politician from Illinois John A. McClernand. Grant and McClernand never did really get along, and after the botched attack McClernand launched at Fort Donelson relations between the two deteriorated even more. Grant simply did not trust McClernand's judgment, since he seemed to be a little too concerned with looking good in newspapers and promoting himself to the people back home. In addition, McClernand and General Smith became engaged in a dispute over seniority, and one thing Grant really did not like was having dissension among his senior officers. With General Smith incapacitated by his steadily worsening leg injury, McClernand, as the only other major general after Grant, would be in command whenever Grant was not present. Not wanting McClernand to be in command of the army, Grant kept him at Savannah so General Sherman would be in charge at the campsite behind Pittsburg Landing.[3]

The one division commander whom Grant was comfortable with was General Sherman, a West Point graduate and professional soldier. But he had been under a cloud from earlier suggestions that he was not mentally stable, and was out to prove his detractors wrong. All the other division commanders, including McClernand, either were political appointees or had little experience in command, or both. Commanding the Fourth Division was forty-seven-year-old Stephen A. Hurlbut, a Republican from Illinois known more for his drinking and unscrupulous land deals than any military knowledge. With General Smith's condition getting worse, Grant knew he would have to replace his most trusted officer with newly promoted Brigadier General William H. L. Wallace. Another Illinois lawyer and non-professional soldier, who was forty-one years old, Wallace at least had fought in several engagements in the Mexican War, although he lacked the experience to fill Smith's shoes. The Sixth Division, which had been formed from the new troops arriving at Savannah, was put under the command of forty-one-year-old Brigadier General Benjamin M. Prentiss, yet another Illinois Republican lawyer who had connections to President Lincoln. Prentiss was also a veteran of the Mexican War, but he and Grant had feuded over seniority the previous year at Cairo and were barely cordial with each other.[4]

While General Grant was getting his army organized at Pittsburg Landing, back in Nashville General Buell finally began moving his Army of the Ohio south to Savannah, where he still believed Grant's army was stationed. Leaving behind a force of about eighteen thousand men to garrison the city, on March 15 Buell's cavalry rode out of Nashville to begin the march to Savannah. The next day the first of the infantry, led by Brigadier General Alexander McCook's Second Division, marched out of Nashville with their first destination being Columbia, a small town on the banks of the Duck River about forty miles from Nashville. Over the next week the rest of the army filed out of Nashville with the divisions of Generals Nelson, Crittenden and Thomas Wood heading south with at least one day between their departures. George Thomas's First Division brought up the rear of the column and did not pull out of Nashville until April 1. Buell also sent General Mitchel's division toward Murfreesboro and then south to Fayetteville to guard the army's flank. General Buell further reduced his force when he ordered General Wood to halt at Columbia to be in position to assist in defending against a possible Confederate advance. These diversions of troops meant that Buell was only going to have four divisions available to join Grant on the advance to Corinth.[5]

Early on March 16 troopers from the 1st Ohio Cavalry galloped across the bridge over the Harpeth River and through Franklin, Tennessee. Stopping briefly outside of the town to give the horses a rest, they soon rode off again, making a dash to secure the two long bridges over the Duck River just outside of Columbia. The troopers were just approaching the outskirts of Columbia when they came upon the bridges already in flames. General McCook's troops, who arrived at the river on the nineteenth, had no choice but to stop where they were. Buell's army had no pontoons and the freezing water was way too deep to attempt to ford. Engineers were sent forward to repair one of the bridges and Buell informed General Halleck that he would probably be delayed four or five days. It began snowing on the twenty-first, and even with one of McCook's brigades assisting, the repair crews faced delay after delay. General Buell arrived on March 26 and, finding the bridge far from completed, advised Halleck that the repairs needed to make the bridge safe for use were more extensive than he had at first believed and that the new completion date was now March 31. If it appeared that Buell was not in any particular hurry to get moving again it is because he was not. As far as he knew, Grant's troops were still centered around Savannah, safely on the east side of the Tennessee River. No one had informed Buell that Grant had crossed his troops to Pittsburg Landing and that he needed to join with Grant's army as quickly as possible.[6]

On March 27 General Buell first learned that Grant's army had crossed the Tennessee and was camped in a vulnerable position on the same side of the river as the Confederate army at Corinth. The water level in Duck River had been slowly falling as work progressed on the bridge, and on the twenty-ninth General Nelson's men stripped off their uniforms and with Jacob Ammen's brigade in the lead waded across a ford through ice-cold waist-deep water. The soldiers made it across the river without too much difficulty, but getting the wagons across proved to be another matter. In many cases empty wagons were turned upside down and set on top of other wagons to keep supplies dry. It was a struggle, but by the time the sun set Nelson's division had made it across the freezing water of the Duck River. The next morning Crittenden's division began crossing at the same ford. The bridge was completed the same day and the Army of the Ohio was finally on the move again after a delay of ten days.[7]

As General Buell's troops moved south of Columbia they turned off the turnpike onto a narrow country road that ran through Waynesboro on an eighty-mile route to Savannah. Nelson's division was over twelve hours ahead of Crittenden and there was nearly six miles between each of Buell's other divisions as they made their way south. There was only the one practical route through a lightly populated region that provided few provisions, and the gap between the divisions was necessary so that each division could be followed by its artillery and supply train. One of the men who made that march, Charles C. Briant of the 6th Indiana, later wrote, "Only one route was practicable, a single, narrow roadway, in poor condition for the ordinary travel of a sparsely inhabited region, and we think the poorest country we ever saw." The army had to wade through swollen creeks and march through heavy mud but was able to make a very respectable twelve miles a day.[8]

Before General Buell learned of Grant's move to the west side of the river he obtained permission from General Halleck to briefly rest his troops at Waynesboro and was considering changing his destination to Hamburg, above Pittsburg Landing, to rest and refit the troops before moving on to join Grant's troops at Savannah. General Nelson, well out in front of the rest of the army, was the only commander who had any sense of urgency in keeping his men moving as quickly as possible. Before Buell had the opportunity to issue orders to stop at Waynesboro, Nelson had marched past that town and was on the road to Savannah. While the other division commanders set a relatively modest pace, Nelson pushed his men ahead through the mud and bad weather, pulling farther and farther away from the rest of the army. It rained almost continuously as the men trudged on; at night there were few dry places to sleep, so many of the men just tried to get warm by gathering around blazing fire made from fence rails gathered along the route. Behind Nelson, Crittenden and McCook began to realize that the army was too spread out and some of Nelson's urgency passed to these divisions as they pushed their men a little harder to catch up with Nelson's men and before Buell was aware of the situation most of his army had passed Waynesboro and could not be recalled, so they pressed on. Despite all the hardships the men had to face on this grueling march, Nelson's advance made it to the vicinity of Savannah on the afternoon of April 5. That night, finally aware of the need for bringing his troops as quickly as possible, General Buell arrived at Savannah, to send his men forward as they gradually arrived.[9]

At the Union campsites near Pittsburg Landing the senior commanders were confident that their position was secure and they were just waiting for Buell's army to arrive so the campaign to Corinth could be continued. General Grant later wrote, "Shiloh was a log meeting-house, some two or three miles from Pittsburg Landing, and on the ridge which divides the waters of Snake and Lick creeks.... Shiloh was the key to our position, and was held by Sherman. His division was at that time wholly raw, no part of it ever having been in an engagement; but I thought this deficiency was more than made up by the superiority of the commander." On April 3, General Sherman wrote to his wife, "We are constantly in the presence of the enemy's pickets, but I am satisfied that they will await our coming at Corinth or some point of the Charleston Road. If we don't get away soon the leaves will be out and the whole country an ambush."[10]

Since General Sherman's division was the first to arrive behind Pittsburg Landing and the first division to set up its camp, the other divisions set up their camps based on Sherman's position. As he was instructed by General Smith, Sherman made his camp far enough inland to make room for the rest of the army when they arrived. As his were the first troops on the ground, Sherman had to cover more territory than he normally would to prevent the Confederates from launching a surprise attack on the other troops as they arrived. There were three important approaches to the campsite that had to be covered, and this spread Sherman's men out dangerously thin. The main road from Corinth was obviously one of the approaches that had to be guarded. Another site that needed watching was a bridge on the Hamburg and Purdy road over Owl Creek about three miles west of the landing. There was also a fordable location about three miles south of the landing across Lick Creek that allowed travel toward both Purdy and Savannah. The main road to Corinth went to the southwest pretty much in between the two creeks. General Sherman assigned three brigades, the 1st, 3rd, and 4th, to protect the Corinth road near the Shiloh meetinghouse, also covering the Owl Creek bridge. Colonel David Stuart's 2nd Brigade was sent over to cover the Lick Creek crossing more than a mile away from the rest of the division. This space between Sherman's main force and Stuart was eventually filled by troops of General Prentiss's newly formed division filing into position as they arrived at the front.[11]

The Federal army that was camped in the woods around Pittsburg Landing was not an organized or cohesive fighting unit. Much like what happened in front of Fort Donelson, new regiments of basically raw recruits were frequently arriving and assigned to divisions as they were needed right up to when the fighting actually began. General Prentiss, himself just promoted to brigadier general, was put in command of the newly formed Sixth Division, made up almost entirely of recently arrived new units. This division had only two organized brigades, and although there were also enough unassigned troops to form a third brigade, there was not enough time to actually develop a command structure for the most recent arrivals.[12]

One of General Hurlbut's men who wrote about his experiences in the Union camps near Pittsburg Landing was Warren Olney of the 3rd Iowa. He especially remembered the weather: "The mud — well, it was indescribable. Though we were only a mile from our base of supplies, the greatest difficulty was experienced in getting camp equipage and provisions."

The troops, and especially the supply wagons, that had been using the few dirt roads had turned those so-called roads into muddy quagmires. Olney continued his comments, writing, "Teams were stalled in the mud in every direction. The principal features of the landscape were trees, mud, wagons buried to the hub, and struggling, plunging mule teams. And the rain! How it did come down! As I recall it, the spring of 1862 did not measure its rainfall in Western Tennessee by inches, but by feet."[13]

Another subject that was frequently written about was the lack of defensive works. Even the most inexperienced soldier had enough common sense to realize that some sort of protection for the camps was better than none, but nothing could be done about it without orders. Lieutenant Colonel Wills De Hass, commander of the 77th Ohio, which had just been assigned to Sherman's division, later noted that when his unit arrived at Pittsburg Landing on April 2 he "found the impression general that a great battle was imminent. Experienced officers believed that Beauregard and Johnston would strike Grant or the Army of the Tennessee before Buell could unite the Army of the Ohio. We found the army at Shiloh listless of danger and in the worst possible condition of defense." De Hass noted that the different division camps were scattered around the area with such large intervals between the camps that made forming a cohesive defensive line nearly impossible. In addition, "[n]ot the semblance of a fortification could be seen, the entire front was in the most exposed condition."[14]

Lieutenant Colonel De Hass also saw that there were too few pickets and they were not far enough out from the camps to give proper warning of an enemy attack. He wondered why there were no cavalry patrols and how the few artillery batteries scattered around at remote locations would have any effect on a large enemy attack. De Hass communicated his concerns to the brigade commander Colonel Jesse Hildebrand, who informed him that nothing could be done about the lack of defensive measures. De Hass concluded, "One day's work in felling trees would have placed the camp in a tolerable state of defense. That a grave military error was committed in disposing the army and neglecting the proper defenses at Shiloh, there can be no questions."[15]

General Sherman's position was a prime example of what was both good and bad about the Federal campsites. Located the farthest from the landing, Sherman's men had a plentiful supply of wood for campfires and water for drinking and cooking. There was sufficient level ground for the camps and a sizeable parade ground on which to drill the men. The surrounding scenery was peaceful and attractive, with clear, sparkling creeks, rugged ravines and thick woods. As far as the comfort of the troops was concerned, this was an admirable place to make camp. However, in a military sense, with no defensive measures taken and the open space between units within Sherman's division and even larger distances between the other divisions the ability to fend off a serious attack was substantially diminished.[16]

There is no sure way to know when Albert Sidney Johnston decided to use Corinth, Mississippi, as the rallying point for his army. The importance of the rail center was so obvious that Johnston was possibly considering pulling his scattered forces together at that location when the retreat first began. General Beauregard suggested that he was the one who recommended Corinth as the best place to gather the troops spread out around Tennessee and for the reinforcements coming in from around the Confederacy to resist the coming Federal advance. Beauregard later wrote that early in March he now had "fair reason to hope that all our forces, including General Johnston's small army, and the troops forthcoming from Tennessee, Alabama, Mississippi and Louisiana, would soon be collected at the point selected by me, and that, should the Federal commander show too much boldness on the West bank of the Tennessee, we could successfully check his course, before allowing him to further develop his ulterior plans."[17]

When General Beauregard first arrived in Tennessee he was both surprised and disappointed by the Confederate military situation in the area. The number of troops available for service was much lower than he had been led to believe, and there were significant shortages of nearly all types of military equipment. Beauregard was by nature vain and short-tempered and had come west to win fame on the battlefield. The forces he observed did not look like they could win much of anything. After the disasters in February, Beauregard learned that the Federals were considering making multiple advances on the Mississippi River to attack the forts at New Madrid and Island No. 10 in addition to the campaign up the Tennessee, which could drive a wedge between General Johnston's forces and those in Western Tennessee. Beauregard later wrote, "It was at this precise moment that I fixed upon Corinth as the best point of concentration on our part, and as the natural Confederate base for any offensive operations of our forces."[18]

Confederate general Pierre G. T. Beauregard. Commanded at Charleston, South Carolina, during attack on Fort Sumter (Library of Congress).

It was quite clear why the sleepy little Northern Mississippi town of Corinth was so important. Just over twenty miles from the Tennessee River, the town was located at the point where two of the nation's major railroads intersected and was the most important railroad center in the Mississippi Valley. The vast majority of the Confederacy's resources and manpower lay between the Mississippi River and the Atlantic Ocean and between the Ohio River and the Gulf of Mexico. The Memphis & Charleston Railroad traversed that entire area from the Mississippi to the Atlantic. The Mobile & Ohio Railroad ran from the Ohio River to the Gulf, and both railroads ran through Corinth, Mississippi. It was mostly because of this transportation situation that Corinth became the focal point for the Confederates to gather for the town's defense and why it was clearly the prime target for a Federal advance up the Tennessee River. Albert Sidney Johnston saw this as clearly as Ulysses S. Grant did, and both men committed their armies to fight for control of Corinth.[19]

Before General Johnston could build up an army strong enough to defend Corinth or take the offensive against Grant's army the troops had to get to Corinth. Johnston's troops coming west from Decatur had about a ninety-mile trip in terrible weather with the column strung out all along the route, an easy target for a quick flank attack. After nearly a week of struggling through terrible roads the advance of Johnston's men arrived at Corinth on March 20, and it took another four days for the rest of the men to arrive. Most of the reinforcements from around the Confederacy had already arrived or would be in camp within a few days, and the entire force was organized into the Army of the Mississippi with four corps commanded by Generals Hardee, Polk, Braxton Bragg, and former vice president of the United States John C. Breckinridge. Breckinridge had replaced General Crittenden, who was dismissed for drunkenness.[20]

This new Confederate army was little more than forty thousand men brought together from different commands in different parts of the South. Few of them had much military experience and even fewer were combat veterans. General Bragg's men had received the best training in their camps but were untested in combat. Most of the troops from Tennessee under Polk and Hardee had spent the majority of their time in the army camped at Columbus or Bowling Green, and the men from the Gulf Coast were little better than raw recruits. The officers, especially the higher-ranking commanders, had never worked together, and the brigade and regimental commanders were almost as new to the army as were their men. There could be no successful offense until these men were organized into an army and had time to work together. A few weeks earlier the slow-moving Federal army had given Johnston time to escape from Tennessee; now they were kind enough to allow him time to transform his collection of amateur soldiers into an army.[21]

Now that the troops were together they had to be formed into an army. General Beauregard observed that most of the men assembled at Corinth were "raw troops, unhabituated to camp life, undisciplined, and hardly drilled," not exactly a ringing endorsement. As he also noted, however, the men who were gathered together "were composed of the best element in the South, and had answered the call of their respective governors, and my own, with the determination of doing their whole duty toward the cause they had espoused." Beauregard knew that these men could be turned into soldiers who might not be the best-looking body of men on a battlefield but would stand up against any foe. With the troops now in camp, hard work lay ahead in organizing and training the men. General Johnston made Beauregard his second-in-command with responsibility "for all orders relative to preparations for the intended movement against the enemy, as well as for all details of organization."[22]

Fortunately for the new army at Corinth, in Braxton Bragg they had one of the best officers in the Confederate army as far as organizing and training new troops went. A graduate of West Point and longtime friend of Jefferson Davis, Bragg would have a long and varied history in the West. Educated and refined, he insisted on hard work and discipline for his troops. Bragg also had a rather unpleasant personality, was tactless to the point of rudeness and totally lacked the ability to simply get along with others. But Bragg was also the best man available to whip the undisciplined men into soldiers. Johnston and Beauregard knew that a great deal of work had to be done before they did any fighting, as Beauregard could see that "with the forces under me, gathered as they had been, and under such difficulties, no chance of success existed, were I to attempt an aggressive movement upon the combined forces under Generals Grant and Buell."[23]

During the last week of March, General Johnston apparently considered turning command of the army at Corinth over to General Beauregard. After all, Johnston probably reasoned, Beauregard had chosen Corinth as the location to gather the forces together. It was Beauregard who arranged the transfers that brought most of the men to Corinth, and he was responsible for organizing and training the new army. In addition to Beauregard's contributions, Johnston felt, and in many cases rightfully so, that he had lost the confidence of the army and the general public. Johnston suggested that he would remain at headquarters running the department and overseeing field operations while Beauregard commanded the army in the field, much like General Halleck's arrangement with his field commanders.

According to one version of the story, Beauregard politely declined the offer and promised Johnston his full support. One of Johnston's aides, Colonel E. W. Munford, remembered the situation a little differently in that Beauregard asked for a day to consider the offer. Beauregard declined Johnston's offer the next day, citing his health as the primary reason, but ever the Southern gentleman, he also graciously commented, "I could not think of commanding on a field where Sidney Johnston was present."[24]

A different version of events was offered by General Johnston's son, William Preston Johnston, who suggested that his father's offer to Beauregard was more of a chivalrous gesture and that he had never really intended to give up overall command. In fact, Johnston certainly knew that his popularity was at a low with the public, and while placing Beauregard in charge of the army may have been Johnston's idea, there was also the possibility that Johnston would be replaced, not by one of his subordinates, but by the president of the Confederacy, Jefferson Davis. There had been rumors that Davis was going to personally assume the military command in the West, and Davis had earlier informed Johnston that he was going to shortly be making a trip to the West. Even before considering giving up the command Johnston wrote to Davis on March 20, "Were you to assume command, it would afford me the most unfeigned pleasure." President Davis decided to cancel the trip west, but Johnston was already thinking about giving up command of the army well before he brought the subject up to Beauregard. In the end, the Confederate command structure remained as it was, with Beauregard continuing as second-in-command. However, considering that he was the officer in whose name orders went out from headquarters, he was responsible for reorganizing the army, and it was Beauregard who devised the plan of attack against Grant's army, it would appear that P. G. T. Beauregard was the army commander in every way but officially.[25]

By March 24 the Confederates believed that Grant had built up his force at Pittsburg Landing to at least forty thousand men, with another division located at Crump's Landing. General Buell's Army of the Ohio was in the vicinity of Columbia and heading south, but the senior Confederate officers were not sure what he was going to do. Some believed Buell was going to slide over and attack the railroad line between Decatur and Stevenson, cutting that important supply link, and then advance on Chattanooga. Most felt that Buell was headed to Savannah to join Grant in an attack on Corinth. If that was the case it was imperative that Johnston attack Grant before Buell arrived. There was a good chance of defeating just Grant's force, but once Buell's men arrived Johnston would be facing a Federal army at least twice the size of his own. If the Confederates were going to make a move against Grant it would have to be soon.[26]

15

Johnston Risks All

Now that Albert Sidney Johnston had gathered troops from all over the South at Corinth, he had to decide what to do with his new army. There were three possible actions open to Johnston. The first and most preferred was to launch an attack on General Grant's forces at Pittsburg Landing before the army of Don Carlos Buell arrived to reinforce Grant. If Johnston tarried too long in Corinth, Buell's troops would eventually join with Grant's and attacking their combined armies was out of the question. The second possibility was that if Buell did reach Grant's, army before the Confederates could launch their attack it was certain that the combined Federal armies would soon be on their way to Corinth, where Johnston would have to defend the vital rail center against a force twice as large as his own, resulting in a siege that could have only one outcome, but at least he would put up a fight and make the Federals pay dearly. The third and least attractive option facing General Johnston was that if he was unable to attack Grant before Buell's forces joined him at Pittsburg Landing then, rather than allowing the army to get trapped in Corinth by an overwhelming enemy force, it would be better to abandon Corinth without a fight and save the army, which would almost certainly end Johnston's military career. Considering his potential options, there was little doubt as to what Johnston was going to do. General Beauregard later wrote about what Johnston planned to do, "By a rapid and vigorous attack on General Grant it was expected he would be beaten back into his transports and the river, or captured."[1]

Time was of the essence and the Confederates needed to act as quickly as possible. But, before attacking anyone, the army had to be reorganized and the troops given as much training as possible considering the time constraints. There was a serious shortage of experienced field officers and so much work that needed to be done to instruct and equip the men that the army was simply unable to leave Corinth when Beauregard had originally hoped they would. As he wrote, "To my extreme disappointment, our forces were not ready and did not make the projected advance as early as I had wished and striven to have it done."[2]

On the night of March 31 a small body of Confederate cavalry scouting the area a few miles out in front of Crump's Landing ran into Federal cavalry on the same mission. A brief skirmish occurred, which was insignificant in itself, but it was enough to alarm General Lew Wallace. It was known that Confederate forces under General Benjamin Frank Cheatham were stationed at Bethel Station, and Wallace now feared that Cheatham was making a move on Wallace's Third Brigade stationed at nearby Adamsville. General Wallace quickly moved his two other brigades to Adamsville, where they arrived during the early-morning hours of April 1. In the meantime Beauregard had instructed Cheatham to make a reconnaissance from Purdy in the direction of the river, emphasizing that he should avoid any engagement with Federal forces. When the sun rose on the first Cheatham's scouts ran into Wallace's entire division drawn up in line of battle near Adamsville. This surprising news was quickly sent to Cheatham, still at Bethel Station, who in turn immediately wired to General Polk that it looked like he was about to be attacked. Both Wallace and Cheatham had misinterpreted the situation, but this quick escalation from a minor cavalry skirmish illustrates how difficult it would be for the Confederates to launch a successful surprise attack.³

It was time for General Johnston to make his move. On April 1 orders were sent out for the First and Third Corps to be prepared to begin the march within the next twenty-four hours. A scouting report had been received that Federal transports and gunboats had advanced up the Tennessee past Yellow Creek on the Confederate right. There was concern that this might be a Federal attempt to flank the Corinth positions or break the Memphis & Charleston Railroad near Iuka. General Breckinridge rushed infantry to Iuka, and by the next morning two full brigades had arrived. It turned out that the Confederates had little to fear from what was actually just a raid, but also on April 2 information was received that did give cause for concern: General Buell's army had crossed the Duck River several days earlier and were closer to Savannah than had been expected. The information about Buell's approach and Cheatham's telegram that General Wallace's division was threatening his front prompted Beauregard to endorse Cheatham's wire: "Now is the moment to advance and strike the enemy at Pittsburg Landing." General Johnston's adjutant Colonel Thomas Jordan took the dispatch with Beauregard's note to Johnston at the Rose house, who then went directly to General Bragg's quarters at the Curlee house. Bragg agreed with Beauregard's assessment, and as Beauregard reported, "It was then, at a late hour, determined that the attack should be attempted at once, incomplete and imperfect as were our preparations for such a grave and momentous adventure. Accordingly, that night at 1 A.M. the preliminary orders to the commanders of corps were issued for the movement."⁴

Colonel Jordan wrote out the preliminary orders to the corps commanders while still in Bragg's room, instructing them to be ready to move out by six o'clock that morning, April 3. This order stated that the corps commanders should "hold their several corps in condition to move at a moment's notice, having forty rounds of ammunition in their cartridge-boxes, and three days' cooked rations in their haversacks; also, sixty rounds of ammunition and uncooked rations in wag-

Confederate general Leonidas Polk. Killed in action outside of Atlanta in 1864 (Library of Congress).

ons." When the time came for the men to use their ammunition forty rounds would prove seriously insufficient, but at this point no one could imagine the fighting that was going to take place. The orders were received by Generals Polk and Hardee before two o'clock and Breckinridge received his by telegraph at Burnsville. After breakfast Johnston and Beauregard met to discuss the plan of operation and were soon joined by Bragg, Hardee, and Polk. Since it would take some time to draw up the formal orders and make copies, General Johnston briefed the corps commanders verbally on their assignments and the order in which the army was to march, so they could begin moving their troops before receiving the written orders. In addition to putting out instructions to the army in Corinth, General Johnston made sure to notify Jefferson Davis that he was leading the army forward to attack Grant's forces at Pittsburg Landing before Buell could arrive.[5]

As the army prepared to move out of Corinth all the roads leading out of the city were jammed with men and wagons. The advance toward Pittsburg Landing needed to be a smoothly, run well-organized march with no room for errors; unfortunately, almost everything that could go wrong did. There were only two roads out of Corinth that led toward Pittsburg Landing; both of them were narrow dirt roads that were currently in terrible condition. The two roads were the Ridge Road, which first headed north and later turned northeast, and the Monterey Road, which started out northeast and turned back to the north at the village of Monterey, where it became the Savannah Road. Leaving Monterey, the Savannah Road intersected with the Ridge Road about four miles from the Federal lines at the James Michie farmhouse.[6]

The order of march would have been confusing to anyone, but it was especially so for the inexperienced field officers who had to lead their men forward. General Hardee was to move his corps out the Ridge Road followed by General Charles Clark's division of Polk's corps. General Cheatham's division, still at Bethel Station, would move on the Purdy road until they came up to the Ridge Road, where they would join with Polk's troops. General Bragg's corps was to leave Corinth on the road to Monterey, and once past the village Wither's division would take the Savannah Road to Michie's. General Daniel Ruggles' division was to continue down the Purdy road from Monterey until they reached the Ridge Road, where Polk was to halt his troops to allow Ruggles to pass. Breckinridge with the Reserve Corps would take the most convenient route from Burnsville to Monterey and then continue to Michie's.[7]

Marching the army out of Corinth quickly turned into a disaster. The orders that had to be written and communicated down the chain of command took longer than had been anticipated and the starting time of 6:00 A.M. had to be postponed. There was a briefing at Beauregard's headquarters for the senior officers at eight o'clock and a new start time of noon was set. When noon arrived, however, the streets were full of men and wagons going nowhere. At first it was believed that Polk's men were blocking the Ridge Road, but it turned out that Clark's troops were camped outside of town. The most likely reason for the delay was simple administrative confusion. Without written orders General Bragg, who was the army's chief of staff, instructed Hardee to start moving his troops as soon as he thought it practical. Hardee did not receive any specific written orders until around 3:00 P.M., which was when his troops finally moved out. Another example of the confusion due to imprecise orders was that General Cheatham was directed to stay in the vicinity of Purdy and Bethel Station until he was convinced there would be no attack on his position. He received no instructions as to how long he was to wait or what route to take to rendezvous with the main army. The problems were not really any one person's fault, because there just had not been enough time to perform all the staff work needed to organize a march of a forty-thousand-man army with all the accompanying artillery and supply wagons.[8]

Knowing from experience that inspirational words can frequently have a positive effect on the morale and enthusiasm of new soldiers, General Johnston wrote out an address to be read to the men:

> I have put you in motion to offer battle to the invaders of your country. With the resolution and disciplined valor becoming men fighting, as you are, for all worth living or dying for, you can but march to a decisive victory over the agrarian mercenaries sent to subjugate and despoil you of your liberties, property, and honor. Remember the precious stake involved; remember the dependence of your mothers, your wives, your sisters, and your children on the result; remember the fair, broad, abounding land, the happy homes, and the ties that would be desolated by your defeat.
>
> The eyes and the hopes of eight millions of people rest upon you. You are expected to show yourselves worthy of your race and lineage; worthy of the women of the South, whose noble devotion in this war has never been exceeded in any time. With such incentives to brave deeds and with the trust that God is with us, your general will lead you confidently to the combat, assured of success.[9]

General Hardee led his men out from Corinth about three o'clock in the afternoon of April 3, marching past Johnston's headquarters with bands playing. About an hour later Bragg's troops began their march out the Monterey Road with two cavalry regiments in the lead. Once they finally got going the Confederates made good time despite the poor condition of the roads. It was well past dark before General Hardee decided to call a halt for the day and moved his men down a side road to camp near a freshwater spring. Clark's division, which was about a half hour behind Hardee, continued on down the Ridge Road, passing Hardee's men in the darkness. About a mile past where Hardee had pulled off the road Clark stopped his troops for the night. About two o'clock in the morning it began to rain heavily for some time, and light rain continued the next morning, making the roads even more difficult to move on than they had been. When Hardee resumed his march on the Ridge Road his men soon ran into Clark's men blocking the road with their wagon train and more time was lost while the wagons were cleared off the road so Hardee's infantry could proceed.[10]

On the morning of April 4 Hardee kept his men moving on the Ridge Road although the continuous rain turned the already-poor roads into quagmires, causing the troops and especially the wagons to advance at a much slower pace than had been planned on. On the Monterey Road the going was no better for Bragg's men. About 8:30 A.M. Brigadier General Jones M. Withers' division passed through Monterey and continued up the Savannah Road to Michie's farm. Ruggles was well behind Withers and was supposed to take the Purdy road past Monterey, but when local citizens informed Bragg of the atrocious condition of that route he ordered Ruggles to follow behind Withers on the Monterey Road instead. This change caused another delay for Clark's division of Polk's corps, since he was waiting at the intersection of the Ridge and Purdy roads to fall in behind Ruggles' men as they passed. Bragg did sent a messenger to Polk to inform him of the change, but it took several hours for the information to pass to Polk and then to Clark and it was not until late afternoon that Ruggles' division was able to arrive at Monterey.[11]

During the evening of the fourth General Hardee's men made their way a short distance past Mitchie's to the Bark Road in the direction of Pittsburg Landing. General Polk continued to follow Hardee and his advance troops reached Mitchie's during the evening.

General Bragg's advance also reached the vicinity of Mitchie's farm during the evening, with the rest of his men coming up during the night. On the night of the fourth the Confederates were spread out, but at least they were close to their point of rendezvous with Bragg on the Savannah and Monterey Road, south of the Bark Road and Polk on the Bark Road, west of Bragg's men, and Hardee was also along the Bark Road closest to Pittsburg Landing. Despite the awful conditions, the men were still in high spirits as they marched and were getting anxious to close with the enemy. Some of the new soldiers relieved their tension by firing their weapons in the air, and while this may have made them feel better, the noise concerned the senior officers who were worried that this could warn the Federals of the approaching Confederates and lose them the element of surprise, upon which the prospects for victory hinged.[12]

Nothing had yet been heard from General Breckinridge during the march, but his men were also on the way to the rendezvous point. Breckinridge had received orders on the afternoon of the third instructing him to march at daylight and be prepared "to meet the enemy in twenty-four hours." With Nathan Bedford Forrest's cavalry leading the way, the Reserve Corps left Burnsville around five o'clock on the morning of the fourth, moving on the roads to Farmington and Monterey. After a long and exhausting march over the same type of miserable, muddy roads that delayed the rest of the army Breckinridge's lead troops arrived in Monterey just before sunset, but the rest of his troops were strung out behind for several miles. At five o'clock that evening General Johnston held a brief meeting with Beauregard and Bragg during which they changed the time for the attack to begin to eight o'clock the next morning. When Breckinridge arrived in Monterey he was informed of the change in plans and for the first time learned of his position in the battle formation. Adding to the discomfort of the exhausted and wet Confederate troops camped out in the open that night, the rain began to come down in torrents and continued through the night and early morning of April 5.[13]

When the lead elements of Johnston's forces stopped for the night on the fourth they were still several miles from the Federal lines that they were originally going to attack on the morning of April 5. The delay had resulted from poor planning at the start and miserable marching conditions caused by the constant rain. The normally poorly maintained country roads were in many places little more than trails through the woods, and they quickly turned into quagmires and in some locations were nearly impassable for wagons, but the tired and muddy columns pressed forward. On the fourth John S. Jackman of Kentucky's Orphan Brigade wrote in his diary about the conditions faced by the Confederates as they marched toward the enemy, "At the outset our road led through a swamp, where, in some places, the mud and water was knee deep every step. The rain continued to pour down all the four noon [forenoon]. I soon regretted that I had started."[14]

During the night orders had been sent out that the troops should be prepared to begin moving forward by three o'clock in the morning, forming their lines as they advanced and launching the assault as early as possible. General Hardee was to form up the first line with as many of his men as needed and send the remainder back to form a second line about a thousand yards behind with Bragg's troops. General Polk was to allow Bragg's men to pass to form the second line; then Polk was to form his men on the left behind Bragg with Breckinridge to his right. As so often happened in Tennessee, the weather became a major factor affecting the Confederate plans. It had been raining all night, and well before the army was to move many of the small streams and ravines that ran across the road became impassable. The advance was postponed until dawn, when General Hardee moved forward, but the roads were is such a poor condition that it was about ten o'clock in the morning before he reached the position where the lines were to be formed and "my corps reached the outposts and developed the lines of the enemy. It was immediately deployed in the line of battle, about one mile and a half east of the Shiloh Church, where Lick Creek and Owl Creek approach most nearly." General Bragg followed Hardee, but with the roads worsening as the men slugged their way through the mud, by the time his lead troops arrived at the assembly point it was already noon and it took the rest of the afternoon, until well after 4:00 P.M., before the rest of Bragg's corps reached their position in line. Obviously there would be no assault on April 5, and it was nearly dark by the time General Polk's troops formed up behind Bragg's line on the left and Breckinridge brought his men up on Polk's right. General Cheatham arrived from Purdy, which he had left just that morning, and rejoined Polk's corps.[15]

The night of the fifth was another miserable experience for the Confederate soldiers waiting in the cold, damp weather. Many of the men were without food, as they had eaten what they carried on their backs during the march or had simply thrown their provisions away as they tried to lighten the load they had to carry as they struggled to move through the deep mud and rain. In his report General Beauregard noted the difficulties the men faced as they moved forward: "The men, however, for the most part, were unused to marching, and the roads, narrow and traversing a densely wooded country, became almost impassable after a severe rainstorm on the night of the 4th." James M. Williams, a private in the 21st Alabama, wrote to his wife about the march to Pittsburg Landing telling her that he had "marched from Corinth last Thursday afternoon towards the enemys lines. Friday we moved two or three miles further through the mud and water.... The rain fell in torrents nearly all night, and we suffered greatly."[16]

The terrible weather and the miscues during the march had some of the senior officers on edge, and around four o'clock that afternoon Beauregard met with Bragg at the intersection of the Corinth and Bark roads. They agreed that the situation look bleak and that perhaps the attack should be canceled. General Polk soon arrived and he and Beauregard, never on friendly terms to begin with, got into a heated discussion. Beauregard blamed Polk for the confusion on the roads during the march, snapping, "I am very much disappointed at the delay which has occurred in getting troops into position." Polk immediately blamed General Bragg for not getting into position soon enough, since Polk could do nothing until Bragg's line was set. General Johnston then came up and the generals held an impromptu conference when General Beauregard surprised everyone present by stating that after all the effort they had made to get to this point he believed the attack should be canceled and the army return to Corinth. Beauregard's suggestion to abandon the attack when the army was so close was based on some quite reasonable concerns he had about the possibility that the attack could not succeed as planned. Everyone was aware that the success of the assault depended largely on achieving surprise when Confederates hit the Federal lines. Beauregard was concerned that the amount of time it had taken the troops to march from Corinth to their current position had most likely made it difficult, if not impossible, to achieve that all-important surprise. Along with the fact that many of the men had run out of food, the wagons with the extra rations and ammunition were too far to the rear to quickly resupply the troops. Perhaps the biggest reason Beauregard believed that there was no chance of surprising the Federal forces was the amount of noise created by many of the untrained men firing their weapons to see if they still worked in the rain and how the sound of this firing must have been heard by Federal pickets. All things considered, Beauregard could not believe that the enemy had not been warned of the army's approach, and thought that when the assault began they would be waiting to slaughter the Confederates from behind stone walls or entrenched positions.[17]

General Beauregard's suggestion to turn back to Corinth received some support during a brief discussion between the corps commanders. The entire foundation of the attack was predicated on achieving the element of surprise. Without that factor, even if the Federal camps were not fortified victory would be difficult. At least two of Grant's divisions were veterans of the Fort Donelson campaign, while few of Johnston's officers and men had ever been under fire and they had little knowledge of battlefield discipline and maneuvers. Johnston listened to the debate for a while, considering the views of the officers who expressed them, but still held out the hope that the enemy was not prepared for an attack. General Johnston asked Polk for his opinion, and he replied that his troops were in good condition and eager for battle, that to retire now would injure their morale, and that he recommended the attack be carried out as planned.[18]

General Johnston ended the debate when he said simply, "Gentlemen, we shall attack at daylight tomorrow," and any thoughts of canceling the attack were over. All the generals at this meeting must have known that launching their men against the Federal camps that morning was the only chance they had to achieve victory. The advance troops of General Buell's army were now quickly closing on Savannah and any more delay could allow him enough time for Grant's army to be sufficiently reinforced to make the assault more difficult. Once Buell's entire army joined Grant's this combined force would be too strong for the Confederates to even consider attacking. Returning to Corinth without a fight was unacceptable to Johnston for several reasons. After the difficult march to reach the point where they were this close to the enemy, then just turning around and making what was certain to be an equally miserable march back to Corinth could very well ruin the army's morale. Considering the low opinion that much of the general public already had of Johnston, to bring his army almost face-to-face with the enemy and then back off would almost surely bring enough condemnation that even his good friend Jefferson Davis would not be able to save Johnston's career. Another question was what would happen to the army once it returned to Corinth. If the troops were not going to be used to fight it is highly likely that some of the states that had weakened their own defenses to supply men to Johnston's army might want those men returned to their former posts. In addition, the whole point of General Grant exposing his army at Pittsburg Landing and Buell marching his troops down from Nashville was to form an army large enough to allow the Federals to capture Corinth. General Johnston knew full well that he could not successfully fight the combined Federal armies and if Corinth was put under siege there could be only one result, losing both the city and the army. In the end there was no other choice he could make, so the assault would take place in the morning. General Johnston flatly stated that "I would fight them if they were a million. They can present no greater front between these two creeks than we can, and the more men they crowd in there, the worse we can make it for them."[19]

The plan of attack was set. The Confederates would advance in long parallel lines stretching across the open plain in front of the Federal camps. General Hardee's corps would lead the assault with a line spread out almost three miles between Owl Creek on the left and Lick Creek on the right. Hardee would be reinforced on the far right by Brigadier General Adley H. Gladden's brigade from Bragg's corps, giving the first line a total of about nine thousand men. About five hundred yards behind Hardee's men General Bragg had over ten thousand men spread out the same as the front line between the creeks. Some eight hundred yards behind Bragg was the third line, consisting of General Polk's nine thousand men on the left and about seven thousand under General Breckinridge on the right. The troops of both Polk and Breckinridge were considered reserves to be sent forward at points where the first two lines needed assistance. Each corps had its own artillery that would accompany the men on the attack, and both flanks were covered by cavalry. Overall there would be nearly forty thousand Confederate soldiers advancing on the Federal camps in the morning.[20]

The formation chosen for the assault was certainly not the best that could have been used. At one time General Johnston had planned on striking the left of the Federal position with a much more concentrated blow to cut them off from their line of retreat at Pittsburg Landing. Advancing across the relatively open terrain in front of the Federal camps in long lines provided no extra force to any specific area and at best would only push the Federal troops back toward Pittsburg Landing, where they could use their fleet of transports to escape or bring up reinforcements. Another problem with the extended lines was that it would be impossible for the corps commanders to know what was going on over the entire length of their lines, especially on the ends. But there was now no time left to make other arrangements. To move forty thousand men into a different formation would probably delay the assault for another day, and Johnston wanted to attack now. General Johnston's son, William Preston Johnston, who was present, later wrote, "Strong reasons demanded an immediate attack, as delay increased the danger of discovery." There is no doubt that this is one of the factors that convinced Johnston to go on with the attack, but he must also have been thinking that even after his long and storied career this moment was what he would be remembered for, and the weight of the Confederacy was squarely on his shoulders. For better or worse, there would be no retreat; the battle would be fought in the morning.[21]

W. J. Worsham of the 19th Tennessee later wrote about that night in front of the Federal camps, "Johnston on Saturday evening had blazed out his lines through the woods right in the face of the enemy, and after dark formed his lines so silently that the enemy, though in cannon shot range, did not hear him. Here we lay all night quietly resting and waiting for the storm next morning, and like the horse, we could almost sniff the coming battle already."[22]

16

The Approaching Battle

The reasoning used by General Beauregard in making his case as to why the attack should be called off was perfectly valid. Despite precautions and orders issued against divulging the presence of the army, there had been little caution exercised on the part of the new and undisciplined troops. Fires had been built, and drums and bugles used freely in a number of regiments, and scattered firing was kept up all night in most of the brigades by men checking to see if their weapons would fire when they needed them. The noise created by the approaching Confederates must have been heard by somebody, and it was difficult for Beauregard to believe that there were no Federal cavalry patrols in the area that could have heard the random musket fire or even discovered the army itself just two miles away from the Federal positions. If Grant's army had created even the most basic defensive works it would have be highly unlikely that the Confederate attack could be successful. As difficult as it is to believe, none of the perfectly reasonable fears that concerned Beauregard came true. Most of the senior Federal commanders had become convinced that the Confederates were in no condition to pull together an army large enough to seriously threaten their position at Pittsburg Landing. It is also likely that the Federal commanders were lulled into a false sense of security by their numerical strength, the fact that General Buell's army was expected to arrive any day and the fact that General Sherman had earlier made a reconnaissance as far as Monterey, about halfway to Corinth, and found no sign of the enemy.[1]

With the Federal camping area fairly ringed by Lick Creek and the Tennessee River on the left and rear and Snake and Owl Creeks on the right, the only practical way for a Confederate force to approach was right in front. Considering all the dense woods, thick underbrush and numerous small streams and ravines that filled the landscape, the overall Federal position was eminently defensible. Unfortunately, the haphazardly located and spread-out campsites occupied by the five divisions at Pittsburg Landing all but negated the natural strength of the position. The two most advanced divisions, the men who would be the first to come into contact with any attacking enemy troops and would naturally bear the early brunt of the onslaught, were those of Generals Sherman and Prentiss. Both of these divisions were made up of the newest recruits, who had never heard or fired a shot in anger.[2]

Most of General Sherman's division was camped a little over two miles from Pittsburg Landing on the right of the army. His men occupied a ridge that was one of the key points to the entire position. On Sherman's left, with a large gap between them, was the division of General Prentiss located about a half mile closer to the landing. Still farther to the left and behind Prentiss was Colonel Stuart's brigade of Sherman's division covering the Hamburg road near Lick Creek. Stuart was pretty much on his own, as he was isolated from the rest of the army by heavy woods and several ravines. General McClernand's division was camped about a quarter mile behind and to the left of Sherman's camp. General Hurlbut's troops were about a mile behind Prentiss, and General Smith's division, now commanded by W. H. L. Wallace, was to the right of Prentiss and behind and a little to the left of McClernand. Grant's sixth division, commanded by Lew Wallace, was still at Crump's Landing, several miles from the rest of the army. General Smith had been replaced by W. H. L. Wallace because his leg injury and worsening infection kept him incapacitated and before the end of April would claim Smith's life. The way the Federal camps were set up, the most experienced troops, McClernand's, W. H. L. Wallace's, and Lew Wallace's divisions, were well away from the front where the fighting would begin.[3]

The Federal commanders were so confident that their camps were safe from enemy attack that no one seemed concerned about the large gaps between the divisions and there had not even been any significant discussions about setting up defensive lines or cooperating with each other in case of an attack. Warren Olney, of the 3rd Iowa, later wrote that from what he could see the various units "camped wherever there was an opening in the woods or underbrush sufficiently large for a regiment." Neither the division nor the brigade commanders appeared to have spent much effort in properly laying out the camps or organizing a plan of defense; instead, "each regiment occupied such suitable ground as presented itself in the neighborhood of the rest of the brigade." There were too few pickets sent out and those who were did not risk going too far from their camp, which prevented the main body of troops from receiving adequate warning in the event of an enemy attack. General Sherman commented on why there were not even the most basic earthworks created to defend the camp, saying that he "acted on the supposition that we were an invading army. We did not fortify our camps against an attack, because we had no orders to do so, and because such a course would have made our raw men timid." It would appear that considering the lack of any defenses at all, most of the other senior officers agreed with Sherman.[4]

Of course the Federal army at Pittsburg Landing was no different from any other large body of soldiers in that the subordinate officers reflected the attitude of the army's commanding officer, and General Grant had little interest in encouraging any defensive notions among his officers or men. Grant was focused on the concept that the army was participating in a major campaign and was just temporarily pausing at Pittsburg Landing waiting for reinforcements before continuing to advance deeper into enemy territory. Grant did have his engineering officer Colonel McPherson look into putting up fortifications, but the best line that would have been practical would have given up most of the flank protection now provided by the creeks. Grant would later write that he "regarded the campaign we were engaged in as an offensive one and had no idea that the enemy would leave strong intrenchments to take the initiative when he knew he would be attacked where he was if he remained." One other reason for not taking the time to build up defensive works was that the majority of the men were new and untrained recruits and Grant believed that "drill and discipline were worth more to our men than fortifications." Whatever the reasoning used, it is quite obvious that the Federal army at Pittsburg Landing was lacking even the most minimal defensive preparation that would be considered prudent for troops in enemy territory.[5]

General Grant did have concerns about the safety of one of his divisions, that of Lew Wallace based at Crump's Landing, several miles from the rest of the army. Grant was afraid that the Confederates "might make a rapid dash upon Crump's and destroy our transports and stores, most of which were kept at that point, and then retreat before Wallace could be reinforced." With Wallace's troops coming into contact with General Cheatham's Confederates on April 1 near Adamsville and several contacts with enemy patrols in that area since then, Grant decided that Crump's Landing might be a more likely target than the main army. The closest division to Lew Wallace's position was that of W. H. L. Wallace, and Grant made arrangements for him to rush reinforcements to Crump's Landing in case of an enemy assault. In a message to W. H. L. Wallace, Grant wrote, "It is believed that the enemy are re-enforcing at Purdy, and it may be necessary to re-enforce General Wallace to avoid his being attacked by a superior force. Should you find danger of this sort, re-enforce him at once with your entire division." When he informed Sherman of this arrangement Grant noted that he did not really expect an attack on Crump's Landing but that "it is best to be prepared."[6]

There were plenty of signs that Confederate forces were near the Union camps if anyone had been paying attention. On Thursday, April 3, one of General Sherman's brigades made a reconnaissance about five miles out from camp on the road to Corinth. Skirmishers from the 48th Ohio made contact with Confederate cavalry and a brief firefight occurred, but since they had firm orders not to be drawn into a pitched battle the Federal troops fell back and returned to camp. The next day, Friday, April 4th, Major Ricker led a force of the 5th Ohio Cavalry on a reconnaissance about two miles out from the picket line and as he reported after passing over a hill his advanced troopers ran into fire from artillery supported by at least two regiments of infantry and a large cavalry force. Ricker quickly brought his men back to the Union picket lines, where he found that the firing had brought General Sherman forward with several regiments of infantry. On his informing Sherman that he had run into the advance of the Confederate army, Ricker wrote, Sherman replied that Beauregard was too intelligent to leave his base of operations to attack the Federal camps and that what Ricker saw was merely a reconnaissance in force. The sounds of the firing that evening sufficiently alarmed the rest of the army that General Hurlbut put his troops on the road to go to Sherman's support. Seymour D. Thompson of the 3rd Iowa remembered that as the regiments moved out they "joined one after another in the column as they took the road. The mud was deep, the artillery wheels sinking nearly to the hubs, and what made it worse, it was already getting quite dark. When we had advanced about three-quarters of a mile, General Hurlbut received orders to turn back." General Sherman considered this a minor skirmish and decided there was no need for any assistance.[7]

The next day Sherman reported this incident to Grant, stating that he believed there were two regiments of infantry and one battery of artillery about two miles in his front but that he doubted that anything more than picket firing would be the result. Sherman remarked, "The enemy is saucy, but got the worst of it yesterday, and will not press our pickets far. I will not be drawn out far unless with certainty of advantage, and I do not apprehend anything like an attack on our position." Earlier in the war General Sherman had come close to having a nervous breakdown. Now that he was in command of troops in the field again, he was determined to remain calm in the face of any danger, especially mere skirmishing. This calm confidence by the division commander out in the most exposed position farthest from Pittsburg Landing only reinforced Grant's own confidence in the safety of the army's position while at the same time over forty thousand Confederates were only about two miles from Sherman's camp.[8]

In addition to Sherman's report on the incident in front of his division, Grant reported to General Halleck on April 5 that he had gone in person to look into reports of attacks on other areas of the front but found nothing to be concerned about, telling Halleck, "I have scarcely the faintest idea of an attack (general one) being made upon us, but will be prepared should such a thing take place." Concentrating on the advance to Corinth and not considering that his position was in any danger from a Confederate attack, Grant also commented that once Buell's troops arrived he intended to send them to Hamburg, about four miles above Pittsburg Landing, because "from that point to Corinth the road is good, and a junction can be formed with the troops from Pittsburg at almost any point." Also on the fifth around noon the first troops of General Nelson's division of Buell's army began arriving at Savannah. Nelson had pushed his division ever since crossing the Duck River and, considering the weather and condition of the roads, had made excellent time. Grant and Nelson stopped by to visit with one of Nelson's brigade commanders, Colonel Jacob Ammen, later that afternoon. Colonel Ammen commented to Grant that his men were not that tired and were perfectly able to continue on to Pittsburg Landing, but Grant replied that there was no hurry and that Ammen should rest his men after their long march: "You cannot march through the swamps; make the troops comfortable; I will send boats for you Monday or Tuesday, or some time early in the week. There will be no fight at Pittsburg Landing; we will have to go to Corinth, where the rebels are fortified. If they come to attack us, we can whip them, as I have more than twice as many troops as I had at Fort Donelson."[9]

Like their generals, many of the men in the Union ranks discounted the threat of an enemy attack. The camps were fairly comfortable and spring was arriving, bringing with it warm, sunny days and blossoming leaves and flowers in the abundant woods. There was regular mail deliveries, and for the men who experienced the cold and misery of Fort Donelson the camps at Pittsburg Landing were quite pleasant. There was always the possibility of action, but as Lucius W. Barber of the 15th Illinois later wrote, "we all knew that a battle was imminent, but never dreamed that the enemy would open the strife. Our great victory at Ft. Donelson had given us great confidence in ourselves and we supposed that we rested in security for the present." A young drummer boy in the 57th Illinois, William W. Cluett, wrote that up until Saturday camping at Pittsburg Landing had been uneventful, although "vague rumors are afloat this evening to the effect that Gen. Albert Sidney Johnston is moving toward the Tennessee River with his entire command. Not much credit is attached to it, however."[10]

Not all the Union soldiers camped at Pittsburg Landing were convinced that their position provided as much security against an enemy attack as was generally believed by the senior officers. Some of the physical attributes of the terrain that appeared to offer protection could also be elements of their defeat. Seymour Thompson was one of those who realized that "with an impassable river immediately in our rear, and an impenetrable forest on either flank, defeat would amount to no less than destruction and capture. The soldiers themselves were not so stupid as not to discern the peril to which we were exposed. Nevertheless, not even the ordinary precautions were taken against it." In addition to the lack of provisions for protecting the camps, many of the men were concerned that the army's headquarters and commanding general were still miles away in Savannah. Who would be in charge of coordinating the different divisions for defense during the crucial first stages of an attack? As Thompson remembered, there had been "rumors that the enemy were evacuating Corinth, and again that he was marching against us. Whatever we believed, we could not deny that if the enemy expected to give us a decisive blow, he would attempt it now." One of Sherman's men, Ephraim J. Hart of the 40th Illinois, remembered that he and his comrades were concerned by the firing they could clearly hear from the skirmish on the fourth but that on Saturday "quiet continued during the day, and many of the boys began to doubt the probability of the rebels troubling us. During the night, however, Company B's boys who were on the front line, were convinced that an enemy was hovering near, as they could hear them moving continuously through the brush."[11]

By April 5 all the signs were there for anyone to see. The multiple skirmishes with the Federal pickets and the frequent sightings of Confederate cavalry riding around the front of the Federal camps should have been obvious indicators that at the very least a large body of enemy troops, if not General Johnston's entire army, was in the immediate vicinity of the still not fully on guard Federal camps. There were some unit commanders, however, who decided to take extra precautions with or without orders to do so. John A. Bering later wrote that in the 48th Ohio their pickets were increased and received orders to notify the regiment's commander, Colonel Peter Sullivan, if any firing occurred during the night, "and it is needless to add, that every one in the regiment felt that we were on the eve of battle. But during the night all was unusually still. No long-roll or bugle-sound disturbed the slumbering camp." Lieutenant Colonel Will De Hass, commander of the 77th Ohio, wrote that at least some preparations were taken in his regiment: "The men were ordered to stack arms in front of their tents, prepared to advance or repel attack, and that if firing were heard during the night to remain quiet, await the long-roll or bugle-call. Every soldier in the regiment felt that a battle was imminent; in an hour the whole camp was asleep. How unconscious of danger lay the army of the Union that night!"[12]

There were many stories and rumors floating around the Federal camps that day, some totally wrong, some containing grains of fact, and some almost prophetic. Seymour Thompson later wrote that in his regiment "[t]here rumors among us that Buell had arrived at Savannah; but no one seemed to feel certain that it was so. From the front there were no tidings of any thing unusual — not an intimation of the nearness of the enemy. Over all was settled a frightful calm. It was that which indicates the gathering storm. Within an hour's march of us the enemy was taking his positions for battle."[13]

In General Prentiss' division the same feeling that a fight was coming seemed to be spreading throughout the camp. Charles A. Morton of the 25th Missouri remembered that on Saturday evening Captain George Donnelly, the brigade's adjutant, "came to the company and said that the enemy was marching on the camp in force, and was within fourteen miles; there would be a battle, and he wanted to see I Company ready." Morton did not know how Donnelly came by this information but noted, "There was no secrecy, the whole regiment anticipated a battle. Some of the officers sat up late, and other remained up all night." Colonel Everett Peabody, commanding the First Brigade, added his concerns about a possible attack and urged that the division be prepared to receive an enemy attack.[14]

With reports of contact with the enemy growing, General Prentiss himself was getting concerned and on Saturday afternoon, in addition to the usual guard, sent troops from the 21st and 25th Missouri Regiments under Colonel David Moore to reconnoiter out in front of the division. Colonel Moore returned about seven o'clock that evening and reported enemy activity out in front of the division, including cavalry patrols. General Prentiss decided he needed more information, so about three o'clock in the morning of April 6 he sent out a detachment of the 25th Missouri commanded by Major James E. Powell. Powell's troops moved out the Corinth road and at 4:55 A.M. they ran into Confederate pickets from General Hardee's corps and firing soon began.[15]

The fight between Major Powell's force and the Confederate pickets began as soon as they made contact, although it was still dark and the firing was pretty much random shooting at gun flashes from the other side. The commander of the Confederate picket line, Major Aaron Hardcastle, reported that "the enemy opened a heavy fire on us at a distance of about two hundred yards" and continued for about an hour, until "about 6:30 A.M. I saw the brigade formed in my rear and fell back." Charles A. Morton of the 25th Missouri remembered that he and his fellow Missourians "drove in the enemy's picket, and developed his main force about one and a half miles from our camp." Hearing the firing, Colonel Peabody sent Colonel Moore back out with troops from the 21st Missouri to reinforce Major Powell. Just as it was getting light enough to see Moore was bringing his men forward to the sound of the firing, he ran into Powell, who was falling back with his wounded. Colonel Moore took over command of both forces and sent back for the remainder of his regiment. This advanced Federal force now consisted of 21st Missouri and several companies each from the 25th Missouri, 16th Wisconsin and the 12th Michigan. Moore formed a line near the northwest portion of Seay Field, where he encountered skirmishers from the 8th and 9th Arkansas regiments. Moore soon discovered that a large body of Confederates was advancing toward his tiny force and he reported, "A terrific fire was opened upon us from the whole front of the four or five regiments forming the advance of the enemy." The fighting continued at this location for about half an hour, during which time Colonel Moore was seriously wounded. General Bragg was as surprised as anyone when the firing began, since he knew the Confederates had not yet begun to advance, and reported "the enemy did not give us time to discuss the question of attack, for soon after dawn he commenced a rapid musketry fire on our pickets."[16]

Confederate general William J. Hardee. Wrote manual for infantry tactics used by both sides (Library of Congress).

Over in the Confederate lines most of the men spent an entirely unpleasant night waiting for the dawn. The night had been clear and cold and the only fires that were allowed had to be in holes in the ground to shield the light from Federal pickets. Most of the men slept in the open on the wet ground, but it is doubtful that many of them got much sleep that night. The Confederates had much more reason to lose sleep that night than did the men in the Federal camps if only because they knew what was going to happen in the morning. One of the questions that had to be on the minds of many of the men lying out in the fields that night was how would they react under fire when the attack began. Would they be able to do their duty, even if it meant death or disfigurement, or would their nerve fail them when the time came? Most of the Confederates waiting for the morning had never fired a shot in anger or even been in the army long enough to get accustomed to firing their weapons. Many of the men wrote letters to their loved ones back home and exchanged promises with friends to send those letters and inform the family back home of how their loved one met a gallant death on the battlefield if one of them failed to survive the battle.[17]

In the predawn darkness of April 6 the woods in front of the Federal camps came alive with thousands of Confederate soldiers eating their cold breakfasts, if they had anything to eat, rolling up their damp blankets and any personal items they might be carrying, and checking their weapons before falling in with their units to form up the lines that were about to advance and begin the battle. As the men stood in their ranks in the dark and wet forests many were probably trying to make their peace with their God or thinking of their loved ones back at home and remembering happier times. Less than two miles away many of the Federal soldiers they would soon be trying to kill were still asleep or just beginning to perform their morning chores, blissfully unaware of what was about to befall them.

The final alignment of General Johnston's army had General Hardee's corps in front with Brigadier General Patrick R. Cleburne on the left, Brigadier General Sterling A. M. Wood to the right and Brigadier General Thomas C. Hindman's brigade next to Wood and Brigadier General Adley H. Gladden from General Bragg's corps moving up to fill in the space on the far right. General Bragg's corps was behind Hardee with Brigadier General Daniel Ruggles' division on the left and Brigadier General Jones M. Withers on the right. Ruggles' division contained brigades commanded by Colonel Preston Pond, Jr., Colonel Randall L. Gibson, and Brigadier General Patton Anderson from left to right. General Withers' division was made up of just two brigades, since Gladden had moved up with Brigadier General John K. Jackson to the right of Gibson and Brigadier General James R. Chalmers on the far right of Bragg's line. Behind Hardee and Bragg, Generals Polk and Breckinridge were formed up as a reserve force.[18]

One of General Bragg's staff officers, Captain S. H. Lockett, was out before dawn with a small party scouting the Federal camps. He later wrote that he clearly saw "a large camp as still and silent as the grave; no signs of life except a few smoldering fires of the last night's supper." Riding to a different location, Lockett "found the cooks of the camp astir preparing breakfast. While we were watching the process reveille was sounded, and I saw one or two regiments form by companies, answer to roll-call, and then disperse to their tents."[19]

Continuing his mission, Lockett shortly came upon another campsite where he witnessed "Federal soldiers cleaning their guns and accouterments and getting ready for Sunday morning inspection." It was getting light by this time and the firing from the skirmishing in front of Prentiss' division could be heard, causing some confusion in the camps, "but it was evident that it was not understood. Soon the firing became more rapid and clearer and closer, and I saw officers begin to stir out of their tents, evidently anxious to find out what it all meant. Then couriers began to arrive, and there was great bustle and confusion; the long roll was beaten; there was rapid falling in, and the whole party in front of me was so thoroughly awake and alarmed."[20]

Many of the survivors of the coming battle would remember the lovely spring sunrise. Ira Blanchard of the 20th Illinois later wrote that the morning "opened beautiful. We were astir early, as Sunday was always inspection day and we had to have our arms, clothing and quarters in the best of order." Not far away from Blanchard and his comrades Lot D. Young of Kentucky's Orphan Brigade saw the sunrise as "so beautiful and lovely that all nature seemed proud and happy. Trees budding, flowers blooming, birds singing, everything seemingly joyful and happy in the bright sunshine of early spring." William Preston Johnston believed that his father was also inspired by the lovely spring morning and as he was mounting his horse confidently told the nearby members of his staff, "Tonight we will water our horses in the Tennessee River." Johnston expected a complete victory by the end of the day, culminating in the destruction or capture of the Federal army at Pittsburg Landing. A little later, however, a more reflective Albert Sidney Johnston told Colonel John S. Marmaduke, a staff officer who had been with the general in Utah, "My son, we must this day conquer or perish."[21]

17

A Lovely Day for a Battle

One of General Prentiss' men, Leander Stillwell of the 61st Illinois, remembered that Sunday morning seemed like Sunday morning back home. During the week there had been all the noise made by the men drilling and wagons going back and forth over the narrow country roads, the drivers cursing at their animals, and the usual buzzing of the camps, "But this morning was strangely still.... Suddenly, away off on the right, in the direction of Shiloh church, came a dull, heavy 'Pum!' then another, and still another. Every man sprung to his feet as if struck by an electric shock." The men in Stillwell's unit looked at one another wondering what could be making that noise as the booms came faster and faster. Stillwell remembered that as they were trying to decide what was going on, "just a few seconds after we heard that first dull, ominous growl off to the southwest, came a low, sullen, continuous roar. There was no mistaking that sound. That was not a squad of pickets emptying their guns on being relieved from duty; it was the continuous roll of thousands of muskets, and told us that a battle was on."[1]

As the firing out in front of his division began to increase in volume General Prentiss sent Colonel Peabody's brigade forward to reinforce Colonel Moore. The addition of these reinforcements only served to broaden the front as more and more Federal troops came on line to oppose the advancing Confederates. The advance Federal troops under Peabody fought stubbornly but were gradually driven back by the overwhelming numbers of General Hardee's Confederates commanded by Brigadier General Sterling A. M. Wood, who were advancing across the fields and through the wooded areas. While Peabody was doing his best to delay the advancing enemy General Prentiss had time to form the rest of his division. By making a stand, then pulling back before being overwhelmed, then repeating the process Peabody's men were able to delay the Confederate advance until about 8:00 A.M., when Peabody's men were finally pushed out of Rhea's field and fell back to join the rest of Prentiss' division near the camps.[2]

While Colonel Peabody's troops were fighting their delaying action General Prentiss sent Colonel Madison Miller with the 2nd Brigade out about three hundred yards in front of the camps to the south side of Spain Field with Captain Andrew Hickenlooper's 5th Ohio Light Artillery stationed on the left of the Eastern Corinth road and Captain Emil Munch's 1st Minnesota Light Artillery on the right of the road. Colonel Miller's troops were almost immediately struck by Brigadier General Adley H. Gladden's brigade and part of Brigadier General James R. Chalmers' brigade that had moved up to the front from General Bragg's line. Captain Hickenlooper remembered that the "banshee-like scream of the hurtling shell, the crash of timber, the volleys of musketry and the cheers of the charging

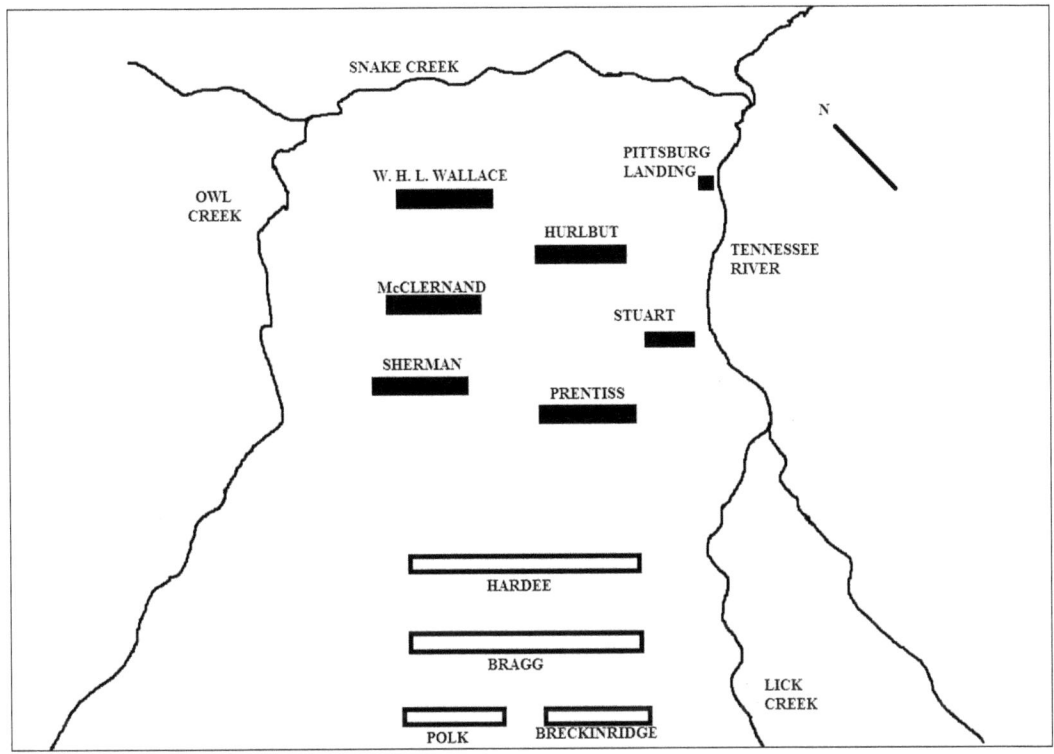

Shiloh — Sunday Morning

regiments, all blended in one mighty rumble and roar." The fighting went back and forth for some time as "several times the enemy essayed to move out from the shelter of the woods across the intervening thickets, but each time our guns — double-shotted with canister — tore great gaps in their ranks and drove them back to cover." Despite the stubborn defense put up by the Federals, the Confederates continued to attack with abandon and after some fierce fighting Miller's troops and the artillery were forced back to the camps where Prentiss had set up his main defensive line. Both Peabody and Miller rejoined the main division lines at about the same time, which was probably fortunate, because Prentiss' line was soon struck by the brigades of Gladden and Colonel R. G. Shaver supported by part of Wood's brigade on the left and on the right by Chalmers' brigade.[3]

Leander Stillwell never forgot his first experience of war. After his regiment took their place in the line they had to just stand there waiting for the approaching enemy. Stillwell and his comrades could see "the blue rings of smoke curling upward among the trees off to the right, and the pungent smell of burning gun-powder filled the air. As the roar came travelling down the line from the right it reminded me (only it was a million times louder) of the sweep of a thunder-shower in summer-time over the hard ground of a stubble-field." Years later Stillwell clearly remembered his thoughts shortly before the firing began in his front: "My mind's eye was fixed on a little log cabin, far away to the north, in the backwoods of western Illinois ... if I only could have been miraculously and instantaneously set down in the yard of that peaceful little home, a thousand miles away from the haunts of fighting men." Also waiting in the Federal line that morning was Charles Morton of the 25th

Missouri, who later wrote that he saw "coming down a gentle slope within easy range the Confederates massed many lines deep." Stillwell later wrote that as they waited "[s]uddenly, obliquely to our right, there was a long, wavy flash of bright light, then another, and another! It was the sunlight shining on gun barrels, and bayonets — and — there they were at last. A long brown line, through the woods they came." When Prentiss' men opened fire Morton saw that "the moving mass was decimated and staggered. Its heavy loss, its very density, prevented a vigorous reply. A heavy fire was poured upon them in their deployment. But soon our men commenced to fall thick and fast. Then we sought the shelter of the trees for we were in heavy oak timber, pretty free from underbrush."[4]

The Confederates came at the advanced divisions of Grant's army like a tidal wave. Although the Federal troops had been given some warning of the attack by the early-morning firing, nothing could have prepared the untrained and inexperienced men for the thousands of enemy soldiers who were now charging toward them. Despite all the delays in leaving Corinth, and the fears of being discovered on Saturday, Albert Sidney Johnston had achieved the surprise that was an integral part of the battle plan. It was not the total surprise of unprepared soldiers that has been written about since the battle, but to the green troops in the two forward Federal divisions the surprise was real enough. While many of the Federal commanders and soldiers were aware that a Confederate attack was possible, few, if any, were prepared for the size and ferocity of the enemy army that now descended upon them. The gap between Prentiss and Sherman allowed the Confederates to hit Prentiss' flank as well as coming in head-on. General Prentiss later reported, "The entire line was under fire, receiving the assault made by the entire force of the enemy advancing in three columns simultaneously upon our left, center, and right." As happened in every division that day, some men would stand and fight and some of the untrained troops would not. On the far left of the division the 61st Illinois briefly held their ground, but soon after the attack began most of the men were heading to the rear, overcome with shock and fear.[5]

This early fighting in front of Prentiss' camp was furious and deadly, with heavy casualties on both sides, including Colonel Peabody and General Gladden. Colonel Francis Quinn, commander of the 12th Michigan, reported that "volley after volley was given and returned and many fell on both sides, but their numbers were too heavy for our forces. I could see to the right and left. They were visible in line, and every hill-top in the rear was covered with them." Leander Stillwell remembered that when the Confederates were in range "we began firing at once. From one end of the regiment to

Union general Benjamin Prentiss. Missouri Republican who ran unsuccessfully for Congress in 1860 (Library of Congress).

the other leaped a sheet of red flame.... We had fired but two or three rounds when, for some reason—I never knew what—we were ordered to fall back across the field and did so. The whole line, so far as I could see to the right, went back. We halted on the other side of the field, in the edge of the woods, in front of our tents, and again began firing." Prentiss held the position in front of the camps for about half an hour when the unsupported flanks began giving way and he was forced to fall back to the campsites before the line was enveloped.[6]

Falling back from tree to tree, disputing every foot of ground, Prentiss' men had no time to form up in a proper line of battle. The men who were still able to fight formed up in small units or fought by themselves, taking cover behind trees and anything else they could find for a little protection. Charles Morton remembered that after falling back from the first line "now we had our camp to defend.... Behind trees in the company streets, and simply tents that screened us from sight, we kept up a constant fire. The enemy could not dislodge us. He dared not charge over the comparatively open ground between us, and for the same reason, as well as because of our disorganized condition and his vastly superior numbers, we could not charge him." To Morton and probably most of Prentiss' men fighting for control of their camps the firing must have seemed to go for hours, but the fighting among the camps lasted only about half an hour. Despite their heavy casualties, the Confederates kept coming, making charge after charge, almost throwing themselves at Prentiss' men until they were attacking over their own dead and wounded who lay all over the field. When enemy troops began coming in on the flanks Prentiss could see that if he didn't fall back the very existence of his division was at risk. About nine o'clock Prentiss pulled out from the camps and withdrew to the reserve area on the left of the division of W. H. L. Wallace. The location that General Prentiss occupied was in the left center of the Federal position. He placed what was left of the division in a wooded area along a sunken road that was a natural entrenchment offering as much protection as any earthworks they could have built. The place that Prentiss occupied between nine and ten o'clock would soon be known as the "Hornet's Nest."[7]

The fighting along the line of Prentiss' division from when his full division first met the main Confederate line to the abandonment of the camps took a little over an hour. There have been many stories of the unpreparedness of the Federal forces and how the Confederate surprise was so complete that Union troops were killed in their tents. While the army as a whole was clearly not prepared for the massive Confederate attack, most of the other stories were just that, stories made up to increase the sensationalism of the accounts of reporters or men who ran away at the first shots trying to divert attention away from themselves. There is little question that when the Confederates hit Prentiss' line at about eight o'clock the regiments in his division were either in line and waiting for the enemy or moving toward the sound of the fighting from the rearmost camp sites. While General Prentiss' division was being engulfed by the Confederate attack on the Federal left early-morning events over in front of General Sherman's division on the right were just as ominous as they had been for Prentiss.[8]

Just as had happened in front of Prentiss' division early that morning, the pickets out in front of General Sherman's division engaged the skirmishers of General Hardee's line as they moved forward through the woods where the strength of the Confederate attack could not be seen or understood. Sherman's division was the most advanced Federal unit on the right positioned to cover the main road to Corinth. Lieutenant Colonel De Hass later wrote that around six o'clock in the morning "we heard dropping shots over the whole of our immediate front and tolerably brisk firing on the left, in the direction of General Prentiss. They had already commenced firing on our pickets, and believed, from the rapid firing on Prentiss' line, that he had been attacked in force." Over in the 48th Ohio the men were having breakfast and noticed that the occasional firing coming from the left was increasing in volume. The Ohioans were ordered to form ranks and during this time, John Bering would later write, "the rattle of musketry and the roar of artillery became almost deafening on our left. In about twenty minutes the pickets in our front commenced firing, which told us the enemy was advancing." When informed of the steadily increasing firing in front of Prentiss' division General Sherman was still not quite convinced that the Confederates were launching an all-out assault but decided it would be wise to be prepared just in case and ordered his troops to form their lines.[9]

General Sherman's defensive lines were formed with Colonel John A. McDowell's brigade on the right with an artillery battery under Captain Frederick Behr on the far right guarding the bridge on the Purdy road over Owl Creek. Colonel Jesse Hildebrand's Third Brigade was posted on the left of the road to Corinth with their right near Shiloh Church. Colonel Ralph P. Buckland's brigade was on the right of the road with its left resting at the meetinghouse. Artillery was placed in several locations to cover as much ground as possible, with one battery commanded by Captain Samuel Barrett posted near Shiloh Church; Captain Allen Waterhouse's battery on a ridge to the left overlooking open ground the Confederates would be crossing with two guns out front in Rhea's field. Most of the 4th Illinois Cavalry were stationed near Shiloh Church. While his troops were forming the lines Sherman sent word back to General McClernand to send forward supporting troops and also to General Hurlbut to support Prentiss. General McClernand acted promptly upon receiving Sherman's request for support and three of his regiments moved up to support Waterhouse's artillery and fill in and extend the line on Sherman's left flank.[10]

Sherman's division was formed up in line of battle a little after seven o'clock and waiting for whatever was going to happen. Sherman was too impatient to just sit and wait, so he rode forward with his staff to investigate the distant firing for himself. About eight o'clock Sherman rode over to the left of his line to Rhea's field to get a good look at the front. They had barely arrived at that location when one of the aides was struck by enemy fire and killed very near the general. It was at this point that, as Sherman later wrote in his *Memoirs*, "I saw the rebel lines of battle in front coming down on us as far as the eye could reach." In his official report Sherman wrote, "I saw the glistening bayonets of heavy masses of infantry to our front in the woods beyond the small stream alluded to, and became satisfied, for the first time, that the enemy designed a determined attack on our whole camp. All the regiments of my division were then in line of battle at their proper posts." Whichever version one cares for, the fact is that William T. Sherman finally believed that the Confederates would attack the Federal army at Pittsburg Landing.[11]

One of the men waiting in Sherman's line for the Confederate attack to begin was Robert H. Flemming of the 77th Ohio, who later wrote about what he saw and felt while standing there as the enemy approached: "The underbrush and timber were pretty well cleared off down as far as the creek in our front, but the large trees were standing. Our pickets were still being driven in, but we could not see anything until our own pickets commenced to emerge from the woods on the far side of the creek. We were crouched down on our knees, with our muskets ready for action as soon as our men came back to the lines and we could see any enemy to shoot at." Flemming experienced his first close call of the day when a musket ball struck the ground right in front of him, showering him with dirt. Not long after this near miss the battle began in earnest: "Finally the enemy's artillery opened, firing over our heads into our camp. The cannon balls commenced cutting the limbs off the trees over our heads, and my particular fear at that time was of being killed by a falling limb. All this time the enemy's artillery was blazing away over our heads, and suddenly the artillery fire trebled in volume, and all the furies of hell broke loose at once could not have made more din."[12]

The first contact with the enemy came on Sherman's left and then the center as the advancing Confederates gradually moved to their left. On the far left of Sherman's line was the 53rd Ohio separated from the rest of Hildebrand's brigade, the 57th and 77th Ohio, by a ravine. With the right of Hardee's line engaged with Prentiss' troops, Cleburne's brigade and part of Wood's struck Hildebrand's and Buckland's brigades and the battle on the Union right was begun.

Confederate general Patrick Cleburne. One of the best Confederate generals, killed at Franklin, Tennessee, in December 1864 (Library of Congress).

Nobody hit the enemy harder than Patrick Cleburne, but his first contact was quickly thrown back. In his official report Cleburne wrote, "Everywhere his musketry and artillery at short range swept the open spaces ... with an iron storm that threatened certain destruction to every living thing that would dare to cross them." One of Cleburne's regiments was the 6th Mississippi and it was on that Sunday morning they earned the nickname "The Bloody Sixth."[13]

Near the center of Cleburne's line was an area of swampy ground that his troops had to go around, with the 6th Mississippi and 23rd Tennessee going to the right and the rest of the brigade to the left, leaving a large gap in Cleburne's lines. As Cleburne's men came up, the Federal lines exploded with fire from artillery and muskets. On the right of Hildebrand's brigade Robert Flemming of the 77th Ohio wrote that as the Confederates came into range "[o]ur fire was too hot for the enemy in our immediate front, and they disappeared from view in the brush beyond the creek. The lull did not last long, however, as they came back with redoubled force, and settled down to that long series of sledgehammer blows, kept up almost incessantly during that long day."[14]

On Cleburne's right the 6th Mississippi and 23rd Tennessee ran into a buzz saw, especially the Mississippians. Earlier that morning as they moved through the woods toward the Federal lines the regiment engaged Sherman's pickets firing at anything that moved. When they finally made their way through the woods and into the light they arrived at Rhea's field, the first regiment of Cleburne's brigade to emerge from the woods. Without waiting for the rest of the brigade the 6th surged forward with their flags waving and hundreds of men shouting the high-pitched rebel yell. Not far behind the Mississippi regiment was the 23rd Tennessee.[15]

Led by Colonel John J. Thornton the 6th Mississippi swept toward the left end of Sherman's line, manned in this area by the 53rd Ohio and Colonel Julius Raith's brigade of General McClernand's division that had come up to fill some of the gap between Sherman and Prentiss. Colonel Raith's brigade was made up of four Illinois regiments, the 17th, 29th, 43rd and 49th supported by Waterhouse's battery. When the Confederates were only about fifty yards from the Federal line both infantry and artillery erupted in a terrific enfilading fire into the Mississippians. Immediately large gaps were torn in Colonel Thornton's line, and the stunned Confederates quickly fell back down the slope to re-form their ranks. In just a few minutes, however, the Confederates advanced again this time being hit with an even more terrible fusillade that all but disintegrated their line, with the survivors ending up in small, disorganized mobs. The ground was covered with dead and wounded Confederates, but the men of the 6th Mississippi rallied and charged again only to be slaughtered again. General Cleburne sadly noted that "under the terrible fire much confusion followed, and a quick and bloody repulse was the consequence." Most of the officers were killed or wounded, including Colonel Thornton, who was wounded, and the losses among the men were horrific; all organization was gone. The survivors fell back to the edge of the woods, done for the day. In less than twenty minutes the 6th Mississippi was all but destroyed. General Cleburne reported that "only when the regiment had lost 300 officers and men killed and wounded, out of an aggregate of 425, ... it yielded and retreated in disorder over its own dead and dying." As if this were not bad enough, almost immediately after what was left of the 6th Mississippi pulled back fresh Confederates took their place and the fighting continued.[16]

One of the regiments that were hit by Cleburne's right was the 53rd Ohio. This was one of the new regiments made up of half-trained men who had never fired a shot in anger or even been in the vicinity of a battle until that Sunday morning. When the attack first began they fired two well-placed volleys, causing severe casualties among the 6th Mississippi especially. But the continued ferocity of the Confederate attacks was apparently too much for their commander Colonel Jesse Appler, who after the second volley shouted to his men, "Fall back and save yourselves." It only took a few minutes for the 53rd Ohio to abandon the front line and head for the rear, although later in the day many of the men returned to the fight at different locations. The defection of the 53rd Ohio left Colonel Raith's troops from McClernand's division defending the left on their own.[17]

Most of General Sherman's regiments, all of whom were new recruits in their first battle, stayed at their posts and fought well. One of Colonel Buckland's men in the 48th Ohio remembered that not long after they took their place in the line on the left of the 72nd Ohio "the rebels, who were not more than a hundred yards distant, opened on our ranks, killing and wounding a number of the regiment at their first fire." Almost simultaneously the Ohioans opened fire, sending a deadly sheet of bullets into the Confederate ranks. Buckland's men "made use of what little shelter the trees and logs afforded, and continued to pour volley after volley into the rebel ranks," but the Confederates continued attacking as more and more came on line. After pulling back from another failed assault the Confederates took cover near the crest of the hill, "returning our fire with that unabating fury that had been thinning our ranks since their first volley."[18]

By about 8:30 A.M. General Cleburne's brigade had been decimated during their continued attacks against the brigades of Hildebrand and Buckland, but they still had plenty of fight left in them. Also about this same time the brigade of Brigadier General Patton Anderson from Bragg's corps had come up and joined the assault on Sherman's lines mostly to the right of the Shiloh meetinghouse against Buckland's brigade. When the 53rd Ohio gave way and fell back out of line the left flank of the 57th Ohio was left exposed. The 23rd Tennessee had been behind the 6th Mississippi on the right of the marsh that split Cleburne's brigade and they had already suffered heavy casualties that morning, but they advanced once more against the left of Sherman's line with the 5th Tennessee and the 15th Arkansas hitting the front and the exposed left of the 57th Ohio. After a brief but violent struggle the Ohioans were also forced to fall back, leaving the left of the 77th Ohio, Hildebrand's last regiment in the line, exposed. Robert Flemming remembered, "This left the left flank of our regiment unprotected, and as a matter of actual fact, the men in the left companies of our regiment had left-faced in their tracks, and were firing at the enemy in the rear of the position first occupied by the Fifty-seventh Ohio."[19]

Not long after nine o'clock Sherman's first line was in serious trouble. Little remained of Hildebrand's brigade on the left and Buckland's brigade was being hit by more and more fresh Confederates as they came up to the fighting line. General Polk's troops were now joining the fighting with Colonel Robert M. Russell's brigade advanced on the right against Sherman's now lightly defended left and Brigadier General Bushrod Johnson led his brigade to the left across the Corinth road to strike the center of Sherman's lines. At about the same time Cleburne and Anderson, having reorganized their remaining troops, joined Russell and Johnson, and this Confederate force would prove to be too much for Sherman's depleted ranks to withstand, although they did not go easily. Among the heavy Confederate casualties were General Johnson and his division commander Brigadier General Charles Clark.[20]

The weak point in the Federal line was on Sherman's left. Only a portion of the 77th Ohio along with what was left of Colonel Raith's troops remained to defend the left flank, not enough men to fight off the overwhelming numbers of fresh Confederate troops who now descended upon them. General Sherman later wrote that the Confederate advance against his left was "so vigorous, and the fire so severe, that when Colonel Raith, of the Forty-third Illinois, received a severe wound and fell from his horse, his regiment and the others manifested disorder." With much of their infantry support gone or greatly diminished, the Federal artillery on the left and center began to suffer from enemy infantry fire. Another Confederate attack led by Colonel Alfred J. Vaughan's 13th Tennessee finally forced the abandonment of the positions on the left. Waterhouse's battery was forced to withdraw shortly, followed by Barrett near the Shiloh meetinghouse. The Confederate infantry continued to press forward against Sherman's remaining troops, and by this time Confederates who had been attacking the right of Prentiss' division, including Wood's brigade, were moving past the left of Sherman's line through the gap between the defenders and threatening to get behind Buckland and McDowell's brigades.[21]

Over on the far right Colonel McDowell's troops had not been engaged with any sizeable enemy force yet, but just as the left of the line was cracking Colonel Preston Pond, commanding one of Bragg's brigades on the far left of the Confederate lines, appeared in McDowell's front, overlapping his right and covering the Owl Creek bridge. Even after the left of his line was turned General Sherman was convinced that the position at Shiloh was so important "that I remained by it and renewed my orders to Colonels McDowell and Buckland to hold their ground." As ten o'clock approached, however, with the Confederates streaming past Sherman's left and Pond's Confederates coming in on the far right Sherman was in very real danger of being flanked on one or both sides. Sherman finally decided that "when the enemy had got his artillery to the rear of our left flank and some change became absolutely necessary" he would order Buckland and McDowell to fall back and form a new line on General McClernand's right near where the Purdy and Hamburg roads crossed the road from Corinth. Although the two front divisions of the Federal army had been forced back, abandoning their camps and suffering heavy casualties, the battle was far from over.[22]

Over on the far left of the Federal position General Sherman's Second Brigade commanded by Colonel David Stuart had been left pretty much on their own with the withdrawal of General Prentiss' troops. The original basic Confederate plan was to push their right along the river to turn the Federal left, cut them off from Pittsburg Landing, forcing them back on Owl Creek, where Grant would be forced to surrender. The stubborn resistance put up by the raw Union soldiers delayed the Confederate move along the river other than two brigades commanded by Generals Chalmers and Jackson from Bragg's corps who made their way to near the mouth of Lick Creek. To meet these two brigades containing nine regiments Colonel Stuart had only three regiments, the 54th and 71st Ohio and the 55th Illinois.[23]

Early in the fighting Colonel Stuart reported that after forming his brigade he rode up to the crest of a hill where he could observe much of the battlefield. What he saw must have been surprising and a little unnerving, as he reported that he saw no Federal soldiers within a quarter of a mile other than "fugitives, making their way to the rear," and that large groups of Confederates were advancing toward his position from two directions. From what Stuart could see, it was obvious to him that "the position of my brigade was inevitably flanked by an overwhelming and unopposed force." Colonel Stuart hurried back to his troops who were already under heavy artillery fire only to find that the 71st Ohio had already fallen back and did not rejoin the brigade. Soon Stuart's other two regiments were engaged with enemy infantry, but he was able to pull them back before being cut off and withdrew to a good position on a hill where the 54th Ohio and 55th Illinois gave a good account of themselves, holding off numerous attacks by Chalmers and Jackson's Confederates and, most important, denying the Confederates access to the Federal left along the river.[24]

18

Fighting and Falling Back

As General Johnston's Confederates were assailing the Federal army at Pittsburg Landing the army's commander was having breakfast at his headquarters at Savannah. General Grant had originally decided to remain at Savannah so he could meet with General Buell as his army came through this area on the way to join Grant's troops. Grant had recently changed his plans, however, and decided to move his headquarters to Pittsburg Landing and take over control of the army in person, primarily because he had learned that John McClernand and Lew Wallace had both been recently promoted to the rank of major general, outranking everyone in the army except Grant himself. This meant that Brigadier General Sherman could no longer be designated as commander of the army when Grant was absent and that one of these new major generals, who were both long on political connections but short on experience in running an army, would be in command of the army when Grant was not on the field, and he was certainly not comfortable with that prospect. Although both men had performed well in their first real battle at Fort Donelson, Grant did not really trust either of them to command the entire army.[1]

The first knowledge anyone at army headquarters in Savannah had that a battle had erupted at Pittsburg Landing was the muffled booming of artillery fire coming from that direction. General Grant and his staff quickly boarded the headquarters ship *Tigress* and headed toward Pittsburg Landing. Just before setting off, Grant sent a quick note to General Nelson, whose division was camped nearby: "An attack having been made on our forces, you will move your entire command to the river opposite Pittsburg." Another message went out to General Buell, who was also in the vicinity although Grant did not know this at the time: "Heavy firing is heard up the river, indicating plainly that an attack has been made upon our most advanced positions. I have been looking for this, but did not believe the attack could be made before Monday or Tuesday. This necessitates me joining the forces up the river instead of meeting you to-day, as I had contemplated." Grant also informed Buell that he had ordered Nelson's division forward toward Pittsburg Landing.[2]

The sound of booming cannon and the rattle of musket fire was first heard in General Nelson's camp at 5:20 A.M., as noted by a staff officer. Shortly thereafter the sounds of battle that were carried through the clean spring air on this beautiful Sunday morning could be heard by troops from Buell's army still several miles from Savannah. General Buell quickly sent out orders to the nearest divisions, those of Generals Crittenden and McCook, to push the men hard toward Savannah, where they could board steamboats for the short trip to Pittsburg Landing.[3]

In Grant's message to Buell he stated that he had "been looking for this," meaning an attack on his troops, which certainly appears to contradict Grant's statement to General Halleck on the fifth that he had no idea a general attack would be made on his position. None of the senior Federal officers involved could say that there had not been enough signs of a Confederate advance toward Pittsburg Landing. Colonel McPherson noted, "It was well known the enemy was approaching our lines, and there had been more or less skirmishing for three days preceding the battle." Yet Grant felt confident that his main force was safe. It is probable that the attack he had been expecting was not against the main portion of the army at Pittsburg Landing but rather against General Lew Wallace's isolated division at Crump's Landing. Grant had even warned General W. H. L. Wallace to be prepared to send reinforcements to Crump's Landing in the event of an enemy attack on that place.[4]

As the *Tigress* made her way up the river the sounds of battle became louder and even more intense. Around 7:30 A.M. Grant's ship pulled up to Crump's Landing next to General Wallace's headquarters boat. Colonel George McGinnis of the 11th Indiana related what he heard as the two generals leaned up against the railings of their respective ships for a quick discussion of the situation. When asked his opinion of the firing Wallace quickly answered, "It's a general engagement." Grant then instructed him to "hold your division in readiness to march on order received." To which Wallace replied, "I am ready now." With Crump's Landing obviously secure Grant continued upriver, arriving at Pittsburg Landing shortly after 8:00 A.M., quickly leaving the steamboat and riding inland to find out what was going on.[5]

Union general Lew Wallace. After mediocre military service would later gain fame as author of novel *Ben-Hur* (Library of Congress).

General Grant and his aides went right to work as soon as they ascended the bluffs above the landing. Considering the severity of the firing and the large number of men engaged, it was clear that one of the first things to do was to begin bringing up more ammunition, and several staff officers went out to organize ammunition trains. Another problem that soon became obvious was the number of men coming back from the front lines, and not just the wounded. Newly arrived troops were put to work in an attempt to stem the flow of men heading toward the river, but this proved to be a waste of effort, as more and more panicked and confused men continued to make their way back from the fighting. Of the five divisions stationed at Pittsburg Landing only General McClernand's division had ever been in combat. The majority of Grant's troops were raw recruits with little or no training and their first experience of battle was one of the most terrible bloodbaths of the entire war. While many people who were not there were later shocked at the number of soldiers who left their units to find safety under the riverbank, it probably should be more surprising that so many more stayed with their units and fought, many to the death.[6]

From reports of subordinates, the constant flow of defeated and discouraged men heading away from the fighting, and what he could see for himself of the fighting it did not take long for Grant to see enough to realize that his army was in real trouble. Once again Grant wrote to General Buell requesting reinforcements be sent up as quickly as possible, saying, "The attack on my forces has been very spirited from early this morning. The appearance of fresh troops in the field now would have a powerful effect, both by inspiring our men and disheartening the enemy. If you will get upon the field, leaving all your baggage on the east bank of the river, it will be more to our advantage, and possible [sic] save the day to us." This was a pretty standard request for reinforcements covering why they were needed and the effect they could have on the battle. The last line of the message, however, shows that General Grant, who would become well known for his calm demeanor in stressful situations, must have been at least a little shaken by the ferocious nature and the size of the Confederate attack: "The rebel forces are estimated at over 100,000 men." During the entire war Grant never overestimated the strength of the enemy he faced as much as he did on this Sunday morning. If he had been his usual calm and rational self he would have realized that General Johnston could not possibly put a force of this size into the field.[7]

Moving around the battlefield with a few aides, Grant visited with his division commanders to get firsthand knowledge of the fighting, and what he learned was not good. This was not a large battle with lines of men firing at each other but rather a series of many small, brutal fights with brigades and regiments slugging it out with one another in open fields and in woods. Since there were no large forces to direct there was little for the army commander to do other than encourage the local commanders and arrange for ammunition and reinforcements to be sent where needed the most. During most of the morning Grant wrote that he was "continuously engaged in passing from one part of the field to another, giving directions to division commanders." Grant met briefly with General Sherman around ten o'clock, but such was his confidence in his subordinate's ability to direct his men in combat that Grant stated that "he never deemed it important to stay long with Sherman." One of the things that Grant learned from his travels around the battlefield was that although the Confederates were just as untrained and inexperienced as his own men, they were fighting as furiously as any men ever did. On the Confederate side William Preston Johnston later wrote, "The fighting was a grapple and a death-struggle all day long, and, as one brigade after another wilted before the deadly fire of the stubborn Federals, still another was pushed into the combat and kept up the fierce assault."[8]

Because of the nature of the terrain the fighting degenerated into a jumble of miniature battles over nearly three miles of woods and fields, hills and ravines where both sides won and lost the same positions over and over. The ground became littered with dead and wounded soldiers and all their accompanying equipment, including broken artillery pieces, caissons, and wagons. Combined with the horrible noises of the screams of the wounded, the constant shrieking of shells and the crack of musket fire made the battlefield probably as close as one could get to hell on earth.

About the same time that General Grant arrived at the scene two brand-new regiments from Iowa, the 15th and 16th, also landed with orders to report to General Prentiss. So new to the army were these men that they did not even have any ammunition for their weapons, receiving their first supply as they were disembarking from the transports. Before they could move out to join Prentiss' men, who had already pushed back from their original positions, the commander of the 15th Iowa, Colonel H. T. Reid, received instructions from a member of Grant's staff to take a position on the bluff above the river "and also to prevent all stragglers from returning from the battle-field to the landing, and to hold ourselves as a reserve." Shortly after they arrived on the bluff both the 15th and 16th Iowa regiments were ordered to leave their positions and, as Colonel Reid remembered, to "advance some two miles, to the support of General McClernand's 1st Division on the extreme right of our lines. The road as we marched was filled with retreating artillery, flying cavalry, straggling infantry, and the wounded returning from the field." Both regiments advanced into heavy firing and "for two hours, from 10 to 12 o'clock, we maintained our position, our men fighting like veterans." Eventually, though, as with so many other Federal regiments that day, the incessant firing and constant Confederate attacks wore the regiments down, and without artillery support the Iowans were in danger of being flanked and cut off as McClernand's line went back and forth with attacks and counterattacks so they had to pull back.[9]

The continuous Confederate attacks made it basically impossible for Federal commanders to build a coordinated defensive line across the battlefield, since the regiments that were holding their positions and stubbornly resisting the furious assaults were frequently being forced to fall back to avoid being flanked and cut off when neighboring units pulled back. For most of the morning that was the story of the battle, with Federal units making a stand and then falling back to make another stand only to be eventually forced from that location also. In addition to losing ground as the casualties grew, each time a unit relocated to make another stand it was made with fewer and fewer men.

By the middle of the morning most of General Sherman's troops had pulled back from their first line. The men on the left had been forced back by the repeated Confederate attacks and Sherman had to pull back the rest of his division to avoid being flanked by the Confederates pouring through gaps in the Federal lines on his left. One of the few units that did not fall back with everyone else was the artillery battery of Captain Samuel E. Barrett. Positioned by the Shiloh meetinghouse, Captain Barrett and his men fought their guns virtually unsupported, stalling the enemy advance in their front. Confederate general Patton Anderson, supported by a section of the Washington Artillery, tried to advance against Barrett's position but was thrown back several times until an assault by troops from different three Confederate brigades was able to dislodge the Federal artillerymen from their position. The Confederates were now in control of Prentiss' and Sherman's first lines of defense, but the fighting was just getting started as General Ruggles noted: "Even after having been driven back from his position the enemy rallied and disputed the ground with remarkable tenacity for some two or three hours against our forces in front and his right flank."[10]

After the initial shock of the massive Confederate attack General Sherman made up for his earlier overconfidence and lack of preparedness. Like virtually all the men under his command, Shiloh was the first major action Sherman had participated in and he handled himself as coolly and calmly as a seasoned veteran. He was all over the field that day encouraging his men as they fought off one Confederate charge after another. When reinforcements came up he was usually there directing them to where they were needed most. And when his men were being pushed back he would rally them to make one more stand. Sherman received two very minor wounds and during the day had three horses shot from under him. But as the Confederates applied more and more pressure Sherman's efforts could only postpone the inevitable, as his rapidly dwindling forces fell back from one position to another.[11]

Behind Sherman's division and to the left was General McClernand's division. McClernand's troops were veterans of the Fort Donelson campaign and were among the best-trained and most dependable men in the army. The sound of the fighting at the front was heard in McClernand's camps well before the men were ordered to form ranks, but there was little concern and no panic. The first news of a serious attack on the front of the army was when a Confederate shell passed over the camp of the 20th Illinois. In the camp of the 18th Illinois in Jones' field the men were in line for Sunday morning inspection when they witnessed men running across the field toward the river. At about the same time as these stragglers appeared McClernand's men received orders to fall in and prepare to move forward.[12]

When Sherman and Prentiss realized they were being attacked in force they both requested reinforcements from the divisions in their rear. Early in the fighting General McClernand sent Colonel Raith's brigade to reinforce Sherman's left and a battery of artillery commanded by Lieutenant George Nispel to assist Colonel Buckland's brigade. McClernand then formed the rest of his division along the Pittsburg road that ran in front of his headquarters, placing the Second Brigade commanded by Colonel C. Carroll Marsh with Captain Jerome Burrows' battery on the right and Colonel Abraham Hare's First Brigade on the left with an open field in his front. Captain Edward McAllister's battery was placed in the northwest corner of that field with another battery commanded by Captain James Timony farther to the right at Water Oaks Pond. When Colonel Raith's brigade fell back from Sherman's line they joined with Marsh's troops on the right. General Hurlbut sent over his Second Brigade commanded by Colonel James C. Veatch to support McClernand's division and they formed up over on the right to support Marsh's brigade.[13]

When General Sherman's two remaining brigades, Buckland's and McDowell's, fell back they stayed on the far right, joining up with the right of McClernand's division about 10:00 A.M. As Sherman's troops were heading backward McClernand's men were moving up to try to form a solid line to stop the still-advancing Confederates. Colonel Marsh reported that just as his men moved into position "the enemy were seen approaching in large force and fine style, column after column moving on us with a steadiness and precision which I had scarcely anticipated."[14]

When they came the Confederates hit General McClernand's lines just as hard as they had struck Sherman and Prentiss a couple of hours earlier. Colonel Marsh reported that just as a battery of artillery was coming to the front to provide additional firepower "the enemy opened on us with a most terrible and deadly fire, unequaled by any which we were under during the subsequent engagement of the day and Monday." One of the men who had to endure that enemy fire was Ira Blanchard of the 20th Illinois, who later recalled that his regiment was positioned to provide support for two artillery batteries and when the enemy came up over a hill they "poured into us a murderous fire.... We gave them the best we had for half an hour, but their fire was telling fearful on our ranks." The Confederate fire was so heavy and accurate that Colonel Marsh stated that "during the first five minutes I lost more in killed and wounded than in all the other actions" his men were involved in during the battle. As Ira Blanchard's unit fell back they passed another line of troops that was briefly holding the Confederates, and hoping to stem the enemy tide at this position their officers "tried to rally the scattered companies again for another stand, but to no avail, as the boys could not be formed under so severe a fire."[15]

As Colonel Hare's brigade moved into position there was already a large formation of Confederate troops lined up across the field. The Confederate line containing troops from both Polk's and Bragg's commands, led by the brigades of Pond and Anderson on their left, came at Sherman and McClernand's troops just as hard as anyone could and the fighting all along the right of the Federal position was deadly for both sides. One of Colonel Veatch's men, Lucius Barber of the 15th Illinois, remembered that once his regiment was in line they had to endure a brief artillery barrage before the Confederate infantry moved forward. Barber later wrote, "The enemy now opened a fire upon us so terrific that our little band seemed likely to be annihilated. Our brave boys were dropping by scores." One of the luckiest men on the battlefield that day, Barber related, "A ball struck the stock of my musket, shivering it and nearly knocking it from my grasp. Another ball passed through my canteen, while another cut the straps to my haversack. Thick as hailstones the bullets whistled through my hair and around my cheek, still I remained unhurt."[16]

The fighting went back and forth as each side launched localized attacks and counterattacks. General McClernand reported that after a successful assault by some of his troops the Confederates came right back and "re-enforced by fresh troops his wavering line was strengthened, and again he commenced turning my right and left, forcing me back." Retreating to a wooded area with an open field in front, McClernand was soon joined by some of Sherman's men and "the contest was again renewed with increased fury on both sides." McClernand also noted that after pushing the enemy back once again, "[w]ithin a radius of 200 yards of my headquarters the ground was almost literally covered with dead bodies, chiefly of the enemy." Not all was blood and terror that morning, as Sergeant Alexander G. Downing of the 11th Iowa wrote in his diary that he had "witnessed a wonderful sight—thickly-flying musket balls, I have never seen hail falling thicker than the minie balls were flying in the air above us."[17]

Despite a most stubborn resistance by individual brigades and regiments, the weight and determination of the Confederate assault gradually forced Sherman and McClernand's men back until they reached the new line being established by Hurlbut and W. H. L. Wallace in the center of the battlefield and formed on the right with McClernand next to Wallace and Sherman extending the line to the right to Owl Creek.[18]

Over on the Federal left General Hurlbut's troops had plenty of time to prepare for the Confederate onslaught. S. D. Thompson of the 3rd Iowa remembered that morning "[a]t about an hour of sun, while we were eating our breakfasts, vollies of musketry were heard in advance, we remarked 'they are skirmishing pretty sharply in front.'" Thompson and his comrades noticed that the firing was growing in volume when "suddenly set in the noise of cannon—jar after jar—quicker and quicker, announcing too truly that the enemy was attacking us in force." Some of the men automatically began to prepare to fall in while others joked and expressed indifference, but Thompson saw through the posing and knew "these manifestations were counterfeits. They lied about the real feelings within. A man may put on the outward appearance of indifference or mirth; but when fortune begins to play freaks with all he has or hopes for, he is seldom mirthful, never indifferent." All over the battlefield that day everyone had to deal with their fears as best they could. Some men could cope with those fears and some could not.[19]

Warren Olney was another Iowan in General Hurlbut's division whose memory of that Sunday morning was still vivid years later: "Our camp was so far back that we heard nothing of this early uproar." Enjoying the fine spring morning, Olney had decided to take a walk down to a creek near his camp when "I had scarcely got out of sight of camp, when the firing toward the front, though faintly heard, seemed too steady to be caused by the pernicious habit which prevailed of the pickets firing off their guns on returning from duty."

Concern, then apprehension and finally alarm were all felt by Olney in just a matter of a few minutes as "presently artillery was heard, and then I turned toward camp, getting more alarmed at every step. When I reached camp a startled look was on every countenance. The musketry firing had become loud and general, and whole batteries of artillery were joining in the dreadful chorus." As the troops were retrieving their weapons, canteens and ammunition boxes the drummers began to beat the long roll to fall in. Olney joined his comrades as "the men, with pale faces, wild eyes, compressed lips, quickly accoutered themselves for battle. The shouts of the officers, the rolling of drums, the hurrying to and fro of the men, the uproar of approaching but unexpected battle, all together produced sensations which cannot be described." It was not long before the men saw wagons with panic-stricken drivers hurling down the road to the landing followed by crowds of men, some wounded and some not, hurrying as quickly as they were able in the same direction. In Olney's camp "uproar and turmoil were all around; but we, having got into line, stood quietly with scarcely a word spoken. Each man was struggling with himself and nerving himself for what bid fair to be a dreadful conflict. What thoughts of home and kindred and all that makes life dear come to one at such a moment."[20]

General Hurlbut quickly led his remaining two brigades, commanded by Colonel Nelson G. Williams and Brigadier General Jacob G. Lauman, and his artillery forward along the Hamburg road. As they came up on the rear and left of Prentiss' second line many of those men were drifting back past Hurlbut's troops with the enemy not far behind. Hurlbut established his line near a peach orchard with Williams' brigade on the south side and Lauman on the west with the right end of his line near the sunken road. The artillery was set up in the field itself. One of Colonel Williams' men, Seymour D. Thompson of the 3rd Iowa, remembered that as they got closer to the front "we met scattered stragglers pouring through the woods." While forming their line Thompson's regiment was on the right of the brigade and "at this time a mass of stragglers hurried pell mell past on our right, whom a field officer was trying to rally." What Thompson saw were the remnants of regiments from Prentiss' right and Sherman's left that had been smashed by the hard-charging Confederates early in the fighting. Thompson and his comrades watched as "[t]hey fled through the woods in panic, like sheep pursued by wolves. Neither commands, threats nor entreaties were of any avail to check them. They had but one thought, to save themselves from the enemy's balls and bayonets."[21]

Once General Hurlbut's troops got their lines arranged they settled in to wait for the Confederates to approach as more and more stragglers in blue uniforms passed their ranks. Soon enough, however, the waiting Federals caught sight of the advancing enemy lines as they came on through Prentiss' abandoned camps. Seymour Thompson remembered that as they waited "the battle rose with great fury to our right. The firing grew into a deafening and incessant roar," but they could do nothing but wait for their turn to endure the same madness. Over in General Lauman's brigade the situation was much the same. As George W. Squier of the 44th Indiana was lying on the ground waiting for the bullets to begin flying he remembered saying a little prayer, "ever kind father preserve me," as he waited anxiously to learn his fate. But like many soldiers, his nervousness disappeared when the firing began and Squier was able to write home after the battle that he was "as cool and composed as if sitting down for a chat or shooting squirrels."[22]

The commander of the 44th Indiana, Colonel Hugh B. Reed, reported that General Lauman's line was formed with the 31st Indiana on the right; then to the left was Reed's regiment, followed by the 25th and 17th Kentucky regiments. Shortly after their skirmishers were forced back, Colonel Reed reported that the 44th and 31st Indiana were "furiously assaulted by the enemy, and as gallantly met, our men behaving in the coolest manner possible, loading and firing with the utmost rapidity; and with so much zeal did they enter in to it, that the officers had only to watch the fight as a matter of interest rather than of duty. The enemy was driven off with immense loss. They again rallied, and charged up to within a few rods of our line, and were again repulsed." The Confederates now changed their angle of attack and struck the two Kentucky regiments on the left, who also opened up a terrific fire. Colonel Reed continued his report saying that "I immediately wheeled two companies of my left wing to the left, and opened upon his flank; his ranks were mown down at each fire, but he still pressed forward; and as bravely was he received. His front rank went down, leaving a line of dead across his front, when he retreated in good order."[23]

General W. H. L. Wallace had hurried forward with two infantry brigades and three batteries of artillery when the fighting first began and took up a position just east of the Duncan field. Colonel James M. Tuttle saw the enemy concentrating in the woods beyond the Duncan field and quickly had his brigade form their line in a wooded area at the edge of the field with his left on an old sunken farm road that curved from the road to Corinth south, then east to the Hamburg–Savannah road. Colonel T. W. Sweeney placed his brigade to the north of the road and the artillery took a position on a ridge behind Tuttle. Wallace's third brigade commanded by Brigadier General John McArthur was split with two regiments guarding the bridge at Snake Creek, one sent to assist Sherman's division, and McArthur and two other regiments posted on the far left of the line. General Wallace's troops were posted almost in the center of the battlefield defending what was the key point of the Federal lines where they waited for the assault that everyone knew was coming. It was at this point that the survivors of General Prentiss' division, probably fewer than one thousand men, took up a position on Wallace's left forming the line that held back the ferocious Confederate attacks until late afternoon.[24]

Not much before ten o'clock General Cheatham was leading a brigade forward on the Confederate right and halted his men in front of the open field owned by farmer Joseph Duncan about three hundred yards wide to survey the area before taking his men out into the open. As he looked out to the front Cheatham could see large numbers of Federal troops taking cover behind a fencerow along an old abandoned sunken road. The roadway was a natural trench line that, along with heavy brush along the fence, provided cover for an excellent defensive position that came to be known as the Hornet's Nest because the men who fought there thought that the buzzing made by the thousands of bullets that were constantly flying through the air sounded like angry hornets. At first Cheatham tried to dislodge the Federal troops with artillery fire, but after about an hour of trading fire with Union artillery the 7th Kentucky and the 6th and 9th Tennessee regiments were sent forward across the open field.[25]

What General Cheatham could not have known was that he was facing a Federal line that stretched nearly half a mile, containing the divisions of Hurlbut on the left, the remains of Prentiss' division in the center, and W. H. L. Wallace's men on the right. General Cheatham's three regiments made it about halfway across the Duncan field when, as Cheatham reported, "another part of the enemy's force, concealed and protected by the fence and thicket to our left, opened a murderous cross-fire upon our lines, which caused my command to halt and return their fire." Cheatham's men advanced no farther and soon they were heading back to their starting point with heavy losses. On the right of Cheatham's line the 6th Tennessee made the best progress through a wooded area but was driven back with the rest of the attackers. General Cheatham tried again with both Tennessee regiments taking advantage of the cover provided by the woods, with the same results. Cheatham just did not have enough manpower to successfully attack the well-protected Union troops. During what was the first of many Confederate attacks against the Hornet's Nest during the day Cheatham's brigade was decimated. The 6th Tennessee alone lost nearly five hundred men in the two assaults. Cheatham pulled his men back to reorganize as other Confederate units came up to continue the attacks.[26]

19

Disaster Approaches

Beginning in the late morning and continuing through the afternoon the Hornet's Nest and peach orchard were the most important positions on the battlefield; they also became the most deadly. For hours the outnumbered men of W. H. L. Wallace, Prentiss' survivors, and Hurlbut's division bravely held back attack after attack by thousands of Confederate soldiers who just as bravely charged the Federal positions time after time, suffering horrendous casualties but always moving forward when ordered. One of General Breckinridge's men who was there was W. J. Worsham of the 19th Tennessee, and he later wrote, "The roar of musketry and artillery, the bursting of shells, and the zip and the whiz of the minnie [sic] balls rendered the scene one that beggars description. We could not drive them by our fire and to charge them seemed like going into the very jaws of death." Another man who advanced on the Federal line was William E. Bevens, a member of the 1st Arkansas in Dan Ruggles' division of Bragg's corps. In his diary Bevens wrote that when his regiment received the first volley from the Union soldiers "[h]ail was nothing to that rain of lead. I looked around and found only four of our company. One was dead, two were wounded and I was as good as dead I thought, for I had no idea I could ever get away."[1]

After General Cheatham's men had been repulsed in the first attack on the Hornet's Nest other Confederate units arrived to continue the assaults. Troops from the brigades of Thomas Hindman, John Bowen, and Cheatham came up to the front and Chalmers and Bowen's brigade advanced against the Federal line but could make no headway against the heavy fire coming out of the center of the position. Colonel John D. Martin took over command of Bowen's brigade after he was wounded and the assault continued unabated. As Martin reported, "They poured upon us a most destructive fire, which we returned with coolness, promptness, and destructive effect," but the Confederates were getting the worst of the carnage and Martin admitted that after many of his officers had been shot and his ranks decimated "at this point we lost about 100 men, and would have been annihilated had not the enemy greatly overshot us." This Confederate attack also made little headway and they eventually began to fall back, being low on ammunition.[2]

Around noon General Bragg had moved over to take command of the Confederate forces to his right after General Polk assumed command in the area to the left of center. Bragg reported that he arrived on the scene shortly after the second failed attack against what would turn out to be "the most obstinate resistance of the day, the enemy being strongly posted, with infantry and artillery, on an eminence immediately behind a dense thicket." Reporting on the failed second assault, Bragg noted that "Hindman's command was gallantly led to the attack, but recoiled under a murderous fire." Hindman was seriously wounded and carried off the field. This was but the start of hours of wasteful attacks on the Hornet's Nest and nearby Federal positions that Bragg set in motion as he noted, "The command soon returned to its work, but was unequal to the heavy task."[3]

Despite the two failed attacks, Bragg continued to launch undermanned piecemeal assaults against the Hornet's Nest. Moving a little to the right, Bragg brought up Colonel Randall Gibson's brigade of Ruggles' division and sent them against the Federal line. General Bragg described what happened in his report as he "threw them forward to attack this same point. A very heavy fire soon opened, and after a short conflict this command fell back in considerable disorder." Colonel Gibson gave a bit more detailed description of the first assault by his troops: "The brigade moved forward in fine style, marching through an open field under a heavy fire and half way up an elevation covered with an almost impenetrable thicket, upon which the enemy was posted. On the left a battery opened that raked our flank, while a steady fire of musketry extended along the entire front. Under this combined fire our line was broken and the troops fell back." William Bevens was a member of Gibson's brigade, and in a diary he wrote that his regiment "went forward into the hottest of the battle where the roar of musketry was incessant, and the cannonading fairly shook the ground. Men fell around us as leaves from the trees." Joseph J. Woods, the colonel of the 12th Iowa, one of Wallace's regiments, reported that the enemy "made a bold attack on us, but met with a warm reception, and soon we repulsed him. Again and again repeatedly did he attack us, trying vainly to drive us from our position. He failed to move us one inch from our position. On the contrary, we repulsed every attack of the enemy and drove him back in confusion."[4]

Confederate general Braxton Bragg. Later commanded Army of Tennessee and was military advisor to Confederate president Jefferson Davis (Library of Congress).

On the left of the Hornet's Nest the Federal line angled backward and crossed the Hamburg–Savannah road, making a sort of L-shaped formation where General Hurlbut's division was defending the ground near the peach orchard. The 44th Indiana had already been in the thick of the fighting at the Hornet's Nest and the regiment's commander, Colonel Hugh B. Reed, reported after they had been moved to their left to support Willard's battery behind General Hurlbut's lines "we were soon charged upon in large force; and here was the most hotly-contested fight of the day, being in an open field, with the exception of a few scattering trees, the enemy far outnumbering us, and fighting with desperate courage, and his fire was fearfully severe; but our officers and men behaved with heroic bravery." Colonel Reed's men were as raw as any of the Federal units and this was their first battle of any kind — certainly none of them had ever witnessed violence on this scale before — but they stood their ground, "never for a moment swerving from their position, pouring in our fire with the coolness of veterans and driving the enemy before them, but again and again with fresh troops they advanced to the charge."[5]

On the far left of the Federal line past where General McArthur's troops were posted Colonel Stuart's brigade was still holding their ground a little in advance of Hurlbut's men at the peach orchard between the left of the Federal line and the river. This was the original route the Confederate attack was supposed to open up so they could cut off the Federal army from the landing and reinforcements or escape. If Stuart was pushed back far enough to break his connection with the rest of the Federal troops on his right the Confederates could swarm in behind the main portions of the Federal line and head straight for Pittsburg Landing unopposed and disaster for Grant's army would follow.[6]

Late in the morning the brigades of Generals Chalmers and Jackson from Withers' division moved over more to the Confederate right to attack Colonel Stuart's position. The Confederates launched a fierce assault on Stuart's outnumbered brigade and forced them back to a new line in a wooded area. With Jackson's Confederates mostly engaged with General McArthur's brigade stationed on the left of the main Federal line, the fighting continued between Stuart and Chalmers. Colonel Stuart reported that when the engagement opened "the enemy's line and ours ... [were] established at a distance of about 150 yards apart. At this point we fought, and held them for upwards of two hours. The enemy's lines were within the edge of a grove, pretty well defended by trees; the space between us was an open, level, and smooth field." By this time Stuart's available force was around eight to nine hundred men in total, but as he wrote, "Inadequate as I knew my force to be, I was encouraged to fight it and hold my position, first with the object of detaining the enemy's forces from advancing toward the river, and secondly because I received a message from General McArthur, who appeared in person somewhere in my vicinity, to hold my position, and that he would support me on my right."[7]

By two o'clock Stuart, who had lost one of his regiments earlier in the day, was just barely holding on to his position with his remaining two regiments, the 55th Illinois and the 54th Ohio. Colonel Stuart had to ask for assistance from McArthur's brigade, who were already engaged with Jackson's Confederates, but the 50th Illinois, commanded by Colonel Moses Bane, shifted to their left to assist Stuart. The Confederates just kept coming at the right of the Federal line and Colonel Bane had barely gotten his men into position when they were hit by a ferocious attack. In just fifteen minutes Bane lost seventy-nine men and had to pull back before his regiment was destroyed. Colonel Stuart continued fighting until his ammunition began to run out and it was time to save as many of his men as possible. Stuart reported, "We had emptied the cartridge boxes of the killed and wounded, and our ammunition was exhausted. Our fire was so slackened from this cause and our losses that I was apprehensive of a forward movement by the enemy, who could easily have overwhelmed us and thrown us into ruinous confusion." After consulting with his regimental commanders around 2:30 to 3:00 P.M. Colonel Stuart was forced to finally abandon his position and fall back. At first he tried to make a stand on a hill to the right, but concentrated enemy artillery fire drove his little force farther back toward the bluffs at Pittsburg Landing.[8]

When Colonel McArthur's position was stuck by Jackson's men he was holding the line with the 9th and 12th Illinois regiments, with the 50th Illinois in reserve. When the 50th fell back from the left by Stuart's position the 9th Illinois stepped up to fill in the line and walked into a hail of gunfire, but McArthur's line held against repeated attacks. After failing to break McArthur's line Jackson halted the attacks momentarily so his units could regroup while he was waiting to be joined by Bowen's brigade from Breckinridge's corps. With the 1st Missouri leading the charge the Confederates hit the left of Hurlbut's line hard. The Illinois troops responded with volley after volley that caused heavy casualties among the attackers, but eventually the strength of the Confederate attack began to tell on McArthur's troops and the 12th Illinois had to fall back. The 9th Illinois was the last to leave their position and got caught in a terrible cross fire, losing more than half of the regiment before they were able to pull back.[9]

General Johnston deemed this area of the battlefield to be so important to the overall success of the attack that shortly after noon he decided to take personal command of the right side of the army. Johnston wanted to break through the area defended by Stuart and McArthur, so after Chalmers and Jackson had been repulsed earlier Johnston sent Bowen's brigade to support Jackson and almost immediately after the brigades of Colonel Winfield Statham and General Adley Gladden launched an attack on the peach orchard. When Colonel Stuart finally fell back he exposed the left flank of McArthur's troops, forcing him to fall back to the north side of the peach orchard. As the Federal left was realigned Lauman's brigade moved over to the left of Hurlbut's division supporting McArthur's troops. Hurlbut moved Williams' brigade to the edge of the peach orchard, and a little after two o'clock the Confederates launched one of the most savage attacks of the day. One of Williams' regiments that met this attack was the 3rd Iowa, and Warren Olney later wrote that although heavy fighting had been taking place on both the right and left his regiment had been left undisturbed until about two o'clock. "Then there came from the woods on the other side of the field, to the edge of it, and then came trotting across it, as fine looking a body of men as I ever expect to see under arms." Soon the Confederate line moved forward across the open field until they were within range of the smoothbore muskets that Olney's regiment was armed with. "Then we rose with a volley right in their faces. Of course, the smoke then entirely obscured the vision, but with eager, bloodthirsty energy, we loaded and fired our muskets at the top of our speed, aiming low, until, from not noticing any return fire, the word passed along from man to man to stop firing." As the smoke cleared in front of their line Olney and his comrades were presented with an awful sight. "They seemed to be piled up on each other in a long row across the field. Probably the obscurity caused by the smoke, as well as the slight slope of the ground towards us, accounted for this piled up appearance, for it was something which could not possibly occur. But the slaughter had been fearful." Here and there a few men could be seen trying to run out of range and occasionally a man who had been lying flat on the ground would get up and try to run, but he would soon be back on the ground, either hit or taking cover from the shots that were sent at him. Olney noted that, "our old fashioned guns, loaded as they were, and at such close quarters, had done fearful execution."[10]

Seymour Thompson of the 3rd Iowa commented on what he witnessed near the peach orchard as the Federal line was attacked again and again, "The fierce yell of the enemy mingled with the increasing din of musketry announced the approach of his assailing columns. The discharge of our artillery could scarcely be heard. Dense clouds of smoke lifted themselves above the combatants.... Suddenly the firing ceased, and a wild shout of triumph caught up by listening comrades, borne far along the line, announced that the assault had been repulsed." The celebration did not last long, however, because the Confederates soon renewed the assault with the same violence as before, and with the same result. For three hours General Bragg virtually threw his men against the Federal lines at the Hornet's Nest and the peach orchard. Out in front of the Federal lines the brush and small trees were cut down as if swept by a gigantic scythe. Thompson said, "Nowhere on all the field of battle did the storm rage so fiercely. Nowhere did the enemy assail and renew the assault with such rage, and nowhere did our troops fight with such inspiring valor."[11]

None of the Federal troops, and only a few Confederates, were aware of it, but a little after two o'clock General Johnston was struck in the leg by a minié ball as he encouraged his men during one of the assaults on McArthur's front. Johnston did not say anything to draw attention to himself, but staff officers saw the army's commander reeling in his saddle as he weakened from loss of blood. Johnston was taken out of the line of fire into a nearby wood where members of his staff helped lower him to the ground and tried to find the wound so he could be treated. The general had been shot in the right leg just below the knee and the bullet had severed an artery. The aides could not find the wound at first, possibly because it was covered by the general's boot. It probably would not have mattered much if they had found the wound, since there was no doctor on the staff to attend to such a serious injury.[12]

Johnston was already unconscious when he was placed on the ground, and repeated attempts to revive him with brandy and other methods by staff members and the general's brother-in-law, Colonel William Preston, proved futile. Albert Sidney Johnston bled to death in just a couple of minutes from a relatively minor leg wound. Not wanting to believe what they had just witnessed, several stunned members of Johnston's staff wrapped him in a blanket to hide his identity and transported the general to the headquarters of General Beauregard, the new commander of the army. Since the death of the army commander could have a devastating effect on troops who were currently engaged in some of the most desperate fighting of the day, Beauregard's first order as commander of the army was to conceal Johnston's death from the troops.[13]

Long after the outcome of the war had been decided there was still some argument about whether or not General Johnston should have been up in the front ranks during the fighting. Normally the commander of an army kept to the rear so he could safely get an overview of the entire battle and make decisions on troop placement and seeing that everything was moving along according to the battle plan. Trying to manage a battle with so many troops involved over so large an area with the constant movement of the lines was a new experience for both Grant and Johnston, and both men spent most of their time out in the field rather than back at their headquarters, although each took a different approach as to how he ran his army. Grant on the one hand, mostly made the rounds of the various commands, meeting with his division commanders, encouraging them to continue fighting and working to get ammunition and reinforcements where they were needed. Johnston, on the other hand, felt it was important for the men to see him in action, leading the way to bolster their morale and confidence. General Beauregard would write that Johnston was "uselessly exposing his person. From where he was, he could not — nor in fact did he ever attempt to — direct the general movements of our forces." While it might be admirable for the commanding general to demonstrate to his men that he was willing to share the same dangers that he was ordering them to face, Johnston's death would have serious consequences for the Confederate army as the battle continued.[14]

Throughout the late morning and into early afternoon the fighting continued all along the Union lines. There would be an occasional lull here and there as units were moved around or ran out of ammunition and had to fall back to be resupplied, but these breaks in the action seldom lasted for any length of time and soon the unit would be back on the front line and the killing would begin again. After repeated attacks on the Federal left, the Hornet's Nest and peach orchard were still in Union hands. Over on the right, however, the divisions of Generals Sherman and McClernand, who had also been engaged in fierce back-and-forth fighting all day, had been gradually pushed back by the continuous Confederate attacks. Ira Blanchard's 20th Illinois had already tried to make a stand at several positions only to fall back each time the rest of McClernand's division was forced back by the frequent enemy attacks. Blanchard later wrote, "Our guns became hot from constant firing. Ammunition had to be brought up from the rear. The ground was covered with the dead and dying. Twas a horrid sight."[15]

The situation along the front lines was little better for the Confederates as they practically flung themselves at the Federal lines in near-suicidal attacks. John Jackman wrote in his diary about how he and his comrades in Kentucky's Orphan Brigade were in the thick of the fighting for much of the day, "Occasionally there would be a lull for a short time; but the cannon were never entirely hushed. They would break out in increased thunder, and the roar of musketry would roll up and down the lines, vibrating almost regularly from one extreme to the other."[16]

By early afternoon the fighting on the Union right was continuing just as fiercely as it had been throughout the morning, even though General Bragg had begun to shift some Confederate units to their right in order to put more pressure on the stubborn Federal defenders in the Hornet's Nest and peach orchard areas. General McClernand reported on the various smaller battles that occurred within the larger scope of the overall fighting, noting that the 11th and 12th Illinois and the 11th Iowa "charged a hostile battery and took it, killing all the artillery horses." Another attack was led by three of his brigade commanders who as they advanced, "heedless of the danger, led their men to the charge amid a storm of bullets and in the face of a battery." McClernand wrote that the engagement continued unabated until "several regiments of my division had exhausted their ammunition and its right flank had been borne back, and it was in danger of being turned, the remainder of my command, with the exception hereafter noticed, also fell back to the camp of the First Brigade." The exception McClernand noted was the 45th Illinois that was holding the enemy off as the other regiments fell back and "only escaped being surrounded and captured by boldly cutting their way through the closing circle of the enemy's lines."[17]

It was around two o'clock in the afternoon when General McClernand formed this defensive position that he called the fifth individual position his troops occupied so far during the battle. With Confederate artillery already firing on this new line McClernand brought forward Captain McAllister's battery and prepared to meet another assault. When the Confederate attack began they were halted by the heavy grape and canister fire from McClernand's artillery until, as he reported, "Deterred from direct advance, he moved a considerable force by the right flank, with the evident intention of turning my left. To defeat this purpose I ordered my command to fall back on the east side of another field in the skirts of a wood. This was my sixth line." Once again Federal troops could not hold a line because the Confederates were able to find room on the flanks to maneuver them out of position without resorting to a bloody frontal assault.[18]

General Sherman reported that late in the morning he had sent Colonel McDowell's troops against the left of the advancing Confederates, pushing them back momentarily, "and then directed the men to avail themselves of every cover — trees, fallen timber, and a wooded valley to our right. We held this position for four long hours, sometimes gaining and at other times losing ground, General McClernand and myself acting in perfect concert and struggling to maintain this line. Colonel McDowell, whose brigade had been little involved in the early fighting and had fallen back with the remainder of the division and now occupied the right of Sherman's line, reported that "about 12:30 o'clock, the enemy, finding no opposition on the right, brought a large force to our right and fronting our flank, causing us to suffer a cross-fire from superior numbers both on the front and flank. It was here that the brigade suffered its greatest loss." McDowell's 40th Illinois had been ordered out to the front to support a battery of artillery, and during this fight they advanced "against the enemy's battery so far as to become entirely separated from the rest of the command" and lost heavily before they were able to make their way back to the main lines.[19]

Another of General Sherman's officers who reported on the various moves his men made during the day was Colonel Joseph Cockerill, commander of the 72nd Ohio. He reported that around noon his men were formed along the Purdy road as instructed, "but so many retiring troops mingled with us we became much broken and separated. I retired about 400 yards by the right flank, and finding the rebels advancing almost parallel with us, we opened fire, which did good service." Shortly after noon Colonel Cockerill joined several other regiments from Sherman's division and "advanced to the northeast across the open fields and into the fire then raging in McClernand's camp." The enemy fire at this point was very heavy, and after a brief contest "[a]ll the troops were forced back to the end of the camp under this tremendous fire, and the loss on both sides must have been heavy. We were compelled to fall back, and I again formed line on the top of the next ridge." Once more the Federal troops tried to put up a fight, stood their ground momentarily, but were again pushed back.[20]

As Sunday gradually slipped into the afternoon the level of fighting and killing all across the battlefield showed no signs of ending or even slowing down a little. Despite mounting losses and Stuart's withdrawal on the left flank, Generals Prentiss, W. H. L. Wallace, and Hurlbut were able to hold most of their positions against a series of ferocious Confederate attacks and the Hornet's Nest and peach orchard were still firmly under Federal control. But how much longer the weary Union soldiers would be able to continue to repel the determined enemy was the question on many minds that afternoon. Over to the right of the Federal lines Generals Sherman and McClernand continued fighting, holding one position against a fierce attack, then launching their own counterattack pushing the Confederates back. Seemingly within minutes, however, General Polk would send forward Pond or Anderson or Wood's brigades again and the relatively few men whom Sherman or McClernand had been able to send forward would either be overpowered or end up with the enemy moving toward their flank and forcing the Union troops to pull back or risk being cut off from the rest of the line. But no matter how hard they defended a position or how many counterattacks they launched, Sherman and McClernand were gradually losing ground and being pushed back toward the Tennessee River.[21]

20

Slaughter in the Afternoon

By mid-afternoon the Confederates began devoting more and more of their forces to breaking the center of the Federal line around the Hornet's Nest and peach orchard positions. Regiments and even brigades were transferred from the front facing Generals Sherman and McClernand to the Confederate right, although by no means did the fighting on the Federal right end. By four o'clock the Federal lines on the right had become unsustainable and both Sherman and McClernand determined to fall back and establish new lines to the north. General McClernand reported that the enemy continued to try to turn his flanks and cut him off from the landing. "To prevent this I ordered my left wing to fall back a short distance and form an obtuse angle with the center, opposing a double front to the enemy's approach. Thus disposed, my left held the enemy in check, while my whole line slowly fell back." McClernand formed his battered troops into another line on good ground with portions of Sherman's division on the right and the 15th and 46th Illinois commanded by Colonel Veatch on the left. Bringing up a few artillery batteries for support, McClernand awaited the next enemy assault, and he did not have long to wait. General Hardee sent Colonel Pond's brigade supported by cavalry commanded by Colonel John A. Wharton against McClernand's line. After a short but heavy artillery barrage, the Confederates came on again. This time, however, as McClernand noted, they changed tactics from flank assaults to a head-on attack on the center of his line: "Advancing in heavy columns led by the Louisiana Zouaves, to break our center, we awaited his approach within sure range, and opened a terrific fire upon him. The head of the column was instantly mowed down; the remainder of it swayed to and fro for a few seconds, and turned and fled." It was now about 4:30 P.M. and this turned out to be the last major fight for McClernand's division. Unfortunately, toward the end of the engagement McClernand learned that "the left, comprising the Fifteenth and Forty-sixth Illinois, was irresistibly swept back by the tide of fugitive soldiers and trains seeking vain security at the landing." These troops falling back created an opening to the right of General W. H. L. Wallace's division defending the Hornet's Nest position.[1]

After this last fight General McClernand was able to re-form his remaining troops with "the right resting near the former line and the left at an acute angle with it. A more extended line, comprising portions of regiments, brigades, and divisions, was soon after formed on this nucleus by the efforts of General Sherman, myself, and other officers. Here, in the eighth position occupied by my division during the day, we rested in line of battle upon our arms." General Sherman reported that late in the afternoon, once he and McClernand learned that General Hurlbut had been pushed back and "knowing that General

Wallace was coming from Crump's Landing with re-enforcements, General McClernand and I, on consultation, selected a new line of defense, with its right covering the bridge by which General Wallace had to approach. We fell back as well as we could, gathering, in addition to our own, such scattered forces as we could find, and formed a new line." This position ran along the Savannah Road, with a view to guarding the bridge by which General Lew Wallace was still expected to join the main army. Once the fighting ended, with Perry Field in front of them and the Savannah Road in their rear, the surviving Federal soldiers kept the Confederates at a respectful distance during the closing hour of the day.[2]

During most of the afternoon General Grant was moving around the battlefield consulting with his commanders and trying to put together some kind of cohesive defense, which proved to be difficult, if not impossible, considering the constantly changing positions of his units. The last time Grant met with General Prentiss that afternoon much of the original Hornet's Nest and peach orchard position had been lost, as the constant Confederate attacks had gradually forced the defenders back on both flanks. At this point in the battle what was left was mostly a salient jutting out from the rest of the Union lines. There was nothing Grant could do to help and little he could say to Prentiss other than to emphasize how important it was to hold the position as long as possible. No doubt both men knew full well that the remaining troops still manning the Hornet's Nest lines were going to be sacrificed so that the rest of the army had time to fall back and regroup at a new defensive position on high ground just in front of the landing.[3]

Among the many Confederate officers who had led their brigades in attacking the Hornet's Nest were Colonel Gibson and Colonel R. G. Shaver of Hindman's division. In their reports these men give a description of what happened to the vast majority of the Confederates assaulting this area of the Federal line defended by W. H. L. Wallace and the remnants of Prentiss' division throughout most of the day. Colonel Shaver launched his brigade against Wallace's position at some time after two o'clock, reporting, "I pressed forward, the enemy remaining close and quiet until my left was within about 50 and my right within about 60 yards from their lines (a dense undergrowth intervening), when a terrific and murderous fire was poured in upon me from their lines and battery. It was impossible to charge through the dense undergrowth, and I soon discovered my fire was having no effect on the enemy, so I had nothing left me but to retire or have my men all shot down." General Bragg had repeatedly sent Gibson's men against the Federal line but only succeeded in getting them slaughtered. Gibson reported that after the first failed assault his men "[s]oon rallied and advanced to the contest. Four times the position was charged and four times the assault proved unavailing. The strong and almost inaccessible position of the enemy — his infantry well covered in ambush and his artillery skillfully posted and efficiently served — was found to be impregnable to infantry alone."[4]

General Cheatham decided to launch another assault about 2:30 P.M., when he instructed Colonel George Maney to take several regiments of his own choosing and attack the center of the Hornet's Nest line. Maney lined up his own 1st Tennessee Battalion on the left with the 9th Tennessee in the center and the 19th Tennessee on the right with the 6th and 7th Kentucky regiments providing support for the attacking troops. Moving forward across an open field, the men of the 19th Tennessee could see troops from an earlier attack by General Breckinridge's men on the left side of the position they were heading for. As the Tennesseans continued moving forward they encountered troops from Colonel Zacariah Deas' Alabama brigade from General Jones Withers' division falling back from their failed attempt to pierce the Federal line. As Maney's line approached the Federal line heavy firing began tearing through their ranks. The Confederates were able to continue advancing until they came to a wooded area west of a cornfield close by the sunken road where they were able to find some protection from the relentless hail of bullets and began exchanging fire with Prentiss and Wallace's troops. Once his men found cover Maney was able to return the 19th Tennessee to Colonel Stratham's brigade.[5]

Colonel Gibson was not the only Confederate officer who finally realized that they were losing hundreds of men and accomplishing nothing in these futile attacks. After the death of General Johnston and General Beauregard's assuming command of the army several changes in commanders and their area of responsibility were made, probably the most significant change being that General Bragg, who had all but destroyed several brigades in his series of attacks against the Hornet's Nest, took over the command of the Confederate far right and Brigadier General Daniel Ruggles took over command in the center, opposite the Hornet's Nest. General Ruggles had seen firsthand the pointless and wasteful attacks on the Federal position. He knew full well how important it was to break the Federal line, but he was also aware of the obvious difficulty in taking the position with infantry alone.[6]

Confederate general Benjamin Frank Cheatham. Division and corps commander with Army of Tennessee till near end of war (Library of Congress).

Sometime after three o'clock Ruggles and General Beauregard sent most of their staff officers out to collect as much artillery as they could find. Fanning out across the battlefield, they gathered batteries, sections, and individual artillery pieces from wherever they could find them. It took almost an hour to amass all the artillery they sent to the right, but now Ruggles was able to bring up about sixty guns, most of which were positioned on the west side of the Duncan field about five hundred yards from the Federal lines. Between four and four thirty the Confederate artillery began a concentrated bombardment against the Federal troops of Wallace and Prentiss who were still manning the Hornet's Nest lines. One of General Polk's artillery commanders, Captain Smith P. Bankhead, later wrote, "The effect of this tremendous concentrated fire was very evident. The reserves, which could be plainly seen going up to Prentice's relief, fell back in confusion under the shower of shot, shell and canister that was poured upon them." The Confederate barrage, which was the largest concentration of field artillery assembled on any North American battlefield up to that time, only lasted about thirty to forty-five minutes, but the havoc it caused achieved the desired results. Most of the Federal artillery that were still supporting the Hornet's Nest lines were driven off and some of the Federal infantry that had been battered by the constant enemy attacks for hours and were now being subjected to the heaviest artillery bombardment to date could see that the end was in sight and began heading to the rear.[7]

Also a little after four o'clock the Confederates launched another attack, with General

Breckinridge sending Stratham's and Bowen's brigades supported by two of Bragg's brigades against the left flank of the now-shrinking Hornet's Nest. The Federal troops on that side of the line received the attacking enemy in the same fashion as they had been for hours, with heavy fire as the yelling Confederates crashed into the Federal line. Smoke lay thick on the heavily wooded terrain and there was confusion everywhere. It was impossible for the brigade commanders to retain command and control functions over their troops. Regiments and even companies fought their own separate little battles with men rushing forward only to be stopped momentarily by enemy fire, then letting loose their own volley and running forward again.[8]

Late in the afternoon on the Federal left near where the line curved toward the river Seymour Thompson was waiting in line with his comrades in the 3rd Iowa of General Hurlbut's division. As the Confederates were preparing yet another assault, Thompson saw "[t]he enemy's infantry in a column of several lines moved to the attack. From our position we could see the immense mass sweeping through the half open woods. The spectacle charmed even the dread it occasioned." While the Confederate infantry was getting ready to move forward the artillery gathered by General Ruggles began to pound the Union positions to soften them up for what Ruggles hoped would be the final assault. Thompson remembered, "Everywhere around us the storm began to rage; shot, shell, grape, canister came howling and whistling through our lines. The very trees seemed to protest against it. Missiles flew everywhere. Lying on our faces we could not escape them." Federal artillery tried to reply, but compared to the Confederate fire they could only put forth a feeble response as horses and men were killed and wounded and guns put out of action under the massive barrage. When the Confederate infantry moved forward they were to the right of the Iowans, and Thompson later wrote, "It is impossible to depict this hour of conflict. All the noises of battle commingled rose in a bewildering roar, and above all we could hear the cries of the combatants as they joined, and the shouts of multitudes announcing a successful or an unsuccessful charge; for we knew not whether these voices were of friends or foes. It was a swift, anxious hour."[9]

By 4:30 P.M. it was obvious that the men of the 3rd Iowa, along with the rest of Hurlbut's troops, were in trouble when enemy troops began coming in from the left of Hurlbut's line. Thompson watched as "[r]egiment after regiment was successively broken from extreme left to right. An enfilading battery opened upon us with canister. Their cartridges exhausted in opposing the flanking fire, and mowed down by the enfilading canister, our troops began to retreat in disorder through the woods." As the men toward the right of Hurlbut's line tried to hold on to their positions a little longer the situation rapidly deteriorated: "Above us the hissing and screaming of missiles; around us the roar of battle rising louder and louder; assailed in front and flank; the enemy to the left crowding our fugitive troops and pressing furiously on our rear; the troops to our right swept back." Under the artillery barrage put together by General Ruggles and the pressure of the infantry attack organized by General Bragg the Federal line on the left finally started to crumble as General Hurlbut's troops began to give way.[10]

General Hurlbut's men fell back and tried to make a stand with the remnants of General Prentiss' troops on their right in an effort to hold the advancing Confederates back long enough for the main portion of the army to form another defensive line. By this time the once impressive battle lines of the attacking Confederates had degenerated into a mass of men charging against the various small Federal units who were taking advantage of the broken terrain to find cover wherever they could. Thompson recalled that, "we no longer had lines of battle, but fought in squads and clusters. The settling smoke obscured the vision. Comrades knew not who stood or fell. All was confusion and chaos around us." Soon another enemy attack separated Hurlbut from Prentiss, and shortly after Confederate troops began closing in on their rear. As Hurlbut's troops continued to fall back, occasionally halting to fire at the pressing enemy, they eventually came to their camps where enemy troops were closing in from different directions. Thompson saw that "[i]n a few moments he would be full in our rear. It was no time to hesitate now. We must run the gauntlet he had prepared for us or be captured. We preferred to take the chances and run." Confederate troops came up in the rear of Hurlbut's fleeing men, forcing them to run for their lives with enemy fire coming in on the flank before the escape route was closed. One of the men who went through that terrifying experience was Warren Olney, who later wrote, "I see the enemy close in on the flank, pouring in their fire at short range. I see our men running for their lives, men every instant tumbling forward limp on their faces, men falling wounded and rolling on the ground, the bullets raising little puffs of dust on apparently every foot of ground, a bullet through my hair, a bullet through my trousers. I hear the cruel *iz, iz,* of the minie balls everywhere." Seymour Thompson also remembered those frightening minutes, "Between these two fires we were completely exposed and suffered our greatest loss. At no time had we been exposed to so thick a fire. More of our men fell within the lines of our own regimental camp than anywhere else upon the field."[11]

Near the center of the position the 61st Illinois of Prentiss' division had been assigned to support a battery of field artillery, and one of the regiment's members, Leander Stillwell, remembered, "Somewhere between 4 and 5 o'clock, as near as I can tell, everything became ominously quiet." About that same time a staff officer met with the battery commander and the regiment's commander, after which the battery limbered up and headed through the woods to the left and rear with the 61st following. Other Federal troops could be seen heading in the same direction and it was quite obvious that they were falling back. Stillwell wrote, "All at once, on the right, the left, and our recent front, came one tremendous roar, and the bullets fell like hail. The lines took the double-quick towards the rear. For awhile the attempt was made to fall back in order, and then everything went to pieces." The narrow road to the landing was crowded with men and guns, wagons and ambulances and all the debris of a beaten army, all the while a storm of lead hail was coming down on them from the rear. Warren Olney remembered that after escaping from the Hornet's Nest enemy troops closed in just behind him and General Prentiss and the remainder of his troops were trapped. "As we passed out of range of the enemy's fire we mingled with the masses of troops scurrying towards the landing, all semblance of organization lost. It was a great crowd of beaten troops. Pell-mell we rushed towards the landing."[12]

After General Hurlbut fell back General Prentiss reported that he and General Wallace "[c]onsulted and agreed to hold our positions at all hazards, believing that we could thus save the army from destruction; we having been now informed for the first time that all the others had fallen back to the vicinity of the river." Not long afterward the withdrawal of General McClernand exposed the right flank of Colonel Sweeny's brigade on the right of Wallace's line and soon Confederate brigades commanded by Colonels Russell and Robert Trabue along with other units, who had been facing McClernand's line, wheeled to their right and advanced against the open right flank of Sweeny's brigade. Soon most of Sweeny's men were streaming back under heavy Confederate attacks. With Sweeny's line dissolving, the door was open for General Ruggles to penetrate to the rear of the Hornet's Nest position.

Colonel Tuttle was able to keep his line together, at least for a little longer, but it was only a matter of time before they would also be overwhelmed. General Prentiss could see that he was about to be attacked from different directions and cut off from the landing and reported that "I found him advancing in mass, completely encircling my command, and nothing was left but to harass him and retard his progress so long as might be possible. This I did until 5:30 P.M., when finding that further resistance must result in the slaughter of every man in the command, I had to yield the fight." Prentiss estimated that he surrendered about twenty-two hundred men.[13]

Seeing the other Federal units withdrawing and leaving his flanks exposed, General Wallace sent out orders for his men to fall back, but before they all could escape the collapsing position he was mortally wounded, and he died a few days later. At his side was his wife, who had come down to the army for a visit. Colonel Sweeny was able to get most of his men away, but only part of Colonel Tuttle's brigade was able to escape, as Tuttle reported that "the Twelfth and Fourteenth, who were delayed by their endeavors to save a battery which had been placed in their rear, were completely cut off and surrounded and were compelled to surrender."[14]

The cost in lives and time to the Confederates was way out of proportion to what they won at the Hornet's Nest and peach orchard positions. The constant attacks had left the fields and woods full of dead and wounded Southerners. Even General Grant, who would soon become accustomed to seeing fields full of slain soldiers, was impressed with the carnage and wrote in his *Memoirs*, "I saw an open field in our possession the second day, over which the Confederates had made repeated charges the day before, so covered with dead that it would have been possible to walk across the clearing, in any direction, stepping on dead bodies without a foot touching the ground. On our side National and Confederate troops were mingled together in about equal proportions; but on the remainder of the field nearly all were Confederate." Another location that grew in legend after the battle was the "Bloody Pond." Located pretty much behind the peach orchard to the left of the center of the line, this was basically a shallow pool of water where many of the wounded from both sides quenched their thirst during and shortly after the battle. During the day so many men approached the pond that the water turned red from the blood that fell into the water.[15]

The capture of the Hornet's Nest ended the last major fighting for the day. It is generally accepted that the courageous stand of the men who defended that line saved the remainder of Grant's army from destruction or surrender. With the Confederates concentrating so much of their strength against this one position, Sherman and McClernand, while they still faced some heavy fighting, were not pressed nearly as severely as they might have been and they had time to begin forming the last line of defense near the river. And it was toward the river and that new line that troops converged from all parts of the battlefield. One of those men was Seymour Thompson, who wrote, "Here the troops were crowded together in disorderly masses. Men were separated from their colors, and mixed in extricable confusion. There were no longer any regiments, brigades or division. All was an immense mob — a great rout, halting because it could retreat no further.... Men looked blankly into each other's countenances, and read only their own dismay."[16]

Recognizing the fact that his troops would probably be pushed farther back by the ferocious Confederates during the late afternoon, Grant had instructed his chief of staff, Colonel Joseph Webster, to build up a last-ditch defensive position to protect the landing. Webster found a good position along the crest of some hills about five hundred yards from the river, where he began gathering artillery that was coming back from the front lines. The semicircular line began at the mouth of Dill Branch on the left. From the river the new Union front extended a mile and a half west-northwest to the Savannah–Hamburg (River) road on the right, where the line overlooked and defended the flooded confluence of Owl and Snake Creeks. Eventually Webster managed to put together a powerful line of artillery consisting of over fifty guns, including Madison's Illinois battery of five 24-pounder heavy siege cannon. As the troops from the left drifted back toward the landing, General Hurlbut's men were placed on the right of the artillery formation and Colonel Stuart's survivors filled in on the left of the artillery. The remnants of General W. H. L. Wallace's division and any other detached units that were able to man the lines to continue the fight were positioned behind and to the left of Hurlbut's men, connecting the line to General McClernand's troops to the right, with Sherman's men defending the far right. It was imperative to keep control of the Savannah–Hamburg or River Road and the bridge over Snake Creek, since this was the route that General Lew Wallace was supposed to use to join the rest of the army. Out in the river the gunboats *Lexington* and *Tyler* were on patrol along the left of the newly formed Federal line, ready to add the firepower of their heavy guns to Colonel Webster's artillery. To even get close to the landing any further Confederate assault would have to overcome massed artillery fire and Federal troops who knew that whatever the outcome, the next fight would be the last of the day and they had nowhere else to retreat to.[17]

21

Grant Hangs On

While General Grant's troops were fighting for their lives in front of Pittsburg Landing across the Tennessee River in and around Savannah, thousands of Federal soldiers from General Buell's army were waiting for transportation to the battlefield. One of General Crittenden's men was William R. Hartpence of the 51st Indiana, who later remembered how helpless he and his fellow soldiers felt as they waited and waited: "Yet, there we lay, along the bank of the Tennessee River, hearing the ponderous booming of cannon and the rainlike whir of musketry, till we were wild with excitement, while our poor boys were being driven back into the river at Pittsburg Landing — while hundreds of lives were going out, and the hopes of thousands more were dying on that bloody field." Through most of the day Hartpence, along with most of Buell's troops, could hear the sounds of battle from across the river and hour after hour they waited for orders to move out, but none came and the frustrated soldiers "trudged up and down, along the eastern bank of the river, or paced back and forth like so many caged animals."[1]

General Buell later wrote that as he waited for transportation to Pittsburg Landing "the firing continued, and increased in volume, I determined to go to the scene of action. Nelson only waited for the services of a guide to march by land. The river bottom between Savannah and Pittsburg Landing was a labyrinth of roads from which the overflows had obliterated all recent signs of travel, and left them impassable except in certain places, and it was with great difficulty that a guide could be obtained." It was not until after 1:00 P.M. that a guide was found and Nelson's division finally began marching south. What passed for roads were so waterlogged and thick with mud that the artillery and wagons had to be left behind. Once Nelson had moved out, General Buell sent orders for the divisions of McCook and Crittenden to push forward as quickly as possible also without their artillery and wagons. Buell and his chief of staff then took a small steamer up the river so Buell could be at Pittsburg Landing when his troops arrived.[2]

One of General Nelson's officers who made that march along the river was Colonel William Grose, commander of the 36th Indiana, and he later remembered that they received orders to begin the march just before one o'clock. The men were getting so anxious to get moving that it took only about ten minutes to get the regiment moving toward the battle. In describing the march Grose noted, "The first half of the way was undulating rolling ground, easy for travel. We descended to the bottom lands along and approaching the river recently overflowed. Here the ground was wet and soft." It took Grose's regiment about three and a half hours to reach the bank opposite Pittsburg Landing. While waiting for transportation across the river Grose could clearly see the opposite shore and that "the river was full of boats, steam up: these and the space between the river and the top of the hill, for half a mile or more in length along the river, were crowded with men in uniforms."[3]

Another man who was marching to the sound of the guns that Sunday was Wilbur F. Hinman of the 65th Ohio. Hinman's regiment was well back in the column, but he remembered the excitement and anxiety of that march: "All that Sunday afternoon we pushed on at a rapid pace with only brief halts for rest. The sound of cannonading continued, louder and clearer as we approached the scene of conflict. We talked bravely to each other, and tried to feel that way, as we moved along with hurrying feet. Faces wore a serious look, and the accustomed jest was rarely heard." Hinman's regiment had not seen any fighting yet and, not knowing the reality of battle, most of the men were looking forward to the new experience. Many expressed concern that the fighting would be over before they arrived on the scene or at least, as Hinman noted, "each man seemed anxious to impress his comrades with the idea that this was what ailed him. I doubt if the world has ever seen more heroic battalions than were ours — at the distance from the field."[4]

General Nelson's advance troops reached a point across the river from Pittsburg Landing just before five o'clock that afternoon and quickly took over some of the steamboats that were constantly ferrying men across the river in both directions. The first of Nelson's troops to cross the river was the brigade of Colonel Jacob Ammen, who noted in his diary that the water appeared to be filled with soldiers in small boats or swimming desperately trying to reach the opposite shore and safety.[5]

Once across the river General Nelson's men were shocked by what they witnessed as they made their way onshore. Thousands of Union soldiers were cowering beneath the shelter of the bluff that ran up from the riverbank to the top of the landing. Robert L. Kimberly of the 41st Ohio would later write that "The bank down to the water's edge was covered with fugitives from the battlefield." As the Ohioans advanced up the riverbank they had to make their way through the mass of frightened and exhausted men sitting and lying everywhere and "the men picked their way among the crowds of runaways. All of them belonged to regiments which had been 'cut to pieces' in the battle — so they said." Leading his men ashore, General Nelson had the same problem as his men and "found cowering under the river bank when I crossed from 7,000 to 10,000 men, frantic with fright and utterly demoralized, who received my gallant division with cries, 'We are whipped; cut to pieces.'" As General Nelson was trying to get some of the fugitives to make way for his own men, Ohioan John A. Cockerill watched as he "drew his sword and rode right into the crowd of refugees, shouting: 'Damn your souls, if you won't fight, get out of the way, and let men come here who will!'" Like most of Buell's men, Colonel Ammen was also appalled at what he saw in the faces of the men gathered along the riverbank: "[S]uch looks of terror, such confusion, I never saw before, and do not wish to see again."[6]

It did not matter what rank was held; everyone who witnessed that scene along the river was shocked and dismayed at the condition and the number of Union troops who ran away from the battlefield and were desperately trying to find shelter from the terrible violence they had seen. When General Grant returned to the landing area to arrange with General Buell for the transportation and placement of his arriving troops, the army commander saw in person the panic on their faces. Grant estimated that there were as many as five thousand of his troops seeking safety under the bluffs who he believed were so "panic-stricken, most of whom would have been shot where they lay, without resistance, before they would have taken muskets and marched to the front to protect themselves." When General Buell landed he was also troubled and angered by the scene that lay out in front of him: "The face of the bluff was crowded with stragglers from the battle.... At the top of the bluff all was confusion. Men mounted and on foot, and wagons with their teams and excited drivers, all struggling to force their way closer to the river." Buell quickly realized that when his men landed they would have to almost fight their way through the crowd of fugitives, and he saw for himself that any attempt to move the men back to their units or toward the battlefield was mostly ignored by the dazed and frightened men and "with few exceptions all efforts to form the troops and move them forward to the fight utterly failed." Grant saw Buell "berating them and trying to shame them into joining their regiments. He even threatened them with shells from the gunboats near by. But it was all to no effect." Nothing was going to get those men to go back to the firing line.[7]

Many officers of various ranks tried to rally the fugitives along the river. One of the Union paymasters, Douglas Putnam Jr., served as an aide to General Grant during the battle and later wrote about what he saw that afternoon: "The space under the bank was literally packed by thousands, I suppose, of men who had from inexperience and fright 'lost their grip,' however, only temporarily. To them it seemed that the day was lost; that the deluge was upon them." There was nowhere else to go; with the river at their backs and almost impassable swamps on both sides along the river many of the stragglers just gave up hope and lay down to wait for whatever fate was in store for them. Putnam remembered "seeing a mounted officer carrying a United States flag, riding back and forth on top of the bank, pleading and entreating in this wise: 'Men, for God's sake, for your country's sake, for your own sake, come up here, form a line, and make one more stand.' The appeal fell on listless ears. No one seemed to respond, and the only reply I heard was some one saying, 'That man talks well, don't he.'"[8]

Most of the officers and men in Grant's army knew that General Buell's Army of the Ohio was going to soon be joining them at Pittsburg Landing before the combined force moved south, but few were aware of when Buell would be arriving. It would probably be fair to say that the reaction of Leander Stillwell was shared by many of the men who were waiting for another Confederate attack on their final line just in front of Pittsburg Landing. Years later Stillwell wrote, "The last place my regiment assumed was close to the road coming up from the landing. As we were lying there I heard the strains of martial music and saw a body of men marching by the flank up the road." Stillwell briefly left his position and walked over to the side of the road to see what unit was moving up. They moved quickly with all their equipment intact and he could see that "they had not been in the fight, for there was no powder-stains on their faces. 'What regiment is this?' I asked of a young sergeant marching on the flank. Back came the answer in a quick, cheery tone, 'The 36th Indiana, the advance guard of Buell's army.'"[9]

Watching Colonel Ammen's troops march by, Stillwell could hardly believe what he had just heard, and it took a moment to realize the implication of what the young sergeant had said. The exhausted soldier from Illinois who had witnessed more horrible sights in this one day than all his previous years never forgot the joy of that moment: "I gave one big, gasping swallow and stood still, but the blood thumped in the veins of my throat and my heart fairly pounded against my little infantry jacket in the joyous rapture of this glorious intelligence. Soldiers need not be told of the thrill of unspeakable exultation they all have felt at the sight of armed friends in danger's darkest hour." Stillwell instinctively knew that the army was not going to be pushed back into the Tennessee River that evening and that the tide of the battle would be different in the morning. He wrote, "Speaking for myself alone, I can only say, in the most heart-felt sincerity, that in all my obscure military career, never to me was the sight of reinforcing legions so precious and so welcome as on that Sunday evening when the rays of the descending sun were flashed back from the bayonets of Buell's advance column as it deployed on the bluffs of Pittsburg Landing."[10]

As General Nelson's troops marched up from the landing they were quickly sent to join the new line set up on the bluffs to the right of Colonel Webster's massed artillery formation. For many years after the battle General Buell and his supporters, on the one hand, believed that his troops had come to the rescue of Grant's beaten army. General Grant, on the other hand, would never admit that his army had actually been beaten and always insisted that Buell's troops were merely reinforcements that aided in resuming the battle the next morning, as Grant had already planned. Based on what took place on the battlefield during the day and what General Buell and his troops encountered as they came ashore at Pittsburg Landing, it is quite understandable how he would come to the conclusion that he did. General Grant, however, had a different view of the situation, as he later wrote that the pathetic scenes at the landing clearly "impressed General Buell with the idea that a line of retreat would be a good thing just then. If he had come in by the front instead of through the stragglers in the rear, he would have thought and felt differently." Grant felt sure that the rear area of the Confederate army was just as confused, contained many stragglers, and in general looked just as bad as the rear of the Federal army. Grant knew that "the distant rear of an army engaged in battle is not the best place from which to judge correctly what is going on in front."[11]

Grant was more correct than he knew, for after the capture of the Hornet's Nest many of the Confederates believed the battle was over and went looking for food in the captured Federal camps. Writing about the overall condition of the Confederate army that evening, General Beauregard stated, "Straggling among the men, which had begun before noon, had now assumed fearful proportions." One of Beauregard's staff officers, Thomas Jordan, reported that "over one-third of the army was scattered in different parts of the field, loading themselves with plunder from the abandoned Federal encampments."[12]

Shortly after the Confederates had neutralized the Hornet's Nest, orders went out to General Bragg's division commanders to organize their troops for one last attack. General Chalmers reported, "It was about four o'clock in the evening, and after distributing ammunition, we received orders from General Bragg to drive the enemy into the river." General Jackson reported that his orders were to "change direction again, face toward Pittsburg, where the enemy appeared to have made his last stand, and to advance upon him, General Chalmers's brigade being again on my right." The relatively small Confederate force made their way toward the right of the landing, forming their line on the south side of Dill Branch along a ridge in front of a steep ravine. As the Confederates moved forward they came under fire from Federal artillery batteries along the bluffs and the gunboats in the river. The ravine had heavy timber and underbrush on both sides and the bottom was fairly obstructed with heavy undergrowth, not the type of terrain conducive to an attack by men who were already exhausted from hours of marching and fighting.[13]

Once more that day the shrill rebel yell was heard as the two small brigades started down the south side of the ravine under increasing heavy artillery fire from the Federal batteries lining the crest of the north side of the ravine. General Chalmers reported that as his men made their way through the tangled undergrowth at the bottom of the ravine and began to move up the north side of the ridge "we were met by a fire from a whole line of batteries protected by infantry, and assisted by shells from the gunboats. Our men struggled

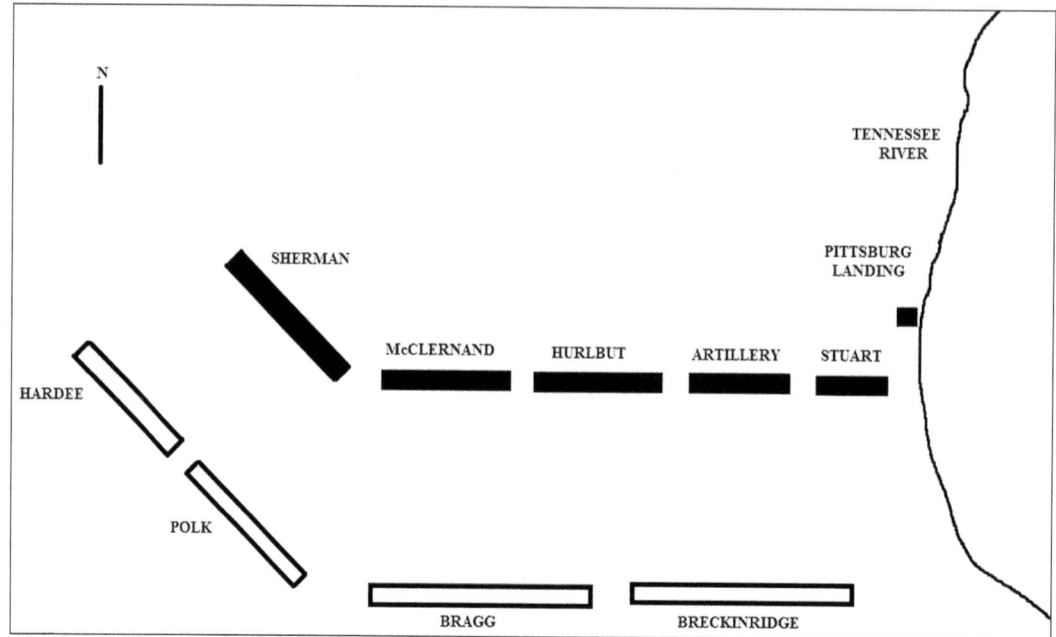

Shiloh—Sunday Evening

vainly to ascend the hill, which was very steep, making charge after charge without success, but continued to fight until night closed hostilities on both sides." The firing was heavy from both sides and Jackson's men soon ran out of ammunition but continued the attack, as he reported, "[W]ith only their bayonets to rely on, steadily my men advanced under a heavy fire from light batteries, siege-pieces and gunboats. Passing through the ravine, they arrived near the crest of the opposite hill upon which the enemy's batteries were, but could not be urged further without support."[14]

There was some support for the Confederate attack close by in the form of two reserve brigades commanded by Colonel Robert Trabue and General John Bowen's brigade now commanded by Colonel John D. Martin. These troops were about three hundred yards behind the attacking troops, but they also came under heavy artillery fire. Colonel Issac Dunlop commanding the 9th Arkansas reported, "Our position became one of extreme peril, placed, as we were, between two batteries, both pouring destructive volley of grape and canister into our ranks. In this position we received orders to fall back and await further orders." With no reinforcements to aid in the assault Chalmers' and Jackson's men were stalled on the side of the ridge under heavy fire.[15]

Among the Federal troops on top of the ridge firing at the Confederates trying to climb the slope were men from the first unit of General Buell's troops to cross the river. When Colonel Ammen's brigade advanced to the bluffs the 36th Indiana commanded by Colonel Grose was sent to support the batteries on the right where the Confederates were working their way through the ravine. Colonel Grose's men arrived on the scene just in time to aid in fighting off Chalmers' Confederates. The fighting in their front lasted less than half an hour, and as Colonel Grose later wrote, "after three or four rounds the enemy fell back. It was then dark." Grose also proudly noted that "no part of Buell's army, except the thirty-sixth Indiana, took any part whatever in the Sunday evening fight at Shiloh."[16]

The final Confederate assault of the day had failed. General Jackson reported that his men were under heavy fire, just hanging on to their positions with no chance to advance farther: "[S]heltering themselves against the precipitous side of the ravine, they remained under this fire for some time. Finding an advance without support impracticable, remaining there under fire useless, and believing any further forward movement should be made simultaneously along the whole line," Jackson decided to obtain orders from General Withers to pull his men back to safety, but before he could contact Withers a staff officer from General Beauregard brought orders to withdraw. General Chalmers' men faced the same challenges, and as night closed in his men also withdrew, with Chalmers reporting, "This was the sixth fight in which we had been engaged during the day, and the men were too much exhausted to storm the batteries on the hill, and they were brought off in good order."[17]

Thomas Jordan noted that General Withers made it clear that had they attempted to force the issue against the Federal batteries where Chalmers and Jackson had been repulsed, "it would have resulted in an awful butchery and dispersion of all employed in so insensate, so preposterous an undertaking; and such must be the verdict of any military man who may studiously read the reports of the subordinate officers of Withers's three brigades, and bear in mind the formidable line of fifty-odd pieces of artillery which Webster had improvised."[18]

The assault on the right was the last organized fighting of the day, and as darkness approached there was no real interest by the Confederate leaders to continue the fighting any further. It would have been difficult for the Confederates to launch any type of coordinated attack even if they had wanted to. Most of the divisions were hopelessly intermingled and the men exhausted. Many regiments were either low or entirely out of ammunition. Perhaps most important was that during this lull in the fighting some regiments began to pull back to the captured Union camps, prompting others to do the same. Typical of the situation was that facing Lieutenant Colonel W. D. Chadwick, commanding the 26th Alabama of General Withers' division, who reported, "Having only about two hundred men left, and seeing that they must all be sacrificed if I remained, without gaining any material advantage, I withdrew them to a wood in the rear of a field and awaited orders. Finding no one to whom I could report, and the men being quite exhausted, I moved back to the enemy's camp."[19]

General Beauregard would receive much criticism for not launching another assault in the early-evening hours, but it was quite obvious that the men were exhausted and too disorganized to mount another serious attack and sending them against the Federal line piecemeal would only get more men slaughtered. He later wrote that "it was 6 o'clock, just before sunset, when I ordered the cessation of hostilities, so that our forces could be withdrawn for rest." Even without Beauregard's order, the fighting was virtually ended by that time, because no one had the strength or desire to continue. One of Beauregard's aides, Alexander R. Chisolm, wrote that he was with Beauregard near Shiloh Church when General Bragg rode up and excitedly stated, "General, we have carried everything before us to the Tennessee River. I have ridden from Owl to Lick Creek, and there is none of the enemy to be seen." Beauregard calmly and quietly replied, "Then General, do not unnecessarily expose your command to the fire of the gun-boats."[20]

Captain Lockett writes that General Bragg first received the order to cease operations from a courier sent by Beauregard and Bragg basically exploded, exclaiming, "My God, was a victory ever sufficiently complete?" But the fact is that even Bragg's staff felt it was time to stop. Colonel David Urquhart wrote, "The plain truth must be told, that our troops at the front were a thin line of exhausted men, who were making no further headway.... Several years of subsequent service have impressed me that General Beauregard's order for withdrawing the troops was most timely."[21]

Staff officer Thomas Jordan also felt that pulling the Confederate troops back that evening was the proper thing to do: "Our troops were scattered. Army, division, brigade and even regimental organizations were broken up for the time to such an extent that any advance, at that hour of the day, in such order or masses as would have promised any substantial advantages, was out of the question." Jordan believed that in addition to the physical exhaustion of the men, "[t]he unavoidable causes of this dis-organization were the rawness of many of the regiments engaged and the densely wooded nature of the battlefield, which made it impossible to mass in due time enough troops for a resolute, sustained, effective assault on the enemy."[22]

Just before dark General Grant had been visiting with his division commanders and had ridden over to the far right to discuss plans with General Sherman. In addition to informing Sherman of the failed attack across the ravine on the left, Grant told him "to be ready to assume the offensive in the morning, saying that, as he had observed at Fort Donelson at the crisis of the battle, both sides seemed defeated, and whoever assumed the offensive was sure to win." In Grant's view, today was just the first phase of the battle; tomorrow would come the climax.[23]

By any reasonable way of measuring, the Federal army had been beaten on Sunday. More than half the army had become casualties or had just run away, the enemy had captured their camps, and the survivors had been pushed back to the Tennessee River, where they still held on to a narrow strip of land just inland from the riverbanks. Despite all these obvious signs of defeat, what counted even more in the end was the fact that Ulysses Grant just refused to accept defeat. Most of the time Grant appeared to be a most ordinary man with a quiet personality who went about his business in a workman-like manner and displayed few traits that would do much to inspire those around him. But on the inside Grant was tough and obstinate, even stubborn, a man who never gave up even when the situation looked darkest. By the force of his will he would hold out a little longer; when the crisis came he kept a clear head and was always ready to take advantage of even the smallest opportunity the enemy might leave open. Grant would later write, "So confident was I before firing had ceased on the 6th that the next day would bring victory to our arms if we could only take the initiative, that I visited each division commander in person before any reinforcements had reached the field." Giving basically the same instructions to each division commander, Grant directed them to "throw out heavy lines of skirmishers in the morning as soon as they could see, and push them forward until they found the enemy, following with their entire divisions in supporting distance, and to engage the enemy as soon as found." As bad as it was on Sunday, just knowing that they would be facing the same type of carnage when the battle resumed in the morning must have weighed heavily on the minds of most of the men on both sides. The battle was not yet finished and in the morning the men in blue would be launching their own attack against an unprepared enemy.[24]

22

A Terrible Night for All

Finally the fighting on this dreadful day was finished. If they were lucky the dazed and exhausted survivors on both sides could rest, have a little something to eat and count their blessings that they had survived one of the most violent days in American history. At the end of the first day of fighting it was now time to take a count of the cost, and it was appalling. First and foremost were the thousands of casualties among the private soldiers on both sides, but the higher-ranking officers also suffered severe casualties. There had been five Union division commanders engaged in the fighting this day; W. H. L. Wallace was dying, Prentiss was a Confederate prisoner, and Sherman had suffered several minor wounds. Nine of the fifteen Union brigade commanders and thirty-three of the sixty-one regimental commanders were dead, wounded or captured. The Confederate casualties among the officers were also severe. Obviously the loss of Albert Sidney Johnston was a blow from which they did not recover, but in addition to the army commander two of the four Confederate corps commanders were wounded. Three of the five division commanders were wounded, four of sixteen brigade commanders were killed or wounded and over twenty regimental commanders were casualties.[1]

Considering the beating the men on both sides had suffered during the twelve hours or so of almost constant fighting it is little wonder that the organization of both armies was severely compromised. Many of the Confederates had been separated from their units during the day, in part from the continued attacks that had them moving all over the battlefield and in part because thousands of them simply stopped when they became too exhausted to continue moving forward or, like many of their Union counterparts, headed for the rear when they became overwhelmed by the horrors of battle. The one major difference between the two armies was that Grant had been able to form his men into a compact line near the river and most of Beauregard's troops were scattered all over the battlefield. The majority of the Confederate troops had either stayed put where they had stopped or pulled back after the fighting ended, so that there was well over a mile-wide gap between the armies during the night. Considering the ferocity of the fighting, the constant changing of positions and the amount of time the men were engaged, it is small wonder that few of the Confederate commanders had been able to keep their units together and many of the officers spent the night trying to pull together their regiments and brigades.[2]

The Federal line was left basically as it was when the Confederates were thrown back from their final assault across the ravine. The majority of the Federal artillery was positioned a little south of Pittsburg Landing, covering the immediate area around the landing and the ravine in its front with General Hurlbut's division formed on the right and McClernand

and Sherman extending the line farther to the right. These three divisions had taken heavy casualties during the fighting, but the composition of the divisions was still intact and their commanders were present and physically able to continue leading their men. The other two divisions that had taken part in the fighting were pretty much gone. The division of W. H. L. Wallace had basically disintegrated after Wallace and most of the senior officers were lost. Most of General Prentiss' division were captured along with their commander after surrendering at the Hornet's Nest. The survivors of these two divisions who were still able and ready to continue the fight were spread out as reserves among the other divisions in the line.[3]

There has always been a great deal of comment on the large number of Union troops who took refuge at the landing and crowded under the bluffs for protection. Clearly many of these men could not deal with the terrible shock of battle and for various reasons simply ran away to seek safety wherever they could find it. The crowds of men who had gathered along the banks of the river were not only those who had fled the battle but also slightly wounded soldiers and noncombatants who provided support to the fighting men but were not meant to take part in battle. There is little doubt that the Confederates also had thousands of stragglers who either fled from the fighting or never advanced to begin with. The main reason why the number of Union troops along the riverbank made such a poor impression was that they were concentrated in a relatively small area around the landing while Confederate stragglers were spread out over several square miles of open territory and the number of these men was not so obvious. By the time darkness fell both Grant and Beauregard would have been lucky to be able to muster much more than half of the men who were in formation that morning and the vast majority of those men were only interested in trying to rest as best they could in the cold, falling rain.[4]

All through the day as his army was being forced back toward the landing General Grant had been waiting for Lew Wallace's Third Division to come up from Crump's Landing and join the rest of the army, but Wallace never arrived, at least not during the fighting. What happened to Wallace and his men that day all but ruined Wallace's reputation as a soldier and created hard feelings toward the general for years to come. Hearing the sounds of the battle, Wallace had his men already prepared to march to whatever position they were assigned when Grant came upriver and ordered Wallace in person to get ready to move but provided no specific instructions. Between 11:30 A.M. and noon one of Grant's staff officers, Captain A. S. Baxter, delivered orders from Grant that the captain wrote on a dirty, wrinkled piece of paper to make sure that he relayed Grant's instructions accurately. After studying the message, Wallace and members of his staff all agreed that the order directed him to "leave a sufficient force at Crump's to guard the public property there, and take the rest of his division and form junction with the right of the army, where he was to form line of battle at a right angle with the river, and act as circumstances required." Wallace asked Baxter how the battle was progressing so far and the captain replied that the enemy was being driven back.[5]

Well aware of the need to bring his troops up to the battlefield as quickly as possible, Wallace chose to take the Purdy road, which was the shortest route "that led directly to the right of the lines as they were established around Pittsburg Landing on Sunday morning, my column started immediately, the distance being about 6 miles." Wallace's division was making reasonably good time as they moved toward the sounds of the battle when another of Grant's aides, Captain W. R. Rowley, caught up to the column and informed the general, "The line to which you are going has been driven back toward the Landing [Pittsburg], and it is a question if we are not to be pushed into the river." This was the first news that Wallace received that he was going in the wrong direction and could very well end up behind the advancing Confederates, cut off from the rest of the army. Rowley informed Wallace that Grant's orders were for him to bring his division to Pittsburg Landing as quickly as possible. Wallace turned his men around and marched over two miles to get back to where they started and then took the River Road to Pittsburg Landing.[6]

As they moved toward the river Wallace's men ran into a terrible section of road near Snake Creek where mud and standing water slowed the march to a crawl. Artillery and wagons got bogged down and soldiers had to frequently stop and help drag them out of swamp-like patches of ground. All this helped to delay Wallace even more, and soon two more of Grant's staff showed up, Colonel James McPherson and Captain John Rawlins, who had been sent to find out what was keeping Wallace and hurry him along. Comments were made that perhaps Wallace had not been pushing his men hard enough, but considering the distances involved and the road conditions it is unlikely that anyone else could have moved much faster. McPherson reported that he believed Wallace said that "his guide had led him wrong, and I was most decidedly of the impression that he had mistaken the road, for his command had already marched a great deal farther than was necessary to reach the battlefield." By the time Wallace's troops arrived at the landing it was too dark to do anything but move into line on the far right of the army.[7]

For many years Lew Wallace was criticized by Grant and others because of his late arrival at the battlefield. Years later, however, after receiving information from the widow of General W. H. L. Wallace showing that Lew Wallace had made the proper preparations to move his troops in the event of an emergency, Grant was honest enough to write that this new information "modifies very materially what I have said, and what has been said by others, of the conduct of General Lew Wallace at the battle of Shiloh. It shows that he naturally, with no more experience than he had at the time in the profession of arms, would take the particular road that he did start upon in the absence of orders to move by a different road."[8]

Once Wallace's troops arrived and took their assigned position in the line Grant's dispositions were finished for the night. With Grant's troops stationed to the right of the main artillery positions more and more of Nelson's division were brought across the river to join Ammen's troops positioned on the left of the artillery. Confident of success the next day, Grant later wrote, "Victory was assured when Wallace arrived with his division of five thousand effective veterans, even if there had been no other support."[9]

During the evening General Buell's forces were constantly streaming across the river to join Grant's battered army. General Nelson was able to get the rest of his division across by late that evening, followed quickly by General Crittenden's troops who arrived on transports sent back to Savannah at Buell's request earlier in the afternoon. General McCook's division, who were the last troops close enough to reach the battlefield by Monday morning, had made a forced march to Savannah, where they arrived late in the evening. Unfortunately, there were no transports available to take them across the river, so McCook simply took control of any boats that came onshore on his side of the river and was able to ferry his men across in piecemeal fashion. General Buell instructed General Nelson to form his division next to the river, which made them the far left of the Federal line. Crittenden's division was assigned to the right of Nelson, but leaving enough room between his men and the artillery for McCook's troops to occupy when they were able to come up later that night.[10]

There had been no formal agreement between Grant and Buell concerning the action each would take in the morning. About the only thing that anyone was sure of was that there would be an attack on the Confederates in the morning and Buell's Army of the Ohio would be on the left. General Buell later wrote that while discussing the day's events with General Sherman he was asked what his plans were for the morning. Buell answered that he "was going to attack the enemy at daylight, and he expressed gratification at my reply, though apparently not because of any unmixed confidence in the result. I had had no consultation with General Grant, and knew nothing of his purpose." Buell also commented that "I presumed that we would be in accord, but I had been only a few hours within the limits of his authority, and I did not look upon him as my commander, though I would zealously have obeyed his orders."[11]

Grant and Buell were not particularly friendly to begin with, and when Grant embarrassed Buell during his trip to Nashville the relations between the two deteriorated even further. Pretty much right after the battle and for years afterward, both men and their many supporters took very different views about how much credit Buell's troops deserved for the victory. Grant would always stubbornly hold to the view that he did not need Buell's troops to beat the Confederates the next day and refused to give anything but a lukewarm recognition of their contribution to Monday's fighting, writing later, "I was glad, however, to see the reinforcements of Buell and credit with them with doing all there was for them to do." It would seem reasonable, however, to believe that even with the addition of Wallace's division, it would have been difficult, if not impossible, for Grant's already beaten and exhausted men to force back the nearly twenty thousand men whom General Beauregard would be able to put in the field the next morning.[12]

The men of both armies spent a spectacularly miserable night trying to get some rest and maybe a little something to eat. All through the night the gunboats *Lexington* and *Tyler* sent their heavy shells over the Federal lines into what were hoped to be the Confederate camps. This shelling had little effect, however, since most of the Confederates had moved back far enough from the Federal lines that the vast majority of the shells fell harmlessly between the armies. Adding to the misery of the soldiers, around midnight a terrific rainstorm hit the area. John Cockerill, a soldier from Ohio, later wrote, "Every few moments I was awakened by a terrible broadside, delivered from the gunboats which lay in the center of the river a hundred yards or so above me." Cockerill complained that what little opportunity the men had for sleep was pretty much ruined because "of this cannonading and the shrieking of the shells." In addition, the constant sloshing of Buell's troops through the mud along with the accompanying noise and curses of the men convinced Cockerill that "there never was a night so long, so hideous, or so utterly uncomfortable." Another Union soldier, William W. Cluett of the 57th Illinois, wrote later that the rain soaked everything and everyone and combined with the horror of the day "the brain was benumbed from cold and hunger; weak men gave way to despair, and strong men cursed the misfortunes that placed our cause in such a position."[13]

The rain added an extra element of frustration to the usual problems involved in trying to move large numbers of soldiers across a river at night. The brother of the commander of Buell's Second Division, Colonel Daniel McCook, would later write about the trials their men faced while trying to make their way to join Grant's men that "before we reached the river the storm burst, the April rain coming down in torrents. In the gloom, blinded by lightning flashes, the troops stumbled and groped their way down the slippery banks." And McCook noted the mental anguish the men went through while waiting to move forward:

22. A Terrible Night for All

"That night was an agony of rumor — rumors of defeat, of panic, of men rushing into the river, of the annihilation of our army, of term of surrender proposed and discussed." Wilbur F. Hinman of the 65th Ohio wrote that as his regiment arrived at Savannah about ten o'clock on Sunday evening they witnessed "the utmost confusion and excitement that it is possible to imagine." Ships of all sizes had been moving back and forth across the river all evening ferrying Buell's troops to Pittsburg Landing and bringing Grant's wounded back across the river. Most of the buildings in the village had been taken over for hospitals, and the bodies of those who had died of their wounds were lying all over the porches and yards. Hinman still remembered years later that "as we marched down the main street toward the river we could hear on every side the groans of the suffering. To us all this was a revelation. We were looking upon the ghastliest picture of war."[14]

The 6th Indiana arrived at Pittsburg Landing during the night and one member of the regiment, Charles C. Briant, later wrote, "I think I give the experience of every member of the old Sixth when I say that the night of the 6th of April, 1862, was the worst night of our entire three years' service." For these new arrivals the terrible weather wasn't even the worst part of what they experienced. With thousands of wounded men to care for, temporary hospitals had been set up in any sheltered location that could be found near the river. Briant's regiment had the poor luck to camp close by one of these hospitals, and all through the night "the groans and shrieks of the wounded and dying drowned every other noise except the pelting rain."[15]

The Federal soldiers were not the only men to suffer that night, since the Confederates faced the same miserable conditions. Writing about the many wounded who lay scattered about the battlefield, Lieutenant Colonel Charles Jones of the 17th Louisiana reported that they "suffered greatly, having nothing to protect them from the rain, which fell in torrents a greater portion of the night. Many of them lay that night in pools of water two or three inches deep." The Confederate soldiers were just as tired and just as hungry as their enemies. The same terrible noise from the wounded and the dying kept them awake as it did many of the Federal soldiers; the only real difference between the men of the two armies was that the Confederates at least had the knowledge that they were the ones who were victorious that day.[16]

Even the generals had nowhere to go to escape the misery of that night. General Grant's headquarters was located a few hundred yards from the river, where he was at least protected from the rain. Like most of his men, however, Grant was unable to sleep because of the storm and the firing of the gunboats and in addition he was also suffering from a painful ankle injury that occurred during the day. The restless general decided to go outside for a bit and took temporary refuge from the storm under a large tree but, as Grant later wrote:

> Some time after midnight, growing restive under the storm and the continuous pain, I moved back to the log-house under the bank. This had been taken as a hospital, and all night wounded men were being brought in, their wounds dressed, a leg or an arm amputated as the case might require, and everything being done to save life or alleviate suffering. The sight was more unendurable than encountering the enemy's fire, and I returned to my tree in the rain.[17]

A little later General Sherman came upon Grant, who was still trying to get comfortable under his tree while the rain continued to pour down out of the black sky. The army's commanding general was just standing there silently smoking his cigar and most probably going over in his mind the events of the day and considering how he would reclaim the battlefield from the enemy in the morning. Having spent most of the day in the thick of the fighting,

Sherman knew as well as anyone how and why the army had been pushed back and just how close they had come to suffering a disaster. The two men, who would become the best of friends and eventually lead the Union armies to final victory, stood around in the rain making small talk for a while. Sherman made a comment on how tough the fighting had been and Grant concurred that at times things looked very dark for the army, but he was confident that in the morning his army would claim the final victory.[18]

A few miles away, in a warm and dry tent in General Sherman's captured camp, the current commander of the Confederate forces, P. G. T. Beauregard, had established his headquarters and was having a relatively pleasant night, at least in comparison to his Federal counterparts. General Bragg and several other senior commanders came by the headquarters tent during the night, and after brief meetings Beauregard was convinced that, at least the men he had spoken to were satisfied with the outcome of the day's fighting. Beauregard later wrote, "No one intimated, directly or indirectly, within my hearing or that of my staff, that the order to cease firing and fall back to the captured camps of the enemy had been given too soon, or that it should not have been given at all."[19]

During the night Beauregard sent a message to Confederate adjutant general Samuel Cooper in Richmond to inform him of the battle and the apparent victory after the first day of fighting: "We this morning attacked the enemy in strong position in front of Pittsburg, and after a severe battle of ten hours, thanks be to the Almighty, gained a complete victory, driving the enemy from every position. Loss on both sides heavy, including our commander-in-chief, General A. S. Johnston, who fell gallantly leading his troops into the thickest of the fight."[20]

General Beauregard had received a message informing him that General Buell's troops who were known to be heading toward Pittsburg Landing were still too far away "and that his main force, therefore, could not reach the field of battle in time to save General Grant's shattered fugitive forces from capture or destruction on the following day." Why the news of thousands of Union soldiers arriving at Savannah and crossing the river to join Grant's troops did not reach Confederate headquarters is a mystery. It is very possible that Beauregard and some of his senior commanders were a little too confident that Monday morning would bring a completion of the victory that had begun on Sunday. Before the Confederates would be completing their victory, however, the troops had to be pulled back together into some semblance of an army. Many of Beauregard's men were scattered all over the battlefield, some had taken refuge in the captured Federal camps looking for food or anything else they could use and others simply stopped where they were when darkness came. In order to make any kind of effective assault on the last Union line in the morning regiments and brigades had to be put back together, and many officers spent most of the night traversing the battlefield trying to rebuild their units. With the original attack formations broken beyond repair, General Beauregard had to make some changes in the command structure of the army. General Hardee was placed in command of the right, replacing General Bragg, who moved over to take command on the left. General Breckinridge was given the responsibility of the far left flank.[21]

As the dark of night gave way to dawn the rain slowly started to subside. The sleepy Confederates began to hear faint sounds of infantry firing in the direction of Pittsburg Landing. The crackle of small-arms fire began to intensify and grow louder, taking many of the Confederates by surprise. It did not take long for the crackle of small-arms fire to intensify, and they were even more surprised by the deeper booming sounds of artillery fire that echoed in the early-morning mists.[22]

23

The Second Morning

Monday morning April 7 dawned cold and wet. The rain had let up, but everyone was pretty miserable from hours of standing or lying in the mud wondering if they were going to survive for another day. There was little real reason for the fighting to continue, but despite all the suffering that occurred on Sunday the leaders of both sides were determined to continue the struggle. General Beauregard had been simply unable to finish the job and destroy General Grant's army the day before, and now that General Buell's troops were arriving and General Lew Wallace's division had finally found its way to the battlefield the chances of a significant Confederate victory had vanished.

General Buell's troops had been arriving at Pittsburg Landing throughout the night and early-morning hours of April 7. About seven o'clock in the morning as Brigadier General Alexander McDowell McCook's troops were disembarking from their transports his men ran into the same appalling scene along the shore as had General Nelson's men earlier that night. David W. Reed of the 77th Pennsylvania later wrote, "As the boats drew near shore, men crowded the banks of the river, preparing to jump aboard, as soon as the vessels got near enough for them to do so. Guards, with fixed bayonets had to be stationed all along the gunwales to keep this mob of frightened and demoralized soldiers off the boats." As the Pennsylvanians reached shore and began to move up the bluff they were greeted with jeers from some of the stragglers who threw out comments like, "Oh! You'll catch it when you get over the hill there," and, "I pity you fellows, you'll never come back again." By the time most of McCook's men were onshore the landing area was simply a mess. Daniel McCook, an aide to his brother, remembered, "At the landing-place confusion was worse than confounded. Rations, forage, and ammunition were trampled into the mire by an excited and surging crowd. Officers were rushing about, endeavoring to collect the stragglers of their commands and lead them into the rapidly-increasing battle."[1]

For most of General Buell's troops this would be their first major battle, and many were anxious to "see the elephant" and prove their courage in the face of danger. As they moved forward toward the battlefield much of this eagerness turned to apprehension as the fear of missing the action began to be shaded by the fear of what could actually happen to them during combat. Some of General McCook's men in the 29th Indiana lost much of their enthusiasm to participate in the battle when they had to march past a large pile of amputated limbs outside a busy field hospital. When they actually got up to the lines there was usually more waiting. The stress of waiting to come to grips with the as-yet-unseen enemy was so great for many soldiers that despite the danger, actually being in combat came as a welcome relief.[2]

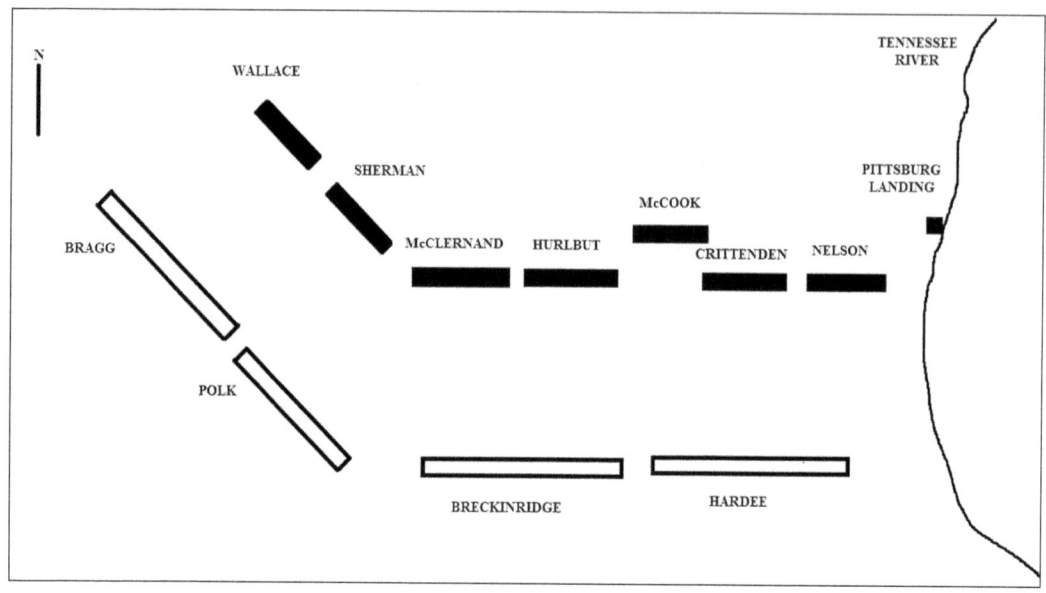

Shiloh — Monday

The Federal troops remained in the same positions they occupied when the fighting ended on Sunday evening. Grant's men in the Army of the Tennessee were on the right with Lew Wallace's fresh troops stationed on the far right and the forces of Generals Sherman, McClernand, and Hurlbut forming to the left in that order. General Buell's Army of the Ohio occupied the left wing of the Federal line, with General McCook's division, who were just arriving when the fighting began, filling in the space on Hurlbut's left and the division of General Crittenden to his left with Nelson's troops on the far left nearest the river. As the fighting continued throughout the day the Federal army would remain basically in these same relative positions, unlike the disorganized shuffling of units that occurred on Sunday.³

The situation in the Confederate

Union general Don Carlos Buell. Relieved of command late in 1862 for being too slow to act on several occasions (Library of Congress).

camps was much different, with confusion being the story everywhere during the early-morning hours. Thousands of stragglers wandered through the fields and woods, units were terribly mixed together and conflicting orders were being sent out from different headquarters. The main priority of the senior officers was to reorganize their troops into some semblance of fighting units, so corps and division commanders just took over whatever units were currently located in their areas regardless of who their original commanders were. During the course of the night and early morning the Confederate army was realigned with General Hardee on the far right taking over command of the brigades of Chalmers and Jackson from Bragg's corps. General Breckinridge was to Hardee's left with General Clark's division from Polk's corps, with the rest of Polk's men coming up a little later in the morning to fill in the space on Breckinridge's left. The far left of the Confederate line was under the command of General Bragg.[4]

Both sides had suffered terrible casualties on Sunday, but the Confederates could not replace their losses. One of the worst-hit units was the brigade of Patrick Cleburne, one of the hardest-fighting generals on either side. He reported that his brigade "was sadly reduced. From near 2,700 I now numbered about 800. Two regiments, the Second Tennessee and the Sixth Mississippi, were absent altogether. Hundreds of my best men were dead or in hospitals, and, I blush to add, hundreds of others had run off early in the fight of the day before." Considering casualties suffered during the fighting and the men who had just run away, both Grant and Beauregard could only put about half the number of men in the field as they had at the beginning of the contest.[5]

Most of the men who had taken part in the first day's fighting were familiar with the difficult terrain that made up much of the battlefield, but Buell's troops were not aware of how broken up the ground in their front was with the many ravines and woods that were scattered all over the area, and they would face the same problems as did the men who had fought on Sunday. On the Federal left most of Nelson's front was open ground, with some thick underbrush and woods between him and Crittenden. Between Crittenden and McCook was more open ground, with another patch of woods to McCook's right between his troops and those of General Hurlbut. As it turned out, General Beauregard had concealed much of his artillery in the wooded areas on the flanks and in the wooded areas in front of Buell's troops on the Confederate right. In addition, a large portion of the Confederate infantry was also stationed on their right. While this made for a strong defensive presence, the real reason Beauregard had strengthened his right was that he intended to complete the original mission of the attack, push the Federal left away from the river, capture Pittsburg Landing, and force a surrender of the trapped Union army. The only problem with this strategy was that Beauregard was unaware that the Federal left was now manned by thousands of fresh troops eager for battle.[6]

General Buell rode out in front of his lines during the night to view the terrain they would be crossing in the morning, but it was too dark to really learn much and he would later admit that "it was my misfortune to know nothing about the topography in front." As had happened on Sunday, the terrain would play an important part in the coming battle. There was little room for large units to do much maneuvering and once again the fighting would degenerate into many small battles between regiment- and brigade-size units, who usually had no idea what was happening to the units on either side because of woods or heavy underbrush.[7]

The odds for victory would have to be with the Federal army on Monday morning. Both the Confederates and Grant's troops were dead tired, while Buell's troops might be tired from their forced marching to the field, but they were sure to be physically and mentally fresher than the men who had gone through Sunday's daylong battle. Even more important than the condition of the men was that now the Federal forces outnumbered the Confederates by a large margin. One more important fact was that Buell's forces had their command structure intact and his men were anxious to participate in their first battle, especially since it clearly appeared that they were saving the obviously beaten Army of the Tennessee from total destruction.[8]

Both Generals Grant and Buell had issued similar orders for the morning: advance and drive the enemy from the ground that they had taken on Sunday. There were no specific orders given to division commanders, just "advance to your front," and there was little or no cooperation between Grant and Buell other than that the Army of the Tennessee would advance on the right and the Army of the Ohio on the left. Considering how much the terrain limited any tactical options, the individual soldier, not the generals, would determine the outcome and as long as the men would stand their ground the fighting would go back and forth until one side gave in and left the field.[9]

As the sun came up, the combined Federal armies were ready to move forward. General Nelson began the advance on the far left along the River Road with Colonel Ammen leading his brigade forward calmly saying to his men, "Now, boys, keep cool; give 'em the best you've got," as he slowly rode back and forth in front of his line. Nelson's men quickly ran into Confederate pickets who were easily brushed aside, and they continued steadily advancing without too much opposition for nearly a mile. At this point General Buell, who was accompanying Crittenden's division, ordered Nelson to halt because he had gone too far out in front of Crittenden, exposing his flank. As it turned out, Nelson's easy advance was due mostly to the fact that the Confederates had pulled out of his front during the night to concentrate their forces in the area of the captured Federal camps.[10]

This early advance by General Buell's troops alerted the Confederates to the fact that they were now facing thousands of fresh Union soldiers. General Beauregard had to make allowances for this fact, and the first change was that the planned attack on the right was clearly not going to happen. The Confederate lines were set up with General Hardee on the right followed to the left by Breckinridge, Polk and Bragg on the far left. The brigades and regiments were somewhat mixed up, with Beauregard ordering the corps commanders to take command of any troops in their vicinity regardless of who they were supposed to report to. Very few brigades were intact, with their regiments being rushed to the front and sent from one part of the field to another when they were needed to reinforce various positions until it was almost impossible to determine where each regiment was at a given time.[11]

Once Crittenden's troops came up on Nelson's right the two divisions advanced together with support from the first troops of McCook's division who had moved up on Crittenden's right. As the Federal line approached the rear of the camps that had been lost on Sunday they encountered heavy fire from General Hardee's Confederates and concentrated artillery fire coming from several locations. At one point not only had Hardee's troops, led by Chalmer's brigade, halted the Federal advance, but also Confederate counterattacks pushed them back in several places. About eight o'clock Nelson and Crittenden began moving forward again with Colonel William B. Hazen's brigade on the right and Colonel Ammen's brigade on the left of Nelson's division. Once again, however, the advance was stalled by heavy artillery fire and then Hardee's infantry came forward to push the Federals back. Colonel Ammen reported that during this period of back-and-forth fighting "the attacks of the enemy are frequent and desperate, but our new troops have the coolness of veterans."

Ammen's flank was partially protected from Confederate infantry by a swampy area to his left, but the Confederate artillery played havoc with Nelson's troops and there was concern that if they could turn Ammen's left then Nelson's entire division would be in danger. General Nelson had no artillery support in the early-morning hours, but Captain John Mendenhall moved up with his battery from Crittenden's division, and along with Captain William Terrill's battery they were able to silence the Confederate artillery and combined to pour such a heavy fire into the advancing enemy that they pulled back and the line was stabilized, but not for long.[12]

About nine o'clock Confederate brigades from Hardee and Breckinridge struck Nelson's troops head-on. Colonel Hazen's brigade was hit hard near the Sunken Road and Mendenhall's artillery was briefly in danger of being overrun. With Hazen leading them in person the 6th Kentucky, supported by the rest of the brigade, struck the advancing enemy with a bayonet charge that drove them back, at least momentarily. Shortly after the Confederates were repulsed they came on again with an even more desperate attack. General Buell reported that "Ammen's brigade, which was on the left, advanced in good order upon the enemy's right, but was checked for some time by his endeavor to turn our left flank and by his strong counter-attack in front." Colonel Ammen reported, "No sooner is our line formed than the enemy assault fiercely, but the brave men and officers of the Tenth Brigade stand cool and firm, and hurl the foe back again and again, as often as he reaches the crest of the small rise immediately in our front." Reinforcements were rushed over from Crittenden's division, and the 2nd Iowa and 15th Illinois from Grant's army were also sent over to support the left. The commander of one of Nelson's regiments, Lieutenant Colonel Nicholas Anderson of the 6th Ohio, reported that during this desperate fighting his men were "continually under a hot and heavy fire, supporting for the greater time Terrill's regular battery, and at one time furnishing a company to manage the guns of said battery, its men having been mostly killed or wounded." General Buell reported that after the Confederate assaults were repulsed Nelson's division moved forward again, pushing the Confederates back close to eight hundred yards aided by the "concentrated fire of Terrill's and Mendenhall's batteries and an attack from Crittenden's division in front." Colonel Hazen reported that during one of the attacks on a Confederate position supported by artillery his men "pushed directly up to the mouths of the guns, which were manned till the cannoneers were cut down by my men."[13]

One of the men who survived the fighting on Sunday was Elisha Stockwell Jr. of the 14th Wisconsin. His regiment was one of several units of Grant's army that had been assigned to the far left of the line to support Nelson's troops and extend the line to the river. Stockwell later wrote that during the early advance on the Federal left "we had lost all formation, and were rushing down the road like a mob." While taking a break at the foot of a hill they were struck by one of the Confederate counterattacks, and while taking cover behind a tree Stockwell turned just in time to see "the colors going out of sight over the hill" as his unit fell back under the heavy enemy fire. Reporting on the involvement of the 41st Ohio, one of Hazen's brigades, Robert Kimberly stated that during the early portion of the advance they easily pushed back the enemy skirmishers but that "the command was inexperienced and the movement quickly went beyond control in a headlong pursuit." With their formation scattered the Confederates launched one of their counterattacks against the Ohioans and, "with fresh troops, seized his ground again, driving back the scattered assailants." One of Crittenden's brigades commanded by Colonel William Sooy Smith was fighting along with Nelson's men during this savage back-and-forth fighting that all but shattered Hazen's brigade along with the brigade of Colonel Sanders D. Bruce. The 41st Ohio lost 140 of 373 men and the 13th Kentucky lost a third of their troops. The fighting in this area continued with both sides launching small but deadly attacks and counterattacks for over an hour until around noon.[14]

While Nelson's and Crittenden's divisions were engaged in fierce fighting on the left of the Federal line near the center, the last of Buell's troops to arrive were having their own problems. General McCook's division had formed on the right of Buell's line to connect with General Hurlbut's troops and began their advance later than the rest of Buell's force. The brigade of Brigadier General Lovell H. Rousseau was stationed on McCook's left and was the lead brigade when McCook moved forward. Unfortunately, as Rousseau's troops advanced they slid a little too much to the right and a gap opened up between them and Crittenden's men. Writing about his first time under fire, Lewis M. Hosea, an officer in Rousseau's brigade, remembered that as their skirmishers began firing there was "a crackling of responses from the woods beyond, but we could see only a little blue smoke rising above the undergrowth and hear the skipping of stray bullets through the branches with a whir of spent force. A stir went through the lines and faces grew pale, for we knew that the battle was sweeping toward us and that these shots were the first sprinkle of the coming storm."[15]

General Beauregard was not slow in taking advantage of this undefended opening between Buell's divisions, and he launched a fierce assault against Rousseau's left flank. Seeing the obvious danger to his entire division, General McCook sent forward the 32nd Indiana commanded by Colonel August Willich to help blunt the Confederate attack, quickly followed by the remainder of Colonel William H. Gibson's brigade. In a very short time the brigades of both Rousseau and Gibson were both heavily engaged as they tried to close the gap between McCook and Crittenden. C. C. Briant of the 6th Indiana remembered the fighting that morning was "charge and counter charge, one continuous roll of musketry, while the artillery rained death and destruction all around us." Lewis Hosea remembered, "The first shock of battle is appalling. The rattle deepens into a roar as men get down to the work of loading and firing rapidly; but it is not alone the noise of firing that appeals. The vicious 'whizz,' and 'zip' past the ears; the heavy 'thud' of bullets that strike the tree-trunks with the force of sledge-hammers — all these make up a horrible din that has no parallel on earth." Once the battle is in progress nothing matters except concentrating on the task at hand, as Hosea later wrote: "After a little the smoke obscures everything and the battle goes on in an ever-increasing acrid fog that would make breathing impossible were it not for the frenzy of battle that seizes upon every other faculty, physical and mental, and makes one oblivious to all other surroundings." Daniel McCook later wrote about waiting for the enemy to close, "All stood awaiting the shock. Then came a deafening crash, the flame from our avenging muskets leaping almost half-way across the field. The sound had scarcely reached its full volume when it was answered by another. Then the roar of battle swelled over all, seemingly filling the firmament.... The line swept back and forth like an undulating thread; there it shrank for a moment; here it bowed toward the enemy."[16]

General McCook's third brigade, commanded by Colonel Edward N. Kirk, was just reaching the front when they were thrown into the battle to replace Rousseau's troops who had to fall back for more ammunition. Almost as soon as Rousseau began to withdraw, the Confederates pressed their attack even more desperately, trying to widen the gap between Crittenden's and McCook's troops even more in order to hit the flank of each with more force. One of Colonel Gibson's regiments, the 49th Ohio, stationed on the left of his line, was forced to fight in several directions at the same time as the enemy came at them from all sides trying to overrun their position and roll up the brigade from the side. Fortunately for McCook's division, Rousseau was able to quickly get his men back to the front line accompanied by two regiments of General Hurlbut's reserve. With his division back to full strength and the addition of the reinforcements, McCook was able to push the attackers back and, with his flanks secure, begin to move forward again.[17]

While General Buell's Army of the Ohio was engaged in heavy fighting on the left of the Federal formation, over on the right General Grant's troops were also heading into battle again. Around dawn, about the same time that General Nelson began his advance, over on the far right of the Federal formation General Lew Wallace opened the fighting by engaging in an artillery duel with a Confederate battery on the bluff behind a ravine in Wallace's front. Wallace reported, "From its position and that of its infantry support, lining the whole length of the bluff, it was apparent that crossing the hollow would be at a heavy loss." It was necessary to destroy or at least force the enemy guns back before Wallace could send his infantry forward, which was relatively quickly accomplished by concentrating the fire from several of Wallace's batteries in a cross fire on the Confederate position, which forced them back far enough for the advance to begin. The first Confederate troops Wallace ran into were Colonel Pond's brigade from Bragg's corps that was on the far left and well in advance of the main Confederate line.[18]

General Wallace's men moved out and with their artillery support gone the Confederate infantry did not put up too much of a fight and Wallace reported that the hill was taken "almost without opposition." Like General Nelson's division on the left, Wallace advanced a little too quickly against light opposition as he tried to get around the flank of Bragg's line and soon was too far ahead of General Sherman's troops on his left and had to halt his advance so that the flanks of his and Sherman's troops were not exposed to enemy counterattacks. General Sherman, who had been waiting for the sound of General Buell's guns before advancing, sent several regiments forward against the same light opposition that Wallace was facing to try to reach the original campsites of Sunday morning. Around ten o'clock when the firing from Buell's troops was at its peak Sherman ordered his troops forward in an all-out attack. Wallace moved forward on the right and Sherman angled a little to his left to remain in contact with General McClernand's right. Sherman had Colonel Buckland's troops out in front, with Colonel Stuart's brigade taking advantage of the cover provided by a wooded area to the right. Once they got going and ran into the main Confederate defenses Sherman noted that his line "advanced slowly and steadily, under a heavy fire of musketry and artillery."[19]

At about the same time that Sherman troops began their advance over to his left General McClernand also began moving his men forward. Just like Wallace and Sherman, McClernand faced little resistance at first and moved slowly toward his abandoned camp, adjusting his lines a few times and using his artillery to provide covering fire for the infantry as they moved forward pushing the defenders back. Upon reaching the rear of his campsites McClernand sent a heavy force of skirmishers out in front of his lines who "advanced through my camp obliquely to the southwest, thus retaking it." By late morning the right wing of the Federal lines was advancing all together as McClernand moved forward "at the same time General Sherman and Wallace were seen advancing in the same direction." General Grant's troops now ran into the Confederate positions that Sherman had noted were forming to the front and McClernand's advance quickly stalled as they ran into the lines manned by many of the Confederates brigades that had forced them back the day before. The 53rd Ohio from Sherman's division ran into such heavy fire that they had to fall back to regroup.

One of Wallace's men, Richard J. Fulfer of the 24th Indiana, later wrote, "The earth shook as if with an earthquake. It seemed as if nothing could live in the hell of fire. One could taste the sulphur and the shell and bullets could have been stirred with a stick." McClernand reported that on his right the advance came to a halt until troops from Colonel Marsh's brigade "opened an oblique fire, which immediately dispersed the enemy in that direction, leaving us in possession of my recaptured camp."[20]

During the time that McClernand was distracted by the fighting for his original camps General Beauregard was taking advantage of the gap that naturally opened between Buell's right and Grant's left. General Polk moved his troops into this gap and launched a series of assaults against both flanks and the fronts of both Federal armies. McClernand had to turn his force to face left so that he could meet the advancing enemy in what he felt was "one of the severest conflicts" of the entire battle. General Cheatham led his Confederates into the center of this assault and called the fighting "the most hotly contested I have ever witnessed."[21]

McClernand's men at first repulsed the enemy advance and then counterattacked and pushed them back. But Polk brought up reinforcements that halted McClernand's troops in their tracks and he admitted, "Our position at this moment was most critical and a repulse seemed inevitable." McClernand requested assistance from General McCook, who was contending with Confederates on his own right flank but was able to send over the Louisville Legion from General Rousseau's brigade to assist McClernand in repelling another Confederate advance. McClernand reported that with the reinforcements "extending and strengthening my line, this gallant body poured into the enemy's ranks one of the most terrible fires I ever witnessed. Thus breaking its center, it fell back in disorder."[22]

As the afternoon began it was becoming obvious that the Federal advantage in numbers was making itself felt. General Beauregard had his exhausted and outnumbered troops fighting for every foot of ground, using local counterattacks to slow the Federal advance and in places push them back, but not for long. As happened on Sunday, much of the fighting took place in relatively small but fierce battles all along the lines. General Cleburne would send his men forward until they were forced back; then General Anderson would hit the advancing Federals a sharp blow at a different location while General Polk sent General Stewart and Colonel Maney forward near the center. A soldier from Wisconsin wrote home explaining what he experienced: "All I know about it is that we drove the rebels & they drove us & then we would drive them again. We were advancing & retreating all the time until afternoon, before we got the upper hand of the Secesh." The men in the 76th Ohio, one of Wallace's regiments, had much in common with most of the Federal units that day. They spent most of the day moving through swamp or wooded areas and up and down ravines, frequently under fire. The officers would order double time to gain a position, then order the men to fall flat to avoid enemy fire, then "up and double quick forward, sometimes filing to the left, then to the right," as Charles Miller remembered, "everywhere taking advantage of deviations of the ground to shelter us from the shot and shell, pressing onward while the enemy gradually fell back, contesting every inch of ground."[23]

Elisha Stockwell Jr. of the 14th Wisconsin later wrote about what he saw that morning as his unit moved forward on the battlefield: "A little farther on we saw lots of dead men scattered through the woods where they had fallen the day before. These were all dressed in blue, but a little farther were some with butternut uniforms mixed among the blue and a little farther nearly all had the butternut uniforms." There was no telling how many more bodies in each color uniform would be added to this grisly scene before the day was over.[24]

24

Reversal of Fortune

By early afternoon it was becoming clear to the Confederate commanders that there was little chance of reversing the flow of the battle and that it was time to consider salvaging what was left of the army before it was too late. Now serving on Beauregard's staff, Colonel Thomas Jordan recorded, "Our losses were swelling, and the straggling was growing more difficult to restrain." Tennessee governor Isham Harris, who had volunteered to work on the staff of General Johnston and was continuing to serve the cause after Johnston's death by working for Beauregard, commented about two o'clock in the afternoon that it appeared to even his untrained eye that the battle was going against them and, according to Jordan, wondered out loud "whether there was not danger in tarrying so long in the field as to be unable to withdraw in good order." Shortly after the governor made this comment Jordan was able to speak with Beauregard and suggested to the army commander, "[D]o you not think our troops are very much in the condition of a lump of sugar thoroughly soaked with water, but yet preserving its original shape, though ready to dissolve? Would it not be judicious to get away with what we have?" General Beauregard had already been contemplating just this idea, because he immediately replied to Jordan, "I intend to withdraw in a few minutes."[1]

General Beauregard had indeed been contemplating the possibility of withdrawal for some time. By late morning it was obvious that the Confederates were facing at least three fresh divisions from General Buell's army in addition to General Wallace's division of Grant's army. It was not just the increased numbers of Federal troops that turned the tide but also the fact that these fresh troops had not been beaten back the day before and their unit organization from division down to company level was intact, something that could not be said for the troops on both sides who participated in Sunday's bloodbath. General Beauregard later wrote that by mid-afternoon as his troops were gradually being pushed back he had "resolved to retire from the field, and thus put an end to a useless loss of life and material." It must have been more than difficult for Beauregard to even contemplate falling back, considering how close the Confederates had come to a spectacular victory, but considering the reality of the situation, he had to acknowledge, "There was now but one course to pursue. It was, while inducing the enemy to believe in a determination on my part to continue the contest, to quietly prepare for a timely and honorable retreat. I acted with much caution and abstained from communicating my intention to the corps commanders."[2]

Over on the left of the Federal lines where General Buell's troops had begun the attack early that morning the fighting had been just as violent as anywhere on the field. The divisions of both Generals Nelson and Crittenden had been moving forward toward the same target, the Hamburg–Purdy road. For most of the day until mid-afternoon both divisions would force the Confederates back only to be forced back again when the enemy counterattacked. With General Crittenden attacking Breckinridge's front moving down the Eastern Corinth road, they were joined by part of McCook's division and advanced across the Duncan field, pushing Breckinridge back to the southwest. Crittenden slowly continued his advance and by mid-afternoon reached the vicinity of the junction between the Eastern Corinth and Hamburg–Purdy roads. In his report Colonel William Sooy Smith, commanding Crittenden's 14th Brigade, wrote how his regiments fared since late morning when they had just barely withstood a furious enemy attack and after some time made an advance of their own toward an enemy artillery battery: "At the head of this column stood a few heroic men, not adequately supported, when the enemy returned to the attack with three fresh regiments in good order. We were driven back by these nearly to the first position occupied by our line, when we rallied and moved forward toward the battery." As they approached the enemy position Captain Mendenhall brought up his guns and soon silenced the Confederate artillery. Colonel Smith also noted that around three o'clock his men "then advanced and captured it the second time, and succeeded in holding it, despite the efforts of the enemy to repulse us. One of the guns was at once turned upon the enemy, and Mendenhall's battery was advanced to nearly the same position and opened fire upon the flank of the enemy's column, then retiring before General McCook's division on our right."[3]

On the far left of the Federal line General Nelson had been going back and forth with enemy troops under Generals Hardee and Breckinridge for most of the morning as he was working his way south toward the junction of the Hamburg–Purdy and Hamburg–Savannah roads. Colonel Ammen, on the far left, described the fighting on his front as he waited for one of the many Confederate attacks: "The enemy is massing in our front, apparently determined to carry our left flank.... On the rebels come with loud shouts, and when they are at the proper place the men of the Tenth rise, the front rank fires, loads; the rear rank fires, &c. The rebels find the aim too accurate and the balls too numerous to continue the advance; they fall back, renew the attack repeatedly, but are each time repulsed." From late morning to mid-afternoon General Hardee sent his troops against Nelson's lines, with the same results as Colonel Ammen reported: "The battle rages with us; no cessation; no diminution of numbers in our front; no appearance of retreat, but evident signs of another attack. They come, but cannot move our line; another effort without success; our left baffles all their courage and skill. We have fought long against superior numbers; the men are weary; ammunition is nearly exhausted." Slowly the Federal line moves forward until they reach Prentiss' camps, where a heavy enemy counterattack pushes Nelson's men back to the woods

Confederate general John C. Breckinridge. Became Confederate secretary of war late in conflict (Virginia Military Institute Archives).

behind the camps, where they hold their ground and regroup. Finally, between two and three o'clock in the afternoon General Nelson's right is reinforced and they begin advancing again. As Colonel Ammen reported, "The troops under my command made a charge; the rebels retreated in haste; disappeared in the forest, and the battle was at an end for that day about 3:30 P.M."[4]

As happened all along the battlefield, regiments charged and then retreated over the same ground multiple times this day. Colonel Sanders D. Bruce, commanding one of Nelson's brigades, reported, "The Second Kentucky at one time during the afternoon charged a battery, took it, spiked one of the guns, and turned another upon the enemy, but were unable to hold it, being fiercely charged in return by their regiments." Colonel Gideon C. Moody commanding the 9th Indiana from Hazen's brigade, reported that after his men ran out of ammunition and were ordered to fall back they were soon rushed forward to support an artillery battery being threatened by an enemy advance: "My men rushed forward, delivering a most destructive fire; charged the enemy with great spirit, driving them back in confusion and with terrible loss; pursued them closely and took another of their batteries, but being without any sufficient support, and the enemy throwing a strong force up a ravine on our left, in order to cut us off, we were compelled to retire." As the afternoon was ending, Colonel William Grose, commanding the 36th Indiana, reported on his regiment's assault on Confederate troops occupying a Federal camp on high ground that "we received orders to charge bayonets upon them, which was commenced in quick-time. As my regiment reached the summit of the eminence the enemy was far out of our reach, moving off, with their battery and infantry in front, their cavalry taking the Corinth road to the left, all in double-quick time."[5]

In the center of the Federal lines where General McClernand continued to advance he began to engage Confederate forces on his left at just about the same time General McCook hit those same enemy troops in their front. Being attacked in front and flank at the same time was too much for the already-exhausted Southerners, and McClernand reported that the attacking Union troops were soon "driving the enemy in the direction his center and left were already retreating." These Confederates were not going to go away that easily, however, and they only fell back a short distance before making another stand. Again it took the combined force of both McClernand and McCook to drive them back from this new position. Just south of the original Federal campsites McClernand ran into heavy artillery fire from several batteries of enemy artillery stationed in nearby woods. He admitted that these guns "were used with most annoying effect" until Federal artillery under Captain Edward McAllister found their range and forced them to withdraw. This was the last major action in this area of the battlefield, as the Confederates were now in full retreat. Around 4:00 P.M. the victorious Union troops had advanced about three miles, basically to about where they were at the beginning of the battle on Sunday morning.[6]

Earlier in the day the vicinity of Water Oaks Pond, about five hundred yards east of the Shiloh meetinghouse, was the scene of some of the most vicious fighting of the entire battle. General Sherman reported, "Here I saw Willich's regiment advance upon a point of water-oaks and thicket, behind which I knew the enemy was in great strength, and enter it in beautiful style. Then arose the severest musketry fire I ever heard, which lasted some twenty minutes, when this splendid regiment had to fall back." It was imperative that General Bragg keep the road to Corinth open, and he formed his lines with artillery firing on any troops who approached the water-oaks area. Sometime after two o'clock Sherman noticed that one of General McCook's brigades "advanced beautifully, deployed, and entered this dreaded woods." Sherman ordered Colonel Buckland and Colonel T. Kilby Smith, who replaced the wounded Colonel Stuart in command of the Second Brigade, to form on the right of McCook's troops, which was Rousseau's brigade, and advance with them. Sherman later wrote about how "Rousseau's brigade moved in splendid order steadily to the front, sweeping everything before it." With Sherman's men joining in the advance, he proudly noted that after some grueling fighting "[a]t 4 P.M. we stood upon the ground of our original line; and the enemy was in full retreat."[7]

One of General Rousseau's men who participated in the advance that so impressed Sherman was Adjutant Lewis Hosea, who remembered, "Between 3 and 4 o'clock in the afternoon we had pushed the enemy, still fighting, back to the vicinity of Shiloh Church." Moving slowly but steadily, Rousseau's troops pushed the Confederates back past the church when, as Hosea watched, "the forces immediately in our front in the vicinity of the road broke in disorder, leaving, however, a considerable body of the enemy on our right against whom the regular battalions right-wheeled and whom we pursued half way through the former camps of Sherman's troops lying parallel with the Shiloh branch, completing the rout of all the enemy's forces in sight."[8]

Adding some of his troops to the advance into the wooded area, General Wallace sent forward two of his brigades commanded by Colonels Morgan Smith and John Thayer. As Wallace reported, "From the time the wood was entered 'Forward' was the only order; and step by step, from tree to tree, position to position, the rebel lines went back, never stopping again." Wallace reported that General Beauregard rode back and forth in front of his and General Sherman's lines encouraging his men to hold their positions, but to no avail. General Wallace reported that while much of the fighting he had witnessed had been "grand and terrible," his troops and the rest of Grant's forces had finally broken the enemy lines and that "[a]s indicated by the sounds, however, the enemy seemed retiring everywhere, cheer after cheer ringing through the woods. Each man felt that the day was ours. About 4 o'clock the enemy to my front broke into rout and ran through the camps occupied by General Sherman on Sunday morning."[9]

Even General Grant participated in the fighting when about three o'clock over on the Federal left he brought up two regiments in person and launched an assault against one of the last enemy positions remaining in that area. The Union troops moved forward with gusto and the Confederates quickly abandoned their position to join the rest of the army as they moved away from the battlefield. Grant later wrote about his charge, "I knew the enemy were ready to break and only wanted a little encouragement from us to go quickly and join their friends who had started earlier."[10]

Earlier that morning General Beauregard had sent couriers back toward Corinth to see whether or not the expected reinforcements under General Earl Van Dorn had arrived. Learning that there was no information about Van Dorn's whereabouts, Beauregard decided it was time to begin withdrawing: "I began seriously the difficult work before me; difficult, because it had to be done without weakness or hesitancy, so as neither to make it appear a defeat in the eye of the enemy, nor a cause of discouragement to our overwrought troops." Once the corps commanders were notified of the plan to fall back they were instructed to "resume the offensive on divers points of the line, with a view to keep our adversary in ignorance of the true motive of our movement." Launching small counterattacks along the line against the pressing Federal forces was imperative to keep them off balance and prevent a coordinated assault that might have devastated the withdrawing Confederate troops. Beauregard noted that his commanders "very ably executed the orders given them; and the retreat was begun by 2:30 P.M. and effected leisurely, quietly, and with much regularity. Although the decision to withdraw the army had been made most of the Confederate troops were still scattered across the battlefield still engaged with advancing Federal troops that it took some time for all the units to receive the order to disengage and pull back."[11]

General Breckinridge was the first to pull his men back from the front so he could set up a rearguard position, troops on his flanks closed in to show a solid although thin front, and once Breckinridge was safely away the next troops to pull back were General Polk's corps, followed by Hardee, with Bragg's troops the last to fall back. General Beauregard later reported, "Soon satisfied that no serious pursuit would be attempted this last line was withdrawn, and never did troops leave a battle-field in better order; even the stragglers fell into the ranks and marched off with those who had stood more steadily by their colors." While the rest of the army continued to fall back, Breckinridge put together a strong defensive position near the same location that the army camped on Saturday night around the crossing of the Pittsburg and Hamburg roads. Usually disengaging from the enemy on an active battlefield is the most difficult part of any retreat, but for Beauregard's weary army this initial movement went even better than could have been hoped for, mostly because, as Beauregard later noted, "[n]o pursuit whatsoever was attempted by the enemy."[12]

Considering General Grant's usual aggressive nature and penchant for taking the offensive, the fact that there was no pursuit of the retreating Confederates that evening is more than a little surprising. The fact is, however, that Grant had very little to chase the enemy with. The surviving troops in Grant's Army of the Tennessee were much too exhausted and disorganized to be able to mount anything in the way of an effective pursuit. Logically, any pursuit would have been made by General Buell's much fresher troops, some of who were just arriving on the field as the Confederates were leaving. Unfortunately, confusion in the command structure and hesitation by several senior officers prevented the Federals from sending out any pursuit immediately after the fighting ended. Grant was technically the senior officer and in overall command of the combined armies, but for some reason he was hesitant to give orders to Buell. After the fighting ended that evening Grant sent a message to Buell saying, "When I left the field this evening my intention was to occupy the most advanced position possible for the night with the infantry engaged through the day, and follow up our success with cavalry and fresh troops expected to arrive." He continued by admitting, "The great fatigue of our men, they having been engaged in two days' fight and subject to a march yesterday and fight today, would preclude the idea of making any advance to-night without the arrival of the expected re-enforcements." Grant decided to wait until morning, when he would be able to put together a strong force of cavalry and infantry that could make a proper pursuit. Another possible reason for delaying the pursuit was that Grant had already received orders from General Halleck not to "advance beyond Pea Ridge, or some point which we can reach and return in a day." General Halleck was already on his way to Pittsburg Landing and was expected any day. Following the orders to stay within a day's march effectively meant there would be no pursuit.[13]

The reality of the situation was that General Grant's troops could not and would not be able to follow the retreating Confederates on Monday evening. If General Buell wanted to send some of his troops after the enemy more the better, but Grant did not want to order Buell to do so. Early the next morning General Sherman led two worn-out brigades along the same route taken by the retreating enemy, but his column was not able to get close enough to them for him to do more than see for himself that they were indeed leaving the area and bear witness to the trail of abandoned equipment they had left behind. Believing that if the enemy rear guard was pressured they might break or at least abandon their artillery, Grant sent a note to Buell asking, "Will you be good enough to order your cavalry to follow on the Corinth road and give two or three of your fresh brigades to follow in support." Clearly Grant was not acting as a commander ordering that action be taken but one officer asking another whom he considered his equal to help if he could.[14]

The lack of pursuit or even cooperation between the two Federal army commanders allowed General Beauregard's beaten troops to escape virtually unscathed after the battle, and one of the best opportunities of the war to seriously damage a retreating Confederate army was missed. Admittedly, Grant's men were exhausted and to ask them to begin a grueling march to catch the retreating enemy would be expecting a great deal, and with Buell's men still coming up his army was also tired and disorganized from the forced marches just to reach Pittsburg Landing and the fighting on Monday, but the Confederates were in just as poor condition, if not worse.

The same Tuesday morning that Grant asked Buell to send out some cavalry to press the retreating enemy troops, General Bragg sent a report to Beauregard while moving on the Corinth road, stating, "Our condition is horrible. Troops utterly disorganized and demoralized. Road almost impassable. No provisions and no forage; consequently everything is feeble. Straggling parties may get in to-night. Those in rear will suffer much.... It is most lamentable to see the state of affairs, but I am powerless and almost exhausted." Bragg said that most of the artillery was being left by the roadside and there were few officers available to direct or control the men. Practically begging for assistance, Bragg wrote, "Relief of some kind is necessary, but how it is to reach us I can hardly suggest, as no human power or animal power could carry wagons over this road with such teams as we have." That same afternoon Bragg sent another message to Beauregard informing the army commander, "We have labored all day trying to bring forward troops, and especially to save artillery. The roads are horrible, and unless we can mend them it is impossible for the artillery to get in. The teams are exhausted by incessant labor and no forage." Bragg also mentioned that he had left General Hardee in command of working parties repairing the roads, but "the men are exhausted, dispirited, and work with no zeal."[15]

On one of General Breckinridge's messages that Bragg forwarded to General Beauregard he added his own note to the original message that he was convinced: "If we are pursued by a vigorous force we will lose all in the rear. The whole road presents the scene of a rout, and no mortal power could restrain it." On that same message General Beauregard wrote his own endorsement: "All is being done that can be done." On the evening of the eighth General Breckinridge, who was still in charge of the rear guard, wrote again admitting that he did not believe his men could withstand a determined attack: "My troops are worn-out, and I don't think can be relied on after the first volley. There is for two days food enough for the men, but the horses are sinking rapidly for want of forage." Luck was with the Confederates that day, however, as the main army was allowed to continue their retreat unmolested.[16]

Roundly criticized for allowing a beaten enemy to escape, General Grant later explained why he did not order any pursuit of the Confederates on that first night, saying, "After the rain of the night before and the frequent and heavy rains for some days previous, the roads were almost impassable. The enemy carrying his artillery and supply trains over them in his retreat, made them still worse for troops following." Grant also stated that "I wanted to pursue, but had not the heart to order the men who had fought desperately for two days, lying in the mud and rain whenever not fighting, and I did not feel disposed to positively order Buell, or any part of his command to pursue." In explaining his decision to simply ask Buell for help, Grant wrote, "Although the senior in rank at the time I had been so only a few weeks. Buell was, and had been for some time past, a department commander, while I commanded only a district. I did not meet Buell in person until too late to get troops ready and pursue with effect; but had I seen him at the moment of the last charge I should have at least requested him to follow."[17]

It was uncharacteristic of Ulysses Grant to hesitate to act or spend time considering the feelings of the men under his command when he had an opportunity to strike a telling blow against the enemy, as he would prove time and again later in the war. He was, however, a stickler for following orders, and one of the factors that may have played a part in not ordering a serious pursuit of the Confederates was a telegram received from General Halleck on the morning of the ninth: "I leave immediately to join you with considerable re-enforcements. Avoid another battle, if you can, till all arrive. We then shall be able to beat them without fail." These instructions certainly seemed to prohibit any major pursuit that might turn into another real battle, even if just with the Confederate rear guard.[18]

The Battle of Shiloh or Pittsburg Landing, the greatest battle fought in North America up to that time, was over and the results shocked and dismayed the entire nation. When the war began most people expected it to be over shortly, after a few minor battles that demonstrated how foolish it was to be fighting each other. Few people on either side expected a bloodbath, but that is what they got at Shiloh, and it was only going to get worse. The combined forces of Grant and Buell lost 1,754 killed, 8,408 wounded, and 2,885 missing, for a total of 13,047. General Beauregard reported his losses as 1,723 killed, 8,012 wounded, and 959 missing, for total casualties of 10,694. The obvious difference in missing was the capture of Prentiss' men at the Hornet's Nest.[19]

Generals Grant and Buell could claim a victory since a surprise attack had been beaten off and the enemy was forced to abandon the field, but it was a close thing. The lack of any obvious gains, coupled with the terrible number of casualties, would soon cause a flood of criticism to come down on both Grant and Beauregard. Eventually, however, the importance of this battle in turning back the Confederate attempt to recapture lost territory in Tennessee and possibly Kentucky would become apparent as the war continued.

25

After Shiloh

The largest and most violent battle that Americans had ever fought was over, but as always in the aftermath of a great battle, much work and suffering was still to come. Several thousand wounded men from both sides had to be cared for by the overwhelmed Union medical staffs. The lucky ones whose wounds allowed them to be moved were sent north to recover in hospitals that, for many, were close enough to their homes to have family visit and help take care of them. The more seriously wounded stayed in the makeshift hospitals in and around the battlefield, where the care was much less satisfactory and the mortality rate was terribly high. The thousands of men who had fled during the battle had to be accounted for and returned to their units. The officers who had clearly shown that they were unfit for command had to be sorted out from those who had done their duty and sent home. And, worst of all, the dead had to be gathered up and identified by burial details. One of the men who had the misfortune to be assigned to one of those details was Judson W. Bishop of the 2nd Minnesota, who remembered, "We had to perform the burial of about 4,000 men, gathering them from every part of the battle field." When possible the bodies of Union soldiers were identified by comrades from their units or their uniform insignia and buried with as much dignity as possible in crudely marked individual graves. Sadly, many of the Federal dead and nearly all the Confederates could not be identified and "they were laid side by side in long pits and were covered, a hundred or more, in one grave."[1]

Even though his army had just barely avoided a disastrous defeat, General Grant was all business and ready to continue the campaign. On April 9 Grant wrote to General Halleck to inform him that through various sources it had been learned that "the enemy intend concentrating upon the railroad at and near Corinth all the force possible." Corinth was now the most important Confederate position in the area and had to be defended at all costs, even if that meant abandoning previously guarded positions. Wanting to continue to press the enemy, Grant wrote, "I do not like to suggest, but it appears to me that it would be demoralizing upon our troops here to be forced to retire upon the opposite bank of the river and unsafe to remain on this many weeks without large re-enforcements." In other words, he wanted more troops to continue the advance toward Corinth.[2]

Also on April 9, Grant began taking steps to improve the condition and discipline of his own troops and the security of the camps. Despite having survived their first battle, the vast majority of Grant's troops were still relatively untrained and discipline was still lax. To cut down on the number of soldiers who would simply decide to take a walk around the countryside or just wanted to get out of some camp duty and also to limit the number of civilian visitors, pickets were set up on the roads in the vicinity to limit travel to and from the camps to those who could produce proper authorization. Orders were also issued to spend more time on improving the generally poor sanitary conditions in the camps, which were the cause of much illness and frequent deaths from a multitude of sicknesses that many of the new recruits were susceptible to. Another problem that continued to vex the Federal camps and Grant ordered ended was the habit of the new soldiers indiscriminately firing their weapons in the air just for fun.[3]

In the days after the battle, as Grant was pulling his battered forces together, General Halleck was on his way to Pittsburg Landing to take over command and large reinforcements were also heading from the Mississippi River to join Grant and Buell. On April 7, as General Beauregard was falling back from Shiloh, Major General John Pope was accepting the surrender of the garrison at Island No. 10, one of the strongest Confederate forts on the Mississippi River. General Pope's army, with a major contribution from Federal gunboats, captured over five thousand enemy prisoners and all the guns and equipment in the fort after a campaign that caused relatively few casualties. Compared with the slaughter at Shiloh that accomplished nothing that could be readily seen by the public, Pope's major success, won with low losses, was acclaimed throughout the North and especially by Henry Halleck.[4]

On April 11 General Halleck arrived at Pittsburg Landing and as the ranking officer in the department naturally assumed command of the combined armies in the field, with Grant and Buell remaining in command of their separate forces. On the fourteenth Halleck wrote to Grant expressing his concerns about the training of the troops and their ability to successfully engage the enemy in another major battle anytime soon: "Immediate and active measures must be taken to put your command in condition to resist another attack by the enemy. Your army is not now in condition to resist an attack. It must be made so without delay." Grant's response was to issue orders to increase the amount of time devoted to training, making the division commanders responsible for the results by ordering that they "will see that as many hours per day as is consistent with the health of the men be devoted to drill and that company commanders excuse no soldier from any part of his duties."[5]

Ten days after Halleck took over command of the army General Pope arrived at Pittsburg Landing with his army of thirty thousand men. General Halleck now commanded nearly one hundred thousand men made up of three individual armies: Buell's Army of the Ohio, Grant's Army of the Tennessee and now Pope's Army of the Mississippi. One question that was on everyone's mind while the troops drilled and drilled more was what Halleck was going to do with this immense force.[6]

Almost as soon as the muskets fell silent a battle with words began, with the blame for the apparent unpreparedness on the first day falling mostly on one man. Many years after the battle Grant wrote that he believed that the battle at Shiloh "has been perhaps less understood, or, to state the case more accurately, more persistently misunderstood, than any other engagement between National and Confederate troops during the entire rebellion." General Sherman also offered his opinion that "probably no single battle of the war gave rise to such wild and damaging reports."[7]

General Grant's refusal to panic in the face of obvious defeat and, of course, Buell's troops who led the counterattack on Monday allowed him to claim a modest overall victory, but in the days immediately following the battle public opinion began to focus on the near disaster of the first day and the appalling number of casualties suffered for no obvious gain.

The pedestal that Grant had been set upon after Fort Henry and Fort Donelson came crashing down under charges of incompetence and drunkenness. Part of the reason for this change in the public's opinion of Grant was based on the horribly high casualties, especially in the soldiers from the Midwest, where the majority of the troops were from. Most of the killed were buried on the field, and about the only information that was distributed throughout the Northern states was lists of names in newspapers. It was much different in the Midwest. Thousands of wounded were streaming north from Pittsburg Landing, and these were not just names in the newspaper; they were sons and husbands, real men whose suffering was real, and they were everywhere. The number of casualties shocked and dismayed the public, and they wanted someone to blame.

Another reason that public opinion turned against Grant was newspaper reports of the battle. Reporters during the Civil War had few restraints, either professional or ethical, to guide their writing. There were some who did their best to accurately report what they saw and heard, but most simply wanted to file interesting and sensational stories to keep their editors happy and keep the public buying their newspapers. Many times high-ranking officers fed inaccurate information to reporters to impress the people back home, and, as usual, the private soldiers knew little about the battle other than what they saw in their own small area but didn't hesitate to spread all kinds of wild rumors they heard from others. General Sherman's intense dislike of reporters was firmly established for the remainder of the war by the misleading and frequently simply inaccurate reporting after the battle. He later wrote that it was "publicly asserted at the North" that the army was completely surprised Sunday morning, "that the rebels caught us in our tents; bayoneted the men in their beds; that General Grant was drunk; that Buell's opportune arrival saved the Army of the Tennessee from utter annihilation, etc." None of this was true and many of these types of accounts were based on rumors and stories from the men who had been among the first to flee the fighting.[8]

Many of the soldiers in the Federal army at Pittsburg Landing, while not having received proper training and having little or no military experience, had common sense enough to see that more could have been done to protect the troops. Charles Morton of the 25th Missouri wrote that "our army was only a rapidly concentrated, badly organized aggregation of armed raw material. The absolute necessity that no battle should be fought before the arrival of Buell's army seemed to forbid scouting or anything that might appear aggressive." This lack of knowledge about enemy movements caused the Federal commanders to be lulled into a false sense of security, and as Morton noted, "in fact, there had been no proper training, and there was no system. The only soldierly quality present was a desire to fight."[9]

Another man who was present at the battle and survived the war was Warren Olney, who later wrote about Pittsburg Landing that "a map of the place selected for the concentration of our army shows that with the proper precautions and such defensive works as later in the war, would have been constructed within a few hours, the place was impregnable." The Confederate attack came at the only point possible due to the creeks and river that protected most of the Federal position. Knowing that there was only one practical route for the enemy to approach made Olney believe that "the complete absence of the ordinary precautions, always taken by military commanders since the beginning of history, is inexplicable." Olney could think of only one reason for this lack of precautions, and "it grows out of the character of General Grant and his distinguished subordinate, and their inexperience. They had had then little practical knowledge of actual warfare. General Sherman, except on one occasion, had never heard a hostile gun fired. They had to learn their art, and the country and their army had to pay the cost of their teaching." While Olney may be correct concerning Sherman's lack of battlefield experience, General Grant had firsthand knowledge of surprise attacks from when the Confederate garrison at Fort Donelson swarmed out of their trenches and broke the Federal lines in their front. Learning that the enemy does not always do what you expect them to do is not a lesson that should have to be repeated too often.[10]

It took only a short time after the battle before a flood of criticism fell on Grant and some of the senior officers. In many cases those doing the commenting were the same men who headed for the rear when the fighting began. Many of the officers in the army received their rank not for their military prowess but rather their political connections or business prominence back home. Those who took to their heels when the fighting began now had to come up with a good reason why they did so to avoid embarrassment and loss of influence in their hometowns. Blaming poor leadership by the army's commanders that resulted in the army being unprepared to receive a surprise attack allowed many to claim they had to follow their men to the rear in order to form a new line on which they could rally and continue the fight. Many of the stories that spread around the North were totally untrue, but the fact is that there had been enough real mistakes and that made it easier to believe even the most outrageous stories and rumors.

General Grant did have many defenders from common soldiers all the way to the top. In July, George Squire wrote to his wife that he and other soldiers who had been at the battle had read "in some of the journals of the day statements that Gen. Grant's army were completely routed, demoralized, and on the point of falling into the hands of the enemy. But that is false. We were not 'whipped,' though driven back." Another one of Grant's defenders was none other than Henry Halleck. While Halleck had no problem criticizing a subordinate, if only to deflect blame from himself, he did stand by Grant concerning the most important complaint being leveled against him, that the army was totally surprised. On May 2 Halleck wrote to Secretary Stanton, "The newspaper accounts that our divisions were surprised are utterly false." Halleck also wrote on June 15 that he was "satisfied from a patient and careful inquiry and investigation that all our troops were notified of the enemy's approach some time before the battle commenced." Halleck also reported to Stanton that the number of men originally reported missing was highly inflated and many of the troops had been scattered and took some time reporting back to their units. He noted, "There seems to have been a morbid desire on the part of some of our officers to make the loss of their particular commands much greater than it really was."[11]

Ulysses Grant is always pictured as a tough, stoic man who cared little about what others said, but he was human, with normal feelings and emotions, and showed a little of that side in a letter to his political sponsor Congressman Washburne on May 14:

> To say that I have not been distressed at these attacks upon me would be false, for I have a father, mother, wife, and children who read them, and are distressed by them, and I necessarily share them in it. Then, too, all subject to my orders read these charges, and it is calculated to weaken their confidence in me and weaken my ability to render efficient service in our present cause. One thing I will assure you of, however,—I can not be driven from rendering the best service within my ability to suppress the present rebellion, and, when it is over, retiring to the same quiet it, the rebellion, found me enjoying. Notoriety has no charms for me, and could I render the same services that I hope has been my fortune to render our just cause without being known in the matter, it would be infinitely preferable to me.[12]

General Grant also commented to Washburne on the decision to make camp at Pittsburg Landing rather than stay on the opposite side of the river, which would have obviously been much safer, that "to have left the field of Pittsburg for the enemy to occupy until our force was sufficient to have gained a bloodless victory would have to leave the Tennessee to become a second Potomac.... Looking back at the past, I can not see for the life of me any important point that could be corrected."[13]

Notwithstanding all the differing opinions of Grant's ability to command an army, there was only one man whose opinion really mattered, Abraham Lincoln. One of the president's friends was journalist and political leader Alexander K. McClure, who was well aware that there were a great deal many influential people around the North calling for Grant's removal and that sentiment "surged against the President from every side, and he was harshly criticized for not promptly dismissing Grant or at least relieving him from his command." Meeting privately with the president, McClure did his best to convince him that removing Grant would do much to improve the president's support, but Mr. Lincoln would have none of it. McClure recounted that Lincoln stated "in a tone of earnestness that I shall never forget: 'I can't spare this man; he fights.' That was all he said, but I knew it was enough, and that Grant was safe in Lincoln's hands against his countless hosts of enemies."[14]

General Grant was not the only officer to receive public condemnation after the battle; there were also a great many questions about the conduct of the Confederate leadership. Considering that Albert Sidney Johnston gave his life bravely leading a charge on the battlefield, his reputation as a great general was relatively secure. Not so for Johnston's successor, General Beauregard. When it became widely known how close the Confederates were to all but destroying Grant's army, but they ended up abandoning the field instead, the consternation over the terrible casualties suffered by the Confederates only added to the criticism of Beauregard. Considering the physically worn-out and totally disorganized condition of the Confederate army on Sunday evening, it would appear quite reasonable that Beauregard would call a halt to the fighting when he did. What he could legitimately be criticized for was continuing to occupy the field with troops who were in desperate need of rest and reorganization before facing what everyone knew would be renewed fighting in the morning.[15]

The one thing that General Beauregard does deserve censure for was the plan of battle itself. The goal of the attack was to drive the Federal left away from the Tennessee River and trap them against the creeks in their rear, forcing surrender. Attacking in long, evenly distributed lines across nearly three miles of front offered little or no opportunity to achieve that goal. The obvious scheme would have been to strengthen the Confederate right to drive a wedge between the main part of the Federal army and the river. That Beauregard devised a poor plan to accomplish this goal is obvious by the results. The fact that General Johnston either acquiesced to Beauregard's plan or, if he had any doubts, did nothing to revise the plan of attack shows either a lack of confidence in his own decision-making ability or too much confidence in his subordinate. Either way, Albert Sidney Johnston was the army commander and by accepting Beauregard's plan also accepted ultimately responsible for the results.[16]

By the end of April the Federal army concentrated around Pittsburg Landing began to stir and it was also clear that General Halleck had decided to personally take command of the army in the field. One of the first actions Halleck took when all the components of the army were assembled was to completely reorganize the structure of the army by rearranging some of the old commands into four parts or wings: right, center, left, and a reserve.

Major General George H. Thomas, one of General Buell's division commanders, was put in command of the right wing that contained his own division and what was left of Grant's Army of the Tennessee less McClernand's and Lew Wallace's divisions. General Buell's Army of the Ohio, less Thomas' division, was designated as the center, with Buell remaining in command. General Pope's Army of the Mississippi remained intact and was now the left wing. The reserve was made up of the divisions of McClernand and Lew Wallace with McClernand in command. The next highest-ranking officer in the department after Halleck was General Grant, who was assigned to command the right wing and the reserve and also fill in as the second-in-command of the entire army.[17]

As one might expect, not all the generals were happy with the new organization of the army. General Buell, for instance, had a legitimate reason to complain, since he had lost one of his divisions, and told General Halleck, "You must excuse me for saying that, as it seems to me, you have saved the feelings of others very much to my injury." Another officer who was not happy with his new assignment was General Grant. His new position as second-in-command made Grant more of a figurehead with nominal authority or responsibility. Grant was not invited to councils of war, orders were not sent through him to the wing commanders and his advice and suggestions were usually ignored, leading Grant to believe he was given a meaningless job and title to keep him out of the way. Grant grew so frustrated and unhappy with his situation that at one point he was actually packing his personal belongings before going on a leave from which he was not planning to return until General Sherman convinced him to give the situation more time before taking such a drastic step.[18]

General Halleck was apparently unaware that Grant was so unhappy with his new role with the army that he was considering leaving, or, considering Halleck's low opinion of Grant, if he did know he did not care. By May 12 the problem was obvious even to Halleck, who wrote to Grant that he was "very much surprised, general, that you should find any cause of complaint in the recent assignment of commands. You have precisely the position to which your rank entitles you." As far as trying to embarrass Grant or injure his reputation went, Halleck did have reason to be offended, since he did support Grant against the worst of the charges after Shiloh, saying, "I have done everything in my power to ward off the attacks which were made upon you. If you believe me your friend you will not require explanations; if not, explanations on my part would be of little avail."[19]

In early May General Halleck was leading his army of nearly one hundred thousand men toward what was still the most important enemy target in his department, the rail center at Corinth. The massive Federal army only advanced a few miles a day, because Halleck insisted on stopping and putting up earthworks every afternoon. While this precaution prevented Halleck from being the victim of a surprise Confederate attack, it also made it difficult, if not impossible, for the Federals to force General Beauregard into a fight where Halleck's numbers would give him an important advantage. Calling the move toward Corinth "a siege from the start to the close," General Grant did not approve of the slow approach but could do nothing about it. Day after day the Federal army moved toward Corinth like the tide rising, slow but unstoppable. General Halleck was not interested in forcing another major battle but rather to maneuver Beauregard out of Corinth or, if he would not leave, lay siege to the town, with Halleck's overwhelming numbers assuring eventual victory.[20]

Corinth was too important to lose without taking desperate measures to hold the town. After General Beauregard warned, "If defeated here, we lose the Mississippi Valley and probably our cause," troops were rushed to Corinth from around the south, including fifteen thousand men from Arkansas under General Earl Van Dorn, bringing the strength of the Confederate garrison to about sixty thousand men. Many thousands of those men, however, were unable to contribute much to the defense of the town. There were still thousands of men recovering from their wounds received at Shiloh, and the living conditions around Corinth were simply appalling. With all the additional troops pouring into Corinth, food was scarce and the water from most wells was dirty and foul smelling; it got so bad that many horses refused to drink and the men had to hold their noses to force down the liquid. Combined with unusually hot weather, the poor water and low rations put thousands of men on the sick lists. Removing the sick from the town and sending them to outlying villages was the only way for them to recover, but many hundreds did not. Almost as many men were lost at Corinth from disease as were lost in the fighting at Shiloh.[21]

No matter the condition of his troops, General Beauregard was committed to defending Corinth. Long lines of fortifications were built north of the town to block the Federal army's direct path to Corinth. The hope was that if the Federals sent out modest-size forces to probe the lines they could be lured into a trap and destroyed by a quick attack, thus reducing the Federal army's manpower and, it was hoped, their will to fight. On May 3 just such an occasion presented itself when General Pope sent a division forward from the main force toward Farmington, about four miles from Corinth. A minor fight developed, but before any major Confederate forces could arrive on the scene Pope was ordered to pull his men back. On the eighth Pope sent two divisions past Farmington to reconnoiter the defenses but was again ordered to return to the Federal lines. On both of these occasions Beauregard attempted to attack the Federal units with General Bragg hitting them from the front while Van Dorn struck them from the flank. Both times, however, Van Dorn was unable to get into position quickly enough and Pope's men fell back before any serious fighting developed. As the massive Union army closed on their target Halleck had earthworks of his own built opposite the Confederate lines to prevent Beauregard from launching an attack on his troops before they were all in position.[22]

As the month of May came to a close it was obvious to Beauregard that Halleck was being too careful to leave any opening for the Confederates to take advantage of. Attacking the more numerous and by now well-entrenched Federal army was simply out of the question. General Beauregard could also clearly see that if he just continued to occupy Corinth eventually so many of his men would be incapacitated, or worse, by illness that any serious Federal attack would probably succeed. In that event he could lose both the town and the army. That could not be allowed to happen; it was time to save the troops while they could still get away. Beginning on May 30 Beauregard used a clever scheme to convince Halleck that trains arriving in Corinth were bringing reinforcements when they were actually evacuating the garrison. This deception worked so well that on the same day that the last of the Confederate troops were leaving Corinth the Federal army was in line and waiting for a battle General Halleck was convinced was about to begin.[23]

When Halleck's troops marched into Corinth all they found was an abandoned town with nothing of military value left behind other than the railroad tracks. Henry Halleck had achieved an almost bloodless significant strategic victory, but not all his subordinates were especially pleased with the outcome. Grant wondered "how the mere occupation of places was to close the war while large and effective rebel armies existed." About fifty miles south in Tupelo, General Beauregard halted the army for rest, quite pleased that he had saved the army to fight another day with presumably a better chance of obtaining a victory.

However, back in the Confederate capital Jefferson Davis, looking over the whole picture, knew what a major blow the Confederacy had suffered with the loss of one of the main rail centers in the West. Shortly after arriving in Tupelo, General Beauregard requested leave to recover from an illness, and while he was recovering President Davis replaced him as army commander with his old friend Braxton Bragg, who in the future would lead the army to both stunning victory and equally stunning defeat.[24]

The horrific battle at Shiloh was the culmination of Grant's river campaign and it brought about a profound change in the thinking of many people in the North who had always believed that the South didn't really mean it and that given time the rebellion would collapse on its own. One of those who experienced this turnaround in their view of the war was Ulysses Grant, who wrote, "Up to the battle of Shiloh I, as well as thousands of other citizens, believed the rebellion against the Government would collapse suddenly and soon, if a decisive victory could be gained over any of its armies." For a brief time Grant thought that the demonstration of Federal power that produced the victories at Fort Henry and Fort Donelson, the loss of Kentucky and much of Tennessee, and the opening of many miles of the Mississippi River to Federal ships, all within a few months, should have been enough to convince most Southerners that they could not win. But what Grant and many in the North did not expect was that the Federal victories in early 1862 only galvanized the South to make a larger commitment to the war effort, and when General Johnston was able to pull together such a large army and, as Grant wrote, "assumed the offensive and made such a gallant effort to regain what had been lost, then, indeed, I gave up all idea of saving the Union except by complete conquest."[25]

Chapter Notes

Chapter 1

1. A. L. Conger, *The Rise of U.S. Grant* (Freeport, NY: Books for Libraries Press, 1970), 42; Benjamin Franklin Cooling, *Forts Henry and Donelson: The Key to the Confederate Heartland* (Knoxville: The University of Tennessee Press, 1987), 1; Stephen D. Engle, *Struggle for the Heartland: The Campaigns from Fort Henry to Corinth* (Lincoln: University of Nebraska Press, 2001), 2.

2. Engle, *Struggle*, 10; Conger, *Rise*, 44; Spencer C. Tucker, *Unconditional Surrender: The Capture of Forts Henry and Donelson* (Abilene, TX: McWhiney Foundation Press, 2001), 14–16.

3. Tucker, *Unconditional Surrender*, 14–16; Conger, *Rise*, 45; United States Naval War Records Office, *Official Records of the Union and Confederate Navies in the War of the Rebellion* (Washington, DC: Government Printing Office, 1894–1922), vol. 25, 474.

4. Tucker, *Unconditional Surrender*, 14; Steven E. Woodworth, *Jefferson Davis and His Generals: The Failure of Confederate Command in the West* (Lawrence: University Press of Kansas, 1990), 21.

5. Tucker, *Unconditional Surrender*, 14.

6. Engle, *Struggle*, 9; Tucker, *Unconditional Surrender*, 14; Woodworth, *Jefferson Davis*, 21–22.

7. Conger, *Rise*, 50–51.

8. Conger, *Rise*, 50–51; Stanley F. Horn, *The Army of Tennessee* (Norman: University of Oklahoma Press, 1968), 16, Engle, *Struggle*, 16; William T. Sherman and John Sherman, "Letters of Two Brothers," *The Century*, January 1893.

9. Fletcher Pratt, *Civil War on Western Waters* (New York: Henry Holt and Company, 1956), 30.

10. Horn, *The Army of Tennessee*, 39–41, 44; Woodworth, *Jefferson Davis*, 35.

11. Woodworth, *Jefferson Davis*, 35–36; Horn, *The Army of Tennessee*, 42–43; Engle, *Struggle*, 16.

12. Kenneth P. Williams, *Grant Rises in the West: The First Year, 1861–1862* (Lincoln: University of Nebraska Press, 1997), 49–50; United States War Department, *War of the Rebellion: A Compilation of the Official Records of the Union and Confederate Armies* (Washington, DC: Government Printing Office, 1880–1901), vol. 4, 255.

13. Horn, *The Army of Tennessee*, 47–48; John Berrien Lindsley, ed., *The Military Annals of Tennessee, Confederate* (Nashville, TN: J. M. Lindsley & Co., Publishers, 1886), 21–22; Christopher Losson, *Tennessee's Forgotten Warriors: Frank Cheatham and His Confederate Division* (Knoxville: The University of Tennessee Press, 1989), 27.

14. Horn, *The Army of Tennessee*, 48; Lindsley, *Military Annals*, 23.

15. Woodworth, *Jefferson Davis*, 30; Engle, *Struggle*, 14–15.

16. Engle, *Struggle*, 12; Horn, *The Army of Tennessee*, 48; Woodworth, *Jefferson Davis*, 30–31.

17. Lindsley, *Military Annals*, 24; Horn, *The Army of Tennessee*, 48–49; Engle, *Struggle*, 14.

18. Losson, *Tennessee's Forgotten Warriors*, 31–32; Woodworth, *Jefferson Davis*, 36; Horn, *The Army of Tennessee*, 50.

19. Steven E. Woodworth, *Nothing but Victory: The Army of the Tennessee, 1861–1865* (New York: Alfred A. Knopf, 2005), 32–33; Cooling, *Forts Henry and Donelson*, 9–10.

20. Tucker, *Unconditional Surrender*, 18; Engle, *Struggle*, 30; James M. McPherson, *Battle Cry of Freedom: The Civil War Era* (New York: Oxford University Press, 1988), 394.

21. Engle, *Struggle*, 30; Henry Coppee, *Grant and His Campaigns: A Military Biography* (New York: Charles B. Richardson, 1866), 35; Tucker, *Unconditional Surrender*, 18–19; John G. Nicolay and John Hay, "Abraham Lincoln: A History, Tennessee and Kentucky," *The Century*, August, 1888; Rowena Reed, *Combined Operations in the Civil War* (Annapolis, MD: Naval Institute Press, 1978), 72.

22. McPherson, *Battle Cry of Freedom*, 393–94; Tucker, *Unconditional Surrender*, 20; John Fiske, *The Mississippi Valley in the Civil War* (Boston: Houghton, Mifflin and Company, 1900), 53; Horn, *The Army of Tennessee*, 51; Engle, *Struggle*, 14.

23. McPherson, *Battle Cry of Freedom*, 393–94; Fiske, *Mississippi Valley*, 53; Horn, *The Army of Tennessee*, 53.

24. Tucker, *Unconditional Surrender*, 21; Horn, *The Army of Tennessee*, 52; Engle, *Struggle*, 15.

25. Charles P. Roland, *Jefferson Davis's Greatest General: Albert Sidney Johnston* (Abilene, TX: McWhiney Foundation Press, 2000), 20; Fiske, *Mississippi Valley*, 53; McPherson, *Battle Cry of Freedom*, 393–94.

26. Horn, *The Army of Tennessee*, 54; Roland, *Jefferson Davis's Greatest General*, 21.

27. James Mason Hoppin, *Life of Andrew Hull Foote, Rear-Admiral United States Navy* (New York: Harper & Brothers, Publishers, 1874), 154, 164; Henry Walke, "Operations of the Western Flotilla," *The Century*, January 1885, 424.

28. Hoppin, *Life*, 165; H. Allen Gosnell, *Guns on the Western Waters: The Story of River Gunboats in the Civil War* (Baton Rouge: Louisiana State University Press, 1949), 45–46.

29. Hoppin, *Life*, 166; Walke, "Operations," 424; Spencer C. Tucker, *Andrew Foote: Civil War Admiral on Western Waters* (Annapolis, MD: Naval Institute Press, 2000), 118, 120–21.
30. Tucker, *Unconditional Surrender*, 36.
31. Tucker, *Unconditional Surrender*, 36–37; Walke, "Operations," 424; Tucker, *Andrew Foote*, 116.
32. Hoppin, *Life*, 154; Tucker, *Andrew Foote*, 118; *Official Records Navy*, vol. 2, 335.
33. Tucker, *Andrew Foote*, 121; Gosnell, *Guns*, 45–46; Walke, "Operations," 424; Hoppin, *Life*, 165.
34. Tucker, *Andrew Foote*, 119–20.
35. Engle, *Struggle*, 12; Cooling, *Forts Henry and Donelson*, 7.
36. Woodworth, *Nothing but Victory*, 6–8; Cooling, *Forts Henry and Donelson*, 7.
37. Woodworth, *Nothing but Victory*, 22–23; Engle, *Struggle*, 10–11.

Chapter 2

1. Nicolay and Hay, "Lincoln: Tennessee," 566–67.
2. Nicolay and Hay, "Lincoln: Tennessee," 567; Cooling, *Forts Henry and Donelson*, 10.
3. Nicolay and Hay, "Lincoln: Tennessee," 567; Thomas Speed, *The Union Cause in Kentucky* (New York: G. P. Putnam's Sons, 1907), 136.
4. Nicolay and Hay, "Lincoln: Tennessee," 568.
5. Albert D. Richardson, *A Personal History of Ulysses S. Grant* (Hartford, CT: American Publishing Company, 1868), 192–93; Nicolay and Hay, "Lincoln: Tennessee," 568–69.
6. Richardson, *Personal History*, 192–93; Nicolay and Hay, "Lincoln: Tennessee," 568–69.
7. Nicolay and Hay, "Lincoln: Tennessee," 568.
8. Albert Sidney Johnston, "Letter from General A. S. Johnston," *Southern Historical Society Papers*, January–June 1877, 128–29.
9. Coppee, *Grant Campaigns*, 37; Lew Wallace, "The Capture of Fort Donelson," *The Century*, December 1884, 286–87.
10. Henry Coppee, *Life and Services of Gen. U.S. Grant* (Chicago: The Western News Company, 1868), 37–38; Gosnell, *Guns*, 46; McPherson, *Battle Cry of Freedom*, 393; James J. Hamilton, *The Battle of Fort Donelson* (New York: Thomas Yoseloff, Publisher, 1968), 24–25.
11. Coppee, *Life and Services*, 37; Horn, *The Army of Tennessee*, 57; Engle, *Struggle*, 47; *Official Records*, vol. 7, 845.
12. Nicolay and Hay, "Lincoln: Tennessee," 575; Jesse Grant Cramer, ed., *Letters of Ulysses S. Grant to His Father and His Youngest Sister, 1857–78* (New York: G. P. Putnam's Sons, 1912), 64; Coppee, *Life and Services*, 18, 24–28.
13. Nicolay and Hay, "Lincoln: Tennessee," 575; Cramer, *Letters*, 65.
14. Nicolay and Hay, "Lincoln: Tennessee," 575; Cramer, *Letters*, 66–67.
15. Conger, *Rise*, 133–34; *Official Records*, vol. 7, 521.
16. Coppee, *Life and Services*, 74; Engle, *Struggle*, 20–21; *Official Records*, vol. 16, pt. 1, 51.
17. Stephen D. Engle, *Don Carlos Buell: Most Promising of All* (Chapel Hill: The University of North Carolina Press, 1999), 130; McPherson, *Battle Cry of Freedom*, 394; Engle, *Struggle*, 21.
18. Engle, *Buell*, 152; *Official Records*, vol. 7, 528–29.
19. Conger, *Rise*, 131–32; *Official Records*, vol. 7, 524, 526.
20. McPherson, *Battle Cry of Freedom*, 395; *Official Records*, vol. 7, 526.
21. *Official Records*, vol. 7, 527.
22. *Official Records*, vol. 7, 527–28.
23. *Official Records*, vol. 7, 528–29.
24. *Official Records*, vol. 7, 532.
25. *Official Records*, vol. 7, 532.
26. *Official Records*, vol. 7, 533.
27. *Official Records*, vol. 7, 535.

Chapter 3

1. Stephen E. Ambrose, *Halleck: Lincoln's Chief of Staff* (Baton Rouge: Louisiana State University Press, 1962), 19; William T. Sherman, *Memoirs of Gen. W. T. Sherman, Written by Himself* (New York: Charles L. Webster & Co., 1891), vol. 2, 248; Pratt, *Civil War*, 53.
2. Hamilton, *Battle*, 18–19.
3. Hamilton, *Battle*, 19–20.
4. Bruce Catton, *Grant Moves South* (Boston: Little Brown and Company, 1960), 118–19; *Official Records*, vol. 7, 533–34; Ulysses S. Grant, *Personal Memoirs of U.S. Grant* (New York: Charles L. Webster & Co., 1885), vol. 1, 285–86.
5. Catton, *Grant Moves South*, 119; Grant, *Memoirs*, vol. 1, 285–86.
6. *Official Records*, vol. 7, 561; Grant, *Memoirs*, vol. 1, 286; Hamilton, *Battle*, 20; Adam Badeau, *Military History of Ulysses S. Grant: From April, 1861, to April, 1865* (New York: D. Appleton and Company, 1885), 25.
7. Conger, 140; *Official Records*, vol. 8, 509–10.
8. Catton, *Grant Moves South*, 129–30; Nicolay and Hay, "Lincoln: Tennessee," 577.
9. Engle, *Struggle*, 40; Grant, *Memoirs*, vol. 1, 287.
10. *Official Records*, vol. 7, 120–21.
11. *Official Records*, vol. 7, 121.
12. Hamilton, *Battle*, 21; Coppee, *Grant Campaigns*, 40; Conger, *Rise*, 140–41; *Official Records*, vol. 7, 571.
13. *Official Records*, vol. 7, 121, 572; Catton, *Grant Moves South*, 130–31.
14. *Official Records*, vol. 7, 575; Hamilton, *Battle*, 21–22.
15. *Official Records*, vol. 7, 121–22, 574, 577; Hamilton, *Battle*, 23.
16. Hamilton, *Battle*, 23; *Official Records*, vol. 7, 580.
17. *Official Records*, vol. 7, 577; Hamilton, *Battle*, 22.
18. *Official Records*, vol. 7, 575, 577; Hamilton, *Battle*, 22; Woodworth, *Nothing but Victory*, 39–40.
19. *Official Records*, vol. 7, 574, 578–79.
20. *Official Records*, vol. 7, 581.

Chapter 4

1. Catton, *Grant Moves South*, 138; Walke, "Operations," 426–27.
2. Henry Walke, "The Gunboats at Belmont and Fort Henry," *Battles and Leaders of the Civil War*, Robert Underwood Johnson and Clarence Clough Buel, eds. (New York: Thomas Yoseloff, 1956), 362; Walke, "Operations," 426–27; Coppee, *Grant Campaigns*, 42; Catton, *Grant Moves South*, 139.
3. Hamilton, 25; Walke, "Operations," 426–27; Coppee, *Grant Campaigns*, 42; Catton, 139.
4. Hamilton, *Battle*, 25; John Y. Simon, ed., *The Papers of Ulysses S. Grant* (Carbondale: Southern Illinois University Press, 1972), vol. 4, 147.
5. Jesse Taylor, "The Defense of Fort Henry," in *Bat-

tles and Leaders of the Civil War, Robert Underwood Johnson and Clarence Clough Buel, eds. (New York: Thomas Yoseloff, 1956), 368; Coppee, *Life and Services*, 41; Catton, *Grant Moves South*, 139; Grant, *Memoirs*, vol. 1, 291.
  6. Coppee, *Life and Services*, 41; Grant, *Memoirs*, vol. 1, 291.
  7. Grant, *Memoirs*, vol. 1, 291; Catton, *Grant Moves South*, 139; Simon, *Papers*, vol. 4, 149.
  8. Hamilton, *Battle*, 26; *Official Records*, vol. 7, 125.
  9. Hamilton, *Battle*, 26; *Official Records*, vol. 7, 125; Coppee, *Life and Services*, 42–43.
  10. Catton, *Grant Moves South*, 141–42; Taylor, "Defense," 369–70; *Official Records*, vol. 7, 139–40.
  11. Hoppin, *Life*, 199–200; Grant, *Memoirs*, vol. 1, 292; Wilbur F. Crummer, *With Grant at Fort Donelson, Shiloh and Vicksburg* (Oak Park, IL: E. C. Crummer & Co., 1915), 19.
  12. Walke, "Gunboats," 362; Taylor, "Defense," 370; Grant, *Memoirs*, vol. 1, 292.
  13. Taylor, "Defense," 370; *Official Records*, vol. 7, 122; Walke, "Operations," 428–29.
  14. Walke, "Operations," 428–29; *Official Records*, vol. 7, 122; Walke, "Gunboats," 363–64.
  15. *Official Records*, vol. 7, 123–24; Walke, "Operations," 431; Hoppin, *Life*, 201; Taylor, 371.
  16. *Official Records*, vol. 7, 123–24, 136; Walke, "Operations," 431; Hoppin, 201; Taylor, "Defense," 371.
  17. Taylor, "Defense," 371.
  18. Badeau, *Military History*, 31–32; *Official Records*, vol. 7, 124.
  19. *Official Records*, vol. 7, 125.
  20. Badeau, *Military History*, 34.
  21. Hamilton, *Battle*, 30–31; Grant, *Memoirs*, vol. 1, 294–95.
  22. Hamilton, *Battle*, 31; Grant, *Memoirs*, vol. 1, 173–75.
  23. Ambrose, *Halleck*, 26; *Official Records*, vol. 7, 583–84.
  24. Ambrose, *Halleck*, 26–27; *Official Records*, vol. 7, 587–88, 593.
  25. Simon, *Papers*, 182; Badeau, *Military History*, 34–35.
  26. *Official Records*, vol. 7, 153–55; Pratt, *Civil War*, 57.
  27. Simon, *Papers*, 182; Badeau, *Military History*, 34–35.
  28. Hamilton, *Battle*, 32–33; *Official Records*, vol. 7, 840, 859, 865.
  29. Hamilton, *Battle*, 38–39; Grant, *Memoirs*, vol. 1, 175; *Official Records*, vol. 7, 174, 599.
  30. *Official Records*, vol. 7, 599.
  31. Badeau, *Military History*, 34.

Chapter 5

  1. Hamilton, *Battle*, 40; *Official Records*, vol. 7, 130–31.
  2. Hamilton, *Battle*, 41.
  3. Woodworth, *Jefferson Davis*, 70–80; *Official Records*, vol. 7, 861; McPherson, *Battle Cry of Freedom*, 397–98.
  4. *Official Records*, vol. 7, 594, 599.
  5. *Official Records*, vol. 7, 600, 603–4.
  6. *Official Records*, vol. 7, 604; Grant, *Memoirs*, vol. 1, 296, 298.
  7. F. H. Magdeburg, "Capture of Fort Donelson," in *War Papers Read Before the Commandery of the State of Wisconsin, Military Order of the Loyal Legion of the United States* (Milwaukee, WI: Burdick & Allen, 1903), vol. 3, 285.
  8. Badeau, *Military History*, 35–36; Grant, *Memoirs*, vol. 1, 289–99; Wallace, "Fort Donelson," 292; Coppee, *Life and Services*, 49–50; Magdeburg, "Fort Donelson," 286.
  9. W. S. Morris, L. D. Hartwell, and J. B. Kuykendall, *History 31st Regiment Illinois Volunteers* (Carbondale, IL: John S. Clark, Printer, 1864), 33; Grant, *Memoirs*, vol. 1, 294–95.
  10. John T. McAuley, "Fort Donelson and Its Surrender," in *Military Essays and Recollections, Paper Read Before the Commandery of the State of Illinois, Military Order of the Loyal Legion of the United States*, vol. 1 (Chicago: A. C. McClurg and Company, 1891), 70–71; Grant, *Memoirs*, vol. 1, 299; Catton, *Grant Moves South*, 155.
  11. Charles C. Nott, *Sketches of the War: A Series of Letters to the North Moore Street School of New York* (New York: Anson D. F. Randolph, 1865), 25.
  12. Nicolay and Hay, "Lincoln: Tennessee," 580; Badeau, *Military History*, 37–38.
  13. Tucker, *Andrew Foote*, 152; *Official Records Navy*, vol. 22, 550.
  14. McAuley, "Fort Donelson," 70; Magdeburg, "Fort Donelson," 286; Wallace, "Fort Donelson," 288–89; Walke, "Operations," 431–32.
  15. Wallace, "Fort Donelson," 288–89; Coppee, *Life and Services*, 50–51; Walke, "Operations," 431–32; Badeau, *Military History*, 36–37.
  16. Wallace, "Fort Donelson," 288–89; Coppee, *Life and Services*, 50–51; Walke, "Operations," 431–32; Badeau, *Military History*, 36–37.
  17. Woodworth, *Jefferson Davis*, 80; Coppee, *Life and Services*, 51–52; Victor Hicken, *Illinois in the Civil War* (Urbana: University of Illinois Press, 1991), 33–34.
  18. Walke, "Operations," 432.
  19. Walke, "Operations," 432–33.
  20. Hicken, *Illinois*, 34; Wallace, "Fort Donelson," 294–95.

Chapter 6

  1. *Official Records*, vol. 7, 172–73, 205–6, 212–13.
  2. *Official Records*, vol. 7, 172–73, 205–6, 212–13; Robert H. Ferrell, ed., *Holding the Line: The Third Tennessee Infantry 1861–1864* (Kent, OH: The Kent State University Press, 1994), 18.
  3. Grant, *Memoirs*, vol. 1, 300; *Official Records*, vol. 7, 172.
  4. Henry I. Smith, *History of the Seventh Iowa Veteran Volunteer Infantry During the Civil War* (Mason City, IA: E. Hitchcock, Printer, Binder, 1903), 42; Coppee, *Life and Services*, 53–54; *Official Records*, vol. 7, 174, 185.
  5. Ferrell, *Holding the Line*, 21–22.
  6. Coppee, *Life and Services*, 55; Wallace, "Fort Donelson," 295.
  7. *Official Records*, vol. 7, 613; Simon, *Papers*, vol. 4, 211.
  8. *Official Records*, vol. 7, 613–14.
  9. Pratt, *Civil War*, 59–60.
  10. Tucker, *Andrew Foote*, 155; *Official Records Navy*, vol. 22, 592; Walke, "Operations," 435; *Official Records*, vol. 7, 166; Gosnell, *Guns*, 68.
  11. Wallace, "Fort Donelson," 299; *Official Records*, vol. 7, 166; Walke, "Operations," 435; Gosnell, *Guns*, 68.
  12. Wallace, "Fort Donelson," 299; *Official Records*, vol. 7, 166; Walke, "Operations," 435; Gosnell, *Guns*, 68; *Official Records Navy*, vol. 22, 592; Pratt, *Civil War*, 59; Tucker, *Andrew Foote*, 156.

13. Walke, "Operations," 433, 435; Tucker, *Andrew Foote*, 155–56; *Official Records Navy*, vol. 22, 587.
14. Walke, "Operations," 433, 435; Tucker, *Andrew Foote*, 156; *Official Records Navy*, vol. 22, 587.
15. Tucker, *Andrew Foote*, 156–57; Walke, "Operations," 433–35; *Official Records*, vol. 7, 166; Pratt, *Civil War*, 60; Gosnell, *Guns*, 68; *Official Records Navy*, Vol. 22, 584–87, 590–92.
16. Pratt, *Civil War*, 60; Tucker, *Andrew Foote*, 157; *Official Records Navy*, vol. 22, 584–86, 590–92.
17. *Official Records*, vol. 7, 159; Grant, *Memoirs*, vol. 1, 305.
18. *Official Records*, vol. 7, 268.
19. Tucker, *Andrew Foote*, 155; Wallace, "Fort Donelson," 415; H. S. Foote, *Report of the Special Committee on the Recent Military Disasters at Forts Henry and Donelson and the Evacuation of Nashville* (Richmond, VA: Enquirer Book and Job Press, 1862), 98–99; Bromfield L. Ridley, *Battles and Sketches of the Army of Tennessee* (Mexico, MO: Missouri Printing and Publishing Co., 1906), 55–56.
20. Ridley, *Battles*, 56; Tucker, *Andrew Foote*, 158.
21. *Official Records*, vol. 7, 268, 281–82; Coppee, *Life and Services*, 57–58; Tucker, *Andrew Foote*, 158–59; Ridley, *Battles*, 56.
22. Morris, Hartwell, and Kuykendall, *History*, 35.

Chapter 7

1. Jeffrey L. Patrick, ed., *Three Years with Wallace's Zouaves: The Civil War Memoirs of Thomas Wise Durham* (Macon, GA: Mercer University Press, 2003), 70.
2. Foote, *Report*, 119; Hicken, *Illinois*, 36; Morris, Hartwell, and Kuykendall, *History*, 35; *Official Records*, vol. 7, 186–87.
3. Morris, Hartwell, and Kuykendall, *History*, 35–36.
4. Hicken, *Illinois*, 36; Foote, *Report*, 120; *Official Records*, vol. 7, 186–87.
5. *Official Records*, vol. 7, 189; Wallace, "Fort Donelson," 301–2; Coppee, *Life and Services*, 58–59.
6. Morris, Hartwell, and Kuykendall, *History*, 34–37.
7. Wallace, "Fort Donelson," 303; Coppee, *Life and Services*, 59; Catton, *Grant Moves South*, 165–66; Tucker, *Andrew Foote*, 159; *Official Records*, vol. 7, 236–37, 244.
8. John Thomas Smith, *A History of the Thirty-first Regiment of Indiana Volunteer Infantry in the War of the Rebellion* (Cincinnati, OH: Western Methodist Book Concern, 1900), 13–14; *Official Records*, vol. 7, 243–44.
9. John Thomas Smith, *History*, 14–15; *Official Records*, vol. 7, 244.
10. *Official Records*, vol. 7, 331; Ridley, *Battles*, 57.
11. Ferrell, *Holding the Line*, 26; *Official Records*, vol. 7, 348.
12. Wallace, "Fort Donelson," 303–4; Coppee, *Life and Services*, 60–61; Catton, *Grant Moves South*, 165–66; Hicken, *Illinois*, 39; *Official Records*, vol. 7, 238.
13. *Official Records*, vol. 7, 238, 252–53, 244; Wallace, "Fort Donelson," 304.
14. Stewart Bennett and Barbara Tillery, eds., *The Struggle for the Life of the Republic: A Civil War Narrative by Brevet Major Charles Dana Miller, 76th Ohio Volunteer Infantry* (Kent, OH: The Kent State University Press, 2004), 18.
15. Ridley, *Battles*, 58.
16. Ferrell, *Holding the Line*, 26, 29.
17. *Official Records*, vol. 7, 283.

Chapter 8

1. Tucker, *Andrew Foote*, 158; Grant, *Memoirs*, vol. 1, 304–5; Wallace, "Fort Donelson," 302; Catton, *Grant Moves South*, 163–64.
2. Grant, *Memoirs*, vol. 1, 304–5; Wallace, "Fort Donelson," 302; Tucker, *Andrew Foote*, 158.
3. Grant, *Memoirs*, vol. 1, 304–5; Wallace, "Fort Donelson," 302; Tucker, *Andrew Foote*, 158; Catton, *Grant Moves South*, 163–64.
4. Hicken, *Illinois*, 39–40; Wallace, "Fort Donelson," 304; Tucker, *Andrew Foote*, 159–60; Grant, *Memoirs*, vol. 1, 305–6.
5. Wallace, "Fort Donelson," 304.
6. Grant, *Memoirs*, vol. 1, 307.
7. Grant, *Memoirs*, vol. 1, 307–8; Adam Badeau, "General Grant," *The Century*, May 1885, 155–56.
8. *Official Records*, vol. 7, 618.
9. Wallace, "Fort Donelson," 305–6; Patrick, *Three Years*, 720.
10. *Official Records*, vol. 7, 239; John Thomas Smith, *History*, 16–17.
11. *Official Records*, vol. 7, 245; John Thomas Smith, *History*, 16–17.
12. Wallace, "Fort Donelson," 306–7; Coppee, *Life and Services*, 61.
13. John H. Brinton, *Personal Memoirs of John H. Brinton: Major and Surgeon, U.S.V., 1861–1865* (1914; repr., Carbondale: Southern Illinois University Press, 1996), 120–21; Coppee, *Life and Services*, 63–64; *Official Records*, vol. 7, 221.
14. Charles F. Hubert, *History of the Fiftieth Regiment Illinois Volunteer Infantry in the War of the Union* (Kansas City, MO: Western Veteran Publishing Company, 1894), 67; Nott, *Sketches*, 30–31.
15. *Official Records*, vol. 7, 377–78, 344.
16. *Official Records*, vol. 7, 333; Ridley, *Battles*, 58–59.
17. Nott, *Sketches*, 32.
18. *Official Records*, vol. 7, 333.
19. Ferrell, *Holding the Line*, 29–30.
20. *Official Records*, vol. 7, 255–56; Edwin C. Bearss, "Unconditional Surrender: The Fall of Fort Donelson," reprinted from *Tennessee Historical Quarterly*, March–June 1962, 3.
21. Bearss, "Unconditional Surrender," 3.
22. *Official Records*, vol. 7, 283.
23. Ferrell, *Holding the Line*, 31.

Chapter 9

1. Bearss, "Unconditional Surrender," 4.
2. Bearss, "Unconditional Surrender," 8; *Official Records*, vol. 7, 287, 295.
3. *Official Records*, vol. 7, 269, 283, 334.
4. *Official Records*, vol. 7, 334; Ridley, *Battles*, 59–60.
5. Bearss, "Unconditional Surrender," 10–11; *Official Records*, vol. 7, 298, 334.
6. *Official Records*, vol. 7, 288, 298, 334; Foote, *Report*, 63–64.
7. Bearss, "Unconditional Surrender," 12; *Official Records*, vol. 7, 334–35, 288; Foote, *Report*, 63–64.
8. Bearss, "Unconditional Surrender," 13–14.
9. *Official Records*, vol. 7, 160–61; Brinton, *Personal Memoirs*, 129–30.
10. Bears, "Unconditional Surrender," 27; *Official Records*, vol. 7, 335.

11. Catton, *Grant Moves South*, 175; *Official Records*, vol. 7, 161.
12. Bearss, "Unconditional Surrender," 15–17.
13. Foote, *Report*, 72–73; *Official Records*, vol. 7, 274–75, 302, 381; Ferrell, *Holding the Line*, 34.
14. Foote, *Report*, 72–73; Bearss, "Unconditional Surrender," 20–21.
15. Bearss, "Unconditional Surrender," 29–30; *Official Records*, vol. 7, 180, 246; Wallace, "Fort Donelson," 308.
16. Bearss, "Unconditional Surrender," 30–31; Lew Wallace, *An Autobiography* (New York: Harper & Brothers Publishers, 1906), 428.
17. Ira Blanchard, *I Marched with Sherman: Civil War Memoirs of the 20th Illinois Volunteer Infantry* (San Francisco: J. D. Huff and Company, 1992), 50.
18. Ferrell, *Holding the Line*, 32–34.
19. Bearss, "Unconditional Surrender," 28–29; *Official Records*, vol. 52, pt. 1, 10, vol. 7, 230, 216.
20. Ferrell, *Holding the Line*, 34.
21. Bearss, "Unconditional Surrender," 35; Catton, *Grant Moves South*, 177–78.
22. Bearss, "Unconditional Surrender," 28; *Official Records*, vol. 7, 626.
23. *Official Records*, vol. 7, 625, 160.
24. *Official Records*, vol. 7, 629.
25. Catton, *Grant Moves South*,181–82; Brinton, *Personal Memoirs*, 142; *Official Records*, vol. 7, 626.
26. Mary A. Livermore, *My Story of the War: A Woman's Narrative of Four Years Personal Experience* (Hartford, CT: A. D. Worthington and Company, 1896), 176–77.
27. Badeau, *Military History*, 54.
28. Badeau, *Military History*, 54–55.
29. Republican Party National Committee, *Life and Services of General U.S. Grant, Conqueror of the Rebellion and Eighteenth President of the United States* (Washington, DC: Philp & Solomons, 1868), 24.

Chapter 10

1. Lynda Lasswell Crist, ed., *The Papers of Jefferson Davis* (Baton Rouge: Louisiana State University Press, 1995), 89; Thomas B. Van Horne, *History of the Army of the Cumberland*, vol. 1 (Cincinnati, OH: Robert Clarke & Co., 1875), 88.
2. Benjamin Franklin Cooling, *Fort Donelson's Legacy: War and Society in Kentucky and Tennessee, 1862–1863* (Knoxville: The University of Tennessee Press, 1997), 10; Van Horne, *History*, 88.
3. Cooling, *Fort Donelson's Legacy*, 10–11.
4. Crist, *Papers*, 89; Cooling, *Fort Donelson's Legacy*, 10.
5. Edward Porter Thompson, *History of the Orphan Brigade* (Louisville, KY: Lewis N. Thompson, 1898), 78–79.
6. Edward Porter Thompson, *Orphan Brigade*, 79; Van Horne, *History*, 88.
7. Larry J. Daniel, *Shiloh: The Battle That Changed the Civil War* (New York: Simon & Schuster, 1997), 45; Cooling, *Forts Henry and Donelson*, 239.
8. John D. Fowler, *Mountaineers in Gray: The Nineteenth Tennessee Volunteer Infantry Regiment, C.S.A.* (Knoxville: The University of Tennessee Press, 2004), 58; Daniel, *Shiloh*, 87; William Preston Johnston, *The Life of Gen. Albert Sidney Johnston* (New York: D. Appleton & Company, 1879), 305; W. J. Worsham, *The Old Nineteenth Tennessee Regiment, C.S.A.* (Knoxville, TN: Press of Paragon Printing Company, 1902), 34.
9. Fowler, *Mountaineers in Gray*, 58; Daniel, *Shiloh*, 87.
10. Daniel, *Shiloh*, 87–88; Edward Porter Thompson, *Orphan Brigade*, 80.
11. Worsham, *Old Nineteenth*, 35; McPherson, *Battle Cry of Freedom*, 402–3; Fiske, *Mississippi Valley*, 64–65.
12. Cooling, *Fort Donelson's Legacy*, 14–15.
13. McPherson, *Battle Cry of Freedom*, 405–6; William Preston Johnston, *Life*, 496.
14. Crist, *Papers*, 88.
15. Crist, *Papers*, 88.
16. Daniel, *Shiloh*, 50.
17. Crist, *Papers*, 92.
18. Crist, *Papers*, 92–93.
19. Crist, *Papers*, 92–93; *Official Records*, vol. 7, 257–58.
20. Foote, *Report*, 171; *Official Records*, vol. 7, 258.
21. Foote, *Report*, 172–73; *Official Records*, vol. 7, 259.
22. Foote, *Report*, 173; *Official Records*, vol. 7, 259–60.
23. Foote, *Report*, 173; *Official Records*, vol. 7, 259–60.
24. Foote, *Report*, 173–74; *Official Records*, vol. 7, 260.
25. Foote, *Report*, 174–75; *Official Records*, vol. 7, 260.
26. *Official Records*, vol. 7, 260–61.
27. Crist, *Papers*, 117.
28. G. T. Beauregard, "The Shiloh Campaign, Part I," *The North American Review*, January 1886, 9.

Chapter 11

1. Coppee, *Life and Services*, 74; *Official Records*, vol. 7, 422–23, 629; Catton, *Grant Moves South*, 184.
2. Hoppin, *Life*, 233–34; *Official Records*, vol. 7, 422–23; Coppee, *Life and Services*, 74.
3. *Official Records*, vol. 7, 424, 648.
4. Daniel, *Shiloh*, 57; *Official Records*, vol. 7, 648–49; Hoppin, *Life*, 233.
5. *Official Records*, vol. 7, 594; Catton, *Grant Moves South*, 186–87.
6. Nicolay and Hay, "Lincoln: Tennessee," 579; *Official Records*, vol. 7, 588.
7. *Official Records*, vol. 7, 587.
8. Nicolay and Hay, "Lincoln: Tennessee," 579; *Official Records*, vol. 7, 593.
9. *Official Records*, vol. 7, 594–95.
10. *Official Records*, vol. 7, 605, 607, 620.
11. Nicolay and Hay, "Lincoln: Tennessee," 580.
12. Nicolay and Hay, "Lincoln: Tennessee," 580.
13. *Official Records*, vol. 7, 595.
14. *Official Records*, vol. 7, 628, 637.
15. Catton, *Grant Moves South*, 188; *Official Records*, vol. 7, 641, 647.
16. *Official Records*, vol. 7, 645–46.
17. *Official Records*, vol. 7, 648.
18. *Official Records*, vol. 7, 648, 655.
19. *Official Records*, vol. 7, 652.
20. Cooling, *Fort Donelson's Legacy*, 19–20; George B. Hodge, *Sketch of the First Kentucky Brigade* (Frankfort: Kentucky Yeoman Office, 1874), 14.
21. Fiske, *Mississippi Valley*, 64–65; Hodge, *Sketch*, 14.
22. Daniel, *Shiloh*, 42–43; Thomas Lawrence Connelly, *Army of the Heartland: The Army of Tennessee, 1861–1862* (Baton Rouge: Louisiana State University Press, 1967), 135–36.
23. Daniel, *Shiloh*, 41, 43; Hodge, *Sketch*, 15; Connelly, *Army of the Heartland*, 135–36; Hoppin, *Life*, 236–37.
24. Hodge, *Sketch*, 14–15; Fiske, *Mississippi Valley*, 64–65.
25. Grant, *Memoirs*, vol. 1, 318–19; *Official Records*, vol. 7, 662–63.

26. Grant, *Memoirs*, vol. 1, 318–19; *Official Records*, vol. 7, 662–63.
27. Catton, *Grant Moves South*, 190–91; Daniel, *Shiloh*, 57–58; *Official Records*, vol. 7, 666; Grant, *Memoirs*, vol. 1, 216–17, 320.
28. Daniel, *Shiloh*, 58.
29. Grant, *Memoirs*, vol. 1, 320; *Official Records*, vol. 7, 670; Catton, *Grant Moves South*, 192; Daniel, *Shiloh*, 58.
30. Daniel, *Shiloh*, 58; Catton, *Grant Moves South*, 192; Grant, *Memoirs*, vol. 1, 217, 321.

Chapter 12

1. Catton, *Grant Moves South*, 193.
2. *Official Records*, vol. 7, 655, 667–68, vol. 52, pt. 1, 217; Catton, *Grant Moves South*, 193–94.
3. *Official Records*, vol. 7, 674.
4. *Official Records*, vol. 7, 674–75.
5. Catton, *Grant Moves South*, 194–95; *Official Records*, vol. 7, 645–46.
6. *Official Records*, vol. 7, 679–80.
7. *Official Records*, vol. 7, 680.
8. *Official Records*, vol. 10, pt. 2, 3, vol. 7, 682.
9. *Official Records*, vol. 10, pt. 2, 6–7.
10. *Official Records*, vol. 10, pt. 2, 4–5.
11. Catton, *Grant Moves South*, 202; *Official Records*, vol. 10, pt. 2, 15.
12. *Official Records*, vol. 10, pt. 2, 15.
13. *Official Records*, vol. 10, pt. 2, 21.
14. *Official Records*, vol. 10, pt. 2, 21.
15. *Official Records*, vol. 10, pt. 2, 22.
16. *Official Records*, vol. 10, pt. 2, 13.
17. *Official Records*, vol. 10, pt. 2, 30, 32, 36; Grant, *Memoirs*, vol. 1, 328.
18. Ambrose, *Halleck*, 39; *Official Records*, vol. 8, 602.
19. Daniel, *Shiloh*, 83; *Official Records*, vol. 10, pt. 2, 28–29.
20. *Official Records*, vol. 7, 683.
21. *Official Records*, vol. 7, 683–84.
22. *Official Records*, vol. 10, pt. 2, 62–63.
23. Grant, *Memoirs*, vol. 1, 327–28.
24. James Grant Wilson, *General Grant's Letters to a Friend, 1861–1880* (New York: T. Y. Crowell & Company, 1897), 7; Brinton, *Personal Memoirs*, 148.
25. Daniel, *Shiloh*, 83–84.

Chapter 13

1. Daniel, *Shiloh*, 73; *Official Records*, vol. 10, pt. 2, 7.
2. Daniel, *Shiloh*, 73; *Official Records*, vol. 7, 674, vol. 10, pt. 2, 7.
3. Pratt, *Civil War*, 63.
4. James Grant Wilson, *The Life and Campaigns of Ulysses Simpson Grant, General-in-Chief of the United States Army* (New York: Robert M. DeWitt, Publisher, 1868), 32; Daniel, *Shiloh*, 75; *Official Records*, vol. 7, 677; J. F. C. Fuller, *The Generalship of Ulysses S. Grant* (New York: Da Capo Press, n.d.), 98; Catton, *Grant Moves South*, 210; D. W. Reed, "Shiloh Campaign and Battle," in *Wisconsin at Shiloh: Report of the Commission*, Frederick H. Magdeburg, compiler (Madison: Wisconsin Shiloh Monument Commission, 1909), 140.
5. Daniel, *Shiloh*, 78; Wallace, *Autobiography*, 444–45; Reed, "Shiloh Campaign and Battle," 140.
6. Daniel, *Shiloh*, 73; Wallace, *Autobiography*, 447; *Official Records*, vol. 10, pt. 1, 9–13, 15.
7. Daniel, *Shiloh*, 81; *Official Records*, vol. 10, pt. 1, 22, 28; Reed, "Shiloh Campaign and Battle," 140–41; Catton, *Grant Moves South*, 210; Sherman, *Memoirs*, vol. 1, 227.
8. Catton, *Grant Moves South*, 210; Daniel, *Shiloh*, 82; *Official Records*, vol. 10, pt. 1, 23.
9. William Conant Church, *Ulysses S. Grant and the Period of National Preservation and Reconstruction* (New York: G. P. Putnam's Sons, 1897), 120; Sherman, *Memoirs*, vol. 1, 256; Reed, "Shiloh Campaign and Battle," 141.
10. Daniel, *Shiloh*, 101–2; *Official Records*, vol. 10, pt. 1, 25, 27; Don Carlos Buell, "Shiloh Revisited," *The Century*, March 1886, 495.
11. Reed, "Shiloh Campaign and Battle," 141; Sherman, *Memoirs*, vol. 1, 261.
12. Reed, "Shiloh Campaign and Battle," 145; Daniel, *Shiloh*, 104; Catton, *Grant Moves South*, 222.
13. Grant, *Memoirs*, vol. 1, 330–31; Reed, "Shiloh Campaign and Battle," 145.
14. Daniel, *Shiloh*, 105; *Official Records*, vol. 10, pt. 2, 45; Fiske, *Mississippi Valley*, 72.
15. *Official Records*, vol. 10, pt. 2, 41.
16. *Official Records*, vol. 10, pt. 2, 46, 49, 52; Fuller, *Generalship*, 100.
17. *Official Records*, vol. 10, pt. 2, 51; Fuller, *Generalship*, 100.
18. David W. Reed, *The Seventy-seventh Pennsylvania at Shiloh* (Harrisburg, PA: Harrisburg Publishing Co., State Printers, 1905), 78; Reed, "Shiloh Campaign and Battle," 141–42; Committee of the Regiment, *The Story of the Fifty-fifth Regiment Illinois Volunteer Infantry in the Civil War, 1861–1865* (Clinton, MA: W. J. Coulter, 1887), 66.
19. David W. Reed, *Seventy-seventh*, 78; Committee of the Regiment, *Story*, 66; Reed, "Shiloh Campaign and Battle," 141–42; George W. Mason, ed., *Illinois at Shiloh: Report of the Shiloh Battlefield Commission* (Chicago: M. A. Donohue & Co., 1905), 10.
20. Fiske, *Mississippi Valley*, 72–73; Mason, *Illinois at Shiloh*, 10.
21. Church, *Grant*, 121; Joseph W. Rich, *The Battle of Shiloh* (Iowa City: The State Historical Society of Iowa, 1911), 48–49.
22. Rich, *The Battle of Shiloh*, 48–50; Church, *Grant*, 122–23.
23. *Official Records*, vol. 10, pt. 2, 55; Fuller, *Generalship*, 100.
24. *Official Records*, vol. 10, pt. 2, 62.
25. Church, *Grant*, 123; Ulysses S. Grant, "The Battle of Shiloh," *The Century*, February 1885, 607.
26. Fiske, *Mississippi Valley*, 72.

Chapter 14

1. Marion Morrison, *A History of the Ninth Regiment Illinois Volunteer Infantry* (Monmouth, IL: John S. Clark, Printer, 1864), 29.
2. Wilson, *Life and Campaigns*, 33; Church, *Grant*, 121–22.
3. Daniel, *Shiloh*, 108–9.
4. Daniel, *Shiloh*, 109.
5. Gerald J. Prokopowicz, *All for the Regiment: The Army of the Ohio, 1861–1862* (Chapel Hill: The University of North Carolina Press, 2001), 95–96; Daniel, *Shiloh*, 112; *Official Records*, vol. 10, pt. 2, 60.
6. Prokopowicz, *All for the Regiment*, 97–98; Daniel, *Shiloh*, 109; *Official Records*, vol. 10, pt. 2, 48, 58–59; Van Horne, *History*, 100–1.

7. Daniel, *Shiloh*, 114; *Official Records*, vol. 10, pt. 1, 329–30; Van Horne, *History*, 102.
8. Daniel, *Shiloh*, 114–15; *Official Records*, vol. 10, pt. 1, 330; William R. Hartpence, *History of the Fifty-first Indiana Veteran Volunteer Infantry* (Cincinnati, OH: The Robert Clarke Company, Printers and Binders, 1894), 34, 36; Charles C. Briant, *History of the Sixth Regiment Indiana Volunteer Infantry, of Both the Three Months' and Three Years' Services* (Indianapolis: Wm. E. Burford, Printer and Binder, 1891), 99.
9. Prokopowicz, *All for the Regiment*, 98–99; Van Horne, *History*, 102–3.
10. Ulysses S. Grant, "The Battle of Shiloh," 596; Brooks D. Simpson and Jean V. Berlin, eds., *Sherman's Civil War: Selected Correspondence of William T. Sherman, 1860–1865* (Chapel Hill: The University of North Carolina Press, 1999), 199.
11. Rich, *The Battle of Shiloh*, 57.
12. Rich, *The Battle of Shiloh*, 47–48.
13. Warren Olney, "'Shiloh': As Seen by a Private Soldier," *A Paper Read Before California Commandery of the Military Order of the Loyal Legion of the United States, May 31, 1889* (n.p., 1889), 5.
14. Wills De Hass, "The Battle of Shiloh," in *The Annals of the War Written by Leading Participants North and South*, Alexander K. McClure, ed. (Philadelphia: The Times Publishing Company, 1879), 679–80.
15. De Hass, "The Battle of Shiloh," 680.
16. Committee of the Regiment, *Story*, 69.
17. Beauregard, "Shiloh, Part I," 16.
18. McPherson, *Battle Cry of Freedom*, 336, 367; Woodworth, *Jefferson Davis*, 95; Beauregard, "Shiloh, Part I," 20.
19. Mason, *Illinois at Shiloh*, 7–8; Beauregard, "Shiloh, Part I," 20; William S. Rosecrans, "Corinth," *The Century*, October 1886, 903.
20. Fowler, *Mountaineers in Gray*, 59; Daniel, *Shiloh*, 88–89; *Official Records*, vol. 10, pt. 2, 327.
21. Roland, *Jefferson Davis's Greatest General*, 54–55; John G. Nicolay and John Hay, "Abraham Lincoln: A History, the Mississippi and Shiloh," *The Century*, September, 1888, 667.
22. Beauregard, "Shiloh, Part I," 19; G. T. Beauregard, "The Shiloh Campaign, Part II," *The North American Review*, February 1886, 159.
23. Fiske, *Mississippi Valley*, 71; Woodward, *Jefferson Davis*, 90–94; Beauregard, "Shiloh, Part I," 20–21.
24. Daniel, *Shiloh*, 95; Alfred Roman, *The Military Operations of General Beauregard in the War Between the States, 1861 to 1865* (New York: Harper & Brothers, 1884), 1:266; *Official Records*, vol. 7, 912.
25. Daniel, *Shiloh*, 96; Johnston, *Life*, 520, 550; Connelly, *Army of the Heartland*, 140–41.
26. Daniel, *Shiloh*, 91; Johnston, *Life*, 520.

Chapter 15

1. *Official Records*, vol. 10, pt. 1, 385; William Preston Johnston, "Albert Sidney Johnston and the Shiloh Campaign," *The Century*, February 1885, 619; Beauregard, "Shiloh, Part I," 22–23.
2. *Official Records*, vol. 10, pt. 1, 385; William Preston Johnston, "Shiloh Campaign," 619; Beauregard, "Shiloh, Part I," 22–23.
3. Daniel, *Shiloh*, 117; *Official Records*, vol. 10, pt. 1, 79; Wallace, *Autobiography*, vol. 1, 545.
4. Daniel, *Shiloh*, 116–17; Beauregard, "Shiloh, Part I," 23; *Official Records*, vol. 10, pt. 2, 381, vol. 10, pt. 1, 385.

5. Daniel, *Shiloh*, 118; Thomas Jordan, "Notes of a Confederate Staff-Officer at Shiloh," *The Century*, February 1885, 594–95; Beauregard, "Shiloh, Part I," 23–24; *Official Records*, vol. 10, pt. 2, 387; Thomas Jordan, "Recollection of General Beauregard's Service in West Tennessee in the Spring of 1862," *Southern Historical Society Papers*, January–December, 1880, 410–12.
6. Daniel, *Shiloh*, 118–19; Connelly, *Army of the Heartland*, 152.
7. Daniel, Shiloh, 119; *Official Records*, vol. 10, pt. 1, 392–93.
8. Daniel, *Shiloh*, 122; *Official Records*, vol. 10, pt. 1, 464, vol. 10, pt. 1, 385–86; Jordan, "Notes," 595–96, 630.
9. *Official Records*, vol. 10, pt. 2, 389.
10. Daniel, *Shiloh*, 122–23; *Official Records*, vol. 10, pt. 1, 567, 607; H. Grady Howell, Jr., *Going to Meet the Yankees: A History of the "Bloody Sixth" Mississippi Infantry, C.S.A.* (Jackson, MS: Chickasaw Bayou Press, 1981), 76.
11. Daniel, *Shiloh*, 123–24; *Official Records*, vol. 10, pt. 2, 390–91.
12. W. H. Polk, "Facts Connected with the Concentration of the Army of the Mississippi Before Shiloh, April, 1862," *Southern Historical Society Papers* 8 (1880): 461; Howell, *Going*, 76; *Official Records*, vol. 10, pt. 1, 567.
13. Daniel, *Shiloh*, 124–25; Edward Thompson, *Orphan Brigade*, 81; *Official Records*, vol. 10, pt. 1, 567, 614, vol. 10, pt. 2, 391.
14. Howell, *Going*, 76; William C. Davis, ed., *Diary of a Confederate Soldier: John S. Jackman of the Orphan Brigade* (Columbia: University of South Carolina Press, 1990), 29–30.
15. Polk, "Facts," 461–62; Daniel, *Shiloh*, 125; *Official Records*, vol. 10, pt. 1, 406, 464, 495, 567; John K. Duke, *History of the Fifty-third Regiment Ohio Volunteer Infantry, During the War of the Rebellion, 1861–1865* (Portsmouth, OH: The Blade Printing Company, 1900), 15.
16. James Dinkins, "The Battle of Shiloh, April 6, 1862," *Southern Historical Society Papers* 31 (1903); *Official Records*, vol. 10, pt. 1, 385–86; John Kent Folmar, *From That Terrible Field: Civil War Letters of James M. Williams, Twenty-first Alabama Infantry* (University: The University of Alabama Press, 1981), 301.
17. Beauregard, "Shiloh, Part II," 161–62; *Official Records*, vol. 10, pt. 1, 463–64; Jordan, "Notes," 631; Daniel, *Shiloh*, 128.
18. Dinkins, "The Battle of Shiloh," 301; Polk, "Facts," 462.
19. William Preston Johnston, "Shiloh Campaign," 621–22.
20. *Official Records*, vol. 10, pt. 1, 386, 567–68; Beauregard, "Shiloh, Part II," 164.
21. William Preston Johnston, "Shiloh Campaign," 620–21; Daniel, *Shiloh*, 119; Johnston, *Life*, 625; *Official Records*, vol. 10, pt. 1, 403.
22. Worsham, *Old Nineteenth*, 36–37.

Chapter 16

1. Ulysses S. Grant, "The Battle of Shiloh," 597; Thomas Jordan, "Battle of Shiloh: Refutation of the So-called 'Lost Opportunity, on the Evening of April 6th,' 1862," *Southern Historical Society Papers* 16 (1888): 204; Sherman, *Memoirs*, vol. 1, 257; George Mason, "Shiloh," in *Military Essays and Recollections, Papers Read Before the Commandery of the State of Illinois, Military Order of the Loyal Legion of the United States* (Chicago, A. C. McClurg and Company, 1891), vol. 1, 95.

2. Ulysses S. Grant, "The Battle of Shiloh," 597; Sherman, *Memoirs*, vol. 1, 257; Mason, "Shiloh," 95; George F. McGinnis, "Shiloh," in *War Papers Read Before the Indiana Commandery, Military Order of the Loyal Legion of the United States* (Indianapolis: Published by the Commandery, 1898), 2.
3. Mason, "Shiloh," 95; McGinnis, "Shiloh," 2; *Official Records*, vol. 10, pt. 1, 112.
4. Warren Olney, "The Battle of Shiloh, with Some Personal Reminiscences," *Overland Monthly and Out West Magazine*, June 1885, 578; Sherman, *Memoirs*, vol. 1, 257.
5. Grant, *Memoirs*, vol. 1, 332–33, 358.
6. Grant, *Memoirs*, vol. 1, 334; *Official Records*, vol. 10, pt. 2, 91.
7. John A. Bering and Thomas Montgomery, *History of the Forty-eighth Ohio Vet. Vol. Inf.* (Hillsboro, OH: Highland News Office, 1880), 18; Duke, *History*, 14; Seymour D. Thompson, *Recollections with the Third Iowa Regiment* (Cincinnati, OH: Published for the Author, 1864), 206–7.
8. *Official Records*, vol. 10, pt. 2, 93–94.
9. *Official Records*, vol. 10, pt. 1, 89, 330–31.
10. Lucius W. Barber, *Army Memoirs of Lucius W. Barber, Company "D," 15th Illinois Volunteer Infantry* (Chicago: The J. M. W. Jones Stationery and Printing Co., 1894), 48; William W. Cluett, *History of the 57th Regiment Illinois Volunteer Infantry* (Princeton, NJ: T. P. Streeter, 1886), 17–18.
11. Seymour D. Thompson, *Recollections*, 205; Ephraim J. Hart, *History of the Fortieth Illinois Inf. (Volunteers)* (Cincinnati, OH: H. S. Bosworth, 1864), 85.
12. Bering and Montgomery, *History*, 19; De Hass, "The Battle of Shiloh," 682.
13. Seymour D. Thompson, *Recollections*, 207–8.
14. Charles A. Morton, "A Boy at Shiloh," in *Personal Recollections of the War of the Rebellion, Addresses Delivered Before the Commandery of the State of New York, Military Order of the Loyal Legion of the United States*, A. Noel Blakeman, ed. (New York: G. P. Putnam's Sons, 1907), 58.
15. Mason, *Illinois at Shiloh*, 16; Alfred T. Andreas, "The 'Ifs and Buts,' of Shiloh," in *Military Essays and Recollections: Papers Read Before the Commandery of the State of Illinois, Military Order of the Loyal Legion of the United States* (Chicago: A. C. McClurg and Company, 1891), vol. 1, 113.
16. Rich, *The Battle of Shiloh*, 54–55; *Official Records*, vol. 10, pt. 1, 464, 603; Reed, "Shiloh Campaign and Battle," 154.
17. Howell, *Going*, 78.
18. David W. Reed, *The Battle of Shiloh and the Organizations Engaged* (Washington, DC: Government Printing Office, 1909), 12.
19. S. H. Lockett, "Controversies in Regard to Shiloh: A Staff Officer's Account of the Attack and Withdrawal," *The Century*, March 1886, 782.
20. Lockett, "Controversies," 782.
21. Blanchard, *I Marched with Sherman*, 53; Lot D. Young, *Reminiscences of a Soldier of the Orphan Brigade* (Louisville, KY: Courier-Journal Job Printing Company, 1918), 26; William Preston Johnston, "Shiloh Campaign," 622.

3. Reed, "Shiloh Campaign and Battle," 154–55; Mason, *Illinois at Shiloh*, 17–18; Andrew Hickenlooper, "The Battle of Shiloh, Part 1—Personal Experiences in the Battle," in *Sketches of War History 1861–1865, Papers Prepared for the Commandery of the State of Ohio, MilitaryOrder of the Loyal Legion of the United States*, vol. 5, W. H. Chamberlin, A. M. van Dyke, and George A. Thayer, eds. (Cincinnati, OH: The Robert Clarke Company, 1903), 414.
4. Stillwell, *Story*, 44–45; Morton, "A Boy at Shiloh," 59–60.
5. *Official Records*, vol. 10, pt. 1, 278; Hicken, *Illinois*, 57.
6. *Official Records*, vol. 10, pt. 1, 278, 280; Stillwell, *Story*, 45.
7. Reed, "Shiloh Campaign and Battle," 154–55; Mason, *Illinois at Shiloh*, 17–18; Morton, "A Boy at Shiloh," 60–61.
8. *Official Records*, vol. 10, pt. 1, 278.
9. Mason, *Illinois at Shiloh*, 18–19; De Hass, "The Battle of Shiloh," 684–85; Bering and Montgomery, *History*, 19–20.
10. Mason, *Illinois at Shiloh*, 20; Sherman, *Memoirs*, vol. 1, 263–64.
11. Rich, *The Battle of Shiloh*, 58–59; Sherman, *Memoirs*, vol. 1, 258; *Official Records*, vol. 10, pt. 1, 249; Edward E. Hale, ed., *Stories of War, Told by Soldiers* (Boston: Roberts Brothers, 1879), 85.
12. Robert H. Flemming, "The Battle of Shiloh as a Private Saw It," in *Sketches of War History 1861–1865, Papers Prepared for the Commandery of the State of Ohio, Military Order of the Loyal Legion of the United States*, vol. 6, Theodore F. Allen, Edward S. McKee, and J. Gordon Taylor, eds., (Cincinnati, OH: Monfort & Company, 1908), 140.
13. De Hass, "The Battle of Shiloh," 685; Reed, "Shiloh Campaign and Battle," 155–56; Howell, *Going*, 82–83.
14. Howell, *Going*, 82–83; *Official Records*, vol. 10, pt. 1, 581; Flemming, "Battle," 141.
15. Howell, *Going*, 82, 85.
16. Howell, *Going*, 86–87; *Official Records*, vol. 10, pt. 1, 581.
17. Hicken, *Illinois*, 56; *Official Records*, vol. 10, pt. 1, 264.
18. Bering and Montgomery, *History*, 19–20.
19. Howell, *Going*, 88; Flemming, "Battle," 141–42.
20. Reed, "Shiloh Campaign and Battle," 155–56; Rich, *The Battle of Shiloh*, 60–61.
21. De Hass, "The Battle of Shiloh," 686; Mason, *Illinois at Shiloh*, 21–22; Hale, *Stories of War*, 86; Sherman, *Memoirs*, vol. 1, 265; Nathaniel Cheairs Hughes, Jr., *The Pride of the Confederate Artillery: The Washington Artillery in the Army of Tennessee* (Baton Rouge: Louisiana State University Press, 1997), 28; *Official Records*, vol. 10, pt. 1, 129–30.
22. Sherman, *Memoirs*, vol. 1, 265; Rich, *The Battle of Shiloh*, 61; Mason, *Illinois at Shiloh*, 26.
23. Rich, *The Battle of Shiloh*, 61; Committee of the Regiment, *Story*, 92.
24. Rich, *The Battle of Shiloh*, 61; *Official Records*, vol. 10, pt. 1, 258.

Chapter 17

1. Leander Stillwell, *The Story of a Common Soldier of Army Life in the Civil War, 1861–1865* (Kansas City: Franklin Hudson Publishing Co., 1920), 42–43.
2. Mason, *Illinois at Shiloh*, 17.

Chapter 18

1. Grant, *Memoirs*, vol. 1, 334–35.
2. *Official Records*, vol. 10, pt. 1, 184–85, pt. 2, 95.
3. Prokopowicz, *All for the Regiment*, 99.
4. *Official Records*, vol. 10, pt. 1, 89, 181.

5. Ulysses S. Grant, "The Battle of Shiloh," 595; *Official Records*, vol. 10, pt. 1, 185; McGinnis, "Shiloh," 8.
6. *Official Records*, vol. 10, pt. 1, 185; Catton, *Grant Moves South*, 225–26.
7. *Official Records*, vol. 10, pt. 2, 95.
8. Grant, *Memoirs*, vol. 1, 343; William Preston Johnston, "Shiloh Campaign," 624.
9. William W. Belknap, *History of the Fifteenth Regiment Iowa Volunteer Infantry* (Keokuk, IA: R. B. Ogden & Son, Print, 1887), 178–80.
10. Hughes, *Pride*, 29; *Official Records*, vol. 10, pt. 1, 471–72, 496–97, 517.
11. McPherson, *Battle Cry of Freedom*, 409; Grant, *Memoirs*, vol. 1, 343.
12. Mason, *Illinois at Shiloh*, 24–25.
13. Reed, "Shiloh Campaign and Battle," 161; Mason, *Illinois at Shiloh*, 25.
14. Sherman, *Memoirs*, vol. 1, 265; Hicken, *Illinois*, 58; *Official Records*, vol. 10, pt. 1, 133.
15. Blanchard, *I Marched with Sherman*, 54; *Official Records*, vol. 10, pt. 1, 133.
16. Mason, *Illinois at Shiloh*, 25–26; Barber, *Army Memoirs*, 53–54.
17. *Official Records*, vol. 10, pt. 1, 116–17; Olynthus B. Clark, ed., *Downing's Civil War Diary by Sergeant Alexander G. Downing, Company E, Eleventh Iowa Infantry* (Des Moines: The Historical Department of Iowa, 1916), 41.
18. Mason, *Illinois at Shiloh*, 25–26; Barber, *Army Memoirs*, 53–54.
19. Seymour D. Thompson, *Recollections*, 210.
20. Olney, "Shiloh," 13–14.
21. Mason, *Illinois at Shiloh*, 33–34; Seymour D. Thompson, *Recollections*, 211–12.
22. Seymour D. Thompson, *Recollections*, 215; Julie A. Doyle, John David Smith, and Richard M. McMurry, eds. *This Wilderness of War: The Civil War Letters of George W. Squier, Hoosier Volunteer* (Knoxville: The University of Tennessee Press, 1998), 10–11.
23. John H. Rerick, *The Forty-fourth Indiana Volunteer Infantry: History of Its Services in the War of the Rebellion* (LaGrange, IN: John H. Rerick, 1880), 46–47.
24. David W. Reed, *Campaigns and Battles of the Twelfth Regiment Iowa Veteran Volunteer Infantry* (Evanston, IL: N.p., 1903), 43–45; Mason, *Illinois at Shiloh*, 33.
25. Losson, *Tennessee's Forgotten Warriors*, 46–47.
26. Losson, *Tennesseee's Forgotten Warriors*, 47; *Official Records*, vol. 10, pt. 1, 438.

Chapter 19

1. Worsham, *Old Nineteenth*, 37; Daniel E. Sutherland, ed., *Reminiscences of a Private: William E. Bevens of the First Arkansas Infantry, C.S.A.* (Fayetteville: The University of Arkansas Press, 1992), 71.
2. *Official Records*, vol. 10, pt. 1, 438, 574, 622.
3. *Official Records*, vol. 10, pt. 1, 466.
4. *Official Records*, vol. 10, pt. 1, 466, 480, 151; Sutherland, *Reminiscences*, 71.
5. *Official Records*, vol. 10, pt. 1, 238–39.
6. Hicken, *Illinois*, 60–61.
7. *Official Records*, vol. 10, pt. 1, 258–59; Reed, "Shiloh Campaign and Battle," 156–61.
8. Reed, "Shiloh Campaign and Battle," 156–61; Hicken, *Illinois*, 60–61; Morrison, *History*, 33–34; *Official Records*, vol. 10, pt. 1, 259.
9. Phil Gottschalk, *In Deadly Earnest: The History of the First Missouri Brigade, CSA* (Columbia, MO: Missouri River Press, Inc, 1991), 89; Reed, "Shiloh Campaign and Battle," 156–61.
10. Olney, "Shiloh," 19–20; Hicken, *Illinois*, 63; William Preston Johnston, "Shiloh Campaign," 626; Mason, *Illinois at Shiloh*, 36.
11. Seymour D. Thompson, *Recollections*, 217–18; Mason, *Illinois at Shiloh*, 30.
12. Olney, "The Battle of Shiloh," 585–86; Hicken, *Illinois*, 63; William Preston Johnston, "Shiloh Campaign," 626.
13. William Preston Johnston, "Shiloh Campaign," 627; Beauregard, "Shiloh, Part II," 171.
14. Beauregard, "Shiloh, Part II," 172.
15. Blanchard, *I Marched with Sherman*, 55–56.
16. Davis, *Diary*, 32.
17. *Official Records*, vol. 10, pt. 1, 117.
18. *Official Records*, vol. 10, pt. 1, 117–18.
19. *Official Records*, vol. 10, pt. 1, 250, 255.
20. *Official Records*, vol. 10, pt. 1, 270–71.
21. Catton, *Grant Moves South*, 232; Olney, "The Battle of Shiloh," 587.

Chapter 20

1. *Official Records*, vol. 10, pt. 1, 118; Reed, "Shiloh Campaign and Battle," 168.
2. *Official Records*, vol. 10, pt. 1, 250; Mason, *Illinois at Shiloh*, 27.
3. Grant, *Memoirs*, vol. 1, 340.
4. *Official Records*, vol. 10, pt. 1, 574, 480.
5. Fowler, *Mountaineers in Gray*, 62; *Official Records*, vol. 10, pt. 1, 439, 455.
6. David W. Reed, *Twelfth Iowa*, 51; Gottschalk, *In Deadly Earnest*, 91; Smith P. Bankhead, "Letter from Colonel Bankhead," *Southern Historical Society Papers*, January 1879, 41.
7. David W. Reed, *Twelfth Iowa*, 51; Gottschalk, *In Deadly Earnest*, 91; Bankhead, "Letter from Colonel Bankhead," 41.
8. Fowler, *Mountaineers in Gray*, 63; *Official Records*, vol. 10, pt. 1, 439, 455.
9. Seymour D. Thompson, *Recollections*, 222–23.
10. Seymour D. Thompson, *Recollections*, 223–24.
11. Olney, "Shiloh," 22; Seymour D. Thompson, *Recollections*, 226–27.
12. Stillwell, *Story*, 48–49; Olney, "Shiloh," 22–23.
13. *Official Records*, vol. 10, pt. 1, 279.
14. Hicken, *Illinois*, 64; *Official Records*, vol. 10, pt. 1, 149.
15. Grant, *Memoirs*, vol. 1, 356; Mason, *Illinois at Shiloh*, 38.
16. Seymour D. Thompson, *Recollections*, 229.
17. Hicken, *Illinois*, 64; Rich, *The Battle of Shiloh*, 72–73; Gottschalk, *In Deadly Earnest*, 93.

Chapter 21

1. Hartpence, *History*, 36–37.
2. Buell, "Shiloh Revisited," 753; Prokopowicz, *All for the Regiment*, 99–100.
3. William Grose, *The Story of the Marches, Battles and Incidents of the 36th Regiment Indiana Volunteer Infantry* (New Castle, IN: The Courier Company Press, 1891), 102–3.
4. Wilbur F. Hinman, *The Story of the Sherman Brigade* (Alliance, OH: Published by author, 1897), 136.

5. Gottschalk, *In Deadly Earnest*, 94; *Official Records*, vol. 10, pt. 1, 333.
6. Robert L. Kimberly and Ephraim S. Holloway, *The Forty-first Ohio Veteran Volunteer Infantry in the War of the Rebellion, 1861–1865* (Cleveland, OH: W. R. Smellie, Printer and Publisher, 1897), 21–22; *Official Records*, vol. 10, pt. 1, 324, 333; John A. Cockerill, "A Boy at Shiloh," in *Sketches of War History 1861–1865, Papers Prepared for the Commandery of the State of Ohio, Military Order of the Loyal Legion of the United States*, vol. 6, Theodore F. Allen, Edward S. McKee, and J. Gordon Taylor, eds. (Cincinnati, OH: Monfort & Company, 1908), 27.
7. Buell, "Shiloh Revisited," 753–54; *Official Records*, vol. 10, pt. 1, 292; Grant, *Memoirs*, vol. 1, 344.
8. Douglas Putnam Jr., "Reminiscences of the Battle of Shiloh," in *Sketches of War History 1861–1865, Papers Read Before the Ohio Commandery of the Military Order of the Loyal Legion of the United States*, vol. 3, Robert Hunter, ed. (Cincinnati, OH: Robert Clarke & Co., 1890), 201–2.
9. Stillwell, *Story*, 53.
10. Stillwell, *Story*, 52.
11. Grant, *Memoirs*, vol. 1, 344–45; *Official Records*, vol. 10, pt. 1, 323.
12. Beauregard, "Shiloh, Part II," 172–73; Thomas Jordan, "The Battle of Shiloh," *Southern Historical Society Papers* 35 (1907): 217.
13. Jordan, "Lost Opportunity," 297–98; *Official Records*, vol. 10, pt. 1, 555.
14. Rich, *The Battle of Shiloh*, 75; Jordan, "Lost Opportunity," 298; *Official Records*, vol. 10, pt. 1, 550–51, 555.
15. Gottschalk, *In Deadly Earnest*, 94; *Official Records*, vol. 10, pt. 1, 624–25.
16. Rich, *The Battle of Shiloh*, 76; *Official Records*, vol. 10, pt. 1, 334.
17. Jordan, "Lost Opportunity," 297–98; *Official Records*, vol. 10, pt. 1, 555.
18. Rich, *The Battle of Shiloh*, 78; Jordan, "Lost Opportunity," 300–1.
19. Jordan, "Lost Opportunity," 299; *Official Records*, vol. 10, pt. 1, 546.
20. Beauregard, "Shiloh, Part II," 173–74; A. R. Chisholm, "The Plan of the Battle and the Withdrawal of the First Day," *The Century*, March 1886, 784.
21. Lockett, "Controversies," 783; Jordan, "Lost Opportunities," 316.
22. Jordan, "Recollection," 416.
23. Sherman, *Memoirs*, vol. 1, 273.
24. Committee of the Regiment, *Story*, 28–29; Ulysses S. Grant, "The Battle of Shiloh," 602.

Chapter 22

1. Gottschalk, *In Deadly Earnest*, 96; Reed, "Shiloh Campaign and Battle," 171; *Official Records*, vol. 10, pt. 1, 101–8, 395, 583–84.
2. Rich, *The Battle of Shiloh*, 79–80; Ulysses S. Grant, "The Battle of Shiloh," 601–2; Coppee, *Life and Services*, 90; Reed, "Shiloh Campaign and Battle," 171.
3. Ulysses S. Grant, "The Battle of Shiloh," 601–2; Coppee, *Life and Services*, 90; Rich, *The Battle of Shiloh*, 79–80.
4. Reed, "Shiloh Campaign and Battle," 171; Rich, *The Battle of Shiloh*, 80–81.
5. McGinnis, "Shiloh," 9–10; *Official Records*, vol. 10, pt. 1, 170; Ulysses S. Grant, "The Battle of Shiloh," 595.
6. *Official Records*, vol. 10, pt. 1, 170; Ulysses S. Grant, "The Battle of Shiloh," 595; Henry B. Carrington, "Major General Lew Wallace at Shiloh," *The Bay State Monthly*, March 1885, 331; McGinnis, "Shiloh," 13.
7. *Official Records*, vol. 10, pt. 1, 170, 181–82; Grant, *Memoirs*, vol. 1, 351; Coppee, *Life and Services*, 91; McGinnis, "Shiloh," 15–16.
8. Ulysses S. Grant, "General Lew Wallace and General McCook at Shiloh," *The Century*, September 1885, 776.
9. Ulysses S. Grant, "The Battle of Shiloh," 601–2.
10. Ulysses S. Grant, "The Battle of Shiloh," 601–2; Van Horne, *History*, 108–9.
11. Van Horne, *History*, 108–9; Buell, "Shiloh Revisited," 771.
12. Grant, *Memoirs*, vol. 1, 348; McPherson, *Battle Cry of Freedom*, 410; Sherman, *Memoirs*, vol. 1, 273.
13. Cockerill, "A Boy at Shiloh," 29; Cluett, *History*, 22.
14. Daniel McCook, "The Second Division at Shiloh," *Harper's New Monthly Magazine*, May 1864, 829; Hinman, *Story*, 142.
15. Briant, *History*, 102–3.
16. *Official Records*, vol. 10, pt. 1, 506, 499, 524; Hughes, *Pride*, 35.
17. Grant, *Memoirs*, vol. 1, 348–49.
18. Catton, *Grant Moves South*, 242.
19. Beauregard, "Shiloh, Part II," 174.
20. *Official Records*, vol. 10, pt. 1, 384.
21. *Official Records*, vol. 10, pt. 1, 387; Connelly, *Army of the Heartland*, 170–71.
22. Hughes, *Pride*, 35; *Official Records*, vol. 10, pt. 1, 499, 524.

Chapter 23

1. David W. Reed, *Seventy-seventh Pennsylvania*, 79; McCook, "Second Division," 830.
2. Prokopowicz, *All for the Regiment*, 105.
3. Grant, *Memoirs*, vol. 1, 350; Van Horne, *History*, 109–10.
4. Beauregard, "Shiloh, Part II," 175, 177; Hughes, *Pride*, 37; Fiske, *Mississippi Valley*, 94.
5. Beauregard, "Shiloh, Part II," 177; *Official Records*, vol. 10, pt. 1, 583.
6. *Official Records*, vol. 10, pt. 1, 293–94; Van Horne, *History*, 111–12.
7. Buell, "Shiloh Revisited," 779; Prokopowicz, *All for the Regiment*, 102.
8. Catton, *Grant Moves South*, 244; Beauregard, "Shiloh, Part II," 177; Van Horne, *History*, 109.
9. Prokopowicz, *All for the Regiment*, 101–2; Buell, "Shiloh Revisited," 779.
10. Grant, *Memoirs*, vol. 1, 349; *Official Records*, vol. 10, pt. 1, 324, 328, 337; Van Horne, *History*, 109–11; Buell, "Shiloh Revisited," 775; Larry J. Daniel, *Days of Glory: The Army of the Cumberland, 1861–1865* (Baton Rouge: Louisiana State University Press, 2004), 81–82.
11. Reed, "Shiloh Campaign and Battle," 172, 175.
12. Grant, *Memoirs*, vol. 1, 349; *Official Records*, vol. 10, pt. 1. 294, 324, 328; Van Horne, *History*, 109–13; Buell, "Shiloh Revisited," 775; Daniel, *Days of Glory*, 81–82.
13. *Official Records*, vol. 10, pt. 1, 336, 341, 343, 345, 294; Van Horne, *History*, 112–13; Daniel, *Days of Glory*, 82.
14. Byron R. Abernethy, ed., *Private Elisha Stockwell, Jr. Sees the Civil War* (Norman: University of Oklahoma Press, 1958), 19; Kimberly and Holloway, *Forty-first Ohio*,

23; Daniel, *Days of Glory*, 82; *Official Records*, vol. 1, 348, 366.
   15. *Official Records*, vol. 10, pt. 1, 295; Van Horne, *History*, 113–14; Lewis M. Hosea, "The Second Day at Shiloh," in *Sketches of War History 1861–1865, Papers Prepared for the Commandery of the State of Ohio, Military Order of the Loyal Legion of the United States*, vol. 4, Theodore F. Allen, Edward S. McKee, and J. Gordon Taylor, eds. (Cincinnati, OH: Monfort & Company, 1908), 198.
   16. *Official Records*, vol. 10, pt. 1, 295; Van Horne, *History*, 113–14; Hosea, "Second Day," 199; Briant, *History*, 108–9.
   17. *Official Records*, vol. 10, pt. 1, 295; Van Horne, *History*, 113–14.
   18. *Official Records*, vol. 10, pt. 1, 170.
   19. *Official Records*, vol. 10, pt. 1, 170, 251; W. H. Chamberlin, *History of the Eighty-first Regiment Ohio Infantry Volunteers, During the War of the Rebellion* (Cincinnati, OH: Gazette Steam Printing House, 1865), 18; Sherman, *Memoirs*, vol. 1, 267.
   20. *Official Records*, vol. 10, pt.1, 119; Richard J. Fulfer, *A History of the Trials and Hardships of the Twenty-Fourth Indiana Volunteer Infantry* (Indianapolis: Indianapolis Printing Co., 1913), 39.
   21. *Official Records*, vol. 10, pt. 1, 119–20, 441.
   22. *Official Records*, vol. 10, pt. 1, 120.
   23. Stephen E. Ambrose, ed., *A Wisconsin Boy in Dixie: The Selected Letters of James K. Newton* (Madison: The University of Wisconsin Press, 1961), 15; Bennett and Tillery, *Struggle*, 28.
   24. Abernethy, *Private Elisha Stockwell*, 16.

Chapter 24

1. Jordan, "Notes," 634.
2. Beauregard, "Shiloh, Part II," 176–77.
3. *Official Records*, vol. 10, pt. 1, 366.
4. *Official Records*, vol. 10, pt. 1, 335–36.
5. *Official Records*, vol. 10, pt. 1, 349, 342, 338.
6. *Official Records*, vol. 10, pt. 1, 120.
7. *Official Records*, vol. 10, pt. 1, 251–52; Sherman, *Memoirs*, vol. 1, 268.
8. Hosea, "Second Day," 206–7.
9. *Official Records*, vol. 10, pt. 1, 172–73.
10. Grant, *Memoirs*, vol. 1, 350–51.
11. Beauregard, "Shiloh, Part II," 178.
12. Beauregard, "Shiloh, Part II," 178; *Official Records*, vol. 10, pt. 1, 388.
13. *Official Records*, vol. 10, pt. 2, 96–97.
14. *Official Records*, vol. 10, pt. 2, 98.
15. *Official Records*, vol. 10, pt. 2, 398–99.
16. *Official Records*, vol. 10, pt. 2, 400.
17. Grant, *Memoirs*, vol. 1, 354–55.
18. *Official Records*, vol. 10, pt. 2, 99.
19. *Official Records*, vol. 10, pt. 1, 108, 395.

Chapter 25

1. Judson W. Bishop, *The Story of a Regiment Being a Narrative of the Service of the Second Regiment, Minnesota Veteran Volunteer Infantry, in the Civil War of 1861–1865* (St. Paul, MN: Regimental Association, 1890), 540.
2. *Official Records*, vol. 10, pt. 2, 99–100.
3. *Official Records*, vol. 10, pt. 2, 100.
4. Walke, "Operations," 439, 442–43; McPherson, *Battle Cry of Freedom*, 415.
5. *Official Records*, vol. 10, pt. 2, 105–6, 109.
6. Grant, *Memoirs*, vol. 1, 371.
7. Grant, *Memoirs*, vol. 1, 369–70; Sherman, *Memoirs*, vol. 1, 272.
8. Sherman, *Memoirs*, vol. 1, 272; Catton, *Grant Moves South*, 253–54.
9. Morton, "A Boy at Shiloh," 67–68.
10. Olney, "Shiloh," 8–9.
11. Doyle, Smith, and McMurry, *This Wilderness of War*, 19; *Official Records*, vol. 10, pt. 1, 99–100.
12. Wilson, *Letters*, 10–11.
13. Wilson, *Letters*, 11–12.
14. A. K. McClure, *Abraham Lincoln and Men of War-Times* (Philadelphia: The Times Publishing Company, 1892), 195–96.
15. McPherson, *Battle Cry of Freedom*, 414; Connelly, *Army of the Heartland*, 168.
16. Daniel, *Shiloh*, 120; Woodworth, *Jefferson Davis*, 96; Roland, *Jefferson Davis's Greatest General*, 323.
17. Grant, *Memoirs*, vol. 1, 371–72.
18. *Official Records*, vol. 10, pt. 2, 144; Sherman, *Memoirs*, vol. 1, 283.
19. *Official Records*, vol. 10, pt. 2, 182–83.
20. Grant, *Memoirs*, vol. 1, 376–77.
21. *Official Records*, vol. 10, pt. 2, 440; Beauregard, "Shiloh, Part II," 181; Douglas Hale, *The Third Texas Cavalry in the Civil War* (Norman: University of Oklahoma Press, 1993), 110–11.
22. Grant, *Memoirs*, vol. 1, 377–78; Beauregard, "Shiloh, Part II," 182.
23. Beauregard, "Shiloh, Part II," 182–83; Grant, *Memoirs*, vol. 1, 379–80.
24. Beauregard, 'Shiloh, Part II," 183–84; McPherson, *Battle Cry of Freedom*, 417.
25. Grant, *Memoirs*, vol. 1, 368.

Bibliography

Books

Abernethy, Byron R., ed. *Private Elisha Stockwell, Jr. Sees the Civil War*. Norman: University of Oklahoma Press, 1958.

Adair, John M. *Historical Sketch of the Forty-Fifth Illinois Regiment*. Lanark, IL: Carroll County Gazette Print, 1869.

Ambrose, D. Leib. *History of the Seventh Regiment Illinois Volunteer Infantry*. Springfield: Illinois Journal Company, 1868.

Ambrose, Stephen E. *Halleck: Lincoln's Chief of Staff*. Baton Rouge: Louisiana State University Press, 1962.

Ambrose, Stephen E., ed. *A Wisconsin Boy in Dixie: The Selected Letters of James K. Newton*. Madison: The University of Wisconsin Press, 1961.

Anderson, Nancy Scott, and Dwight Anderson. *The Generals–Ulysses S. Grant and Robert E. Lee*. New York: Wings Books, 1994.

Badeau, Adam. *Military History of Ulysses S. Grant: From April, 1861, to April, 1865*, 3 vols. New York: D. Appleton, 1885.

Barber, Lucius W. *Army Memoirs of Lucius W. Barber, Company "D," 15th Illinois Volunteer Infantry*. Chicago: The J. M. W. Jones Stationery and Printing Co., 1894.

Basler Roy P., ed. *The Collected Works of Abraham Lincoln*, 8 vols. New Brunswick, NJ: Rutgers University Press, 1953.

Bearss, Edwin C. *The Fall of Fort Henry*. Dover, TN: Eastern National Park and Monument Association, 1963.

Belknap, William W. *History of the Fifteenth Regiment, Iowa Veteran Volunteer Infantry*. Keokuk, IA: R. B. Ogden & Son, Print, 1887.

Bennett, Stewart, and Barbara Tillery, eds. *The Struggle for the Life of the Republic: A Civil War Narrative by Brevet Major Charles Dana Miller, 76th Ohio Volunteer Infantry*. Kent, OH: The Kent State University Press, 2004.

Bering, John A., and Thomas Montgomery. *History of the Forty-Eighth Ohio Vet. Vol. Inf.* Hillsboro, OH: Highland News Office, 1880.

Bishop, Judson W. *The Story of a Regiment Being a Narrative of the Service of the Second Regiment, Minnesota Veteran Volunteer Infantry, in the Civil War of 1861–1865*. St. Paul, MN: Regimental Association, 1890.

Blanchard, Ira. *I Marched with Sherman: Civil War Memoirs of the 20th Illinois Volunteer Infantry*. San Francisco: J. D. Huff, 1992.

Bouton, Edward. *Events of the Civil War*. Los Angeles: Kingsley, Moles & Collins Co., Printers, 1906.

Boyd, James P. *The Life of General William T. Sherman*. Philadelphia: Publishers Union, 1891.

Boyd, James P. *Military and Civil Life of Gen. Ulysses S. Grant*. Philadelphia: Garretson, 1885.

Briant, Charles C. *History of the Sixth Regiment Indiana Volunteer Infantry, of Both the Three Months' and Three Years' Services*. Indianapolis: Wm. E. Burford, Printer and Binder, 1891.

Brinton, John H. *Personal Memoirs of John H. Brinton: Major and Surgeon U.S.V., 1861–1865*. New York: The Neale Publishing Company, 1914. Reprint. Carbondale: Southern Illinois University Press, 1996.

Byers, S. H. M. *Iowa in War Times*. Des Moines, IA: W. D. Condit, 1888.

Carpenter, John A. *Ulysses S. Grant*. New York: Twayne Publishers, 1970.

Catton, Bruce. *Grant Moves South*. Boston: Little, Brown, 1960.

Chamberlin, W. H. *History of the Eighty-First Regiment Ohio Infantry Volunteers, During the War of the Rebellion*. Cincinnati, OH: Gazette Steam Printing House, 1885.

Church, William Conant. *Ulysses S. Grant and the Period of National Preservation and Reconstruction*. New York: G. P. Putnam's Sons, 1897.

Clark, Olynthus B., ed. *Downing's Civil War Diary by Sergeant Alexander G. Downing, Company E, Eleventh Iowa Infantry*. Des Moines: The Historical Department of Iowa, 1916.

Cluett, William W. *History of the 57th Regiment Illinois Volunteer Infantry*. Princeton, NJ: T. P. Streeter, 1886.

Coffin, Charles Carleton. *Four Years of Fighting: A Volume of Personal Observation with the Army and Navy*. Boston: Ticknor and Fields, 1866.

Committee of the Regiment. *The Story of the Fifty-fifth Regiment Illinois Volunteer Infantry in the Civil War, 1861–1865*. Clinton, MA: W. J. Coulter, 1887.

Conger, A. L. *The Rise of U.S. Grant*. Freeport, NY: Books for Libraries Press, 1970.

Connelly, Thomas Lawrence. *Army of the Heartland: The Army of Tennessee, 1861–1862*. Baton Rouge: Louisiana State University Press, 1967.

Coolidge, Louis A. *Ulysses S. Grant*. Boston: Houghton Mifflin, 1917.

Cooling, Benjamin Franklin. *Fort Donelson's Legacy: War and Society in Kentucky and Tennessee, 1862–1863*. Knoxville: The University of Tennessee Press, 1997.

Cooling, Benjamin Franklin. *Forts Henry and Donelson: The Key to the Confederate Heartland*. Knoxville: The University of Tennessee Press, 1987.

Cope. Alexis. *The Fifteenth Ohio Volunteers and Its Campaigns.* Columbus, OH: Published by the author, 1916.

Coppee, Henry. *Grant and His Campaigns: A Military Biography.* New York: Charles B. Richardson, 1866.

Coppee, Henry. *Life and Services of Gen. U.S. Grant.* Chicago: The Western News Company, 1868.

Cramer, Jesse Grant, ed. *Letters of Ulysses S. Grant to His Father and His Youngest Sister, 1857-78.* New York: G. P. Putnam's Sons, 1912.

Crist, Lynda Lasswell, ed. *The Papers of Jefferson Davis.* Baton Rouge: Louisiana State University Press, 1995.

Crooker, Lucien B., Henry S. Nourse, and John G. Brown. *The Story of the Fifty-Fifth Regiment Illinois Volunteer Infantry in the Civil War 1861-1865.* Clinton, MA: W. J. Coulter, 1887.

Crummer, Wilbur F. *With Grant at Fort Donelson, Shiloh and Vicksburg.* Oak Park, IL: E. C. Crummer, 1915.

Dana, Charles A., and James H. Wilson. *The Life of Ulysses S. Grant: General of the Armies of the United States.* Springfield, MA: Gurdon Bill & Company, 1868.

Daniel, Larry J. *Days of Glory: The Army of the Cumberland, 1861-1865.* Baton Rouge: Louisiana State University Press, 2004.

Daniel, Larry J. *Shiloh: The Battle That Changed the Civil War.* New York: Simon & Schuster, 1997.

Davis, William C., ed. *Diary of a Confederate Soldier: John S. Jackman of the Orphan Brigade.* Columbia: University of South Carolina Press, 1990.

Deming, Henry C. *The Life of Ulysses S. Grant, General United States Army.* Hartford, CT: S. S. Scranton, 1868.

Dodge, William S. *History of the Old Second Division, Army of the Cumberland, Commanders: M'Cook, Sill, and Johnson.* Chicago: Church & Goodman, 1864.

Doyle, Julie A., John David Smith, and Richard M. McMurry, eds. *This Wilderness of War: The Civil War Letters of George W. Squier, Hoosier Volunteer.* Knoxville: The University of Tennessee Press, 1998.

Duke, John K. *History of the Fifty-Third Regiment Ohio Volunteer Infantry, During the War of the Rebellion, 1861-1865.* Portsmouth, OH: The Blade Printing Company, 1900.

Duncan, Thomas D. *Recollections of Thomas D. Duncan: A Confederate Soldier.* Nashville, TN: McQuiddy Printing Company, 1922.

Dyer, Frederick H. *A Compendium of the War of the Rebellion.* Des Moines, IA: The Dyer Publishing Company, 1908.

Engle, Stephen D. *Don Carlos Buell: Most Promising of All.* Chapel Hill: The University of North Carolina Press, 1999.

Engle, Stephen D. *Struggle for the Heartland: The Campaigns from Fort Henry to Corinth.* Lincoln: University of Nebraska Press, 2001.

Estvan, Bela. *War Pictures from the South.* New York: D. Appleton and Company, 1863.

Evans, Clement A., ed. *Confederate Military History*, vol. 3. Atlanta: Confederate Publishing Company, 1899.

Ferrell, H. Robert, ed. *Holding the Line: The Third Tennessee Infantry 1861-1864.* Kent, OH: The Kent State University Press, 1994.

Fiske, John. *The Mississippi Valley in the Civil War.* Boston: Houghton, Mifflin, 1900.

Folmar, John Kent. *From That Terrible Field: Civil War Letters of James M. Williams, Twenty-first Alabama Infantry.* University: The University of Alabama Press, 1981.

Foote, H. S. *Report of the Special Committee on the Recent Military Disasters at Forts Henry and Donelson and the Evacuation of Nashville.* Richmond, VA: Enquirer Book and Job Press, 1862.

Force, Manning F. *From Fort Henry to Corinth.* New York: Charles Scribner's Sons, 1881.

Fowler, John D. *Mountaineers in Gray: The Nineteenth Tennessee Volunteer Infantry Regiment, C.S.A.* Knoxville: The University of Tennessee Press, 2004.

Fox, William F. *Regimental Losses in the American Civil War, 1861-1865.* Albany, NY: Albany Publishing Company, 1889.

Fulfer, Richard J. *A History of the Trials and Hardships of the Twenty-Fourth Indiana Volunteer Infantry.* Indianapolis: Indianapolis Printing Co., 1913.

Fuller, J. F. C. *The Generalship of Ulysses S. Grant.* New York: Da Capo, n.d.

Garland, Hamlin. *Ulysses S. Grant: His Life and Character.* New York: The Macmillan Company, 1920.

Gosnell, H. Allen. *Guns on the Western Waters: The Story of River Gunboats in the Civil War.* Baton Rouge: Louisiana State University Press, 1949.

Gottschalk, Phil. *In Deadly Earnest: The History of the First Missouri Brigade, CSA.* Columbia, MO: Missouri River Press, Inc., 1991.

Grant, Ulysses S. *Personal Memoirs of U.S. Grant.* New York: Charles L. Webster, 1885.

Grose, William. *The Story of the Marches, Battles and Incidents of the 36th Regiment Indiana Volunteer Infantry.* New Castle, IN: The Courier Company Press, 1891.

Hale, Douglas. *The Third Texas Cavalry in the Civil War.* Norman: University of Oklahoma Press, 1993.

Hale, Edward, E., ed. *Stories of War, Told by Soldiers.* Boston: Roberts Brothers, 1879.

Hamilton, James J. *The Battle of Fort Donelson.* New York: Thomas Yoseloff, Publisher, 1968.

Hancock, R. R. *Hancock's Diary: Or a History of the Second Tennessee Confederate Cavalry.* Nashville, TN: Brandon Printing Company, 1887.

Hannaford, Ebenezer. *The Story of a Regiment: A History of the Campaigns, and Associations in the Field, of the Sixth Regiment Ohio Volunteer Infantry.* Cincinnati, OH: Published by the author, 1868.

Hart, Ephraim J. *History of the Fortieth Illinois Inf. (Volunteers).* Cincinnati, OH: H. S. Bosworth, 1864.

Hartpence, William R. *History of the Fifty-first Indiana Veteran Volunteer Infantry.* Cincinnati, OH: The Robert Clarke Company, Printers and Binders, 1894.

Hicken, Victor. *Illinois in the Civil War.* Urbana: University of Illinois Press, 1991.

Hinman, Wilbur F. *The Story of the Sherman Brigade.* Alliance, OH: Published by author, 1897.

Hodge, George B. *Sketch of the First Kentucky Brigade.* Frankfort: Kentucky Yeoman Office, 1874.

Hoppin, James Mason. *Life of Andrew Hull Foote, Rear-Admiral United States Navy.* New York: Harper & Brothers, 1874.

Horn, Stanley F. *The Army of Tennessee.* Norman: University of Oklahoma Press, 1968.

Howell, H. Grady, Jr. *Going to Meet the Yankees: A History of the "Bloody Sixth" Mississippi Infantry, C.S.A.* Jackson, MS: Chickasaw Bayou Press, 1981.

Howland, Edward. *Grant as a Soldier and Statesman.* Hartford, CT: J. B. Burr, 1868.

Hubert, Charles F. *History of the Fiftieth Regiment Illinois Volunteer Infantry in the War of the Union.* Kansas City, MO: Western Veteran Publishing Company, 1894.

Hughes, Nathaniel Cheairs, Jr. *The Pride of the Confederate Artillery: The Washington Artillery in the Army of*

Tennessee. Baton Rouge: Louisiana State University Press, 1997.

Johnson, R. W. *A Soldier's Reminiscences in Peace and War.* Philadelphia: J. B. Lippincott, 1886.

Johnston, William Preston. *The Life of Gen. Albert Sidney Johnston.* New York: D. Appleton, 1879.

Jones, Thomas B., and Benjamin Dornblaser. *Complete History of the 46th Regiment Illinois Volunteer Infantry.* Freeport, IL: W. H. Wagner & Sons, Printers, 1907.

Kimbell, Charles B. *History of Battery "A" First Illinois Light Artillery Volunteers.* Chicago: Cushing Printing Company, 1899.

Kimberly, Robert L., and Ephraim S. Holloway. *The Forty-first Ohio Veteran Volunteer Infantry in the War of the Rebellion, 1861–1865.* Cleveland, OH: W. R. Smellie, Printer and Publisher, 1897.

Kiner, F. F. *One Year's Soldiering, Embracing the Battles of Fort Donelson and Shiloh.* Lancaster, PA: E. H. Thomas, Printer, 1863.

Kiper, Richard L. *Major General John Alexander McClernand, Politician in Uniform.* Kent, OH: The Kent State University Press, 1999.

Lindsley, John Berrien, ed. *The Military Annals of Tennessee, Confederate.* Nashville, TN: J. M. Lindsley & Co., Publishers, 1886.

Livermore, Mary A. *My Story of the War: A Woman's Narrative of Four Years Personal Experience.* Hartford, CT: A. D. Worthington, 1896.

Longacre, Edward G. *General Ulysses S. Grant: The Soldier and the Man.* Cambridge, MA: Da Capo, 2006.

Losson, Christopher. *Tennessee's Forgotten Warriors: Frank Cheatham and His Confederate Division.* Knoxville: The University of Tennessee Press, 1989.

Luvaas, Jay, Stephen Bowman, and Leonard Fullenkamp, eds. *Guide to the Battle of Shiloh.* Lawrence: University Press of Kansas, 1996.

Mason, George W., ed. *Illinois at Shiloh: Report of the Shiloh Battlefield Commission.* Chicago: M. A. Donohue, 1905.

McClure, A. K. *Abraham Lincoln and Men of War-Times.* Philadelphia: The Times Publishing Company, 1892.

McMurray, W. J. *History of the Twentieth Tennessee Regiment Volunteer Infantry, C.S.A.* Nashville, TN: The Publication Committee, 1904.

McPherson, James M. *Battle Cry of Freedom—the Civil War Era.* New York: Oxford University Press, 1988.

Morris, W. S., L. D. Hartwell, and J. B. Kuykendall. *History 31st Regiment Illinois Volunteers.* Carbondale: Southern Illinois University Press, 1998.

Morrison, Marion. *A History of the Ninth Regiment Illinois Volunteer Infantry.* Monmouth, IL: John S. Clark, Printer, 1864.

Nash, Howard P. *A Naval History of the Civil War.* New York: A. S. Barnes, 1972.

Nevin, David. *The Road to Shiloh: Early Battles in the West.* Alexandria, VA: Time-Life Books, 1983.

Nott, Charles C. *Sketches of the War: A Series of Letters to the North Moore Street School of New York.* New York: Anson D. F. Randolph, 1865.

Patrick, Jeffrey L., ed. *Three Years with Wallace's Zouaves: The Civil War Memoirs of Thomas Wise Durham.* Macon, GA: Mercer University Press, 2003.

Perret, Geoffrey. *Ulysses S. Grant: Soldier & President.* New York: Random House, 1997.

Pollard, Edward A. *The First Year of the War.* Richmond, VA: West & Johnston, 1862.

Pratt, Fletcher. *Civil War on Western Waters.* New York: Henry Holt, 1956.

Prokopowicz, Gerald J. *All for the Regiment: The Army of the Ohio, 1861–1862.* Chapel Hill: The University of North Carolina Press, 2001.

Reed, David W. *The Battle of Shiloh and the Organizations Engaged.* Washington, DC: Government Printing Office, 1909.

Reed, David W. *Campaigns and Battles of the Twelfth Regiment Iowa Veteran Volunteer Infantry.* Evanston, IL: N.p., 1903.

Reed, David W. *The Seventy-Seventh Pennsylvania at Shiloh.* Harrisburg, PA: Harrisburg Publishing Co., State Printers, 1905.

Reed, Rowena. *Combined Operations in the Civil War.* Annapolis, MD: Naval Institute Press, 1978.

Republican Party National Committee. *Life and Services of General U.S. Grant, Conqueror of the Rebellion and Eighteenth President of the United States.* Washington, DC: Philp & Solomons, 1868.

Rerick, John H. *The Forty-Fourth Indiana Volunteer Infantry: History of Its Services in the War of the Rebellion.* LaGrange, IN: John H. Rerick, 1880.

Rice, DeLong. *The Story of Shiloh.* Nashville, TN: Brandon Printing Company, 1919.

Rich, Joseph W. *The Battle of Shiloh.* Iowa City: The State Historical Society of Iowa, 1911.

Richardson, Albert D. *A Personal History of Ulysses S. Grant.* Hartford, CT: American Publishing Company, 1868.

Richardson, Albert D. *The Secret Service, the Field, the Dungeon, and the Escape.* Hartford, CT: American Publishing Company, 1865.

Ridley, Bromfield L. *Battles and Sketches of the Army of Tennessee.* Mexico, MO: Missouri Printing & Publishing Co., 1906.

Roland, Charles P. *Jefferson Davis's Greatest General: Albert Sidney Johnston.* Abilene, TX: McWhiney Foundation Press, 2000.

Roman, Alfred. *The Military Operations of General Beauregard in the War Between the States, 1861 to 1865.* 2 volumes. New York: Harper & Brothers, 1884.

Sherman, William T. *Memoirs of Gen. W. T. Sherman, Written by Himself.* New York: Charles L. Webster, 1891.

Simon, John Y., ed. *The Papers of Ulysses S. Grant.* Carbondale: Southern Illinois University Press, 1972.

Simpson, Brooks D. *Ulysses S. Grant: Triumph Over Adversity, 1822–1865.* Boston: Houghton Mifflin, 2000.

Simpson, Brooks D., and Jean V. Berlin, eds. *Sherman's Civil War: Selected Correspondence of William T. Sherman, 1860–1865.* Chapel Hill: The University of North Carolina Press, 1999.

Smith, Henry I. *History of the Seventh Iowa Veteran Volunteer Infantry During the Civil War.* Mason City, IA: E. Hitchcock, Printer, Binder, 1903.

Smith, John Thomas. *A History of the Thirty-first Regiment of Indiana Volunteer Infantry in the War of the Rebellion.* Cincinnati, OH: Western Methodist Book Concern, 1900.

Speed, Thomas. *The Union Cause in Kentucky.* New York: G. P. Putnam's Sons, 1907.

Stevenson, Thomas M. *History of the 78th Regiment O. V. V. I.* Zanesville, OH: Hugh Dunne, 1865.

Stillwell, Leander. *The Story of a Common Soldier of Army Life in the Civil War, 1861–1865.* Kansas City: Franklin Hudson, 1920.

Stuart, Addison A. *Iowa Colonels and Regiments: Being a History of Iowa Regiments in the War of the Rebellion.* Des Moines, IA: Mills, 1865.

Sutherland, Daniel E., ed. *Reminiscences of a Private:*

William E. Bevens of the First Arkansas Infantry, C.S.A. Fayetteville: The University of Arkansas Press, 1992.

Thompson, Edward Porter. *History of the First Kentucky Brigade.* Cincinnati, OH: Caxton Publishing House, 1868.

Thompson, Edward Porter. *History of the Orphan Brigade.* Louisville, KY: Lewis N. Thompson, 1898.

Thompson, Seymour D. *Recollections with the Third Iowa Regiment.* Cincinnati, OH: Published for the Author, 1864.

Tucker, Spencer C. *Andrew Foote: Civil War Admiral on Western Waters.* Annapolis, MD: Naval Institute Press, 2000.

Tucker, Spencer C. *Unconditional Surrender: The Capture of Forts Henry and Donelson.* Abilene, TX: McWhiney Foundation Press, 2001.

United States Naval War Records Office. *Official Records of the Union and Confederate Navies in the War of the Rebellion.* Washington, DC: Government Printing Office, 1894–1922.

United States War Department. *War of the Rebellion: A Compilation of the Official Records of the Union and Confederate Armies.* Washington, DC: Government Printing Office, 1880–1901.

Van Horne, Thomas B. *History of the Army of the Cumberland,* vol. 1. Cincinnati, OH: Robert Clarke, 1875.

Vaughan, Alfred J. *Personal Record of the Thirteenth Regiment, Tennessee Infantry.* Memphis. TN: Press of S. C. Toof, 1897.

Victor, Orville J. *Incidents and Anecdotes of the War.* New York: James D. Torrey, Publisher, 1866.

Wallace, Lew. *An Autobiography.* New York: Harper & Brothers, 1906.

Williams, Kenneth P. *Grant Rises in the West: The First Year, 1861–1862.* Lincoln: University of Nebraska Press, 1997.

Wilson, James Grant. *General Grant.* New York: D. Appleton, 1897.

Wilson, James Grant. *General Grant's Letters to a Friend, 1861–1880.* New York: T. Y. Crowell, 1897.

Wilson, James Grant. *The Life and Campaigns of Ulysses Simpson Grant, General-in-Chief of the United States Army.* New York: Robert M De Witt, Publisher, 1868.

Woodbury, Henry H. (apparent author). *Complete History of the 46th Illinois Veteran Volunteer Infantry.* Freeport, IL: Bailey & Ankeny, Printers, 1866.

Woodworth, Steven E. *Jefferson Davis and His Generals: The Failure of Confederate Command in the West.* Lawrence: University Press of Kansas, 1990.

Woodworth, Steven E. *No Band of Brothers: Problems in the Rebel High Command.* Columbia: University of Missouri Press, 1999.

Woodworth, Steven E. *Nothing but Victory: The Army of the Tennessee, 1861–1865.* New York: Alfred A. Knopf, 2005.

Worsham, W. J. *The Old Nineteenth Tennessee Regiment, C.S.A.* Knoxville, TN: Press of Paragon Printing Company, 1902.

Wright, Charles. *A Corporal's Story, Experiences in the Ranks of Company C, 81st Ohio Vol. Infantry.* Philadelphia: James Beale, Printer, 1887.

Wright, Thomas J. *History of the Eighth Regiment Kentucky Vol. Inf.* St. Joseph, MO: St. Joseph Steam Printing Company, 1880.

Young, Lot D. *Reminiscences of a Soldier of the Orphan Brigade.* Louisville, KY: Courier-Journal Job Printing Company, 1918.

Articles

Andreas, Alfred T. "The 'Ifs and Buts,' of Shiloh." In *Military Essays and Recollections: Papers Read Before the Commandery of the State of Illinois, Military Order of the Loyal Legion of the United States,* vol. 1. Chicago: A. C. McClurg, 1891.

Badeau, Adam. "General Grant." *The Century,* May 1885.

Bankhead, Smith P. "Letter from Colonel Bankhead." *Southern Historical Society Papers,* January 1879.

Bearss, Edwin C. "Unconditional Surrender: The Fall of Fort Donelson." Reprinted from *Tennessee Historical Quarterly,* March–June 1962.

Beauregard, P. G. T. "The Shiloh Campaign, Part I." *The North American Review,* January 1886.

Beauregard, P. G. T. "The Shiloh Campaign, Part II." *The North American Review,* February 1886.

Buell, Don Carlos "Shiloh Revisited." *The Century,* March 1886.

Byers, S. H. M. "Some War Letters." *The North American Review,* March 1887.

Carrington, Henry B. "Major General Lew Wallace at Shiloh." *The Bay State Monthly,* March 1885.

Chisholm, A. R. "The Plan of the Battle and the Withdrawal of the First Day." *The Century,* March 1886.

Cockerill, John A. "A Boy at Shiloh." In *Sketches of War History 1861–1865, Papers Prepared for the Commandery of the State of Ohio, Military Order of the Loyal Legion of the United State,* vol. 6, Theodore F. Allen, Edward S. McKee, and J. Gordon Taylor, eds. Cincinnati, OH: Monfort, 1908.

"Coming Up at Shiloh." *The Continental Monthly,* October 1884.

Dawes, E. C. "My First Day Under Fire at Shiloh." In *Sketches of War History 1861–1865, Papers Prepared for the Ohio Commandery of the Military Order of the Loyal Legion of the United States,* vol. 4, W. H. Chamberlain, ed. Cincinnati, OH: The Robert Clarke Company, 1896.

De Hass, Wills. "The Battle of Shiloh." In *The Annals of the War Written by Leading Participants North and South,* Alexander K. McClure, ed. Philadelphia: The Times Publishing Company, 1879.

Dinkins, James. "The Battle of Shiloh, April 6, 1862." *Southern Historical Society Papers* 31 (1903).

Flemming, Robert H. "The Battle of Shiloh as a Private Saw It." In *Sketches of War History 1861–1865, Papers Prepared for the Commandery of the State of Ohio, Military Order of the Loyal Legion of the United States,* vol. 6, Theodore F. Allen, Edward S. McKee, and J. Gordon Taylor, eds. Cincinnati, OH: Monfort, 1908.

Grant, F. D. "Halleck's Injustice to Grant." *The North American Review,* December 1885.

Grant, Ulysses S. "The Battle of Shiloh." *The Century,* February 1885.

Grant, Ulysses S. "General Lew Wallace and General McCook at Shiloh." *The Century,* September 1885.

Heard, S. S. "Letter from Colonel S. S. Heard." *Southern Historical Society Papers,* January 1879.

Hickenlooper, Andrew. "The Battle of Shiloh, Part 1– Personal Experiences in the Battle." In *Sketches of War History 1861–1865, Papers Prepared for the Commandery of the State of Ohio, Military Order of the Loyal Legion of the United States,* vol. 5, W. H. Chamberlin, A. M. Van Dyke, and George A. Thayer, eds. Cincinnati, OH: The Robert Clarke Company, 1903.

Hickenlooper, Andrew. "The Battle of Shiloh, Part 2– General Review of Reports of the Battle." In *Sketches of War History 1861–1865, Papers Prepared for the Commandery of the State of Ohio, Military Order of the Loyal Legion of the United States*, vol. 5, W. H. Chamberlin, A. M. Van Dyke, and George A. Thayer, eds. Cincinnati, OH: The Robert Clarke Company, 1903.

Hosea, Lewis M. "The Second Day at Shiloh." In *Sketches of War History 1861–1865, Papers Prepared for the Commandery of the State of Ohio, Military Order of the Loyal Legion of the United States*, vol. 4, Theodore F. Allen, Edward S. McKee, and J. Gordon Taylor, eds. Cincinnati, OH: Monfort, 1908.

Johnston, Albert Sidney. "Letter from General A. S. Johnston." *Southern Historical Society Papers*, January–June 1877.

Johnston, William Preston. "Albert Sidney Johnston and the Shiloh Campaign." *The Century*, February 1885.

Jones, D. Lloyd. "The Battle of Shiloh." In *War Papers Read Before the Commandery of the State of Wisconsin, Military Order of the Loyal Legion of the United States*, vol. 4. Milwaukee, WI: Burdick & Allen, 1914.

Jordan, Thomas. "The Battle of Shiloh." *Southern Historical Society Papers* 35 (1907).

Jordan, Thomas. "Battle of Shiloh: Refutation of the So-called 'Lost Opportunity, on the Evening of April 6th,' 1862." *Southern Historical Society Papers* 16 (1888).

Jordan, Thomas. "Notes of a Confederate Staff-Officer at Shiloh." *The Century*, February 1885.

Jordan, Thomas. "Recollection of General Beauregard's Service in West Tennessee in the Spring of 1862." *Southern Historical Society Papers*, January–December, 1880.

Lawrence, Eugene. "Grant on the Battle-Field." *Harper's New Monthly Magazine*, July 1869.

Lockett, S. H. "Controversies in Regard to Shiloh: A Staff Officer's Account of the Attack and Withdrawal." *The Century*, March 1886.

Magdeburg, F. H. "Capture of Fort Donelson." In *War Papers Read Before the Commandery of the State of Wisconsin, Military Order of the Loyal Legion of the United States*, vol. 3. Milwaukee, WI: Burdick & Allen, 1903.

Magdeburg, F. H. "The Fourteenth Wisconsin Infantry at the Battle of Shiloh." In *War Papers Read Before the Commandery of the State of Wisconsin, Military Order of the Loyal Legion of the United States*, vol. 3. Milwaukee, WI: Burdick & Allen, 1903.

Mason, George. "Shiloh." In *Military Essays and Recollections, Papers Read Before the Commandery of the State of Illinois, Military Order of the Loyal Legion of the United States*, vol. 1. Chicago: A. C. McClurg, 1891.

McAuley, John T. "Fort Donelson and Its Surrender." In *Military Essays and Recollections: Papers Read Before the Commandery of the State of Illinois, Military Order of the Loyal Legion of the United States*, vol. 1. Chicago: A. C. McClurg, 1891.

McCook, Alexander M. "Six Weeks in the Mud." *Overland Monthly and Out West Magazine*, March 1869.

McCook, Daniel. "The Second Division at Shiloh." *Harper's New Monthly Magazine*, May 1864.

McGinnis, George F. "Shiloh." In *War Papers Read Before the Indiana Commandery, Military Order of the Loyal Legion of the United States*. Indianapolis: Published by the Commandery, 1898.

Morton, Charles A. "A Boy at Shiloh." In *Personal Recollections of the War of the Rebellion, Addresses Delivered Before the Commandery of the State of New York, Military Order of the Loyal Legion of the United States*, A. Noel Blakeman, ed. New York: G. P. Putnam's Sons, 1907.

Nicolay, John G., and John Hay. "Abraham Lincoln: A History, Tennessee and Kentucky." *The Century*, August 1888.

Nicolay, John G., and John Hay. "Abraham Lincoln: A History, the Mississippi and Shiloh." *The Century*, September 1888.

Olney, Warren. "The Battle of Shiloh, with Some Personal Reminiscences." *Overland Monthly and Out West Magazine*, June 1885.

Olney, Warren. "'Shiloh': As Seen by a Private Soldier." *A Paper Read Before California Commandery of the Military Order of the Loyal Legion of the United States May 31, 1889* (n.p., 1889).

Perry, Leslie J. "The Rise of General Grant." *The Century*, November 1896.

Polk. W. M. "Facts Connected with the Concentration of the Army of the Mississippi Before Shiloh, April, 1862." *Southern Historical Society Papers* 8 (1880).

Putnam, Douglas, Jr. "Reminiscences of the Battle of Shiloh." In *Sketches of War History 1861–1865, Papers Read before the Ohio Commandery of the Military Order of the Loyal Legion of the United States*, vol. 3, Robert Hunter, ed. Cincinnati, OH: Robert Clarke, 1890.

Reed, D. W. "Shiloh Campaign and Battle." In *Wisconsin at Shiloh: Report of the Commission*, Frederick H. Magdeburg, compiler. Madison: Wisconsin Shiloh Monument Commission, 1909.

Rosecrans, William S. "Corinth." *The Century*, October, 1886.

Sandidge, L. D. "Letter from Captain Sandidge." *Southern Historical Society Papers*, January 1879.

Shanks, W. F. G. "Recollections of Grant." *Harper's New Monthly Magazine*, June 1865.

Sherman, William T., and John Sherman. "Letters of Two Brothers." *The Century*, January 1893.

Taylor, Jesse. "The Defense of Fort Henry." In *Battles and Leaders of the Civil War*, 4 vols., Robert Underwood Johnson and Clarence Clough Buel, eds. New York: Thomas Yoseloff, 1956.

Thrall, James C. "Letter from Captain James C. Thrall." *Southern Historical Society Papers*, January 1879.

Truman, Ben C. "A Spectacular Battle and Its 'Ifs.'" *Overland Monthly and Out West Magazine*, August 1889.

Walke, Henry. "The Gunboats at Belmont and Fort Henry." In *Battles and Leaders of the Civil War*, 4 vols., Robert Underwood Johnson and Clarence Clough Buel, eds. New York: Thomas Yoseloff, 1956.

Walke, Henry. "Operations of the Western Flotilla." *The Century*, January 1885.

Wallace, Lew. "The Capture of Fort Donelson." *The Century*, December 1884.

Wright, Marcus J. "The Battle of Belmont." *Southern Historical Society Papers* 16 (1888).

Index

Adamsville, Tennessee 108–10
Ammen, Col. Jacob: arrives at Pittsburg Landing 119, 157, 158, 165; attack on Monday 172, 173, 178, 179; in line 160; on march 102
Anderson, Lt. Col. Nicholas 173
Anderson, Brig. Gen. Patton 122; attack on left 138, 148; Monday 175; Shiloh 130, 131, 136
Appler, Col. Jesse 130
Army of Tennessee 6, 7
Army of the Mississippi 105, 185, 189
Army of the Ohio: march to Corinth 185, 189; march to Pittsburg Landing 99, 101, 102, 104, 107; Monday assault 170, 172, 175; Pittsburg Landing 158, 166
Army of the Tennessee 104, 170, 172, 181, 185, 186, 189
Athens, Alabama 70

Baldwin, Col. W.E. 47, 48
Bane, Col. Moses 144
Bankhead, Capt. Smith P. 151
Barber, Flavel 58, 59; Fort Donelson 41, 42, 50–52; surrender 65
Barber, Lucius 119, 138
Bark Road 111–13
Barrett, Capt. Samuel 128, 131, 136
Baxter, Capt. A.S. 164
Beauregard, Gen. G.P.T. 22–24, 31, 105, 159, 183; Corinth 74, 75, 104, 106, 190; counterattack 174, 176; criticism of 188, 189; and Davis 72, 73; and Johnston 69–71, 106, 107; Johnston killed 146, 151; march to Shiloh 108–10, 112, 113; Monday morning 169, 171, 172; overnight 166, 168; pull back 161–64; replaced 191; retreat 182; turn back 113, 114, 116, 118; withdraws 177, 180–82
Behr, Capt. Frederick 128
Belmont, Missouri 13, 16, 24
USS *Benton* 11, 53
Bering, John A. 120, 128

Bethel Station, Tennessee 93, 108–10
Bevens, William E. 142, 143
Bishop, Judson 184
Blanchard, Ira 64, 122, 137, 147
Bloody Pond 154
Bowen, Brig. Gen. John: Hornet's Nest 152, 160; Shiloh 142, 145
Bowling Green, Kentucky 5, 14–20, 31, 72, 77, 79, 81, 106, cut off 21–23, 33; cut railroad 24, 25; retreat from 61, 67–69, 73, 76, 78, 80, 83; transfer troops to Fort Donelson 32–35, 37
Bragg, Major Gen. Braxton assault begins 121, 122, 124, 130–32, 138; to Corinth 71, 72, 74, 106, 109, 190, 110; evening assault 159, 161, 168; Hornet's Nest 142, 143, 145, 147, 150–52; Monday on left 168, 171, 172, 175, 179; replaces Beauregard 191; retreats 181, 182; to Shiloh 111–15
Briant, Charles C. 102, 167, 174
Brinton, Dr. John 90
Brown, Col. John C. 50, 51
Brown, Major William 47, 64
Bruce, Col. Sanders D. 173, 179
Buchanan, James 38
Buckland, Col. Ralph P. 128–31, 137, 175, 180
Buckner, Brig. Gen. Simon Bolivar Fort Donelson 37, 39, 46, 49, 50, 51, 57, 58; in Kentucky 14, 21, 32; negotiate terms 59–62, 63, 66, 73, 74
Buell, Major Gen. Don Carlos 17, 19, 82, 83, 166, 183; correspondence with Grant 133, 135, 181, 182; correspondence with Halleck 18, 25, 31, 78; correspondence with Lincoln 17–19; correspondence with McClellan 16, 23, 77, 78; diversion 31, 35, 71, 73; Halleck in command 89, 185, 189; Nashville 77, 78, 81, 82; and Nelson 82, 119; Pittsburg Landing 101–03, 107, 109, 114, 156–60, 165, 167; plan to

join Grant 96, 99, 100; Shiloh 166, 169–74, 176, 177, 181–83, 183
Burnsville, Tennessee 94, 110, 112
Burrows, Capt. Jerome 137

Cairo, Illinois 4, 7, 13, 14, 16, 18, 23, 25, 31, 32, 35; railroads 12; repair ships 38, 53
USS *Carondelet* 11, 32, 44, 45; Fort Henry 26, 28, 29; Fort Donelson 39, 42, 43, 44
Chadwick, Lt. Col. W.D. 161
Chalmers, Brig. Gen. James R.: assault on right 132, 142, 144, 145; during night 171; evening assault 159–61; in line 122, 124, 125
Cheatham, Brig. Gen. Frank: Bethel Station 108–10; engages Lew Wallace 109; Hornet's Nest 140–42, 150; joins army 110, 113, 118; Monday 176
Cheatham, R. B. 80
Chisolm, Alexander R. 161
USS *Cincinnati* 11, 29, 38; Fort Henry 26, 28
Clark, Brig. Gen. Charles 171; Shiloh 110, 111; wounded 131
Clarksville, Tennessee 15, 82, bridges destroyed 30, 33–36, 76, escape to 32, 46, 64, 65, 69; occupied 77–79, 84, 86, 87
Cleburne, Brig. Gen. Patrick R. 171; Monday 176; Shiloh 122, 129–31
Cluett, William 119, 166
Cockerill, John 157, 166
Cockerill, Col. Joseph 148
Columbia, Tennessee 6, 102, 107; Duck River 101
USS *Conestoga* 10; Cumberland River 76; Fort Donelson 38, 43; Fort Henry 26, 28, 32
Cook, Col. John: Fort Donelson 36, 56, 57, 65; Fort Henry 28
Cooper, Gen. Samuel 14, 15, 168
Corinth, Mississippi 21, 106, 110, 118, 119, 120, 127, 128, 131, 132,

209

140, 178, 179, 182; Confederate base 94, 102, 104–08, 180, 190; Johnston retreat 70, 71, 74, 85; march to Shiloh 111, 113, 114, 116, 126; Union target 92–97, 99, 101, 103, 109, 184, 189, 190
Crittenden, Major Gen. George B. 70, 73; replaced 106
Crittenden, Brig. Gen. Thomas L.: Kentucky militia 13; march to Pittsburg Landing 101, 102, 133, 156, 165; Monday morning 170–174, 178
Cruft, Col. Charles: Fort Donelson 36, 55, 56, 64; reinforces McClernand 49–51
Crummer, Wilber 28
Cullum, Brig. Gen. George, W. 20, 35; Fort Donelson 42; Grant's reports 86; Nashville 76, 82, 84

Davis, Jefferson 7, 107, 110, 114; and Bragg 106; and Johnston 8, 9, 71–73, 74; Kentucky 13; replaces Beauregard 191
Deas, Col. Zacariah 150
Decatur, Alabama 70, 105, 107
De Hass, Lt. Col. Wills: Pittsburg Landing 104, 120, 127, 128
USS *DeKalb* 11
Dennison, William 3
Dill Branch 155, 159
District of West Tennessee 76
Donnelly, Capt. George 120
Dove, Commander Benjamin 38
Dover, Tennessee 25, 31, 36, 39, Forrest 63; Fort Donelson 38; hotel 46, 62, 65; road to Nashville 42, 45
Downing, Alexander 138
Duck River 32, 101, 102, 109, 119
Duncan, Joseph 140
Duncan Field 140, 151, 178
Dunlop, Col. Issac 160
Durham, Thomas 47, 55

Eads, James B. 9, 10
Eastport 32
Eastport, Mississippi 84, 92–94
18th Illinois Infantry: Fort Donelson 48; Shiloh 137
18th Tennessee Infantry 49
8th Arkansas Infantry 121
8th Illinois Infantry 36, 48
8th Kentucky Infantry CSA 56
8th Missouri Infantry 36, 55, 56
11th Illinois Infantry 36; Fort Donelson 48; Shiloh 147
11th Indiana Infantry: Fort Donelson 46, 55; Shiloh 134
11th Iowa Infantry 138, 147
USS *Essex* 11, 38; Fort Henry 26, 28, 29

Fayetteville, Alabama 70, 101
15th Arkansas Infantry: Fort Donelson 56; Shiloh 131

15th Illinois Infantry 119; Shiloh 138, 149, 173
15th Iowa Infantry 134, 136
5th Ohio Cavalry 93, 94, 95, 118
5th Ohio Light Artillery 124
5th Tennessee Infantry 131
50th Illinois Infantry: Fort Donelson 57; Shiloh 144
58th Illinois Infantry 50
58th Ohio Infantry 50
55th Illinois Infantry 132, 144
51st Indiana Infantry 156
51st Virginia Infantry 48
54th Ohio Infantry 132
57th Illinois Infantry: Fort Donelson 50, 119; Shiloh 166
57th Ohio Infantry 129, 131
56th Virginia Infantry 48
53rd Ohio Infantry 129, 130, 175
1st Arkansas Infantry 142
1st Minnesota Light Artillery 124
1st Mississippi Infantry Fort 56
1st Missouri Infantry CSA: Nashville 80; Shiloh 145
1st Nebraska Infantry 36, 50, 51
1st Ohio Cavalry 101
1st Tennessee Artillery 28
1st Tennessee Battalion 150
1st Texas Infantry 56
Flemming, Robert 128, 129, 131
Florence, Alabama 20, 32, 34, 93
Floyd, Brig. Gen. John B. 30; escape 63, 64, 73; Fort Donelson 32, 37, 38, 39, 45, 46, 51, 58; Nashville 73, 74, 80; surrender 60–62
Foote, Flag Officer Andrew Hull 10, 11, 23; Cumberland raid 76, 77, 79, 80, 99; failed attack 44, 45; Fort Donelson 31, 32, 35–37, 39, 42; to Fort Henry 24, 26, 28; meets Grant 53, 55
Forge Road 48, 51, 58, 59
Forrest, Col. Nathan Bedford: escape 63; Fort Donelson 39, 48, 62; Nashville 80; Shiloh 112
Fort Heiman 15, 21, 28, 30
Fort Henry 15, 21, 20, 22, 25, 31–37, 39, 41–43, 45, 66, 68, 69, 71, 74, 77, 84, 87, 92, 95, 186, 191; defense 27, 28; Grant campaign 23, 24, 26, 27; naval attack 29; surrender 30
Fort Donelson 15, 21, 27, 31, 32, 38, 42, 60, 66–69, 71–74, 76–81, 93, 99, 100, 103, 114, 119, 133, 137, 162, 186, 187, 191; Confederate assault 51, 53, 54, 58; naval action 43, 45; plan of attack 34–36, 39; problems for Grant 84–90; reinforcements 35, 37; surrender 60–62, 64; troops' positions 42, 45
Fort Pillow 7, 85, 92
40th Illinois Infantry 119, 148
48th Illinois Infantry 40
48th Ohio Infantry 118; Shiloh 120, 128, 130
45th Illinois Infantry: Fort Donel-

son 40; Fort Henry 28; Shiloh 147
41st Ohio Infantry 157, 173
44th Indiana Infantry: Fort Donelson 49, 56; Shiloh 139, 140, 143
49th Illinois Infantry 36; Fort Donelson 40, 55; Shiloh 130
49th Ohio Infantry 174
46th Illinois Infantry: Fort Donelson 50; Shiloh 149
43rd Illinois Infantry 130
14th Iowa Infantry 57
14th Mississippi Infantry 49
14th Wisconsin Infantry 173, 176
4th Illinois Cavalry 95, 128
4th Mississippi Infantry 56
Frémont, Major Gen. John C. 7, 8, 10, 11, 13, 14, 16, 19
Fulfer, Richard 176

General Field Orders No. 1 27
General Field Orders No. 5 33
Gibson, Col. Randall L. 122, 143, 150, 151
Gibson, Col. William H. 174
Gladden, Brig. Gen. Adley H. 114, 122, 124, 125; wounded 126, 145
Grant, Major Gen. Ulysses S. 15, 16, 21, 22, 32, 98, 101, 102, 114, 159, 162, 166, 184, 185; Ammen 119; Belmont 13, 16; Buckner 39, 65; and Buell 83, 133, 135; casualties 154, 183; changes view of war 191; Clarksville 76, 77; Corinth 95, 189, 190; correspondence with Cullum 42, 76, 82, 66, 85–88, 90, 92, 96–98, 119, 184, 185, 189; correspondence with Halleck 21, 23, 24, 30, 33, 36, 42; correspondence with Washburne 90, 187, 188; criticism of 186, 187; district command 76; division commanders 100; and Foote 31, 32, 53; Fort Donelson 30, 31, 36, 37, 39, 41, 42, 45, 49, 54, 55, 62, 63; Fort Henry 22–27; General Field Orders No. 5 32, 33; and Halleck 84, 85, 86, 88, 89, 90, 189; on Johnston 9; leaves army 189; and Lew Wallace 117, 118, 134, 164, 165; Lincoln support 188; major general 66, 67, 80; and McClernand 54; message to troops 66; and Nelson 78, 81, 82, 119, 133; over confident 118, 119; Paducah 14; Pittsburg Landing 95, 96, 116–19; and Prentiss 150; Savannah 100, 133; to Sherman 100; Shiloh 98, 99, 103, 126, 154, 157, 158, 162, 163, 165, 167, 168, 170, 172, 175, 176, 180, 181–83, 185; and Smith 98; staff officers 95; strategy 20, 21; Tennessee expedition 77, 92; *Tigress* 133; visits commanders 135, 146, 150; visits Nashville 82, 90; and Wallace 54

Index

Grose, Col. William 160; to Pittsburg Landing 156; Shiloh 179
Gwin, Lt. William 92; Pittsburg Landing 93

Halleck, Major Gen. Henry W. 8, 89; advance on Tennessee 92; command in field 185, 188; to Corinth 189, 190; correspondence with Alonzo Thomas 89, 90; correspondence with Buell 18, 19, 25, 31, 78, 102, 189; correspondence with Cullum 84; correspondence with Foote 23, 24, 35, 76; correspondence with Grant 21–25, 30, 33, 35, 42, 66, 78, 85–88, 90, 92, 96, 97, 98, 118, 119, 181, 183–85, 189; correspondence with Lincoln 18, 19; correspondence with McClellan 16–18, 22, 23, 35, 77–79, 85, 86, 89; correspondence with Stanton 79, 80, 187; and Grant 23, 32, 67, 76, 77, 84, 93; and McClellan 16–18; Pittsburg Landing 181, 183, 185; promotes self 78, 79; strategy 17, 18, 20
Hamburg, Tennessee 97, 98, 102, 103, 119, 132, 139, 140, 143, 155, 178, 181
Hanson, Col. Roger 57, 58
Hardcastle, Major Aaron B. 121
Hardee Major Gen. William 50, 72; assault begins 124, 127, 129; at Bowling Green 15, 34, 35; command center 149; command right 168, 171, 172; corps command 106; Monday 173, 178; retreat 181, 182; to Shiloh 110–13, 114, 120, 122
Hare, Col. Abraham 137
Harris, Isham G. 6, 7, 13, 177; leaves Nashville 80
Hart, E. J. 119
Hartpence, William R. 156
Hay, John 78
Haynes, Major Charles 93
Haynie, Col. Isham 40
Hazen, Col. William B.: Monday assault 172; on right 173, 179
Head, Col. John 47
Heath, Col. Thomas 95
Hickenlooper, Capt. Andrew 124
Hickman Creek 38
Hildebrand, Col. Jesse 104, 128, 129–31
Hillyer, Capt. W. S. 95
Hindman, Brig. Gen. Thomas C.: Hornet's Nest 142, 150; in line 122
Hinman, Wilbur F. 157, 167
Hitchcock, Brig. Gen. Ethan Allen 77, 78
Hornet's nest 127, 140, 141, 142, 147, 148, 150, 153, 183; capture 154, 159, 164; Confederate assault 142, 143, 145, 149–52, 154
Hosea, Lewis M. 174, 180

Hubert, Charles F. 57
Hunter, Major Gen. David 7
Huntsville, Alabama 70
Hurlbut, Brig. Gen. Steven A. 93; arrives Pittsburg Landing 94, 95, 100; falls back 139, 149, 152, 153; final line 155, 163; Monday advance 170, 171, 174, 175; new commander 101, 103; peach orchard 138, 139, 140, 142–45, 148; position 117, 118; supports Prentiss 128, 137

Island No. 10 7, 13, 15, 85, 92, 105, 185

Jackman, John S.: march from Nashville 112; Shiloh 147
Jackson, Brig. Gen. John K. 144, 145; evening assault 159–61; Shiloh 122, 132, 171
Johnson, Brig. Gen. Bushrod R.: Fort Donelson 39; Shiloh 131; surrender 62, 66
Johnston, Gen. Albert Sidney 8, 9, 58, 61, 66; address to troops 111; cancels attack 113, 114; Corinth 99, 104–06; correspondence with Davis 72–75; criticism of 71, 72; Floyd 38; Fort Donelson 32, 34, 35, 37; gives up command 106, 107; Kentucky 14; mortally wounded 146; Nashville 80–82; retreats south 67–71; Shiloh 109–12, 114, 115, 122, 123, 126, 145; strategy 15
Johnston, William Preston 107; Shiloh assault 115, 122, 135
Jones, Lt. Col. Charles 167
Jordan, Col. Thomas: retreat 177; Shiloh 109, 159, 161, 162

Kentucky Orphan Brigade CSA: Nashville 69; Shiloh 112, 121, 147
Kimberly, Robert 157, 173
Kirk, Col. Edward N. 174

Lauman, Col. Jacob G.: advance on left 56, 57; to Fort Donelson 36; garrison 65; reinforces Prentiss 139, 145
Lee, Gen. Robert E. 9
USS *Lexington* 10, 21, to Fort Donelson 38; to Fort Henry 26, 28, 32; Pittsburg Landing 155, 166; on Tennessee 92, 93
Lick Creek 97, 103, 113, 114, 116, 117, 132, 161
Lincoln, Abraham: generals act 17–19, 25; Grant 67, 78, 80, 89, 101, 188; Halleck 8, 11; Kentucky 13, 16; McClellan 88; volunteers 3, 6
Livermore, Mary 66
Lockett, Capt. S. H. 122, 162
Logan, Col. John 48
Louisiana Zouaves 149
USS *Louisville* 11, 44; Fort Donelson 35, 38, 43

Louisville Legion 176
Louisville & Nashville Railroad 15

Magoffin, Beriah 6, 13
Maney, Col. George: Hornet's Nest 150, 151; Monday 176
Marmaduke, Col. John S. 123
Marsh, Col. C. Carroll 137, 176
Martin, Col. John D. 142, 160
Mayfield, Kentucky 21
McAllister, Capt. Edward 137, 147, 179
McArthur, Brig. Gen. John: Fort Donelson 36, 45, 47–49; garrison 65; Shiloh 140, 144–46
McCausland, Col. John 64
McClellan, Major Gen. George B. 21, 22, 88, correspondence with Buell 16–18, 22, 23, 35, 77–79, 85, 86, 89; correspondence with Halleck 16–18, 22, 23, 35, 77–79, 85, 86, 89; general-in-chief 8; Grant 85–87; plans in the West 23, 31, 35, 77–79; replaced 89, 96
McClernand, Major Gen. John A. 24, 93, 117; to Corinth 189; Fort Donelson 30, 36, 39–42, 45, 46–50, 55; Fort Henry 26–28; meets Grant 54; Monday assault 170, 175, 176; to Pittsburg Landing 96, 100, 101, 117; Shiloh 128, 130, 132, 134, 136–38, 148, 149, 150, 153–55, 163
McClure, Alexander K. 188
McCook, Brig. Gen. Alexander: Monday assault 170, 172, 174–76, 178–80; to Pittsburg Landing 101, 102, 132, 156, 165, 169
McCook, Col. Daniel: arrives Pittsburg Landing 166, 169; Monday assault 174
McDowell, Col. John A.: Pittsburg Landing 95; Shiloh 128, 131, 137, 147, 148
McGinnis, Col George 134
McPherson, Col. James B. 98, 117, 134; and Lew Wallace 165
Memphis, Tennessee 5–7, 21, 69, 77, 79, 80, 92, 94
Memphis & Charleston Railroad 92, 93, 95, 105, 109
Mendenhall, Capt. John 173, 178
Michie, James 110, 111
Mill Springs 22, 83
Miller, Charles Dana: Fort Donelson 51; Shiloh 176
Miller, Col. Madison 124, 125
Mitchel, Brig. Gen. Ormsby 82, 101
Monterey, Tennessee 95, 110, 112
Monterey Road 110–12
Moody, Col. Gideon C. 179
Moore, Col. David 120, 121, 124
Morris, W. S. 36, 47
Morrison, Marion 100
Morrison, Col. William R. 36, 40
Morton, Charles: about organiza-

tion of army 186; Shiloh 120, 121, 125–27
Morton, Oliver P. 6, 12
USS *Mound City* 11
Mound City, Illinois 45
Munch, Capt. Emil 124
Munford, E. W. 107
Murfreesboro, Tennessee 69, 70, 73, 82, 101

Nashville, Tennessee 4, 5, 9, 32–35, 68, 72, 74, 84, 85, 114, 166; Confederate retreat 42, 45, 46, 52, 61, 63, 64, 69–71, 73, 83, 99; Grant's problems in 85, 87, 89, 90; industry 5, 21, 34; panic in city 80, 81; Union capture 67, 76–79, 81, 82, 95; Union target 7, 16–18, 22
Nelson, Brig. Gen. William: Fort Donelson 78, 81; Monday assault 170, 171–75, 178, 179; Nashville 81, 82, 90; Pittsburg Landing 101–03, 119, 133, 156, 157, 159, 165, 169
New Madrid, Missouri 7, 13, 15, 25, 85, 105
Nicolay, John G. 78
19th Tennessee Infantry 70, 115; Shiloh 142, 150, 151
9th Arkansas Infantry 121, 160
9th Illinois Infantry: Fort Donelson 48, 100; Shiloh 144, 145
9th Indiana Infantry 179
9th Tennessee Infantry 140, 150
Nispel, Lt. George 137
Nott, Capt. Charles C. 37, 57, 58

Oglesby, Col. Richard 24; to Fort Donelson 36, 41; under attack 47–49
Olney, Warren 103, 104, 117, 138, 139; position 186, 187; under attack 145, 153
Owl Creek 97, 103, 113, 114, 116, 128, 131, 132, 138, 155, 161

Paducah, Kentucky 4, 14; Grant occupies 14, 18, 21, 25–27
Panther Island 28
Paulding, Lt. Commander Leonard: commander of *Cincinnati* 26; commander of *St. Louis* at Fort Henry 38
Peabody, Col. Everett casualty 126; early fighting 124, 125; in Shiloh camp 120, 121
Peach orchard 139, 142–45, 147, 149, 150, 154
Phelps, Lt. Seth L.: command *Tyler* at Fort Henry 26; on Cumberland 31, 32; surrender of Fort Henry 29
Pillow, Brig. Gen. Gideon J.: Columbus 13; Fort Donelson 37, 39, 46, 47, 49–52, 56, 59, 63, 64, 70, 73; Grant's opinion of 30, 36; surrender 60–62; Tennessee 6, 7

USS *Pittsburg* 11; Fort Donelson 35, 38, 43, 44
Pittsburg Landing 92–94, 104, 113, 117, 118, 128, 134, 156, 168, 171, 181–83, 185, 186, 188; Buell arrival 119, 156–59, 167–69; Confederate target 108–12, 115, 123, 132, 133, 144; final line 163; Grant arrives 133; Lew Wallace 164, 165; location 94, 95, 97, 99; Union camps 95, 97, 98, 100–03, 107, 114, 116, 117, 119
Polk, James K. 7; Grant visits widow 82
Polk, Major Gen. Leonidas: Belmont 16; Columbus 13–15, 71; command West 7, 8; corps command 106; joins battle 131, 138, 142, 148; Monday morning 171, 172, 176; retreat 181; to Shiloh 110–15, 122
Pond, Col. Preston Jr. 122, 131, 138, 148, 149, 175, 179
Pope, Major Gen. John: Corinth 190; joins Halleck 189; on Mississippi 85, 185
Porter, Admiral David 3
Porter, Capt. William: command of *Essex* 26; Fort Henry 29
Powell, Major James E. 120, 121
Prentiss, Brig. Gen. Benjamin M. 150, 151; casualties 183; Hornet's Nest 140, 142, 148, 152–54; morning assault 122, 124–26, 127–32, 135, 136; new division 100, 103; prisoner 163, 164, 178; reinforcements 137, 139; Shiloh position 116, 117, 120
Purdy, Tennessee 93, 97, 98, 100, 103, 109–11, 113, 118, 128, 132, 148, 164, 178
Putnam, Douglas, Jr. 158

Quinn, Col. Francis 126

Raith, Col. Julius 130, 131, 137
Rawlins, Capt. John A. 26, 95; finds Lew Wallace 165
Reed, David 169
Reed, Col. Hugh P. 139, 140, 143
Reid, Col. H. T. 136
Rhoads, Lt. Col. Frank L. 48
Ricker, Major Elbridge: cavalry raid 94; patrol at Shiloh 118
Ridge Road 110, 111
Riley, F. A. 44
Rogers, Capt. John 9, 10
Ross, Col. Leonard F. 55
Rousseau, Brig. Gen. Lovell H. 176; Monday assault 175, 175, 180
Rowley, Capt. William R. 95; with Lew Wallace 164, 165
Ruggles, Brig. Gen. Daniel: artillery on Hornet's Nest 152, 153; command in center 151; march to Shiloh 110, 111; Shiloh assault 122, 136, 142, 143
Russell, Col. Robert M. 131, 153

USS *St. Louis* 11; Fort Donelson 35, 37, 43, 44, 53; Fort Henry 26, 28, 29
Savannah, Tennessee 86, 92–97, 156; Buell destination 102, 103, 107, 109, 112, 114, 119; Grant headquarters 98, 100–02, 133; McCook arrives 165, 167; Nelson arrives 119; road 110, 143, 150, 155
Savannah Road 110, 111, 140, 143, 150, 178
Scott, Thomas A. 6, 79, 80
2nd Iowa Infantry: Fort Donelson 57, 58, 65; Shiloh 173
2nd Kentucky Infantry CSA 57
2nd Kentucky Infantry USA 179
2nd Minnesota Infantry 184
2nd Tennessee 171
2nd U.S. Cavalry 9
17th Illinois Infantry: Fort Donelson 40, 55; Shiloh 130
17th Kentucky Infantry: Fort Donelson 49; Shiloh 139
17th Louisiana Infantry 167
7th Illinois Infantry 36
7th Iowa Infantry 36
7th Kentucky Infantry CSA 140, 150
71st Ohio Infantry 132
72nd Ohio Infantry 130, 148
77th Ohio Infantry 104, 120; Shiloh 128, 129, 131
77th Pennsylvania Infantry 169
76th Ohio Infantry: Fort Donelson 50, 51; Shiloh 176
Shaver, Col. R. G. 125, 150
Shelbyville, Alabama 70
Sherman, John 5
Sherman, Brig. Gen. William T.: after Shiloh 186, 187; Confederate assault 126–32, 136, 137, 138, 140, 147, 148; with Grant 135, 162, 189; Monday advance 170, 175, 179–81; new line 149, 154, 155; overnight 167, 168; Pittsburg Landing 96–98, 100, 101, 103, 104, 116–18; rivers 3, 5; strategy 20, 78, 93; Tennessee raid 93–95
Shiloh 9, 103, 104, 160, 165, 183, 185, 189–91; artillery position 136; casualties 183; church 97, 113, 124, 128, 131, 136, 161, 179, 180
16th Iowa Infantry 135, 136
16th Wisconsin Infantry 121
6th Indiana Infantry 102; Shiloh 167, 174
6th Kentucky Infantry CSA 150
6th Kentucky Infantry USA 173
6th Mississippi Infantry: casualties 130, 171; Shiloh 129
6th Ohio Infantry 173
6th Tennessee Infantry 140, 141
68th Ohio Infantry 50
65th Ohio Infantry 157, 167
61st Illinois Infantry 124, 126, 153
Smith, Brig. Gen. Charles F. 32,

84, 86, 96, 98, 100; Fort Donelson 36, 37, 45, 47, 54–59; Fort Henry 21, 22, 24–28, 30; injured 93; to Nashville 82, 83; Pittsburg Landing 95, 103, 117; replaced 101; surrender 62, 63, 66, 79; Tennessee expedition 86, 88, 95
Smith, Col. Morgan L.: Fort Donelson 36, 55, 56, 64; Fort Henry 28; Shiloh Monday 180
Smith, Col. T. Kilby 180
Smith, Col. William Sooy 173, 178
Snake Creek 97, 103, 116, 140, 155, 165
Squier, George W. 141
Stanton, Edwin 66, 67; correspondence with Halleck 79, 80, 86, 89, 187
Statham, Col. Winfield 145, 152
Stemble, Commander Roger 26
Stevenson, Alabama 69, 70, 107
Stillwell, Leander: reinforcement 158; Shiloh 124, 125, 126, 153
Stockwell, Elisha Jr. 173, 176
Stuart, Col. David: falls back 145, 148, 155; Monday assault 175; protects left flank 132, 144, 145; left at Shiloh 103, 116, 117; wounded 180
Sullivan, Col. Peter 120
Sweeney, Col. T. W. Shioh 140

Taylor, Capt. Jesse 26, 29
Terrill, Capt. William 173
Thayer, Col. John M.: Fort Donelson 36, 50, 51, 54, 64; Shiloh 180
3rd Iowa Infantry 103, 117, 118; Shiloh 138, 139, 145, 152
Third Mississippi Infantry 56
Third Tennessee Infantry 41, 49–51, 58, 65
13th Kentucky Infantry USA 174
13th Tennessee Infantry 131
30th Tennessee Infantry 57
31st Illinois Infantry 36; Fort Donelson 47, 48
31st Indiana Infantry 36; Fort Donelson 49; Shiloh 139, 140
32nd Indiana Infantry 174
32nd Tennessee Infantry 51
36th Indiana Infantry 156, 158, 160, 179

Thomas, Brig. Gen. George H.: Corinth 189; Mill Springs 22; to Pittsburg Landing 101
Thomas, Brig. Gen. Lorenzo 89
Thompson, Lt. Egbert 38
Thompson, Seymour D.: camp at Shiloh 118–20; Shiloh 138, 139
Thornton, Col. John J. 130
Tigress 133, 134
Tilghman, Brig. Gen. Lloyd 15; Fort Henry 27, 28; surrender 29, 30
Timony, Capt. James 137
Trabue, Col. Robert: Hornet's Nest 153; Shiloh evening assault 160
Tuttle, Col. James M.: Hornet's Nest 154; Shiloh 140
12th Illinois Infantry 36; Shiloh 144, 145, 147
12th Iowa Infantry 143
12th Michigan Infantry 121, 126
20th Mississippi Infantry 47, 64
20th Illinois Infantry 64; Shiloh 122, 137, 147
25th Kentucky Infantry USA: Fort Donelson 49; Shiloh 139
25th Missouri Infantry USA 120, 121, 125, 186
21st Alabama Infantry 113
21st Illinois Infantry 16
21st Missouri Infantry USA 120, 121
24th Indiana Infantry 176
29th Illinois Infantry 130
29th Indiana Infantry 169
26th Alabama Infantry 161
26th Mississippi Infantry 47, 48
26th Tennessee Infantry 47, 48
23rd Tennessee Infantry 129, 131
USS *Tyler (Taylor)* 10, 11; Fort Donelson 43; Fort Henry 26, 28; Pittsburg Landing 92, 93, 155, 166

Urquhart, Col. David Shiloh 161

Van Dorn, Major Gen. Earl 180, 190
Vaughan, Col. Alfred J. 131
Veatch, Col. James C. 137, 138, 149

Walke, Commander Henry: commands *Carondelet* 26; Fort Donelson 44; Fort Henry 28, 29
Wallace, Major Gen. Lew 93, 133, 134; about Grant 54; confronts Cheatham 108, 109, 117, 118; to Corinth 189; criticism of 165; Crump's Landing 100, 108; Fort Donelson 36, 37, 39, 42, 45, 49–51, 54–56, 64; to Fort Henry 66; Monday advance 175–77, 180; to Pittsburg Landing 150, 155, 164–66, 169, 170
Wallace, Brig. Gen. William H. L.: commands division 93, 101; Fort Donelson 36, 48, 50; Fort Henry 24; Hornet's Nest 138, 140, 142, 143, 148–51, 153–55; mortally wounded 154, 163; position on field 117, 118, 127, 134
Washburne, Elihu B. 90, 187, 188
Washington Artillery CSA 136
Water Oaks Pond 137, 179
Waterhouse, Capt. Allen 128, 130, 131
Webster, Col. Joseph D. 54, 95; Shiloh line 154, 155, 159, 161
Wharton, Col. Gabriel 48, 64
Wharton, Col. John A. 149
Williams, James M. 113
Williams, Col. Nelson G.: peach orchard 145; reinforces Prentiss 139
Willich, Col. August: Monday assault 179; Shiloh 174
Withers, Brig. Gen. Jones M. 111, 122, 144, 150, 161
Wood, Brig. Gen. Sterling A. M. 122, 124, 125, 129, 131, 148
Wood, Brig. Gen. Thomas, J. 101
Woods, Col. Joseph J. 143
Worsham, W. J.: to Corinth 70; Shiloh 115, 142
Wynn's Ferry Road 39, 46, 49–51, 64

Yates, Richard 2
Young, Lot D. 122

Zollicoffer, Brig. Gen. Felix 14